PERICLES ON STAGE

PERICLES
ON STAGE

POLITICAL
COMEDY IN
ARISTOPHANES'
EARLY PLAYS

MICHAEL VICKERS

University of Texas Press, Austin

♾ The paper used in this publication

meets the minimum requirements of

American National Standard for Information Sciences —

Permanence of Paper for Printed Library Materials,

ANSI Z39.48-1984.

Library of Congress

Cataloging-in-Publication Data

Vickers, Michael J.

Pericles on stage : political comedy in

Aristophanes' early plays / Michael Vickers.

p.   cm.

Includes bibliographical references and indexes.

ISBN 0-292-78727-8 (alk. paper)

1. Aristophanes — Political and social views.

2. Political plays, Greek — History and criticism.

3. Greek drama (Comedy) — History and criticism.

4. Athens (Greece) — Politics and government.

5. Politics and literature — Greece — Athens.   6. Pericles,

499–429 B.C. — In literature.   I. Title.

PA3879.V53   1997

882'.01 — dc20   96-16242

FOR SUSAN

CONTENTS

CHAPTER 10
Pericles at Sparta: Aristophanes' *Birds* II
171

PREFACE

According to an anonymous *Life* of Aristophanes, when Dionysius the tyrant of Syracuse wanted to know about the government of Athens, Plato sent him a copy of Aristophanes' *Clouds*. That we do not know whether Dionysius I or II was in question does not alter the apparent fact that Plato considered *Clouds* to be a play with political content. The story is rarely if ever discussed today, not least because it runs counter to the widespread view that even if Aristophanes did write "political" plays, *Clouds* is not one of them. The story is, moreover, "late," and since "the ancient lives of the poets contain an uncomfortably high proportion of fiction and guesswork" (Lloyd-Jones and Wilson 1990, xiv), it will be said that it can be safely disregarded.

But what if it can be shown that *Clouds* is political — and not only *Clouds,* but other plays in the Aristophanic corpus? The purpose of this book is to present the case that in his earlier plays, Aristophanes provided a commentary on the day-to-day political concerns of Athenians, and that he did so by exploiting the public images of the two most prominent Athenian politicians of the second half of the fifth century, namely, Pericles and his ward Alcibiades. In *Clouds* and elsewhere, Aristophanes examines in considerable detail the public and private morality of these two individuals. He achieves this by playing on elements that rarely figure in conventional histories, for many historians today prefer to establish what actually happened — as though one could ever really tell — and tend to be impatient with anything that smacks of gossip. The usual procedure is to weigh up the evidence for and against the historicity of tales that occur in the substantial anecdotal tradition, and to dismiss as "inventions of comic writers" those which seem to be altogether far-fetched, or for which the evidence appears to be conflicting. In a work such as this, one can be content merely to record the fact that a particular tale was told about Pericles or Alcibiades in antiquity, and if it seems to have an echo or — more accurately — a prefiguration in Aristophanes, then one can be reasonably sure of the historicity of the gossip, even if the question of whether the incident, allegation, imputation, or slur was actually true remains open.

What is attempted here is in effect a kind of political biography using in a completely new way one of our principal contemporary witnesses, Aristophanes. The picture will be exaggerated, but nonetheless real. Through Aristophanes' eyes, it is possible to gauge the reaction of the Athenian public to the events that occurred in the years following Pericles' death in 429 B.C., to the struggle for the political succession, and to the problems presented by Alcibiades' gradual emergence as one of the most powerful figures in the state. Aristophanes dramatizes the debate across the generation gap by personalizing the issues in a way that has frequent echoes in the anecdotal tradition relating to both Pericles and Alcibiades.

To argue for the omnipresence of Alcibiades in the plays that were written at the time of his political activity is difficult enough, for although there is ancient testimony in support of this view, political allegory is today very much out of favor with most students of the classical past. To include Pericles as well is doubly difficult, for the reader has to be persuaded not only that Greek comedy was a rather more pointedly political business than most modern scholars have thought, but also that Pericles, whose reputation is today that of a secular saint, was mercilessly lampooned even after his death. There is, however, a sufficiently large overlap between the scurrilous tales told of Pericles and his extended family and the twists and turns of Aristophanes' plots to justify the case made here, and antipathy to political allegory can be shown to have rather more to do with the history of scholarship than with a respect for evidence. This is not a commentary on Aristophanes, but is simply intended to put Pericles (and Alcibiades) firmly back in the picture. There are thus many aspects of Aristophanes' sophisticated humor that are not touched upon. There is also a good deal of repetition — on Aristophanes' part — in his exploitation of Pericles and Alcibiades' peculiarities and idiosyncrasies. In mitigation, it should be recalled that although this book will take but a few hours to read, the material to which it relates was spread out over several years. The audiences will doubtless have looked forward to seeing how stock motifs, such as the shape of Pericles' head or Alcibiades' speech defect, were exploited in each new play.

It is hoped that this work will reach an audience beyond those who have a reading knowledge of Greek, and for this reason most Greek words have been transliterated. I have used a system I first saw employed by John Scheid and Jesper Svenbro. Greek names have usually been Latinized, since the book is written in English.

It will be clear from text and notes how much I owe to previous writers, but my frequent criticisms of Sir Kenneth Dover require some qualification. To paraphrase Russell Meiggs on Jérôme Carcopino, I have come to disagree with all the main hypotheses of his work on Aristophanes, and almost all of my references are critical. But the work of few scholars has excited me more, and this would have been a more prosaic and superficial study if Dover had not stimulated me to ask difficult questions and to risk bold answers.

This book was written during leave from my employment at the Ashmolean Museum, Oxford, some of it in the incomparable surroundings of the Fondation Hardt in Geneva, where my visits were sponsored by the British Academy and the Fonds national suisse de recherche, and some of it at the Institute for Advanced Studies at the Hebrew University in Jerusalem, where I had the honor of being a Visiting Scholar in 1993. Debts of gratitude are owed to the Librarian of the Ashmolean Library and his staff for their unfailing courtesy. Many thanks are also due to Frederick Ahl, Ernst Badian, Mary Beard, Peter Bicknell, Edmund Bloedow, Ewen Bowie, Roger Brock, Mortimer Chambers, Michael Chase, Stephen Colvin, David Crystal, Peter Derow, Karl Galinsky, David Gill, Michael Flower, George Forrest, Clive Foss, Don Fowler, David Gribble, Edith Hall, Eric Handley, William Heckscher, Jeffrey Henderson, Gabriel Herman, Michael Inwood, Thomas DaCosta Kaufmann, Peter Levi, the late David Lewis, François Lissarague, Cyril Mango, Harold B. Mattingly, Roger Moorey, Oswyn Murray, William Murray, Robin Osborne, Martin Ostwald, Douglass Parker, Maurice Pope, Roy Porter, Nancy Ramage, Walter Redfern, John Richmond, Ralph Rosen, Ingrid Rowland, Igor Ševčenko, Andrew and Susan Sherratt, Christiane Sourvinou-Inwood, Philip Stadter, Barry Strauss, Ronald S. Stroud, Daniel P. Tompkins, Robert Wallace, David Warrell, Nigel Wilson, Martin Winkler, and Norman Yoffee for (in various measure) advice, encouragement, and fruitful skepticism. Brigadier G. O. Cowan, Director of Army Medicine at the Royal Army Medical College, London, provided useful leads on scholarship relating to the Athenian plague. Anonymous readers for the press made many valuable comments and suggestions for improvement. My thanks also go to those members of the University of Texas Press, Joanna Hitchcock, Leslie Tingle, Tayron Cutter, Ali Hossaini, and Nancy Bryan, who made a long and complicated task—at least for me—almost a pleasure. Special thanks are due to Sherry Wert for exemplary copy editing. If there are any remaining shortcomings, they are to be laid at my door. I was greatly helped, too, by being able to read prior to publication Barry Strauss's *Fathers and Sons and the Crisis of Athenian Ideology* and Robert Wallace's "Private Lives and Public Enemies." I shall, moreover, be forever indebted to my late friend and colleague E. D. Francis for having taught me to be aware of the underlying patterns of Greek discourse, and for giving me some valuable leads in the early stages of this research. But these debts are as nothing compared to what I owe to my patient wife, Susan Vickers, to whom this work is dedicated.

ABBREVIATIONS

The following list contains those abbreviations used in the notes. Abbreviations for ancient authors are otherwise as listed in LSJ or OCD^2, although the names of Aristophanes' plays are given in English, in full.

Alc.   Plutarch, *Life of Alcibiades*

CAF   T. Kock, ed., *Comicorum Atticorum Fragmenta,* 3 vols. (Leipzig: Teubner, 1880–1888)

CGFP   C. Austin, ed., *Comicorum Graecorum Fragmenta in Papyris Reperta* (Berlin and New York: de Gruyter, 1973)

DK^6 H. Diels and W. Kranz, eds., *Die Fragmente der Vorsokratiker,* 6th ed. (Berlin: Weidmann, 1951–1952)

FCG   A. Meineke, ed., *Fragmenta Comicorum Graecorum,* 5 vols. (Berlin: G. Reimer, 1839–1857)

FGrH   F. Jacoby, ed., *Fragmente der griechischen Historiker* (Berlin: Weidmann; and Leiden: E. J. Brill, 1923–1958)

FHG   C. Müller, *Fragmenta Historicorum Graecorum* (Paris: A. F. Didot, 1841–1870)

HCT   A. W. Gomme, A. Andrewes, and K. J. Dover, *A Historical Commentary on Thucydides,* 5 vols. (Oxford: Clarendon, 1948–1981)

IG   *Inscriptiones Graecae*

LSJ   H. G. Liddell, R. Scott, and H. S. Jones, *A Greek-English Lexicon,* 9th ed., with supplement (Oxford: Clarendon, 1968)

ML   R. Meiggs and D. M. Lewis, *A Selection of Greek Historical Inscriptions* (Oxford: Clarendon, 1969)

*OCD*²   N. G. L. Hammond and H. H. Scullard, *The Oxford Classical Dictionary,* 2d ed. (Oxford: Clarendon, 1970)

PCG   R. Kassel and C. Austin, eds., *Poetae Comici Graeci* (Berlin and New York: de Gruyter, 1983–)

Per.   Plutarch, *Life of Pericles*

RE   A. Paully, G. Wissowa, W. Kroll, *Real-Encyclopädie der klassischen Altertumswissenschaft* (Stuttgart: Alfred Druckenmüller, 1894–1980)

TGF   A. Nauck, *Tragicorum Graecorum Fragmenta,* 2d ed. (Leipzig: Teubner, 1889)

NICIAS, LAMACHUS, AND ALCIBIADES
Political Allegory in Aristophanes

Aristophanes wrote in dangerous times. Attacks on contemporaries had to be carried out with considerable discretion. This was especially advisable since "the kind of person who [was] usually lampooned on the stage [was] rich, or aristocratic, or powerful."[1] Aristophanes had sailed close to the wind at the celebration of the Great Dionysia of 426 B.C. when he lampooned the demagogue Cleon in the *Babylonians,* and was prosecuted for his pains.[2] Even power legally used could be frightening. The means by which the powerful might be successfully ridiculed is indicated by the plot summary of a play by Aristophanes' older rival Cratinus, which came to light on a papyrus fragment first published in 1904. Cratinus "satirized Pericles with great plausibility by means of *emphasis,* because he brought the war on the Athenians."[3] "Emphasis" was a technical term meaning "innuendo," or even "subliminal suggestion," rather than "explicitness" as it does today.[4] It was defined by Quin-

---

1. [Xen.] *Ath. pol.* 2.18, written in c. 430 B.C.: on the date, see Ostwald 1986, 182 n. 23.
2. *Acharnians* 377–382, and Schol. 378; *Acharnians* 502–503, and Schol.; Ostwald 1986, 207.
3. *POxy.* 663, 44–48; *CGFP,* 70; Cratin. *Dionysalexandros* i, *PCG.*
4. "We [today] are simply not attuned to writing which proceeds by indirect suggestion rather than by direct statement. . . . When we 'emphasize' something, we proclaim it to our readers, leaving no doubt that we want its presence known. The ancient writer does the exact opposite": Ahl 1984, 179; 1991, 22–24.

tilian as "the process of digging out some lurking meaning from something said,"[5] and Demetrius the rhetorician (writing in the fourth century B.C.) stated that "the effect of an argument is more formidable (*deinoteros*) because it is achieved by letting the fact make itself manifest (*emphainontos*) rather than having the speaker make the point for himself."[6] According to a tradition that may go back to Aristotle, the device was one of the distinguishing characteristics of Greek comedy, which "differs from abuse, since abuse delivers the insults in an unconcealed manner, whereas comedy needs what is called *émphasis*."[7] "Emphasis," moreover, contributes greatly to the allegorical pictures Aristophanes creates. Hidden meaning, innuendo, and double entendre are, however, not to everyone's taste today. It will be explained presently how this came about, and when the break with the pattern that had prevailed in antiquity occurred.

Very occasionally, Aristophanes will make explicit what was either implicit or self-evident (in view of the masks and costumes the actors wore). Near the beginning of *Peace*, two slaves are busy feeding the dung beetle on which Trygaeus will fly up to Olympus. One of them says: "Some bright spark in the audience may be saying 'What is this about? What does the beetle mean?'" The other replies that the person sitting next to him will declare, "It seems to me that he is hinting at Cleon, saying that he shamelessly eats dung" (*Peace* 43–48). The word for "hint" is *ainíttetai*, cognate with *aínigma* ("enigma" or "riddle"). Cleon was a politician much hated by Aristophanes, but he had died a few months before *Peace* was performed in 421 B.C. The procedure to which Aristophanes here draws specific attention is not confined to this passage, but (or so it will be argued in this book) is widespread throughout Aristophanes, where it is usually put across "emphatically." For want of a better term, I have called it "political allegory."

The most powerful Athenian politician during much of Aristophanes' lifetime was not Cleon but Alcibiades, who had been Pericles' ward, and who began to lay claim to Pericles' political mantle during the 420s. He was elected general for 420/19 B.C., and was to be re-elected for the next five years, before going into exile in 415 B.C.[8] There are enough stories about Alcibiades' role in the theatre to justify the assumption that it would have been wise to make any attacks on him covert. He is said—and even if the stories were *ben*

5. Quint. *Inst.* 9.2.64 (trans. Ahl 1984, 176).
6. Demetr. *Eloc.* 288 (trans. Ahl 1991, 22–25).
7. *Tractatus Coislinianus* 31–32 Koster. On the possible derivation of the *Tractatus* from Aristotle's lost *Poetics*, see Janko 1984. Cf. *Per.* 16.1: in describing the way in which comic writers lampooned Pericles, Plutarch calls their technique *parémphasis*.
8. Develin 1989, 142–150.

trovate, they indicate the kind of man the ancients considered Alcibiades to have been—to have beaten up a rival *choregus* "before the audience and judges," ([Andoc.] 4.20–21),[9] to have prevented Aristophanes from winning first prize for *Clouds* in 423 B.C. by intimidating the judges (*Clouds, Arg.* 5 Coulon), and to have gone to the Record Office and "expunged with his wetted finger" an indictment against the comic poet Hegemon of Thasos (the officials were afraid to renew the charge "on account of Alcibiades") (Ath. 9.407c). Eupolis, another comic writer, clearly went too far in the *Baptae* when he drew Alcibiades' especial anger by "openly lampooning his *traulotēta*" (Tzetz. XIAi 89 Koster).

Traulotēta was a speech defect whereby *rho* is pronounced as *lambda:* such a confusion could deliver meanings in Greek as different from each other as "Kids fly free" and "Kids fry flea" in English. In Alcibiades' own mouth the disorder was not considered especially offensive by contemporaries, "but was thought to be full of charm, and to have added persuasiveness (*pithanótēta*) to his discourse" (*Alc.* 1.6). The phenomenon is not uncommon, even today: "Many politicians and others dependent on public esteem go in for lisps, stutters and bizarre pronunciations . . . and these afflictions may serve to make the sufferer more likeable."[10] It was presumably because it was to his social and political advantage to do so that Alcibiades' son later adopted both his father's distinctive gait and his mode of speech: *klasaukheneúetai te kaì traulízetai* ("he bends his neck in an affected way and pronounces *rho* as *lambda*"; Archipp. *PCG* 48 *ap. Alc.* 1.8). Traulism, or lambdacism, was a speech mannerism peculiar—in the 420s B.C.—to Alcibiades.[11] Aristophanes draws specific attention to it in the *Wasps,*[12] where a slave says that he saw in a dream a certain Theorus with the head of a *kórax* (crow). Then (44–45) Alcibiades is supposed to have said to him *traulísas* ("lambdacizing"): *holâis; Théolos tèn kephalèn kólakos ékhei* ("Do you see Theolus? He has the head of a flatterer"). He should have said: *horâis; Théōros tèn kephalèn kórakos ékhei* ("Do you see Theorus? He has the head of a crow"). There are special reasons why the lambdacism is spelled out here (and these will be discussed in Chapter 7). Normally, lambdacism would not have been indicated

9. For arguments in favor of the authenticity of this speech, see Raubitschek 1948; Furley 1989; cf. *Alc.* 16.5; Dem. 21.147.

10. Sayle 1988, 10.

11. Alcibiades the younger, Demosthenes (see Stanford 1967, 152 n. 10 for refs.), and Aristotle (Diog. Laert. 5.1) also shared the same speech impediment (which is often translated "lisp" for want of a more accurate term). For a good discussion of the condition, see O'Neill 1980 (a reference I owe to the kindness of David Crystal).

12. *Wasps* 42–46; cf. *Clouds* 862–864 and 1381–1384 (discussed below in Chapters 3 and 7).

in the text, as Quintilian explains: *lambdakismós,* along with iotacism, a soft voice, and broad pronunciation (and Quintilian uses the Greek words for these expressions, though he wrote in Latin) "happen through sounds, and . . . cannot be shown in writing because they are errors in speech and of the tongue."[13]

The impediment was an obvious handle for mockery on the stage (and elsewhere), and playwrights (and others) exploited the possibilities for double meanings presented by Alcibiades' idiolect. We find Aristophanes doing so from *Knights* onward. His rival Eupolis clearly got Alcibiades' goat in *Baptae.* Not only does Alcibiades seem to have punished Eupolis (having some of his cronies "baptize" the poet in the sea),[14] but he is said to have "passed a law to the effect that comedy should no longer be written openly, but figuratively" (Tzetz. XIAi 97–98 Koster). The authority for this statement is very late, but if, as seems likely, the *Baptae* was performed during the year or two preceding the Sicilian expedition,[15] there may be support—albeit flimsy[16]—in the legislation passed in 415 B.C. and associated with the name of Syracosius. This stated that it was henceforth illegal to lampoon people on stage by name (*mè kōmōideîsthai onomastí tina;* Schol. *Birds* 1297).

There has been no end of scholarly debate over the meaning of Syracosius' legislation.[17] Since some thirty-seven Athenians are mentioned in *Birds,* performed in the following year (414 B.C.), it has been suggested that the legislation was a dead letter, if it existed at all. The absence from *Birds* of the names of any of those found guilty of parodying the Eleusinian Mysteries or the mutilation of the Herms has been noted, and the law has been held to have applied to them: that *they* should not be mentioned on the stage.[18] This may be to miss the point; the reality may have been that Aristophanes was simply obeying the law in not mentioning by name those who were being seriously lampooned—namely, the "rich, the aristocratic, and the powerful." Aristophanes is in any case said, albeit by the same late authority, to have

13. Quint. *Inst.* 1.5.32; Ahl 1991, 96. Quintilian's statement will account for the lack of any indication of lambdacism in some lines of Eupolis (*PCG* 385) that Meinecke (*FCG* 3:368) plausibly suggested were spoken by Alcibiades and another. It is not a question of the feature "not being sustained": Halliwell 1990, 76.

14. Tzetz. XIAi 89 Koster: "Baptize me on stage and I will soak you in salt water"; an authentic couplet, according to West 1972, 29–30; 1974, 17.

15. Storey 1990; 1993.

16. Halliwell (1991, 55–56) well shows how flimsy the evidence is.

17. Halliwell (1991, 54–66) has captured the essence of a discussion that at times verges upon the theological.

18. Sommerstein 1986, 101–108, with references to earlier literature.

been among those who practiced symbolic satire after 415 B.C. (Tzetz. XIAi 99–100 Koster). It will be argued below that many of the names of real people who are specifically mentioned are simply vehicles for the lampooning of the major targets. The latter, and not the individuals concerned, are properly the *kōmōidouménoi* ("those who are satirized").

Alcibiades' apparent absence from comedy has been a matter for frequent comment. Thus: "Aristophanes makes surprisingly few references to the aristocratic Alcibiades,"[19] "Alcibiades appears surprisingly infrequently in Aristophanes and the fragments of other dramatists,"[20] and "Alcibiades, however surprisingly, does not appear to have been a particularly appealing butt for comic poets at any point in his career."[21] Then, "references made by Athenian dramatists to Alcibiades in the years 414–411 B.C. are only to be found in a very limited quantity,"[22] and in the specific context of *Birds,* it was noted long ago that Alcibiades is nowhere mentioned by name.[23] Scholarly surprise was due to the fact that Alcibiades not only was "rich, aristocratic, and powerful," but also was the most controversial individual of his age, having been elected one of the three generals for the Sicilian expedition (a campaign he had done much to promote); having been suspected of involvement in various acts of impiety before the departure of the fleet; having been recalled from Sicily to stand trial; having jumped ship and gone into exile at Sparta; having advised the Spartans on the most effective ways to defeat Athens; and having, so rumor had it, seduced and gotten with child Timaea, the wife of the Spartan king.

THE PROBLEM WITH POLITICAL ALLEGORY

Birds in fact provides a useful testing ground for theories of allegory in Greek drama. There is nothing new in seeing the play as an allegory in which Alci-

19. de Ste. Croix 1972, 361.

20. Heath 1987a, 34. For a good account of the places where Alcibiades is mentioned specifically in Aristophanes, see Moorton 1988, 345–359. They are not many, however; cf. Hertzberg 1853, 15: "—auch bei Aristophanes wird Alkibiades verhältnissmässig selten erwähnt."

21. Halliwell 1991, 61.

22. Hertzberg 1853, 303. Cf. Halliwell 1991, 60, on "comic poets' particular silence about the controversial figure of Alcibiades during [the] period [415–411]."

23. By Droysen (1835, 161–208). This can only in part have been due to the difficulty of fitting *Alcibiádēs* into verse (noted by Critias 4 [West]); *ho Kleiníou* ("son of Cleinias") could be (and was) employed instead.

biades underlies the hero Peisthetaerus, but "the majority of scholars today . . . flatly reject a political reading";[24] *Birds* has "no strong and obvious connection with a topical question of public interest";[25] "attempts to find in *Birds* any extensive allegorical comment . . . are unconvincing."[26] Allegorical readings had their advocates — in some quarters at least — during the eighteenth and nineteenth centuries. Perhaps the most influential work in this respect was J. W. Süvern's study of *Birds* of 1827, which appeared in an English translation in 1835,[27] but which is now generally dismissed as an analysis that "in its failure to persuade posterity, remains a warning against eagerness to credit the play with an explicit political design."[28] Süvern was reacting against the position adopted by A. W. von Schlegel earlier in the century: "that the *Birds* was nothing more than the fantastic exuberance of poetic genius, soaring with light wing into an airy region of its own creation, but yet with a shrewd eye for the follies of a world from which it pretends to have shaken itself free."[29] This, however, is the position taken by most scholars today; Cedric Whitman went even further, maintaining that "the theme of the *Birds* is absurdity itself . . . it is about meaninglessness."[30] The nineteenth-century dichotomy between "allegory" on the one hand and "fantastic exuberance" on the other was neatly categorized by the Swiss scholar H. Köchly in political terms, as a division between Right and Left.[31] This is in many ways a useful model, for it is possible to perceive a growing dislike for allegory as one of the elements in the secular clash between the old truth and the new, between faith and science, between conservatives and liberals.

Greek studies developed in northern Europe during the sixteenth and seventeenth centuries as a means of challenging the traditional authority of the Roman church. The Greek New Testament of Martin Luther was the weapon used to attack an institution whose spiritual claims appeared to rest on a Latin pun.[32] The Renaissance tradition of cloaking secrets in the fabric of fables was

24. Konstan 1990, 187; he cites with evident approval Whitman 1964, 169: "*Birds* . . . is strangely free of political concerns." For an exception to the general trend, see Arrowsmith 1973.

25. Sommerstein 1987, 1.

26. Dunbar 1995, 3.

27. Süvern 1827; 1835.

28. Dobrov 1990, 214; cf. Arrowsmith 1970, 7.

29. Merry 1904, 18, characterizing Schlegel 1809.

30. Whitman 1964, 179.

31. "Wie bei einer parlamentarischen Versammlung, so treten auch hier zunächst in schärfstem Gegensatz eine *Rechte* und eine *Linke* sich gegenüber": Köchly 1857, 1.

32. "*Tu es Petrus et super hanc petram aedificabo ecclesiam meam,*" inscribed around the base of the dome of St. Peter's. On the connection between Protestantism and Greek studies, see Lloyd-Jones 1982, 19; cf. Bernal 1987, 193–194.

a potent one,[33] but its practitioners served a largely courtly public. The court ethos "cherished the display of wit and playful forms of expression that led to deeper truths."[34] Classical scholarship had begun in this tradition, but was going in another direction. At the end of the seventeenth and in the early eighteenth century there was a "diminishing tolerance of error, an increasing demand for precision,"[35] coupled with a growing skepticism with regard to the claims made in some quarters regarding the authenticity of certain ancient texts. The Whig scholar Richard Bentley presented powerful arguments against those who believed that the letters of Phalaris were by the sixth-century B.C. tyrant of Sicilian Acragas. The essay in which Bentley methodically demolished his Tory opponents' case is a classic of its kind.[36] The creation of the science of *Altertumswissenschaft* in early-nineteenth-century Germany and its attendant specialization led to what its proponents regarded as an increased rigor in the treatment of ancient literature.[37] But a "science" that had begun as a defense of the Word of One God was perhaps ill-equipped to understand a culture that worshiped many gods.

A love of Greece was also a means by which liberals expressed their opposition to an *ancien régime* that reckoned its descent from exiled Trojans,[38] and whose members derived moral and ethical truths from emblem books and amused themselves with riddles. Both emblem books and riddles were to lose their status under the new order.[39] Puns went the same way. The Whig wit, the Reverend Sydney Smith (1771–1845), had

> very little to say about puns; they are in very bad repute, and so they *ought* to be. The wit of language is so miserably inferior to the wit of ideas, that it is very deservedly driven out of good company. Sometimes, indeed, a pun makes its appearance which seems for a moment

33. Wind 1966.

34. Kaufmann 1990, 72; cf. Winkler 1991, 35–37.

35. R. H. Griffith 1945, 156.

36. Bentley 1699; 1883.

37. Pfeiffer 1976; Wilamowitz-Moellendorff 1982; Bernal 1987.

38. "The Greek cause was supported in England by . . . Whigs and Radicals": Blake 1982, 32. On the supposed Trojan descent of, e.g., the Habsburgs, see Laschitzer 1888 (esp. pl. 1: "*Hector Priami Magni Regis Troianorum Fil[ius]*"); cf. MacDougall 1982.

39. See the Chronological Index in Heckscher, Sherman, and Ferguson 1984, 81–90: emblem books published in the sixteenth century take up 2½ pages, in the seventeenth century 4, in the eighteenth century 1½, and in the nineteenth less than 1. On riddles, see Bryant 1990, 51: "With the coming of the nineteenth century there began a decline in the esteem in which the riddle was held."

to redeem its species; but we must not be deceived by them; it is a radically bad race of wit.[40]

Classics, meanwhile, had become a subject whose principal pedagogical aim was to teach the young to express themselves unambiguously; ambiguity in ancient literature consequently tended to be overlooked. Since "hidden meanings" were in essence "kitsch,"[41] they came to be disregarded, even derided.[42] Puns might be explained away as "accidental";[43] when this was clearly impossible — as with those of Aristophanes — they might be dismissed as "rarely sophisticated."[44] But then, "few scholars are so Oedipal as to seek what they consciously do not wish to find."[45] If it is true that "tyrants and terrorists pun sparingly,"[46] their opponents often find ambiguity to be an effective means of safe criticism. Allegory — and certainly political allegory — went out of scholarly fashion; it was only tolerated in the form of what De Quincey called "impersonated abstractions."[47]

AMBIGUITY IN GREECE

By contrast, the ancient Greeks were very keen on ambiguity — in its place — and on disguising (or enhancing) fact with fiction. A prime example is to be found in the *Protagoras,* where Plato makes the Abderite philosopher ask his audience whether he should make his case *mûthon légōn* ("in the form of a myth") or go through it in a factual way (Pl. *Prt.* 320c). His listeners choose the myth. Isocrates, writing in the fourth century B.C., put matters very nicely when speaking of *logoùs amphibólous* ("ambiguous words"): "arguments the employment of which, when one contends in court over contracts for his own advantage, is shameful and no slight token of depravity but, when one

40. S. Smith 1886, 241–242.

41. If Roy Pascal is correct that "the recommendation of obsolete values is the essence of kitsch": 1973, 38; cf. 294–295.

42. Dover 1958, 235.

43. Contrast, "The pun is not natural, it is an art form and thus not careless": Ahl 1988, 25; cf. Vendryes 1921, 209; Redfern 1984, 15.

44. Dover 1968, 96.

45. Ahl 1988, 21–23.

46. Hall 1984, 100.

47. De Quincey 1857, 281; cf. Newiger 1957. The primary sense of "allegory" in *OED*[2] (s.v.) is "description of a subject under the guise of some other subject of aptly suggestive resemblance."

discourses on the nature of man and of things, is fine and philosophical."[48] Poetry was another area where ambiguity might exist. W. B. Stanford, writing in prewar Trinity College, Dublin, amid the last vestiges of the *ancien régime,* and in the city of those consummate wordplayers James Joyce and Myles na Gopaleen, was one of the few to recognize the fact:

> No *genre* of Greek poetry is entirely free from deliberate ambiguities, whether trivial puns, superstitious or sophistical etymologies, cryptic oracles, diplomatic evasions, cunning and deceptive equivocations, humorous or cacemphatic *doubles entendres,* unconscious foreshadowings of catastrophe, allusive phrases, associative meanings and vaguenesses, or any other of the manifold devices of ambiguity in its widest sense. Simpler lyric poetry had least of it, drama most.[49]

These devices might be employed in the service of political allegory in both serious and comic contexts. A good example of the former is to be found in Bacchylides' *Dithyramb for the Athenians* (18 Snell), written in the late 470s B.C. apparently employing the career of Theseus as a graceful tribute to Cimon, his family, and his exploits.[50] The conjunction of a *kuneàn Lákainan* ("Laconian cap") and an *oúlion Thessalàn khlamúd'* ("woolly [or 'deadly'] Thessalian cloak") must allude, albeit "emphatically," to Cimon's twin sons Lacedaemonius and Oulius, and to their brother Thessalus. John Barron has persuasively argued that references to "Lemnian fire" in Theseus' eyes and his "auburn" hair refer to Cimon's parents, Miltiades, the captor of Lemnos, and Hegesipyle, a Thracian princess. The message of these lines must be that Cimon "is a second Theseus": appropriate for one who brought Theseus' bones to Athens in the 470s B.C.[51] Bacchylides' other Thesean dithyramb (17 Snell) has been called "a manifesto for the Delian League," and describes a scene that was also depicted in a mural in Cimon's Theseum, namely the hero's visit to the underwater realm of his father Poseidon. Again certain words in the poem stand out, and can only be explained by reference to Cimon. Theseus visits his *hippíou* ("horsey") father: Cimon's family was the "horsiest" in Athens (his grandfather Cimon had won the Olympic chariot race in 536, 532, and 528 B.C. with the same team of mares; Hdt. 6,103.2–3).[52] Amphitrite places a distinctive garment, an *aïóna,* around him. The word is exceptionally rare, and must play on *Ēïōn,* Eion, the city on the

48. Isoc. 21.240; cf. Stanford 1939, 13.
49. Stanford 1939, 181–182.
50. Barron 1980; Francis 1990, 53–66.
51. Barron 1980, 2.
52. Ibid., 3.

Strymon that was the site of the Delian League's first victory, won under Cimon.[53] Elsewhere, a dead Trojan named Eioneus ("the man of Eion") was included by Polygnotus in the mural decoration of the Lesche of the Cnidians at Delphi (Paus. 10.27.1), and his presence, too, must reflect Cimon's first great triumph; by allusive means, an allegorical equation is thus made between Cimon's victory at Eion and the Sack of Troy.[54] Myth could indeed be "readily adjusted or invented in the service of state, family or politics."[55]

The same "emphatic" approach to historical events and the individual's role in them was employed by writers for the Athenian comic stage. Instead of graceful compliments, however, insults were the common coin. Wordplay, ambiguity, and "emphasis" lent themselves admirably to a "discourse on the nature" of particular individuals, and were especially useful when those who were "rich, aristocratic, and powerful" were in the line of fire. Much hinges on the level of sophistication of Aristophanes' audience. There are those who would see them as peasants,[56] but this is perhaps an instance of the "impoverishment of the past," to which I have alluded elsewhere,[57] and to which there are welcome signs of reaction.[58] Rather, Aristophanes was writing for an audience that included many who were urbane and politically aware, alert to any nuance, equivocation, or ambiguity; in short, "sophisticated." He was not writing for peasants and potters.

Much of what is imputed by these various means is at the level of gossip, and much may well never have actually occurred in real life. Some incidents or conceits in any case had their origins in the exaggerations of comic writers—frequently grounds for dismissing elements of the anecdotal tradition out of hand, but in the present context all to the good. But although the historicity of some of the events and imputations discussed here may be open to question, the historical significance of the fact that such things were said, joked about, or even believed should not be overlooked. As G. M. Young once observed: "The real, central theme of History is not what happened, but

53. Ibid., 4; Francis 1990, 62.
54. Barron 1980, 4; Francis 1990, 62, 95.
55. Boardman 1982, 1. For excellent discussions of the topic, see Francis 1980; 1990.
56. E.g., Dover 1972, frontispiece, where the reader is invited to "contemplate the expression" on the face of a modern Greek peasant in order to "imagine the people who constituted the greater part of Aristophanes' audience."
57. Vickers 1987c; 1990b; 1990c; Vickers and Gill 1994.
58. Notably Goldhill 1987, esp. pp. 58–59, where he criticizes the view that the "requirements of performance before a mass audience preclude, or at any rate severely limit, the possibilities of complex, problematic or obscure expression in the tragic texts"; the same considerations apply to comedy.

what people felt about it when it was happening."[59] And the role of gossip in a "shame-honor" culture such as that of ancient Athens should not be underestimated. If gossip did indeed "play with reputations,"[60] how much more effectively could this be achieved on the comic stage. If "talk dragged details of men's private lives into the public arena for inspection and condemnation,"[61] writers of comedy will have capitalized on the fact. In a society that "lacked organized news media,"[62] the comic theatre will have served as an effective means of dissecting rumor and gossip. It will be taken for granted in what follows that if there is a prefiguration in comedy of a story preserved in the anecdotal tradition, then the two are related. Whether the prefiguration or the story has a basis in fact will not be my concern. All I hope to demonstrate is that there is a sufficiently large overlap between tales told about members of Pericles' extended family and the plots and situations that occur in Aristophanes' extant plays to justify a belief in political allegory.

It was probably with good reason that Aristotle mentions Pericles' ward Alcibiades in his analysis of the difference between poetry and history:

> The historian and the poet do not differ in that they use metrical or unmetrical language. . . . The difference is that the one tells of events that have happened, the other of such as might happen . . . poetry expresses the universal, history particulars. Now, "the universal" consists in describing the kind of things that a person of a certain character would say or do probably or necessarily. . . . An example of the particular is what Alcibiades did, or what was done to him. (Arist. *Poet.* 9,2–4)

It is tempting to think that Aristotle is implicitly saying that the poet (he is speaking of the dramatic poet) shows the kind of thing that someone like Alcibiades might say or do, given his known propensities.[63] This is what the Antiochene polymath Libanius seems to have implied centuries later when he posed the rhetorical question: "What play did not include [Alcibiades] among the cast of characters? Eupolis, Aristophanes, did they not show him on the

59. G. M. Young, cited in Marcus 1966, III. Cf. Strauss 1990, 122: "The truth of [the anecdotes about Alcibiades' youthful adventures] hardly matters; much more important is that Alcibiades elicited them."

60. Spacks 1985, 4; cf. Hunter 1990. Aspasia provides a prime example; see M. M. Henry 1995, 19–28.

61. Hunter 1990, 322.

62. Ober 1989, 148.

63. Cf. Else (1957, 313), who argues that the reason why Alcibiades is given as the example of a historical individual by Aristotle is "because he was a favorite and conspicuous butt of the Old Comedy."

stage? It is to him that comedy owed its success" (Lib. fr. 50β [5.644.5–7]). Given the information available to Libanius (the libraries of late-Roman Athens and Antioch will have contained rather more primary literature than is available to us),[64] it is possible that he knew what he was talking about. It is also the case that Libanius has regularly been given short shrift by the learned, ever since his professors at Athens criticized him for skipping their lectures so that he could do his own research.[65]

ALLEGORY IN *BIRDS*

It is a far from new idea that *Birds* is a parody of the situation in which Alcibiades found himself in 414 B.C. The idea was first put forward in modern times by Jacques le Paulmier de Grentemesnil.[66] The Jesuit scholar Pierre Brumoy developed it at length in 1730, and variants have been proposed by Süvern, Köchly, Blaydes, and others.[67] A few years ago, I wrote an essay in similar vein,[68] but not only did I ignore le Paulmier, Brumoy, and Süvern (whose works are discussed more fully in Chapter 9), but I also overlooked the full implications of another study, which I now find to be full of good sense. This was Barry R. Katz's demonstration that the three gods, Poseidon, Heracles, and the Thracian Triballus, who make representations to Peisthetaerus at *Birds* 1565–1691, are allegories of Nicias, Lamachus, and Alcibiades, the three generals who had been appointed to command the Athenian expeditionary force sent to Sicily in 415 B.C. I was already convinced that Peisthetaerus himself embodied many recognizable characteristics of Alcibiades,[69] and had not yet fully realized the extent to which Aristophanes might have reflected different facets of the same individual by means of different characters (who might even be on the stage at the same time).

Such "polymorphic characterization," as I have called it, might recently have seen an exploration of, say, the political career of Baroness Thatcher by means of the interaction of an Iron Lady, of St. Francis of Assisi, and of Queen Boadicea (embodying the belligerent, charitable, and patriotic per-

---

64. Cf. Norman 1960, 122–126.

65. Norman 1965, 13–15.

66. le Paulmier de Grentemesnil 1668, 750.

67. Brumoy 1730 (*non vidi*); 1780, 12:138–219; Süvern 1826; Köchly 1857; Blaydes 1882.

68. Vickers 1989b.

69. For a reworking of the case, see Chapters 9 and 10.

sonae of the former British prime minister). It was the perfect dramatic vehicle for representing a figure as multifaceted as Alcibiades, compared in antiquity to Proteus (Lib. *Decl.* 12.42 [5.558.16]) and a chameleon (*Alc.* 23.4),
and supposedly descended from Daedalus (Pl. *Alc.* 1.121).[70] It is a principle
that can easily encompass both Peisthetaerus and the Triballian as reflections
of Alcibiades. It is also — as we shall see — a principle that solves the problem
of "discontinuity" that is supposed to afflict Aristophanes' plots.

Katz's argument is that "Aristophanes, amidst much comic foolery, intended his divine embassy of Poseidon, Heracles, and Triballos, who come to
Cloudcuckooland to treat for peace, to remind his audience of the curious
troika placed in charge of the Sicilian expedition" — of Nicias, Lamachus,
and Alcibiades.[71] And this is achieved very effectively. Poseidon's apparent
leadership of the group reflects the unofficial seniority due to his age enjoyed
by Nicias, and the way in which he is outvoted by his fellow envoys recalls
how Nicias in Sicily had been outvoted by his fellow generals; his concern for
propriety and decorum reflects a trait of Nicias, and his remark about the
Triballian, "O Democracy, where will you lead us if the gods elect *him*"
(1570–1571), reflects Nicias' opposition both to Alcibiades and to the Sicilian
expedition. The unintelligibility of the Triballian's speech (which is very brief
and mostly gibberish) is associated by Katz with Alcibiades' speech defect,
and with his practice of hesitating in a speech and searching for the right
word; his cloak may allude to Alcibiades' liking for long, trailing robes. Then
Heracles' impatient desire immediately to strangle Peisthetaerus (1575) recalls
Lamachus' proposal for a direct attack on Syracuse. Poseidon's reminder that
the gods had been sent to make peace (1577) recalls Nicias' relatively pacific
proposal on the same occasion, and the rough character of Heracles well corresponds to that of Lamachus, the tough "professional" soldier. The possibility that Heracles will be poor (1644) perhaps alludes to Lamachus' well-known
poverty: he was so badly off that whenever he was elected general he would
ask "the Athenians to advance him some money to provide him with clothes
and shoes" (Plut. *Nic.* 15.1). Heracles' apparent eagerness to get a good meal
may have something to do with Aristophanes' lampoon elsewhere of Lamachus' debts, his gluttony, and his dependence on state pay.

Such, in outline, is Katz's case. He also suggests that a reason for the Triballian's reticence, his presence on stage as a virtual "silent partner," might be
to highlight the absence of Alcibiades from Athens.[72] But if the tradition that

70. Hertzberg (1853, 14) speaks of Alcibiades' "geistige Elasticität."
71. Katz 1976, 353.
72. Ibid., 358.

Peisthetaerus reflects the personality of Alcibiades is a valid one (on which see Chapter 9), the latter individual will already have been effectively present on stage. Aristophanes shows Peisthetaerus dressed as a swallow (1412), a bird whose twittering was regularly described in the same words (*traulízein* and *traulós*) as Alcibiades' speech defect. Peisthetaerus is characterized as a despot, the tyrant of Cloudcuckooland, recalling the fears expressed on the eve of the departure of the fleet for Sicily that Alcibiades was aiming at tyranny in Athens (Thuc. 6.15). The case has also been made (and will be made more fully below) that *Birds* lampoons an Alcibiades at Sparta who has bamboozled his hosts and dishonored Timaea, the Spartan queen.[73] For present purposes, this is of secondary importance; one of the objects of this Introduction is to reinforce Katz's arguments so as to make it appear on balance likely that Aristophanes did employ political allegory.

Aristophanes uses both parallel situations and characteristic language to show the three gods as Nicias, Lamachus, and Alcibiades. Nicias was currently the admiral of the Athenian fleet in Sicily. If Aristophanes' idea of a marine god (*theós*) played on this, it was a witty conceit. Nicias was also notoriously superstitious. He kept a soothsayer in his house, was much given to divination (*theiasmôi;* Thuc. 7.50.4; cf. 7.77.2), and "never disregarded religious observances and omens" (Plut. *Crass.* 38.2). Poseidon's objection (1567) to the Triballian's wearing his cloak *ep' aristér'* ("on the left" or on the side that "bode ill," was "sinister" or "ominous")[74] may allude to Nicias' habitual superstition. Similar considerations perhaps govern Poseidon's injunction (1568) to the Triballian to shift his cloak *epì dexián* ("to the fortunate side").[75] Poseidon's concern with neatness (cf. 1573) recalls furthermore how Nicias had tidied up the Delian festival, making what had been a disorderly affair a stately procession (Plut. *Nic.* 3.5). The Triballian's *himátion* perhaps echoes the Alcibiadean reality even more than Katz thought, for not only did Alcibiades wear a "purple robe which he trailed through the Agora" (*Alc.* 16.1), but no fewer than twenty-two of his *himátia* had been put up for sale by public auction a few months before the performance of *Birds*. The details were recorded on an inscription visible to all.[76]

"How like Laespodias you are!" Poseidon complains of the Triballian at *Birds* 1569. Laespodias was to be Nicias' fellow general for the year 414/13 B.C.,

---

73. Brumoy 1780, 12:184; Vickers 1989b; see Chapters 9 and 10.

74. LSJ s.v. *aristerós*.

75. Cf. LSJ s.v. *dexiós* II: "fortunate, esp. of the flight of birds and other omens." The gods' ambassadorial status (*presbeúomen*, 1566) perhaps recalls Nicias' service as one of the envoys (*présbeis*) he had persuaded the Athenians to send to Sparta in 420: Thuc. 5.46.2.

76. Pritchett 1956, 167, 190–210; 1961, 23; cf. Lewis 1966.

although his campaigning was in Laconia rather than Sicily (Thuc. 6.105.2). His infirmity (Laespodias is supposed to have had a gammy leg; Schol. *Birds* 1569), and the Triballian's supposed resemblance, may be an exaggerated allusion to Alcibiades' gait, which (together with his diction) was later to be imitated by Alcibiades Junior. It was said of the latter that "he walks (*badízei*) in an affected way, dragging his *himátion* behind him, so as to resemble his father" (Archipp. *PCG* 48 *ap. Alc.* 1.8).

Aristophanes' allegory may be rather more sophisticated than this, and perhaps operated on more than one level. In keeping with the subtext of the play, the ambassador gods are characterized as Spartan deities. Heracles was believed to have been the ancestor of a line of Spartan kings,[77] Poseidon had important sanctuaries at Cape Taenarus and at Sparta itself,[78] and the Thracian Triballians were probably allies of the Spartans.[79] There may also be a pun on the name *Trib*-allian and the *tríbōn* — a simple cloak, but characteristic of Sparta. (The Spartan way of life was characterized as "barley bread and a *tríbōna* [Spartan cloak]").[80] Alcibiades in exile had for the moment thrown in his lot with the Spartans, and it might have been diverting to see the men who had been his co-generals in 415 B.C. doing the same, but in the safe, fictional world of the stage. Again, this is secondary to the principal purpose of this Introduction, except that it serves to explain why Heracles expresses the wish (1575) to "strangle" Peisthetaerus: "strangling" was the regular form of capital punishment at Sparta (cf. Plut. *Agis* 19.6, 20.1, 20.5), and Alcibiades had recently been condemned to death in absentia by the Athenians. The reason Heracles wants to kill Peisthetaerus is because he is blockading (*apoteikhísas*) the gods (1576). It may be more than a coincidence that Lamachus was building an *apoteíkhisma* ("fortification wall") on Euryalus above Syracuse at the time *Birds* was performed (Thuc. 6.99.1), whereas Alcibiades conspicuously was not.

Poseidon reminds his companions that they are ambassadors for peace (1577). This might not be just a reflection of Nicias' relatively peaceable approach to his Sicilian adversaries,[81] but also an allusion to Nicias' activities as a peacemaker in the 420s B.C., which culminated in the Peace of Nicias, of

---

77. Hdt. 8.131; Paus. 3.1.5; Ath. 12.535b; *Alc.* 23.8.

78. Paus. 3.25.4; cf. 3.12.5, 3.14.2. Poseidon's shrine at Taenarus included the cave wherein Heracles was said to have taken Cerberus prisoner: Guarducci 1984, 101.

79. Thucydides speaks of the Triballoi defeating Sitalces, the Athenians' Thracian ally, in 424 (4.101.5).

80. Plut. *Cleom.* 16.7; cf. *lakōnízein kaì tríbōnas ékhein* ("to behave like a Spartan and wear a simple cloak"), [Dem.] 54.34.

81. Cf. Katz 1976, 361.

which Lamachus was a cosignatory.[82] Heracles' interest in the meat Peisthetaerus is cooking does, as Katz suggested, recall Aristophanes' lampoon of Lamachus in *Acharnians* (of 425 B.C.), but there is more that might be said. Lamachus' being deprived of a feast because he had to go on maneuvers at *Acharnians* 1085–1142 was presumably a jibe at his dependence on state support, and the information imparted by a servant at *Birds* 1589 that "there is no oil in the flask" may also find an explanation in *Acharnians,* where the lampooned Lamachus polishes his shield with oil (*Acharnians* 1128). Lamachus could, moreover, be mentioned by name in 425 B.C. because it was not yet against the law to do so — or because he was neither rich, nor aristocratic, nor powerful.

Poseidon (probably; the Ravenna and Marcian manuscripts are unclear as to who delivers the speech at 1591–1595) tells Peisthetaerus that the divine envoys have not come to make war for personal gain (*ou kerdaínomen*); one of the accusations that Nicias made against Alcibiades when the Sicilian expedition was debated was that he was in it to serve his own ends (*idíōn héneka kerdôn;* Plut. *Nic.* 12.4; cf. Thuc. 6.15.2). "Pools of water in the marshes, and halcyon (*alcuonídas*) days" will be granted in exchange for peace. There may be a pun here on Alcibiades' name, as well as a reference to his current place of refuge, for Sparta was exceedingly swampy (cf. Strabo 8.5.1), and there was even a marsh next to one of the kings' houses (Xen. *Lac.* 15.6), where Alcibiades was currently outstaying his welcome. The claim that Poseidon and Heracles have come as plenipotentiaries (*autokrátores*) may allude not only to the current status of Nicias and Lamachus as generals possessing full powers (*autokrátoras;* Thuc. 6.8.2; cf. Plut. *Nic.* 12.6), but also to an occasion in 420 B.C. when Alcibiades had caused Nicias great embarrassment by persuading Spartan ambassadors plenipotentiary (*autokrátores;* Thuc. 5.45.1; cf. 46.1), who had come to discuss outstanding differences after the Peace of Nicias, publicly to deny their true position. The result was a complete breakdown of the peace with Sparta, and its replacement — at Alcibiades' prompting — with a peace with Argos (Thuc. 5.45–46). Alcibiades' fooling of the Spartan envoys had been achieved by means of "deceit and oaths" (Plut. *Nic.* 10.4; cf. Thuc. 5.45.2), and there may be something of this in Peisthetaerus' mention of "mortals who swear false oaths" (1609) and of perjury (1611). Then, oaths sworn "by the Raven" (1611) may be an "emphatic" allusion to a bad portent that had been observed at Delphi (the Raven was Apollo's bird) just before the departure of the fleet for Sicily. Ravens had pecked the golden fruit from

82. Thuc. 5.16.1, 19.2, 24.1, 43.2; Plut. *Nic.* 9.9; *Alc.* 14.2.

a sacred palm tree (Plut. *Nic.* 13.5; *Mor.* 397f.).[83] That ravens might peck the perjurer's eye out (1613) brings the response from Poseidon, "By Poseidon you speak sense in that at least."

Heracles goes along with whatever Peisthetaerus says (1603, 1614; cf. 1626–27, 1675, 1685), perhaps reflecting the relationship between Lamachus and Alcibiades; at the council of war at Rhegium at which Lamachus had spoken in favor of a quick attack on Syracuse, he "nevertheless gave his own voice for the proposal of Alcibiades" (Thuc. 5.50.1). It is Heracles who is open to Peisthetaerus' persuasiveness, and who is won over by his arguments, ludicrous as they are. The fantasy always has a basis in reality. Thus Poseidon and Peisthetaerus argue that if Zeus should die, Heracles will be a pauper on the grounds that as a bastard he cannot inherit (1641–1650). "Me, a bastard? What are you saying?" asks Heracles with some bewilderment (1651). If the historical Lamachus was in question, everyone in the audience will have been puzzled as well, for Lamachus was certainly legitimate.[84] Peisthetaerus explains: "Because you are the son of a foreign (*xénēs*) woman" (1652) — grounds for illegitimacy, and hence loss of citizen's rights. Lamachus' *father* was in fact called *Xeno*phanes (Thuc. 6.8.2), which may explain the conceit.

The scene is full of puns, many of them the result of a confusion of *lambda* and *rho* in the mouth of Peisthetaerus. This kind of wordplay quickly palls today,[85] so I shall limit this particular discussion to two examples. First, at 1657–1658, Peisthetaerus refers to Poseidon being the first (*prôtos*) to claim Heracles' father's money (*khrēmátōn*). *Hoûtos ho Poseidôn plōtós* (for *prôtos*), however, would mean "Poseidon here afloat" — appropriate enough, given Poseidon's watery sphere. Second, Heracles' father's money (*khrēmátōn*), when lambdacized, produces a play upon *klēmátōn* ("shoes").[86] This might well be

83. Nicias had himself dedicated a bronze palm tree on Delos: Plut. *Nic.* 3.7.

84. Kirchner 1901–1903, no. 8981. For an interesting footnote to the bastardy of Heracles, see Callaghan 1990.

85. Cf. two modern examples: "Eleanor Roosevelt, discussing democracy with an oriental ambassador, asked: 'And when did you last have an election?' The diplomat, with some embarrassment, answered, 'Before blekfast'": Redfern 1984, 164. Or the "Japanese" joke attributed to Woody Allen: "What is the difference between pussy and sushi?" "Rice."

86. Hsch.; see LSJ s.v. *klêma* III (and cf. *kleímata* and *klíma* VI). If *klêma* does indeed mean "shoe," the judgment of Biel (1779–1780, 2:205; followed by M. Schmidt 1860, 493; and Latte 1966, 489) that Hesychius (who glosses *kleímata, klêma,* and *klímata* as *hupodéma/ta* ["shoe/s"]) misunderstood Jeremiah 48:32 (*klímata soû diêlthe thálassan* ["your branches passed over the sea"]) requires reassessment. Since the context there concerns "the vine of Sibmah," it is difficult to see how a confusion with shoes could ever have arisen. Best to take Hesychius at face value, with LSJ s.vv. The same "shoe" joke is repeated at 1666; by 414 B.C. it will have been

a witty allusion to Lamachus' poverty, which was so extreme that he had to ask the state for shoe money whenever he was elected general (Plut. *Nic.* 15.1).

Barbarous language was likened by the Greeks to the twittering of swallows.[87] *Traulízein,* the Greek word for Alcibiades' speech impediment, was also used for "the twittering of swallows," and *this* is probably the linguistic association Aristophanes makes between Alcibiades and the Triballian (who has already been called *barbarôtaton* ["extremely barbarous"] at 1573) when the latter speaks gibberish, as much as alluding to Alcibiades' occasional hesitancy of speech.[88] The discussion between Heracles and Poseidon as to what the Triballian might have said in the lines (1678–1679) that Benjamin Bickley Rogers translated as "Me gulna charmi grati Sovranau Birdito stori,"[89] and William Arrowsmith as "Gleep? Schnoozer skirt wotta twatch snock! Birdnicks pockle. Ugh,"[90] has Heracles making an interpretation favorable to Peisthetaerus, but Poseidon objecting that he said the opposite, and continuing (1681), "unless he said to *badízein* ('walk') like the swallows." If, as was suggested above, the debate of the gods is based on the council of war held by Nicias, Lamachus, and Alcibiades at Rhegium, this line (which nearly every editor from Bentley onward has tried to emend)[91] can stand, and be seen as a witty allusion (1) to Alcibiades' proposal to *badízein* against the Syracusans (after having won over the Syracusans' allies, beginning with the Messenians; Plut. *Nic.* 14.3), (2) to his "migration" (or desertion) from the Athenians, and perhaps (3) to Alcibiades' "funny walk," to which Aristophanes apparently drew attention at the beginning of the scene under discussion.

"Swallows" are mentioned again in the following line (1682), and Heracles soon falls in once more (1685–1687) with Peisthetaerus' demand for *Basíleia* ("Sovereignty"). That Poseidon admits that he is outvoted (and cf. 1630) could well reflect the outcome of the Rhegian meeting, for the policy adopted on that occasion was that of Alcibiades. Lamachus threw his lot in with Alcibiades, who then sailed off to try to persuade the Messenians to join the Athenians (Thuc. 6.50.1).[92] Not long after this, Alcibiades was recalled to

---

a hoary one (see Chapters 2 and 3). For an attested pun involving a play on *kappa* and *chi,* see Pherecyd. *ap.* Diog. Laert. 1.119, where *Krónos* is turned into *Khrónos* (cited by Tate 1927, 215 n. 2).

87. E.g., Aesch. *Ag.* 1050; Schol. *Birds* 1680: *barbarízein khelidonízein.*

88. Cf. Katz 1976, 357.

89. Rogers 1906, 223.

90. Arrowsmith 1970, 130.

91. Blaydes 1882, 167–168, thus lists half a score of such changes to the manuscript reading. Cf. Dunbar 1995, 124, 736–737.

92. But *ouk épeithen* ("he did not persuade [them]").

Athens to face charges that were clearly derived from the Athenian public's fear that he was aiming at tyranny; but he escaped from his escort and duly "migrated." The way, however, that Poseidon appears to say, in effect, "I wash my hands of the whole business" (1683–1684), should relate as much to the way Nicias had declined sole command of the Sicilian expedition (Thuc. 6.23.3)[93] as to his resignation to the will of his colleagues at Rhegium. Not only is Katz's case fully vindicated, but it is clear that Aristophanes' political allegory closely reflects the nuances of the politics of the year before *Birds* was performed.

If the evidence presented here is cogent, then political allegory may be present to a degree hitherto unsuspected. Line by line, word by word, nuance by nuance, Aristophanes creates complex and diverting images based on the recent adventures of Athens' most prominent son. He holds Alcibiades up to ridicule by means of "emphasis" and the witty use of allusive language, while also poking gentle fun at the foibles of Nicias and Lamachus. He seems to distance himself, for whatever reason (personal safety, obeying the law with regard to satirizing by name) by employing allegory. Or rather, he does not distance himself, but engages in an analysis of what happened that is richer and more evocative (and safer) — thanks to ambiguity at whatever level — than any explicit account of the council of war at Rhegium might have been. Nor can it reasonably be claimed that "the passage do[es] not inevitably call Alcibiades to mind, and need not do so to be dramatically effective."[94] Rhegium will have been one of the last pieces of hard news — as opposed to rumor and gossip — that the Athenians had received about Alcibiades. It should also be clear that the number of puns, double meanings, and potential political references in the scene at *Birds* 1565–1693 is too large to attribute merely to coincidence. (Or to put matters another way: if the parallels noted by Katz and the present writer were not contrived, then Aristophanes was being particularly insensitive.)

The reason for this preliminary excursus is to suggest that if political allegory can be shown to exist in the play of all plays that is supposed to lack any "explicit political design,"[95] or that has "no strong or obvious connection with a topical question of public interest,"[96] then it is not altogether unrea-

---

93. Cf. the occasion in 425 when Nicias publicly relinquished the command against the Spartans in Sphacteria in favor of Cleon (Thuc. 4.28, an act that Plutarch thought foolish centuries later (Plut. *Crass.* 36.1).

94. Moorton 1988, 348, epitomizing Westlake 1980, 42, 47, and 49 n. 32, on a different, but related, topic.

95. Dobrov 1990, 214.

96. Sommerstein 1987, 1.

sonable to look for a similarly "emphatic" or allegorical commentary on recent history in earlier plays; nor is it unreasonable to find echoes of Aristophanes in Thucydides, who will have known how to read such allegory. We cannot hope to catch every allusion, but we are fortunate in that we possess something of the rich anecdotal tradition relating to the principal personalities whose policies, idiosyncrasies, and scandalous activities are lampooned by Aristophanes, namely Alcibiades, his guardian Pericles, and Cleon. Pericles was of course dead by the time Aristophanes wrote, but so, too, was Cleon when lampooned in *Peace.* The use — the indiscriminate use, some might say — of the anecdotal tradition raises questions of method that will be discussed in Chapter 1.

PERICLES ON STAGE

PERICLES AND ALCIBIADES
ON STAGE

If even Aristophanes' *Birds,* a play that has been widely held to be "strangely free of political concerns,"[1] and to be "about meaninglessness," whose theme has been held to be "absurdity itself,"[2] can be shown in reality to bear closely upon events that occurred a few months before it was performed, then all prejudices regarding political allegory in Old and Middle Comedy need to be set aside. And that there are prejudices in this matter can be easily shown from the way in which the story of Plato's gift of a copy of *Clouds* to Dionysius I or II of Syracuse has been handled by scholars. The story was mentioned briefly in the Preface, but it bears looking at in greater detail. The account appears in two versions of the anonymous *Life* of Aristophanes, but it is such an extraordinary and unexpected tale that commentators have ignored it, editors have expunged it, and it is actually omitted from a recent English translation of the medieval Greek text. The information comes in a passage where the fame of Aristophanes is under discussion:

> The fame of the poet was so great that it reached the Persians, and the king of the Persians asked whose side the comic writer was on. And they say that when Dionysius the tyrant wanted to know about Athenian government (*tèn Athenaíon politeían*), Plato sent him Aristophanes' play about the denunciation of Socrates in the *Clouds* (*tèn Aristophánous poíēsin, tèn katà Sōkrátous en Nephélais katēgorían*), and advised

1. Whitman 1964, 169.
2. Ibid., 179.

him to learn about their government by studying [Aristophanes'] dramas (*tà drâmata autoû*). (*Vit. Ar.* 28.46–48 Koster; cf. 29a. 33–35)

There can be little doubt that this is the meaning of the Greek as it stands, but the very thought of Plato disseminating the work that had done his intellectual hero so much harm has been so repugnant that some scholars have attempted to avoid its implications. Thus in the editions of W. Dindorf and F. Dübner, the reference to *Clouds* was left out,[3] whereas J. van Leeuwen proposed an emendation that had Plato presenting the works of Aristophanes to the Syracusan tyrant *minus* the offending play ("Which is what you might expect from Plato").[4] W. J. K. Koster printed the text translated above,[5] but M. Lefkowitz in her translation of Koster's text felt free to omit the reference to *Clouds*.[6] She clearly had good precedents, but it is difficult to imagine the circumstances in which the story could have been made up on the basis of internal evidence from the plays, which is the usual source of many of the undeniable fictions to be found in the lives of the Greek poets,[7] and it is a counsel of despair to emend (or ignore) a text without very good reason. It will be argued that Plato could well have made a gift of the kind described, and that whether or not he actually did, *Clouds* and other plays in the Aristophanic corpus are of a sufficiently political character to make the Syracusan story plausible. *Clouds,* or so it will be argued in Chapters 2 and 3, examines the public and private morality of Pericles and Alcibiades, two individuals against whom charges of tyranny were made.[8] If so, it would have been an eminently suitable gift for a Syracusan tyrant.

There is a mass of hitherto unconsidered evidence to support a case for Aristophanes having written plays that are intensely political: *Spitting Image*[9] rather than *The Muppets,* reflections of current events rather than sheer fantasy (or philosophical or literary criticism). First though, it must be asked why the connections made here have not been noted before. It has, I believe, much to do with what has been well described as "the classicist's hesitancy, widespread though not universal, to study stylistic elements other than those

3. Dindorf 1838; Dübner 1842.
4. Van Leeuwen 1908, 172–173.
5. Koster 1975, 135.
6. Lefkowitz 1981, 171.
7. Lefkowitz 1981.
8. E.g., Cratin. *PCG* 258 *ap. Per.* 7.1; *Per.* 12.2; *Com. adesp.* 60 *CAF* 3.411 *ap. Per.* 16.1; Val. Max. 8.9 ext. 2; cf. Ehrenberg 1954, 85; Ahl 1991, 47 (Pericles); Thuc. 6.15.2–4; cf. Seager 1967 (Alcibiades).
9. British Central Television's popular show in which puppets based on recognizable politicians acted out fantastic variations on recent news events.

sanctioned by tradition."[10] But apart from most classicists' distaste for political allegory, there has been an undeniable tendency to view Aristophanes' plays in the way in which they have always been viewed since scholars began writing about them: giving outlines of the plot based on the extant text, indicating the date of performance and the success or otherwise where known, and adding a commentary on *realia* mentioned in the play.[11] It is a rare plot summary that says what the purpose of an ancient comedy is, namely, who is the target. In fact, only the plot summary of Cratinus' *Dionysalexandros* does this, stating that the target was Pericles, "satirized because he brought the war on the Athenians."[12] This is what I believe to have been the purpose of *Acharnians* as well; and other plays in the Aristophanic corpus are similarly political, frequently dwelling on Pericles and members of his extended family, especially on his ward Alcibiades.

There is, though, the idea abroad that there is something exceptional about *Dionysalexandros,* that it somehow departs from the norm in being a "mythological burlesque," of a kind we supposedly do not otherwise possess.[13] But once the possibility of political allegory is accepted, the available evidence seems to point in the direction of *Dionysalexandros* being the norm rather than the exception, the publication of its plot summary in 1904 coming too late to influence what by then had become an entrenched position. Studies devoted to "the comic hero,"[14] Aristophanic "imagery" and "dramaturgy,"[15] or supposed *kōmōidouménoi,*[16] which assume that the constituent parts of the Aristophanic corpus can be reduced to a kind of "Lego set," are of limited use. It is as though one were to take a motor car apart and, having carefully laid the pieces side by side, claim that the workings of the internal combustion engine had been satisfactorily explained. There is little in the way of such analysis in this book; simply a description of how Aristophanes' powerful humor moves, and succeeds in going places that other forms of discourse could not approach.

10. Tompkins 1972, 183.

11. Cf. Stadter 1989, lxiv: Old Comedy was not considered proper for after-dinner entertainment in the second century A.D., "because it is too intense, too indecent, and 'every person would need a grammar-teacher beside him, to explain who Laispodias is in Eupolis, and Cinesias in Plato [the comic poet], Lampon in Cratinus, and each of the others made fun of in comedy, so that our dinner party would become a grammar-school, or the jokes would mean less [Plut. *Mor.* 712a].'"

12. *POxy.* 663, 44–48; *CGFP* 70; Cratin. *Dionysalexandros* i, *PCG.* See further Appendix A below.

13. Taplin 1986, 167; Rosen 1988b, 49.

14. E.g., Whitman 1964.

15. E.g., Taillardat 1965; Thiercy 1986.

16. E.g., Storey 1989.

It has been wisely said that "wordplay, and the study of it, can give access to the implicit," [17] and the way in which Aristophanes employs "emphasis" has already been indicated in the Introduction. Although allegory, ambiguity, and puns are not respectable in some academic quarters, there are welcome signs of change. The very fact that the question "Who is Dicaeopolis?" can be posed (as it has been recently) [18] — and answered with the names of historical individuals — suggests that allegory may still have its friends. Walter Redfern, Frederick Ahl, and Jonathan Culler have done much to create a renewed interest in wordplay as an important aspect of many literatures. [19] Ahl's work in particular is of special significance in that it shows how extensive was the role of wordplay in both Greek and Roman society. Jeffrey Henderson has done much to elucidate the double meanings that were engendered by comic poets in the realm of obscene language, and Ralph M. Rosen has shed new light on the origins of obscene usage in the genre of iambic abuse a century or so earlier. [20] John Barron and E. D. Francis have elucidated the political allegory of Bacchylides' Thesean dithyrambs. [21] Benyamin Shimron has recently shown that "Herodotus . . . smiles with a purpose," that he uses "sarcasm, wit, simple jokes . . . irony [and] puns" to make more serious points. [22] Even Thucydides was not above punning, [23] and may even have lampooned Alcibiades' mode of speech (see Chapter 2). Plato's *Cratylus* is a work based on wordplay of a kind that clearly went down well in the fifth or the fourth century B.C., and whatever its precise significance might have been, it was composed on the principle that ambiguity can be an efficient means of communication that can greatly enrich what is being said. [24] It is against this back-

17. Redfern 1984, 26.

18. E. L. Bowie 1988; Sutton 1988.

19. Redfern 1984; Ahl 1984; 1985; 1991; Culler 1988.

20. Henderson 1975; 1987; Rosen 1988a; 1988b.

21. Barron 1980; Francis 1990, 53–64; and see the Introduction.

22. See "The Uses of Humour" in Shimron 1989, 58–72; on seriousness in comedy, see Henderson 1990.

23. J. E. Powell 1937, 103; Shimron 1989, 71.

24. Cf. Hutchinson 1983, 106: "The pun brings in another level (or levels) of meaning to a text, and an author may exploit this second level in a single occasion, on several separate occasions, or continually. Puns, employed in a sustained and intricate manner, will allow him to narrate on several levels simultaneously."

ground of the humor of ambiguity being used to make serious points[25] that we should perhaps view Aristophanes' extremely complex, subtle, and sophisticated wordplay.

One way in which Aristophanes generated double meanings was, as we have already seen, by exploiting Alcibiades' distinctive speech mannerism. The resulting words are not only Greek, but are entirely consistent with the anecdotal tradition relating to Alcibiades. The dramatic device was well known in antiquity: when the rhetorician Hermogenes had to give an example of parody in Old Comedy, he chose Alcibiades' speech mannerism and the double meanings generated thereby (Hermog. *Meth.* 34). It is important to realize that such wordplay cannot occur accidentally; it is not inherent in the Greek language to deliver double entendres whenever there is a potential confusion of *rho* and *lambda*. There is thus no wordplay of this kind to be found, for example, in *Iliad* 1, *Agamemnon,* or *Dyscolos.*[26] Nor is there any in *Acharnians,* a play Aristophanes wrote before Alcibiades' entry into politics.[27] Lambdacism is not usually indicated in the text (Quint. *Inst.* 1.5.32), but will have been added by the actor.

Aristophanes exploits other features of Alcibiades' mode of speech as well, notably his frequent use of *kaí* ("and") to begin sentences, of paratactic constructions (sentences held together internally by means of "and"), and of the grammatical form known as the potential optative (an overly polite way of giving orders). These occur, as Daniel Tompkins has demonstrated,[28] in Alcibiades' speeches in Thucydides, a writer who, if Hermogenes (as opposed to Dionysius of Halicarnassus [*Pomp.* 776 (=p. 114, 26 Rhys Roberts)]) is to be believed, regularly imitated the manner of speech of his speakers (Hermog. *Meth.* 31).[29] Not only does the application of Alcibiades' speech patterns to

25. Cf. Hutchinson 1983, 104 (citing Mahood 1957, 164): "Seriousness may also be present in the pun, a quality with which it is not commonly associated"; Denniston 1952, 136: "'Punning' . . . is an unfortunate description because it connotes for us a humorous intention, while by the Greeks it was frequently regarded as a means of attaining truth, or as aesthetically valuable in itself.'"

26. I am grateful to Ernst Badian for making me perform this exercise. It is also worth mentioning that puns can work despite conflicting accentuation; attested examples include: *léidion* and *elaidíou* (Ath. 13.582d–e), *sigē̂* and *Sígeion* (Ath. 13.584e), *hetaírōn* and *hetairôn* (Men. 323 Koerte *ap.* Ath. 13.571e), *Dêmos kalós* and *kēmòs kalós* (Ar. *Wasps* 99). Cf. Ahl 1991, 44: "Ancient authors routinely disregard differences in vowel quantity when making wordplays."

27. Alcibiades' vocabulary was already mocked in Aristophanes' *Banqueters* of 427 B.C.: Ar. *PCG* 205, 5–6; the play is too fragmentary to judge whether other kinds of wordplay were employed.

28. Tompkins 1972.

29. Cf. Tompkins 1972, 37; and Francis 1991–1993.

Aristophanes provide us with an element of relative objectivity, or an "external control, evidence independent of our reading of the play,"[30] but it also quickly emerges that there is much to be said for the allegorical approach. Far from being an uncontrollable, amorphous mess, the resultant material possesses an internal consistency that can be controlled against the historical record, albeit that record may be the exaggerated one of the anecdotal tradition.

Perhaps the closest parallel today for the kind of dramatic performance that was Athenian comedy is the British medical school pantomime. The humor is Aristophanic, or worse, and the characters are often based on recognizable individuals.[31] The process of composition has been well described as follows:

> Not many people know how hard it is to carry out the [Medical School Dramatic] Society's pantomime. The wretched producer must write or persuade friends to write a brilliant script in good time for rehearsal, laboriously collecting jokes through the long English winter to adorn the highly original plot. . . . At the last minute the script will have to be spiced with the very latest gossip, not all that easily come by when rehearsals absorb all leisure time. He must exercise his clinical observation, not only on the various hospital departments as he comes freshly to them, looking for suitable targets for lampoon, but also he must watch and know well his contemporaries, trying to discern which of them can carry out these tricky bits of mimicry.[32]

Mutatis mutandis, this is how Aristophanes must have gone about the task of writing a comedy, devising a clever plot, and exercising his powers of observation in noting the peculiarities of his targets. The only difference was that he had experienced actors, rather than medical students, to perform his plays.

ALCIBIADES AND PERICLES

It is a matter of historical record that Pericles was lampooned on the Athenian stage. Plutarch's *Life* is a rich source of quotations from "comic poets,"

30. Cf. Heath 1987a, 8.
31. E.g., "The most popular song [in the Oxford Medical School's 1961 pantomime] was undoubtedly 'A luvverly bunch of foetuses'": Anon. 1961, 17. In the same production, "Gerald Funny" was a lightly disguised Gerald Honey, a Senior Registrar.
32. Anon. 1959.

including Cratinus, Telecleides, Eupolis, and Hermippus, as well as Aristophanes, who attacked him. J. Schwarze has recently studied these attacks,[33] and believes that the great majority of such references belong either to the period when Pericles was struggling with Thucydides son of Milesias for control of Athenian politics or to the very end of his life, when Athens was at war with the Peloponnesian League. But so far as Aristophanes is concerned, Schwarze only discusses those passages where Pericles is actually mentioned, without considering the possibility that the statesman's personality might be the basis for posthumous lampoons beyond his appearance as himself in Eupolis' *Demi*. Eupolis' conceit, which involved the resurrection of the statesmen of the past with a view to showing up the worthlessness of those of c. 412 B.C., was well known in later antiquity. It was the *locus classicus* of the device known as *idolopoeia*, whereby characters were brought back from the dead in order to make a contemporary point.[34] Although *de mortuis nil nisi bonum* may be the rule today,[35] it certainly was not so in antiquity: the equation of Cleon and a dung beetle discussed at the beginning of the Introduction is enough to demonstrate that; nor, if the argument presented here is correct, can it any longer be said that "Pericles' . . . death save[d] him from Aristophanes' relentless blows."[36] Although there was an Athenian law of apparently long standing forbidding verbal abuse of the dead (Dem. 20.104),[37] it has recently been shown that "sufficiently striking examples [of comic denigration of the dead exist] to suggest that fear of legal prosecution was not operative."[38]

It will be argued below that the dead Pericles is the principal target of *Acharnians,* but that the very-much-alive Alcibiades comes increasingly to the fore in the plays of the later 420s B.C., in fact from *Knights* onward. In *Knights* (725 and 1215), an "Alcibiadean" figure addresses a "Periclean" one as *ô patér* ("Father") and *ô pappídion* ("Daddikins"), and in *Clouds* and *Wasps* he plays the part of a son to a "Periclean" father. Indeed, for much of the nine-

---

33. Schwarze 1971; cf. Rosen 1988b, 49–58.

34. Aristid. 3.487; Hermog. *Prog.* 9; Aphth. *Prog.* 11. Cf. Aristid. 2.322 (on Pl. *Epist.* 8.355a: Dion resurrected to talk to the Syracusans); Crat. *PCG* 87 (*Chirones*: Solon brought back from the dead "ut Pericleae licentiae priscae vitae disciplinam opponeret," *CAF* 1.82); Pl. *Menex.:* where Aspasia and Socrates are brought back to life; see further Loraux 1981, 471 n. 308.

35. With certain exceptions: The proposed London show *And Now, Maxwell—the Musical* was going to have "a small chorus of former *Daily Mirror* workers who confront Maxwell about their pensions": *The Independent on Sunday* (6 Sept. 1992), 1.

36. Solomos 1974, 60.

37. Halliwell 1991, 49.

38. Ibid., 51.

teenth century it was common to see Alcibiades "coming forward" in the character of Pheidippides in *Clouds*.[39] It is perfectly easy to see why, and the idea even appealed to Alcibiades' foremost modern biographer, J. Hatzfeld, who only rejected it on the grounds that in no way could Strepsiades correspond to Alcibiades' physical father, Cleinias.[40] There are, however, several reasons why he could correspond to Pericles, in whose house Alcibiades grew up, and who played the de facto role of a father.[41] It has even been suggested that Deinomache, Alcibiades' mother, was once married to Pericles.[42] Whether or not this was the case, it is a filial nexus that links junior and senior characters in three of the plays discussed here: *Knights, Clouds,* and *Wasps*. The "heroic and frightening" nature of filial rebellion in the 420s B.C., and "the claims of the young to an early assumption of their political patrimony,"[43] are given added point by being shown on the stage in a personalized way. Then in *Peace*, Alcibiades comes to the fore, while "the Olympian" underlies the characterization — appropriately enough — of a god, albeit a minor one. In *Birds*, an echo of Pericles as the leader of his people plays opposite a tyrannically inclined Alcibiades. Characters representing Periclean ideals are used increasingly as a foil for Alcibiadean values, and become less and less objects of ridicule in their own right.

POSTHUMOUS PARODY OF PERICLES

It is, though, a large step from seeing the live Pericles satirized to having him lampooned when dead. It is not simply a question of taste; the way the story of Pericles has generally been told is that although he had his problems in the later 430s B.C., and fell into political disfavor for a few months in the early 420s, he regained popularity and persuaded a repentant people to legitimize his son by Aspasia on his deathbed.[44] If the hypothesis put forward here is

---

39. Donaldson 1860, 185; and see Chapters 2 and 3.

40. Hatzfeld 1951, 34.

41. "Periclès, tuteur d'Alcibiade et son parent, joue pour lui le rôle d'un père": Loraux 1981, 467. Strauss (1990, 122) regards Pericles as one of Alcibiades' "surrogate fathers." For discussions of the precise relationship between Pericles and Alcibiades, see W. E. Thompson 1970 and Cromey 1984.

42. Cromey 1984; Podlecki 1987, III; cf. Stadter 1989, 238, 332.

43. Strauss 1990, 118–119; cf. 1993.

44. A picture we owe largely to Grote (1870, 5:428–442).

correct, a sizable portion of the Athenian populace was unforgiving or callous enough to welcome the sight of a Pericles viciously lampooned at the Lenaean festival of 425 B.C., so that the judges granted Aristophanes first prize. It is only when Pericles' successors revealed themselves to be made of baser material that Aristophanes began to employ Periclean imagery in a slightly more positive light.

What evidence do we therefore have for posthumous parody? Eupolis is not exactly complimentary toward Pericles in Eupolis' *Demi* of c. 412 B.C., with its abusive references to his "bastard" son, his "harlot" wife, and the peculiar shape of his head (Eup. *PCG* 110, 115).[45] The but recently dead Cleon is explicitly lampooned in *Peace,* as we have already seen; and perhaps the best-known example of the genre is the parody of Aeschylus and Euripides in *Frogs,* the one long dead, the other only recently departed. *Dionysalexandros* may be another posthumous lampoon of Pericles (Appendix A), and "the depredations of the Achaeans" mentioned in the plot summary, a topical allusion to the Spartan invasions of 428 (Thuc. 3.1.1) or 427 (Thuc. 3.26.1), rather than those of 431 or 430 B.C.[46]

PERICLES' REPUTATION

Pericles today is a figure whom it is customary to regard with respect,[47] but it is clear that there was a strong critical tradition in ancient historiography.[48] The encomia of Pericles that we find in Thucydides and Plutarch—his "gentleness and mildness of spirit," his bravery, his incorruptibility, his charity, his "nobility and power"—clearly belong to a tradition other than that of the "offensive jests" and the "hostile stories" that Plutarch also records, in addition to information he supplies concerning the day-to-day opposition to Pericles' policies conducted by Thucydides son of Milesias.[49] Above all, it is the

45. Nicias, too, "has an important role" in *Demi* (de Romilly 1963, 202 n. 2); he had died but a couple of years earlier.
46. Cf. Schwarze 1971, 24; Handley 1982, 115.
47. Vogt (1960) is one of the very few to have criticized Pericles in modern times. But "the case," notes de Romilly (1963, 375), "is not quite new, as one can see from fifth-century evidence."
48. Stadter 1989, xliii–xliv (on Plutarch's treatment of hostile testimony), lxii (on Stesimbrotus), lxxvi–lxxvii (on Duris of Samos).
49. Cf. Gomme *HCT* 1:74; Stadter 1989. There is also an undertone of criticism in Pl. *Grg.* 515e, 518e; cf. Schreiner 1968, 10.

sympathy that Thucydides the historian[50] and Plutarch[51] clearly show for Pericles that has colored later views of the statesman; and if it is true, as has been persuasively argued,[52] that Alcibiades was one of Thucydides' principal informants, then we may perhaps see not only a "magnification of Alcibiades' part in shaping events"[53] as the product of such an association, but also the favorable press that Pericles received at the historian's hands. Pericles' virtues, moreover, must have become more manifest as Alcibiades' vices became increasingly apparent.

Nor should it be forgotten that Pericles only became a hero in modern eyes with George Grote. William Mitford, for example, writing in 1829, could still charge Pericles with having "deprav[ed] the Athenian constitution, to favour that popular power by which he ruled, and [having] reviv[ed] that pernicious hostility between the democratical and aristocratical interests, first in Athens, and then, by the Peloponnesian war, throughout the nation."[54] How different (and deliberately so) Grote's tribute to a "life, long, honourable, and useful."[55] It is nevertheless true that "it is hard to take much interest in Pericles if we have no longer description of him than that he was 'an Athenian statesman of democratic tendencies, who was a great patron of arts and letters.'"[56] The tales preserved about him give another, frequently salacious and sometimes brutal, side to his character; these underlie many of Aristophanes' plots and allusions.

Those used to the "plaster saint" image of Pericles will doubtless be repelled by some of the dirt Aristophanes throws at the dead statesman. The symptoms of the plague, for example, are a constant motif (and one suspects that Plutarch's *poikílai metabolaí* ["varied symptoms"; *Per.* 38.1] is based on a knowing reading of the "emphasis" of Thucydides' description of the effects of the malady [Thuc. 2.49], placed as it is after Pericles' Funeral Speech [Thuc. 2.35–46] and shortly before the report of his final speech and Thucydides' appraisal [Thuc. 2.60–65]). There is much "cripple-teasing" of a

---

50. E.g., Thuc. 2.65; though Thucydides is not wholly uncritical: see Hussey 1985, 123 n. 11. Thucydides only grudgingly includes Pericles among the statesmen he calls *xunetoí* ("intelligent"), deeming him *mè axúnetos* ("not unintelligent"): Thuc. 2.34.6; Hornblower 1991, 124–125, 294.

51. Stadter 1989, xxxviii–xliv.

52. E.g., by Brunt (1952, 59–96) and Bloedow (1973).

53. Brunt 1952, 89.

54. Mitford 1829, 2:403.

55. Grote 1870, 2:432.

56. Robinson 1916, v.

kind familiar in eighteenth-century political cartoons.[57] In addition to mockery of Pericles' congenitally misshapen head, such plague symptoms as sores and ulcers, blindness, forgetfulness, and the loss of the genitalia are distastefully employed as vehicles for criticism of Pericles' reputation.

Far worse, from the point of view of Pericles' political reputation, is the constant harping on his alleged mistreatment of Samian prisoners in 439 B.C. According to the tale Plutarch tells (though he claims not to believe it himself), these unfortunates were tied to planks in the Agora at Miletus, and were left in the open for ten days before being beaten to death with wooden clubs, and their bodies cast away unburied.[58] The source was Stesimbrotus of Thasos who (like Aristophanes in *Clouds;* see Chapters 2 and 3) wrote a "contemptuous review of the education and training of Athenian leaders."[59] There are hints that eyebrows were raised almost immediately at Athens: at the funeral ceremony for Athenians fallen at Samos, Cimon's sister Elpinice is supposed to have said to Pericles: "A fine exploit and one worthy of garlands, Pericles, to lose many of our brave fellow-citizens, not fighting with Phoenicians or Medes, as my brother Cimon did, but *katastrephómenos* ['subduing' (or 'torturing')] our allies and our kith and kin" (*Per.* 28.5–6).[60] *Stréphein* ("twist" or "torture") occurs frequently in Aristophanic contexts where Periclean characters are being delineated, the most obvious one being Strepsiades' name in *Clouds.* "Pieces of wood" also figure large from time to time, notably in *Wasps,* when Bdelycleon uses a lump to force the head of the Periclean Philocleon back down the chimney from which it has emerged. Stories of torture do not necessarily have to be true, but the fact that they were told at all — and that they formed the basis of posthumous mockery—puts Pericles in a novel light, and raises questions as to whether his *auctoritas* depended upon respect generated by fear as much as upon admiration.

---

57. E.g. Stevens and George 1870–1954; George 1959; Rodnan 1961; Atherton 1974; Brewer 1986. Thanks are due to Roy Porter for these references.

58. Duris *FGrH* 76 F 67 *ap. Per.* 28.2–3. The story has often been doubted (Grote [1870, 5:292], whose aim was to rehabilitate Pericles, omits it altogether, as do Kagan [1990] and duBois [1991]). Cantarella (1984, 52–53 n. 60) leaves the question open. Keramopoullos (1923) rejects the whole idea. For Meiggs (1972, 192), "the substance of the story rings true," and Stadter (1989, 258–259) believes "it likely that Duris' story is at least partially true."

59. Stadter 1989, lxii, following Schachermeyr 1965.

60. Plutarch compares Pericles' exploits at Samos with Q. Fabius Maximus' recapture of Tarentum, an event that gained Fabius a reputation for cruelty: *Plut. Fab.* 29.1; cf. 22.5.

It has been well said that "it was the comic poet who gave communal expression to the social currents running beneath the surface of public discourse."[61] The civic aspect of the great dramatic festivals cannot be overemphasized, with (at least at the Great Dionysia) libations poured by the ten generals, the public display of the annual tribute in the theatre, the announcement of the names of civic benefactors, and the parade in full armor of young men whose fathers had died in battle and who had been raised at public expense.[62] For example, in 404 in *Frogs,* Aristophanes made an appeal for the return of those who had been deprived of civic rights. The success of the play, which won its author a crown of olive leaves ("equal in honor to a gold crown"), and the almost unheard-of privilege of a repeat performance (*Vit. Ar.* 28.39–43; 29.28–31 [Koster]), suggest that comedy might have served on other occasions as a commentary on matters of topical civic concern: to make people laugh at exaggerations of individuals and events, but with a fundamentally serious motive. We may perhaps begin to see the Athenian stage as a forum for "experimental politics,"[63] either to investigate what a given individual might or might not do, given the historical circumstances and his (or her) own tendencies and proclivities (cf. Arist. *Poet.* 9.1–4), or to put speeches into the mouths of individuals who were for one reason or another—exile or death, for example—absent from the city. That such an individual was usually "rich, or aristocratic, or powerful," and that (if a law of Thurii is any guide) it was "adulterers and the politically over-active" (Plut. *Mor.* 519b) who were lampooned, will have added a certain zest to such events. It is usual to say that comedy served as a "safety valve"; it may have done so, but more important was the way it served as a sanction that was far less harsh than ostracism or death, but was a sanction all the same.

It is important, however, to remember that Aristophanes' own political views are irrelevant;[64] or rather, to acknowledge that whatever they may have been, it is methodologically sounder, advantageous even, to ignore them, especially in the case of plays that—like *Acharnians* and *Knights*—won first

61. Henderson 1987, xxx–xxxi. On the civic aspect of Athenian drama, see further Macleod 1982; Goldhill 1987, 58–76; Henderson 1990.
62. Goldhill 1987.
63. Cf. Vickers 1989a, 65.
64. Cf. Gomme 1962; for another view, see de Ste. Croix 1972; and for another, Fisher 1993.

prize. For unless some external factor intervened,[65] we can be reasonably sure that whatever the playwright might include with a view to winning the dramatic victory would have reflected the current outlook of a majority of Athenians. The judges were chosen by lot,[66] and were thus likely to be as fair a cross-section of the Athenian body politic as anyone could have wished.[67] Whether Aristophanes' satire had any noticeable political effect is perhaps another matter. The only example I have found is an imputation that Alcibiades was shirking military service in 425 B.C. (*Acharnians* 1048–1068) that *may* have led to his enrollment in the brigade of knights by the following year. The one apparent attempt at a patriotic appeal to Alcibiades to change his policy with regard to the Peace of Nicias (in *Peace*) failed completely. But then Jonathan Swift, for all his satirical writing, only achieved the repeal of a single tax in the whole of his lifetime.

It is equally fruitless to attempt to assess the historical accuracy of allegations made about Pericles and his ward. Much of the gossip may well have had its origin in the exaggerations of comic writers. For this study, the sources of the anecdotes are of secondary importance. This is a logical procedure so long as one is not attempting to establish historical truth, simply the early existence of a piece of gossip. The discussion of a typical example will help to elucidate the issues involved. The precise source of a story told by Frontinus of Pericles is, and will doubtless remain, a mystery,[68] and yet the tale would seem to bear upon Aristophanes' *Clouds*. It has, however, never (at least to my knowledge) been brought into play in this context. It goes as follows: "Pericles, when a thunderbolt struck his camp and terrified his soldiers, calling an assembly, struck fire by knocking two stones together in the sight of all his men. He thus allayed their panic by explaining that the thunderbolt was similarly produced by the contact of the clouds" (Frontin. *Str.* 1.11.10). Pericles' practical-mindedness and lack of superstition is diametrically opposite that of Strepsiades at *Clouds* 385, who is unwilling to believe in Socrates' explanation that clouds make a noise when they collide with each other (383–384). In Chapters 2 and 3, it will be argued on other grounds that the character of Strepsiades is a comic Pericles, and there can be no reason for not taking Frontinus' story as corroborative evidence for such a view. Even if the tale was made up after the performance of *Clouds* in order to illustrate Pericles' interest in natural philosophy, Pericles is still there, and that is all that

65. As in the case of *Clouds:* see Chapter 3.
66. Pickard-Cambridge 1968, 95–96.
67. On the underlying principles of lottery, see Pope 1986; 1989.
68. On Frontinus' sources, see Bendz 1963, 7–8.

is necessary. Posthumous invention is, however, unlikely, and it is probably safer to think of it as the kind of story about Pericles that Aristophanes used as the basis for his plot. Either way, the tale is Periclean in character, and helps to justify the argument I shall be running. This example also includes a specimen of the comic technique described by Gilbert Murray, in which "a man from Aberdeen was represented as wildly scattering his money" in a twentieth-century farce.[69] Aristophanes frequently takes a known characteristic of a historical individual and either exaggerates it (as in the case of Cleon in *Knights*) or reverses it (as here). Any such reversal has of course to be a complete one for it to work effectively. It will henceforth be referred to as the "Hermogenes principle," in respect of the third item in a list drawn up by Hermogenes the rhetorician (writing in the second century A.D.) of the ways in which writers of Old Comedy made their audiences laugh: by means of parody, by means of the unexpected, and by means of images that were diametrically opposed to what was being represented (Hermog. *Meth.* 34). The "Hermogenes principle" only works, moreover, if the characterization has been firmly established already.

Our principal source of information concerning Pericles and Alcibiades is Thucydides, whose work was heavily utilized by Plutarch. In addition, however, Plutarch made substantial use of contemporary sources.[70] Pericles' latest biographer has, moreover, said of the *Life of Pericles* that it possesses "great value. Plutarch had an excellent library containing many works now lost to us, some written by contemporaries of Pericles and by men of the next generation. He read the inscriptions and ancient documents and saw paintings, sculptures, and buildings that no longer exist. When used with care, his work is an outstanding source of authentic information."[71] Much the same might be said of Plutarch's *Life of Alcibiades*,[72] which quotes from contemporary playwrights, and writers such as Antisthenes, Antiphon, and Lysias, who knew Alcibiades personally. Other sources used by Plutarch include the work of later writers such as Satyrus and Duris of Samos. Another important text is the speech against Alcibiades attributed (though not universally) to Andocides: [Andocides] 4. At best, this speech was written in 417 B.C.;[73] at worst, it is a literary forgery of the early fourth century B.C., when two anti-

---

69. Murray 1933, 86.

70. Stadter 1989, lix; cf. lviii–lxxxv.

71. Kagan 1990, xii.

72. See Levi 1967, 132: "Le fonti per la storia di Alcibiade sono di ottima qualità"; cf. Russell 1972, 117–129. Prandi 1992, 281–292, has a useful discussion of Plutarch's sources.

73. So Schroff 1901; Raubitschek 1948; Furley 1989.

Alcibiadean speeches wrongly attributed to Lysias were also composed.[74] Either way, it is a reliable source for gossip, if not for history. Plato is another rich source, especially for Alcibiades. The *Symposium,* for all that it was probably a literary contrivance,[75] encapsulates the essence of the man, and whether or not the dialogues that bear Alcibiades' name, the first and second *Alcibiades,* are actually by Plato, they depend to a greater or lesser degree upon the anecdotal tradition.[76] In this context, Plato probably ranks as a historical novelist rather than a historian, but again, the truths of fiction can be more telling than those of purely documentary sources.[77] Xenophon has much that is relevant in the *Hellenica* and *Memorabilia,* and Isocrates and Demosthenes reflect a surprisingly favorable fourth-century view.[78] Libanius is a rich and as yet largely unexploited source of Alcibiadiana,[79] and though the "situations in [his] declamations may be fictitious, the persons and the general framework are historical."[80] An unexpected by-product of this study of Aristophanes has been to open up the possibility that among contemporary writers who used Aristophanes' plays as source material were Thucydides and Xenophon. These will be discussed in more detail below.[81]

POLYMORPHIC CHARACTERIZATION

Reference has already been made to the phenomenon of "polymorphic characterization," which — it will be argued — was exploited in all of the plays discussed here. The technique — of reflecting different facets of the same individual by means of different characters — is rarely if ever used today, but in Aristophanes' hands it was an effective way of revealing different sides of a person's character. It was the perfect dramatic vehicle for representing a figure as multifaceted as Alcibiades, or one whose character was as complex as that of Pericles. Moreover, polymorphic characterization provides a solution to

74. Maidment 1941, 538–539.
75. Blanckenhagen 1992.
76. Strycker 1942; Bluck 1953. David Gribble is currently preparing a study of Alcibiades in the Socratics.
77. Cf. Cobb 1986.
78. Cf. Bruns 1896, 489–530, 557–585.
79. Rendered the more accessible thanks to Schouler 1984, esp. 626–634.
80. Wolf 1954, 236 (reprinted in Fatouros and Krischer 1983, 75).
81. On Plato's likely dependence on Aristophanes, see Brock 1990; Vickers 1994.

the problem of the supposed lack of unity that has often been felt to mark Aristophanes' plots.[82] Far from being loosely structured or broken-backed, they are as tight as a drum. If, for example, in *Clouds* Pericles and Alcibiades underlie *both* Strepsiades and Pheidippides *and* the Stronger and Weaker Arguments, there is continuity, rather than discontinuity—or even "irrelevance" or "inconsequentiality."[83] It is all the more necessary to insist on this, as the supposed formlessness of Aristophanes' plots has recently given rise to consideration of the possibility that unity might not have been an aesthetic ideal in antiquity.[84] On a smaller scale, the "trivial inconsistencies" that Aristophanes might have removed by a "stroke of the pen"[85] prove not to be "mistakes," but to reflect the historical reality of the imperfect world in which Pericles, Alcibiades, Aristophanes, and his audience lived.

ARISTOPHANES' OBSCENITY

Aristophanes emerges from this study not only as the writer of plays that are rather more political documents than is usually held to be the case, but as considerably more "Aristophanic." He can be seen as a rather more skillful wordsmith than some would have us believe, a practitioner of extremely complex imagery, a master of tight plot construction, and a writer capable of a verbal savagery not seen since Hipponax. This invective is frequently hidden in allegory and wordplay, presumably in order to evade taboos and charges of making false accusations. Instead of being generalized "flights of fancy," Aristophanes' plots have specific, individual targets in view, and the insults hurled by his characters are far from random. Aristophanes' obscenity is never, as has been claimed, "simply gratuitous."[86] Nor is there any obscenity for obscenity's sake (Aristophanes has even been accused of *coprolalia*)[87]; every barb is carefully honed. Once again, it is necessary to stress this, for

82. E.g., Norwood (1931, 302): "We must recognise that the structure of [Aristophanes'] dramas is on the whole loose and faltering"; Henderson (1987, lx), who speaks of Aristophanes' "inconsequentiality of plot"; Brock (1986, 24): "Aristophanes' plays are generally regarded as loosely, even tenuously, plotted."
83. Cf. Harriott 1986, 172; Süss 1954.
84. E.g., Konstan 1985, 45. In defense of unity, see A. M. Bowie 1987; Heath 1987a, 43–54.
85. Norwood 1931, 299; cf. Dover 1972, 44, 59–65.
86. Henderson 1975, 96.
87. Dracoulidès 1967, 25–47.

there has been a tendency to equate obscenity with unruliness, and by extension with lack of form.

The stress laid upon the supposed sexual excesses of Pericles and Alcibiades in the plays considered here tends to support the recent hypothesis that the existence of a law at Thurii (founded in 443 B.C. with considerable Athenian participation; cf. Diod. 12.35.2), which restricted dramatic ridicule of citizens to *moikhoì kaì polupragmónes* ("adulterers and those who were overly active in political matters"; Plut. *Mor.* 519b), may point to similar legislation at Athens.[88] The contemporary public images of both Pericles and Alcibiades will have qualified them in the adultery class, and Pericles was outspoken in his criticism of *apragmosúnē* ("a lack of concern for politics").[89]

Aristophanes' obscenity is, moreover, highly moral; or at least the stance he adopts is one that can be construed as such.[90] This may seem an odd thing to say, for "morality" and "obscenity" are today usually polar opposites, although there are occasional exceptions. High moral ground and filthy language can coexist; see Mr. Bernard in Mordecai Richler's *Solomon Gursky Was Here:*

> Mr. Bernard, in his forties then, rocking on his tiny heels before the towering marble fireplace, seething. Young Lionel seated on the sofa, unperturbed, riding it out with a supercilious smile. When without warning an exasperated Mr. Bernard strode toward him, unzipped his fly, yanked out his penis, and shook it in his son's face. "I want you to know, you whoremaster, that in all my years this has only been into your mother. God bless her," and zipping up again, tearful, adding, "and to this day she has the only cunt still good enough for Bernard Gursky. Respect. Dignity. That you still have to learn. Animal."[91]

Aristophanes' position is identical, and in an identical spirit he exploits Pericles' notorious tendency to *aphrodisia* and his equally well known — in antiquity at least — criticism of paedophilia.[92] It is with a view to making the audience laugh by showing up Alcibiades' immorality that Aristophanes descends to the gutter, and not because "[he] wrote just as obscenely as he could on every possible occasion."[93]

---

88. Cf. Henderson 1990; add Thuc. 3.34 (on the [re-] foundation of Notium in 427 B.C., to which the Athenians "gave laws like their own").

89. Thuc. 2.40.2, 63.2, 64.4; cf. Carter 1986.

90. Cf. Rosen 1988b.

91. Richler 1990, 198.

92. *Per.* 8.8; Cic. *de Off.* 1.40; Val. Max. 4.3. ext. 1. This evidence is overlooked by Dover (1978).

93. Eugene O'Neill, cited by Davies (1992, 76).

B. B. Rogers has some interesting pages on the essentially moral tone of Aristophanes' plays. In the context of a discussion of the probably apocryphal story of the austere St. John Chrysostom's liking for the poet, he lists various respectable folk—Plato, Archbishop Marco Musuro, Bishop Christopher Wordsworth—who admired Aristophanes, and quotes William Sewell on the subject:

> Men smile when they hear the anecdote of one of the most venerable Fathers of the Church, who never went to bed without Aristophanes under his pillow. But the noble tone of morals, the elevated taste, the sound political wisdom, the boldness and acuteness of the satire, the grand object, which is seen throughout, of correcting the follies of the day and improving the condition of his country,—all these are features of Aristophanes which, however disguised, as they intentionally are, by coarseness and buffoonery, entitle him to the highest respect from every reader of antiquity.[94]

It is from such a standpoint that Aristophanes elaborates on the excesses of two of the most "rich and powerful" citizens of Athens, and especially their sexual excesses.

THE TEXT OF ARISTOPHANES

The manuscript tradition relating to Aristophanes is unusual in that there is only one manuscript that contains all eleven of the extant plays, and that is also the sole source for one of them. This is the tenth-century Codex Ravennas (R), which only became widely known to scholars in 1796,[95] and whose status has been controversial ever since. The feature that has helped give R a bad name is the frequency with which elementary mistakes occur. Incorrect accents,[96] wrong (or missing) breathings, mistaken word breaks, and faulty punctuation[97] abound. If there is such a profusion of small mistakes, how

94. Rogers 1910a, liv.
95. Clark 1871.
96. Cf. Elliott 1914, xviii n. 1: "R is the worst manuscript I have read as regards accents."
97. Cf. Starkie 1909, 32: "[In R] punctuation-marks are scattered as if out of a pepper-caster"; nevertheless, Starkie was inclined to "respect [the] accuracy of R" (1909, lxxvii), concluding that its errors "though numerous are mostly trivial."

much greater the chance of large ones, is the way one senses the game has often been played, with the result that the idiosyncratic readings and line assignments of R have been largely disregarded. R's relatively late appearance on the scene may also have contributed to the comparative neglect of its qualities: norms of Aristophanic textual criticism had been well established by 1796.

The "peculiar readings" of R, which "represents a different tradition from all the other MSS,"[98] are often, however, rather more knowing and playful than those to be found elsewhere. A good example occurs at *Acharnians* 126, where Dicaeopolis (who "comes forward" as a caricature of Pericles) is speaking. *Strageúomai* is the word in question, and it is uttered by Dicaeopolis just after he has heard that the fraudulent Persian ambassador is to be entertained at dinner in the Prytaneum, the building where public officials had free meals. "Do you think I *strageúomai* here, when no welcoming door is shut to them?" he says. The other manuscript tradition reads *strateúomai* ("serve in the army"), which is less than satisfactory, and Küster's emendation *straggeúomai* ("loiter") is generally accepted. This is probably in essence correct (in that this is the principal meaning), but *strageúomai* would have additionally played on *stratēgós* ("general")—the office Pericles filled for many years—and on *geúomai* ("taste" or "eat")—a reference to one of the main themes of the play; Dicaeopolis' greed for all kinds of food is a caricature of Pericles' concern for Athens' grain supply.

Another variant reading in *Acharnians* peculiar to R plays knowingly on Alcibiades' position in 425 B.C. It will be argued in Chapter 5 that the scene at 1048–1068, where a bridegroom asks for a ladleful of peace so that he can stay at home and screw, and his bride asks how she can make her husband's cock stay at home, is a commentary on Alcibiades' draft-dodging, his recent marriage, and his early infidelities. At 1061–1062, Dicaeopolis says that he will give the bride some peace for her alone, "for," according to all the manuscripts, "a woman is not *axía* ['worthy'] of the war." Blaydes emended *axía* to *aitía* ("to be blamed for"),[99] and most critics followed him.[100] But Alcibiades' *axíoma* ("reputation") was the reason he was granted the prize of valor at Potidaea in 431 B.C. over the individual who had really earned it,[101] and

98. Elliott 1914, xx.

99. Blaydes 1845, ad loc.

100. See Elliott (1914, 175), who would translate *hotiề gunế 'sti toû polémou t' ouk axía* as "She is a woman and unable to bear the ills of war"; but even he rejected *axía* in favour of *aitía*.

101. Pl. *Symp.* 219e; Diog. Laert. 2.23; *Alc.* 7.5; Antisth. Fr. 33 Caizzi *ap.* Ath. 5.216c; Isoc. 16.29–30.

Thucydides makes oblique allusions to the fact.[102] That the writer of the source of R was aware of this is clear from his use of the conjunctive *dé* where the rest have *te* ("and"). *Te* would have caused line 1062 to mean "for she is a woman *and* not . . . ," whereas *dé* would make it absolutely clear that someone other than the bride was in question. For all his manliness, Alcibiades was on occasion characterized as a woman: Libanius' account of the youthful Alcibiades wearing women's clothes[103] is corroborated by Plutarch's assertion that if you examined Alcibiades' behavior at Sparta closely, you would say, "It is the woman of old."[104] If Alcibiades was the "woman" in question who was "not *axía* ['worthy'] of the war," this *dé* was a conjunction not without effect, for by the next year Alcibiades was a member of the brigade of knights, fighting bravely at Delium (*Alc.* 7.6; Pl. *Symp.* 221a).

The identifications of speakers in R are often sound, and can serve as a helpful guide when the line assignments are disputed. Many of these identifications have fallen into disuse, but some of them are perhaps worthy of respect. A good example of the way in which R helps to resolve problematical identifications is at *Knights* 432ff., where the Alcibiadean Sausage-seller[105] draws attention to his wares—*állantas,*—setting up a crescendo of references to *tálanta* ("talents"). R has Paphlagon accusing the Sausage-seller of having stolen "many talents" (435) from the Athenian state: this could be an allusion to Alcibiades' role of *táktēs* ("tribute assessor") in 425 B.C., when he is supposed to have been guilty of embezzlement.[106] Then at *Knights* 438, according to R (and other manuscripts) but few editors, Paphlagon asserts that the Sausage-seller took ten talents from Potidaea. The customary attribution of the line to the Sausage-seller has generated much debate as to how and when Cleon could have done this,[107] but we have already seen how Alcibiades was present at Potidaea, and was unfairly granted the prize of honor. That Alcibiades was probably intended here is confirmed by the allusion to

102. E.g., Thuc. 5.43.2, 6.15.3, 6.16.2; cf. Vickers 1995a.

103. E.g., Lib. fr. 50β [11.643.8–11]: "[Alcibiades] . . . had intercourse with courtesans, suffering terrible things before he was old enough, but performing worse, and boasted that dressed in women's clothes, though a male, he attended symposia undetected."

104. *Alc.* 23.5–6. For the medieval tradition (brought to my attention by Martin Ostwald) that Alcibiades actually was a woman, see Thuasne 1923, 624–643.

105. On the identification, see Chapter 6 below.

106. [Andoc.] 4.11. Alcibiades' participation has been doubted by, e.g., Maidment 1941, 551; and Andrewes in *HCT* 4:49—and believed in by, e.g., Ostwald 1986, 293; Develin 1985, cf. Develin 1989, 131; Ellis 1989, 31. On the reliability of [Andoc.] 4, see Raubitschek 1948; Furley 1989.

107. Cf. Sommerstein 1981, 166.

the Alcmaeonid curse at 445–446: Alcibiades was of Alcmaeonid descent on his mother's side (*Alc.* 1.1; Isoc. 16.25), whereas the association of the Sausage-seller with the curse has caused general puzzlement.[108]

In the matter of dialects, the manuscripts (with R as bellwether) are a rather more trustworthy guide to what Aristophanes actually wrote than are most printed texts. If a dialect form occurs at all, editors eager to display their learning have tended to impose that form on the other lines spoken by the same character. What was lightly salted has often been rendered indigestible. B. B. Rogers is one of the few editors to be sound on this.[109] Of course, actors may well have taken up the hints (usually given in the first few lines after a character's entrance), but that (like lambdacization) should not give rise to emendation. W. B. Stanford once likened ancient texts to "a tape-recording waiting to be played on someone's vocal organs";[110] even more happily, he might have compared them to a score waiting to be interpreted.

For many reasons, therefore, I propose in what follows to favor the readings and line allocations of R.[111] With all its faults, R preserves something of the authentic flavor of Aristophanes' political comedy. Most printed texts of Aristophanes resemble the horse designed by a committee; the Ravenna codex, by contrast, is the nearest we shall ever get to a thoroughbred.

There is little that is fundamentally new here. It should not be necessary to justify fidelity to manuscript readings, and Aristophanes' treatment of Pericles and Alcibiades is not without parallel elsewhere in his work. Few would dispute that in *Clouds* Aristophanes takes Socrates as the peg upon which to hang all kinds of sophistical nonsense; all that is being argued in this book is that he took some even more prominent figures ("the rich and powerful") as pegs upon which to hang generalizations about various interests and issues of concern to contemporary Athenians. Anyone who can tolerate a *portmanteau* Socrates, or indeed a Paphlagonian Cleon, should have few difficulties in seeing Periclean and Alcibiadean reflections of Athenian fathers and sons, or of old and new politicians.

108. See ibid., 167.
109. And see the sensible remarks of Colvin 1995.
110. Stanford 1967, 3.
111. And surely someone could prepare a lightly corrected printout; it would be a valuable contribution to Aristophanic scholarship.

PERICLES AND
ALCIBIADES AT THE
PHRONTISTERY
Aristophanes' *Clouds* I

Aristophanes' *Clouds* was performed at the City Dionysia in 423 B.C. (although the text we have is probably of a revision carried out in c. 418/17 B.C.).[1] It was thus the third of Aristophanes' extant plays to be performed. Since, however, it serves best to answer the question raised at the beginning of Chapter 1 concerning the political relevance of Aristophanes' plays in general (and of *Clouds* in particular), it will be treated first.

Recent commentators on *Clouds* have tended to overlook the story that "Socrates' lovers . . . especially those in the circle around Alcibiades" prevented the poet from winning first prize (*Clouds, Arg.* 5 Coulon). Nor do we hear much today of a view that enjoyed a certain vogue in the nineteenth century, namely that Pheidippides in *Clouds* "came forward in the character of Alcibiades, who had the same love for horses and bore a similar relation to Socrates."[2] Considerable evidence for an equation between Pheidippides and

1. For the issues involved, see Henderson 1993.
2. E.g., Donaldson (1860, 185), who continues: "At the same time, the prominent part which Alcibiades was beginning to take in public affairs, and the influence he possessed over the young men of his own age, pointed him out as their most adequate representative"; cf. Thirlwall (1845–1852, 3:278): "It is hardly possible to doubt that under this character the poet meant to represent Alcibiades"; Hertzberg 1853, 67 n. 56.

Alcibiades was spelled out by J. W. Süvern in 1826,[3] and it is perhaps surprising that such an equation is rarely even discussed.[4] The explanation may lie in the evident fact that *Clouds* is thought to be primarily an attack on the historical Socrates,[5] and that to allow references to other historical characters might weaken any defense of the philosopher.[6] It will be argued in what follows that this is perhaps to miss the point of what appears to be a play with a much wider political objective.

Süvern's arguments may be summarized thus: Pheidippides' mother was a niece of a Megacles (46–47), a name that is repeated frequently throughout the play (70, 124, 815). He was also descended from Coesyra (48, 800). Alcibiades' mother was a daughter of Megacles (*Alc.* 1.1), and Coesyra was a prominent member of the Alcmaeonid clan. The *hipp*- element in Pheidippides' name may, moreover, have recalled Hipparete, daughter of Hipponicus, who was Alcibiades' wife (*Alc.* 8.4; Isoc. 16.31), not to mention his own keenness for horses. Alcibiades' disdain for gymnastic contests, and his preference for the breeding of race horses (Isoc. 16.33), may, in view of the low esteem in which gymnastic exercises are held by some in *Clouds,* also be relevant.

Süvern notes that a Pheidippus is mentioned by Homer (*Il.* 2.678) as the son of Thessalus from whom the Thessalian Aleuad dynasty claimed descent;[7] this is another possible allusion to Alcibiades, in that Satyrus records the fact that when Alcibiades was in Thessaly, "in his horse-breeding and chariot-racing, he was more horsemanlike than the Aleuadae" (Satyr. *FHG* 3.160 *ap.* Ath. 12.534b). Süvern sees a reference to Alcibiades' well-known speech impediment[8] in the baby-talk at 1381–1384. He also regards Aristophanes' failure to win the prize for *Clouds* through the machinations of Alcibiades as grounds for believing that the latter was lampooned in the person of Pheidippides. He notes, too, that Alcibiades and Socrates had recently been in the

3. Süvern 1826; 1836.

4. Some exceptions: Leeuwen (1898, 16, 139, 141), Boruchovich (1959), Turato (1972, 99–100), Montuori (1974, 171), and Ambrosino (1986–1987, 101–102) accept the equation; Schmid and Stählin (1929–1948, 4/1:248), and Moorton (1988) do not. Alcibiades is not mentioned in the context of Pheidippides by either Dover (1968) or Sommerstein (1982). O'Regan (1992, 155) refreshingly speaks of "Alcibiades' subterranean presence as a model for Pheidippides."

5. E.g., Dover 1968, vi.

6. For such a defense, see Dover 1968, xxxii–lvii; for other views: Havelock 1972, 1 nn. 1–6; Montuori 1974; 1981; Nussbaum 1980 (who speaks [p. 45] of an "uncritical adulation" of Socrates); Tomin 1987.

7. Discussed most recently by Panagl (1983, 303).

8. *Wasps* 44–48; *Alc.* 1.6–7 (and see the Introduction); Leeuwen 1898, 139, 141; Vickers 1987b.

news when the younger had saved the older man's life at the battle of Delium in 424 B.C. (*Alc.* 7.6).

Süvern believes that the distinctly Socratic conversation between Alcibiades and Pericles recorded by Xenophon (*Mem.* 1.2.40–46) makes the subject of Alcibiades' education directly relevant to *Clouds,* and he notes that the conversation was characterized by Pericles himself as *sophízesthai* ("philosophiz[ing]"; *Mem.* 1.2.46). Likewise, he regards the story of Alcibiades' injunction to Pericles to find ways of not rendering his accounts (*Alc.* 7.3; Diod. 12.38) as an indication of the way in which Alcibiades' mind was widely thought to work, especially if Alcibiades had, in the years immediately preceding *Clouds,* been a *táktēs* entrusted with a revision of the tribute of the Delian League ([Andoc.] 4.11). Some of these points are stronger than others, but together they constitute a case that deserves serious consideration.

TRAULISM, AND SOCRATIC SHOES

One of Süvern's suggestions in particular deserves closer study, namely that when Strepsiades reminds Pheidippides at *Clouds* 1381 of his childish speech impediment (*traulízontos*), Aristophanes is making an allusion to the way Alcibiades spoke (*Wasps* 44–48; *Alc.* 1, 6–7). In line 1382, Strepsiades quotes the way in which his infant son had asked for a drink: *brûn.* If, however, he lambdacized the word in question, it will have sounded as *plún:* "give me a bath." [9] If so, reference may have been made to Alcibiades' love of bathing, an activity for which he was later to be criticized (Plut. *Mor.* 235a).

Lambdacism as an explanation of *traulízontos* at 1381–1382, moreover, may help to clarify a notorious crux at 869–872, in the lines spoken when Socrates first meets Pheidippides. At 862 Strepsiades has reminded his son that as a lambdacizing six-year-old (*hexétei . . . traulísanti*) he once persuaded his father to buy him a toy chariot, an appropriate gift if the infant Alcibiades is in question. [10] If, moreover, there was a reason for drawing attention to the speech defect shared by both the juvenile Pheidippides and the mature Alcibiades, it may have been to set up lambdacizing wordplay at 870ff.

9. With overtones perhaps of "give me a good telling off": cf. LSJ s.v. *plunō,* II; and Vickers 1987b, 143. The baby-talk at *Clouds* 1381–1382 is not referred to by the otherwise comprehensive Ferguson (1977).

10. For an excellent discussion of the chariot-racing world of the adult Alcibiades, see Schaeffer 1949–1950.

First, though, some relevant background information. Socrates was criticized for always drawing illustrations from "shoemakers, carpenters and smiths."[11] Whether or not the first *Alcibiades* (the dramatic date of which is late in the lifetime of Pericles) is actually by Plato, Socrates there mentions shoes or shoemakers seven times ([Pl.] *Alc.* 1.125a, 128a, 128c, 129d), and the story was told that "when Alcibiades offered [Socrates] a large piece of ground to build a house upon, he said, 'But if I wanted shoes, and you had given me a piece of leather to make myself shoes, I should be laughed at if I took it'" (Diog. Laert. *Socrates* 9.1). Elsewhere, the comic writer Ameipsias charges Socrates with wearing a cloak of so coarse a cut that a shoemaker must have given him it as an insult (Amips. *PCG* 9; Diog. Laert. 2.27). It is therefore surprising that the scene in *Clouds* where Socrates is said to have made waxen flea-slippers (149–152) to measure how far a flea had jumped from his head to Chaerephon's[12] is not as a matter of course adduced as an example of Socrates' evident interest in footwear and shoemaking,[13] for all that he himself allegedly went barefoot (103, 363).

At 868–869, Socrates states that Pheidippides is still a child, and is not familiar (*tríbōn*) with the rigging (*kremathrôn*) in his establishment. That what Pheidippides says in line 870 is shocking is clear from Strepsiades' reaction in 871, and that his pronunciation is idiosyncratic is shown by Socrates' reaction at 872. Commentators today usually take Socrates' remark as referring to the quality of Pheidippides' vowels,[14] but Strepsiades' reference to traulism alerts us to the likelihood that Pheidippides' consonants are in question and that we ought perhaps to think in terms of lambdacism. If so, Pheidippides' reply (870), *autòs tríbōn eíēs àn, ei krémaió ge* ("You could do with being hung up and beaten as soundly as a fuller beats a dirty cloak"[15]), may have been heard as *autòs thlíbōn eíēs àn, ei klémaió ge* ("May you be a wanker yourself, if you go on about shoes"), where *tríbōn* is pronounced as *thlíbōn*, and *krémaió ge* as *klémaió ge*. *Kleímata, klêma,* and *klíma* are, as we have already had occasion to note, all words for "shoe."[16] All would agree that Socrates ridicules Pheidippides at 872 by mimicking his childish pronunciation, but critics have made heavy weather of what several manuscripts, including the Ravenna

---

11. E.g., Xen. *Mem.* 1.2.37; cf. ibid., 4.4.5; Pl. *Symp.* 221e; *Grg.* 447e, 489e–491a; Ael. *VH* 2.1.

12. Cf. Pl. *Grg.* 447e (where Socrates speaks of shoes and a cobbler to Chaerephon).

13. On which see further Lang 1978.

14. E.g., Starkie 1911, 197; Stanford 1967, 142; Dover 1968, 206; Sommerstein 1982, 203.

15. Translated by Sommerstein (1982, 203).

16. LSJ; Hsch. s.vv. Cf. the likely pun on *khrēmata* ("money") and *klēmata* ("shoes") at *Birds* 1657 (apparently in the context of a Lamachus who once asked the state for "shoe money") discussed in the Introduction, and the similar pun at *Wasps* 102–103 treated in Chapter 7.

codex, record as *idoù krémaió g'*. If, however, we allow for lambdacization, the audience may have heard *idoù klēmaíon* ("just listen to that 'shoey'") — appropriate enough if Alcibiades' speech mannerism and Socrates' frequent references to "shoes" and "cobblers" are at issue. Linguistic characterization such as this can be found elsewhere,[17] and the "shoe" motif recurs throughout *Clouds*.

For all that "Aristophanes' puns are seldom sophisticated,"[18] it might be worth observing not only that a *tríbōn* was the garment regularly worn by the historical Socrates (Pl. *Prt.* 335d) but also that he is said to have slept under one together with the young Alcibiades, an occasion from which Plato later made Alcibiades claim to have emerged unscathed (Pl. *Symp.* 219b). If Aristophanes was alluding to what was probably a well-known nonevent, lambdacism at *Clouds* 870 would have added a further level of meaning, with its suggestive allusion to what Aristophanes thought Socrates actually did beneath the *tríbōn* he shared with his youthful companion. If this analysis is valid, the judgment of Athenaeus may require some modification: "No comic poet has said anything about what Plato tells of Socrates: that he . . . lay with Alcibiades under the same cloak. And yet this would of necessity have been shouted from the rooftops by Aristophanes who was present at Plato's symposium" (Ath. 5.219b). Strepsiades' horror (871) would have been an effective way of drawing particular attention to what Pheidippides seems to have implied: the "emphatic" equivalent of "shouting from the rooftops." Nor should we expect any lambdacization to appear in the text, in the light of Quintilian's observation (*Inst.* 1.5.32) that it was not the kind of thing that was written down.

STREPSIADES AND PERICLES

This is by way of indicating that there may be more than "a brief and incomplete allusion"[19] to Alcibiades in the person of Pheidippides, and it will be argued in what follows that *Clouds* is concerned in part at least with the bad habits Aristophanes thought Alcibiades had picked up from his teachers. But

---

17. Cf. Woodruff 1982, 126–127: "Even if the *Hippias Major* is a forgery, it represents mannerisms [which are] distinctively Hippian. . . . Certain striking mannerisms occur frequently in Hippias' speech and in Socrates' speech when he is mocking Hippias"; cf. Brock 1990, 47–48.
18. Dover 1968, 96.
19. Hatzfeld 1951, 34.

if Pheidippides does indeed "come forward in the character of Alcibiades," whom might Aristophanes be thought to be advancing in the person of Strepsiades? Certainly not Alcibiades' physical father Cleinias, who fell at Coronea in 447 B.C. (*Alc.* 1.1) (and this was J. Hatzfeld's only reason for dismissing an equation between Alcibiades and Pheidippides).[20] There was, however, another who — as we have seen — played for Alcibiades "the role of a father," namely Pericles, in whose house Alcibiades spent his boyhood years (Pl. *Prt.* 320a; Diod. 12.38.2).

Pericles had of course been dead for some time when *Clouds* was performed, but as we have already had occasion to note, death did not prevent Pericles being the butt of comedy. There are sufficient references in *Clouds* to Strepsiades' morbidity to enable us to believe that Aristophanes' original audience might have thought of him as one brought back from the dead. From the "endless night" of lines 2–3, such allusions permeate the play: "*apóllumai* ('I'm fit to perish')" (16),[21] "the evil which has *apolóleken* ('ruined' or 'killed') me" (26); "*kataphrúgei* ('burn to a cinder')" (396: perhaps with an allusion to a funeral pyre); "I'll look half a corpse" (504);[22] "I will call him back *pròs tò phôs* ('to the light')" (632), but perhaps with the implied meaning "from the dead";[23] "I died recently" (726); "No one is going to prosecute me when I am dead" (782); "*apò gàr oloûmai* ('I shall be destroyed')" (792); "You waste my livelihood by washing yourself as though I were dead" (838);[24] "Shall I tell the coffin-makers of my father's illness?" (846); "You'll be dead" (1436); "*apò gàr oloûmai* ('it will be the death of me')" (1440).[25] If these are allusions to the dead Pericles, then Strepsiades' statement that he lives "a long way off in the countryside" (138) might refer to Pericles' tomb in the fields near the Academy (Paus. 1.29.3).

Süvern came close to seeing Pericles in Strepsiades,[26] and it is tempting to pursue this idea, for Strepsiades shares many of the characteristics attributed to Pericles, and the plot deals with concerns that were his. For all that he was "rich and of noble birth" (*Per.* 7.2), Pericles was regarded as being careful with his money, if not actually stingy, and especially so within his domestic circle. His family "complained at his exact regulation of his daily expenses,

---

20. Ibid.; cf. Turato 1972, 100; Ambrosino 1986–1987, 103–104.
21. Sommerstein 1982, 13.
22. For another interpretation, see Dover 1968, 60–61.
23. Cf. LSJ *pháos* Ib.
24. Following Sommerstein 1982, 202.
25. Ibid., 149.
26. "Hier setzt sich der Alte wie in die Stelle des Perikles": Süvern 1826, 39 (on *Clouds* 859). O'Regan (1992, 65) notes the "shadow of Pericles" over Strepsiades.

which allowed none of the superfluities common in great and wealthy households, but which made debit and credit exactly balance each other" (*Per.* 16.5, 36.2). Strepsiades' parsimony is no secret. He upbraids a slave for having used too thick a wick in a lamp (57), a vessel with Periclean resonance (*Per.* 16.9; and see Chapter 7), and admits to being niggardly (421). Strepsiades' patronymic "son of Pheidon ('Thrifty')" (134) conveys the same notion,[27] as does that of Pheidippides ("son of one who begrudges expenditure on horses").

One of the side effects of the plague was forgetfulness: "Some had no sooner recovered than they were seized with a forgetfulness of all things and knew neither themselves or their friends" (Thuc. 2.49.8; cf. *Per.* 38.3–4). If Pericles underlies the figure of Strepsiades, the forgetfulness motif in *Clouds* might be relevant to the pathology of the statesman's illness (other plague allusions will be discussed below). At 129–130, Strepsiades complains that he is "old, forgetful, and slow"; at 414, the Chorus promise Strepsiades success so long as he has a good memory; at 482–483, Socrates says to Strepsiades, "I want to find out . . . whether you have a good memory," and at 631 he condemns him for having forgotten things before he has learned them; at 685, Strepsiades is unable to recall his lessons; at 854–855, he complains that he forgets everything he is taught.

The shape of Pericles' head was the basis for much comic humor. It was "long out of all proportion" (*Per.* 3.3),[28] and was likened to a squill (*Per.* 3.4), a vegetable rather like an onion; it is tempting to view Strepsiades' comment at 188–190 that he knows where some lovely big bulbs grow as a reference to the Periclean cranium. Pericles' self-consciousness with regard to his "blemish" had the effect that sculptors usually showed him with his head covered (*Per.* 3.3–4), and if Pericles underlies the figure of Strepsiades, there may be an allusion to this when the latter expresses surprise (268) that he has left home without even a cap.

A rather more serious reason may underlie Strepsiades' name, usually translated "son of Twister," and to which attention is drawn by means of variants of the word "twist" throughout the play (e.g., 36, 88, 434, 450, 776, 792, 1455).[29] The name also means "son of Torturer," and thus recalls the punishment Pericles is supposed to have meted out to Samian prisoners in the Agora at Miletus in 439 B.C. Plutarch, as we saw, disbelieved these ugly stories, but

27. Strepsiades' demotic *Kikkunnóthen* ("from Cicynna") may be a pun on *Kekhēnóthen* ("from the Openmouthenians") (trans. Sommerstein 1982); cf. the description of Athens as *hē Kekhēnaiōn pólis* at *Knights* 1263.
28. Cf. Gonick 1987, 13; Cohen 1991.
29. Cf. Sommerstein 1982, 161.

true or false, they seem to have had a wide circulation, for they frequently contribute to the characterization of Periclean figures in Aristophanes. Strepsiades' name thus perhaps expresses the idea that he is not the innocent victim he claims to be.

STREPSIADES, PERICLES, AND PHILOSOPHY

Though Pericles kept his domestic financial affairs on an even keel, he is said to have been troubled by worries over the public accounts, and the stories of the young Alcibiades suggesting that the best thing might be for him to think of ways in which he could arrange not to have to present the accounts at all (*Alc.* 7.5; Diod. 12.38; cf. Chapter 4) are perhaps even more pertinent to *Clouds* than Süvern thought. Strepsiades' accounts are an issue (19–20), and his debts are a constant theme throughout *Clouds*.[30] The whole object of the education of father and son is to find clever arguments that will help Strepsiades evade his creditors, and they take lessons in philosophy toward this end. We recall Pericles' association with Pythocleides and Damon ("a sophist of the highest order"), who was (probably) ostracized for all that he attempted to disguise his sophistry with musical education;[31] with Zeno, from whom he learnt the "strength of a two-edged tongue" (*Per.* 4.4; compare Strepsiades' boast that his son "gleams with a two-edged tongue," 1160); with Protagoras, skilled in "making wrong appear right" (Arist. *Rh.* 1402a23);[32] and especially with Anaxagoras, a philosopher whom Pericles greatly admired (Plut. *Them.* 2), and through whose influence he both became deeply interested in grand speculations (*meteōrologías kai metarsioleskhías*) and developed "an elevation and sublimity of expression far removed from vulgarity and low buffoonery" (*Per.* 5.1). In the *Phaedrus* (269e–270a), Plato makes Socrates explain how Anaxagoras influenced Pericles, "imbuing him with *meteōrología.*"[33] It was Anaxagoras, too, who said to Pericles that "those who want to use a lamp supply it with oil" (*Per.* 16.9). Whether at the level of the lamp or of meteorology, these interests are surely reflected in certain passages in *Clouds*, namely, *tà metéōra prágmata* (228); *metéōron* (264); *metéōroi* (266); *ándras meteōrophénakas* (333); *meteōrosophistôn* (360); *meteōristheís* (404); *meteórōn* (490);

---

30. E.g., 16–17, 34–35, 244–245, 436, 487, 1131–1144, 1214–1302.
31. *Per.* 4.1; [Pl.] *Alc.* 1.118c; Arist. *Ath. Pol.* 27.4; Wallace 1991.
32. Cf. Dover 1968, xxxvii.
33. Edmunds 1987b; see, too, Ostwald 1986, 268–269.

and *tôn meteórōn pragmátōn* (1284). The author of the first *Alcibiades* makes Alcibiades describe Pericles' education very concisely: "[Pericles] did not become a philosopher (*sophós*) by himself; he lived with many philosophers including Pythoclides and Anaxagoras, and still, at the age he is, he takes lessons from Damon for this purpose" ([Pl.] *Alc.* 1.118c). The only place we ever hear of Pericles and Socrates together is—significantly perhaps, in the light of the shoemaking theme that runs through *Clouds*—in the shop of Simon the cobbler (Plut. *Mor.* 776b),[34] in later tradition a devoted follower of Socrates,[35] and a person who is supposed to have rejected an offer of support from Pericles by saying that he would never sell his freedom of speech (Diog. Laert. 2.123).

If Strepsiades was indeed set up as Pericles, it must have been highly amusing to watch an analogue of a man known as "the Olympian," whose speech was likened to thunder and lightning, being persuaded that Zeus did not exist, and that thunder was but a magnified fart. The very name of the play, *Nephélai,* has an Olympian ring to it, for it recalls Zeus' most famous title, the Homeric *Nephelēgeréta Zeús* ("Cloud-gathering Zeus"). It also recalls Cratinus' characterization of Pericles as a "mighty tyrant whom the gods call *Kephalēgerétan* ('[the] head-gathering [one]' [an abusive reference to Pericles' peculiar cranium])" (*PCG* 258; *Per.* 3.5). Strepsiades is very interested in the fact that the Clouds are women (314–357). Women were never far from Pericles' mind; Aristotle's pupil Clearchus put matters very succinctly: "Pericles was much given to *aphrodisia*" (*FHG* 2.314 *ap.* Ath. 13.589d). The Clouds' promise to grant Strepsiades *kléos* ("fame") "as broad as the heavens among mortals" (460–461) simply repeats the elements of Pericles' name, *perí* and *kléos*—"far-famed." Pericles' liking for the ladies may also underlie the scene in which Strepsiades is taught the difference between masculine and feminine, a scene that includes the statement, "I *know* which names are feminine!" (683).

SOCRATES

Aristophanes could have chosen Socrates as the appropriate philosophical peg upon which to hang all the sophistical "business" since he was in all likelihood

34. Cf. Thompson 1960; Stadter 1989, 68.
35. A tradition analyzed by Hock (1976).

a visitor to Pericles' house,[36] the venue of Socrates' philosophical intercourse with Aspasia,[37] with whose aid he is said to have "hunted down" the youthful Alcibiades, of whom he was inordinately fond (Ath. 5.219e; cf. Pl. *Prt.* 309a–c). Socrates, moreover, was generally believed — rightly or wrongly — to have had a pernicious influence on the politics as well as the morals of Alcibiades and other young men in his circle. The statement of Socrates in the first *Alcibiades* that Alcibiades would never achieve his tyrannical objectives without Socrates' help ([Pl.] *Alc.* 1.105b–e) represents a view of the philosopher that was widely held at Athens,[38] one that was to be a contributory factor in his condemnation in 399 (Pl. *Ap.* 23d). But rather than being a faithful image of Socrates, Aristophanes' clever conceit may instead be a witty cento of allusions to several representatives of the new learning that was, rather in the manner of Giuseppe Arcimboldo's learned exercises with fruit, flowers, and vegetables,[39] formed into a portrait of the son of Sophroniscus.

PHEIDIPPIDES, ALCIBIADES, ET AL.

Similarly, Pheidippides seems to incorporate features of personalities other than Alcibiades. For example, we hear of Xanthippus, Pericles' eldest son, "a spendthrift by nature," not being able to "bear with his father's stingy ways and the small amount of money which he allowed him." Xanthippus borrowed money from a friend, as though Pericles had asked him to do so. "When the friend asked for the money back again, Pericles brought a lawsuit against him, at which the young Xanthippus was enraged and abused his father, sneering at his way of life, and his discussions with sophists" (*Per.* 36.4). There are resonances of this in the plot in general, and in some of the views

36. Cf. A. E. W. Taylor 1926, 75–76: "The appearance of [Callias] and his brother among the associates of Socrates [in the *Cratylus*] is one of the many indications that the philosopher stood early in life in close relations with the Periclean circle."

37. Busolt 1893–1904, 3/1:510–513.

38. Cf. Montuori (1974, 170), who adds that Plato is said to have approached Socrates "because he was master in the art of politics" (Pl. *Epist.* 7 [324c]), and that Critias may have had good reason to forbid Socrates to "teach the art of words" to "the young" (Xen. *Mem.* 1.2.31, 33), having (with Alcibiades) himself had the benefit of a political education from Socrates (Xen. *Mem.* 1.2.15–16).

39. See the catalogue of the exhibition in the Palazzo Grassi, Venice: Rasponi and Tanzi 1987, esp. Kaufmann 1987; Kaufmann 1990; Winkler 1991.

expressed by Pheidippides in particular.[40] It was Xanthippus' wife's "expensive habits" that caused his financial embarrassment, and knowledge of this may have enriched Aristophanes' caricature of the Periclean household. Pericles' inheritance had, moreover, been a public issue in the last months of his life, when the statesman had successfully pleaded with the people to allow his son by Aspasia to be granted citizenship (*Per.* 37.2–5). It might appear that Aristophanes has taken the notion of "filial relationship to Pericles" and created another arcimboldesque portrait, this time in the image of Alcibiades.

The occasion for the play may have been Alcibiades' own money troubles. Although he was supposed to have inherited a large fortune (100 talents is the figure we hear),[41] Alcibiades never seems to have lived within his means. Toward the end of his life, he was given an annual income of fifty talents by the Persian satrap Pharnabazus (Nepos *Alc.* 9), but he can rarely have been as rich as this, much as he will have wanted to be. He was suspected of having abused his tenure of the office of *táktēs* in 425 B.C. in order to extort money from the allies whose tribute he and his colleagues were supposed to reassess ([Andoc.] 4.11). His recent[42] marriage to Hipparete, the daughter of a "man of great wealth and noble birth" (*Alc.* 8.1), seems only to have added to Alcibiades' financial requirements. Not content with a dowry of ten talents, he demanded and received an additional ten from his in-laws on the birth of his and Hipparete's first child. Alcibiades' hubristic behavior, however, is said (albeit by a somewhat biased source) to have so disturbed his brother-in-law Callias that the latter made his family fortune over to the state should he die childless, lest Alcibiades kill him in order to lay hands on it ([Andoc.] 4.15; *Alc.* 8.4). It is not unreasonable to suppose, therefore, that Alcibiades was in financial difficulties in the late 420s B.C.[43] He was certainly in debt in 415 B.C. as a result of his "devotion to horse-racing and other pleasures which outran his means" (Thuc. 6.15.3; cf. 6.12.2), and although he had by this time laid on

40. Stadter (1989, 327) raises an interesting question in his discussion of this story. "Is our whole story here taken from a comic scene, in which Pericles or a surrogate drives off his creditors?" The answer may well lie in the Creditor scene in *Clouds*. Indeed, Stadter notes that the Creditor's words at *Clouds* 1267–1268 ("order your son to pay back the money he received as a loan") fit Plutarch's anecdote very well, and that Strepsiades' behavior resembles that of Pericles. Millett (1991, 67) has also noted the "broad parallel" between "Strepsiades' woes" and the tale of Xanthippus' indebtedness as told by Plutarch.

41. Lys. 19.52; cf. Vickers 1990b for some comparative Athenian fortunes; and in general, J. K. Davies 1984.

42. See Chapter 5, n. 76 below, for an argument that would place the marriage before the winter of 425/24 B.C.

43. Cf. Ambrosino 1986–1987, 102: "E probabile che all'epoca delle *Nuvole* il dispendio [di Alcibiade] fosse notorio."

a flamboyant performance and lavish entertainment at the Olympic games of 416 B.C. (*Alc.* 11.1–3), it was already clear in 423 B.C. — in the light of his family's traditional interest in chariot-racing[44] — in what direction he was heading, even if Aristophanes' revision of *Clouds* (the version we probably have) was carried out as early as 419 or 418 B.C.[45]

If reference was indeed being made to Alcibiades' spendthrift ways, and if Pericles underlies Strepsiades, two things are being said at once: (1) that Alcibiades is running up debts now (but in a way that used to upset his guardian), and (2) that he tries to avoid his debts by using the kinds of clever argument that he and Pericles learned from the teachers they frequented. Alcibiades' current excesses are accordingly laid at the door of Pericles.[46] But the younger man's lawlessness and hubristic behavior eventually prove too much even for Strepsiades/Pericles, so that the latter finally burns down the source of all the trouble in a symbolic rejection of the philosophies he had once fostered. Not that there is any evidence of Pericles having given up his philosophic connections; the conflagration seems to have been used as a dramatic device to suggest that even Pericles would be disgusted at Alcibiades' current practices. It may even have its origin in the story that the Athenians publicly burned Protagoras' books[47] — assuming, of course, that this happened at all.[48]

OLYMPIAN ZEUS

We have already had occasion to mention that Pericles bore the nickname "the Olympian": a "childish and pompous" epithet, according to Plutarch (but one that he believed to be justified by Pericles' manifest virtues; *Per.*

44. Alcibiades' uncle Megacles had scored an Olympic chariot-racing victory in 424 B.C., and his grandfather Megacles was victorious in the Pythian games (Pind. *Pyth.* 7). *His* great-grandfather Alcmaeon's wealth enabled him to breed horses and to be the first Athenian to win at Olympia (Hdt. 6.125; Isoc. 16.25; cf. Blakesley 1854, 160 n. 281). See too, Thuc. 6.16.1; and *Clouds, Arg.* 5 Coulon. All were doubtless aware of the tradition that the Alcmaeonids were descended from *hippota* ("horseman") Nestor.

45. Dover 1972, 104; Henderson (1993, 600) argues for 418/17.

46. Cf. 1454–1455: "These problems are your responsibility, because you twisted yourself [*strepsas seauton* (for the violent undertone, see Chapter 1)] towards evil affairs."

47. Cic. *Nat. D.* 1.63; Diog. Laert. 9.52; cf. Dodds 1951, 189. Starkie (1911, 308–309, following Göttling) thinks the allusion may be to some haughty Pythagoreans who were burned to death in their house at Croton in the 430s B.C.

48. The historicity of story is disputed: see Wallace 1993, 133–135, 149–150.

39.2). Olympian Zeus figures large in *Clouds,* but rarely if ever in a favorable context. Strepsiades' first words, *Ioù, ioú. ô Zeû basileû* ("Alas, alas, O lord Zeus"; 1–2), set the scene. They are especially appropriate if Pericles is the object of Aristophanes' attentions, for apart from alluding to the statesman's nickname, they draw attention to another epithet — *basilikḗ* ("royal") — which Plutarch applied to the form of government that existed at Athens during Pericles' ascendancy (*Per.* 15.1; cf. Hermipp. *PCG* 47.1). The same point is made at 153. Pericles is said always to have prayed before business (*Per.* 8.6); this may be why Strepsiades declares (127) that *euxámenos* ("having prayed to the gods"), he will go and get himself taught at the Phrontistery.

The dialogue between Strepsiades and the Student he meets there concerns natural phenomena — insects and reptiles — deemed "Mysteries" by the adept (143). This allows Aristophanes to make fun of Chaerephon, Socrates' close associate, to introduce the theme of farting (160–166) — taken up in a big way at 293–295 and 382–397 — and perhaps most important of all, to introduce a discussion that may have parodied those of Pericles with Anaxagoras. Though "How then did he measure it?" may not have been "the question which a real Strepsiades would have asked,"[49] it is one that Pericles might have posed.[50]

Once installed in the Phrontistery, Strepsiades expresses great interest in a map of the world, which the Student explains to him.[51] His questions, however, consistently bear on well-known aspects of Pericles' career. He asks whether geometry is any use for measuring out land for cleruchies (203), a scheme of land apportionment with which Pericles had been closely associated.[52] On learning that it could measure any land, he remarks, "A democratic and useful ploy" (205), with an interesting paradox if M. Montuori is correct in seeing geometry as an aristocratic, as opposed to a democratic, avocation.[53] Pericles' democratic affectations, of course, need no gloss.[54] Strepsiades cannot see any jurymen at Athens (208); Pericles had instituted payment for jury service at Athens as a means to gain political influence (*Per.* 9.3). In case anyone might miss the point, Pericles is actually mentioned at 213 (cf. 859) as having been responsible for "laying out" Euboea (as indeed he was,

49. Dover 1968, xl.
50. The discussion of the intestinal arrangements of gnats and their connection with lawsuits (159–168) may also parody Pericles' interest in natural philosophy.
51. Socrates and Alcibiades once discussed a map of the world: Ael. *VH* 3.28.
52. *Per.* 9.1, 11.5, 23.4, 34.2; and perhaps the *hóroi* discussed in Chapter 5 are relevant here.
53. Montuori 1974, 237–238.
54. Cf. *Per.* 7.3, 14, 15.1–2, 17.1, 23.1.

when he suppressed a revolt in 446 B.C.).[55] Strepsiades wants Sparta to be moved away from Attica as far as possible; the average Athenian's view of the enemy was held in an intense form by Pericles.[56]

If Pericles does underlie Strepsiades, it is amusing to see the latter swearing by Zeus and threatening to hit the student for not moving Laconia further away; and even more so to see him kowtowing before Socrates, who greets him from on high, as though he were the god and Strepsiades a mere mortal. It is interesting to note in this context that Semonides fr. 1.3 contrasts Zeus with *ephḗmeroi* ("mortals").[57] The images in real life of Socrates and Pericles are here ludicrously reversed. Socrates' first short speech (227–234) is supposed to be based on theories first formulated by Diogenes of Apollonia, a philosopher who flourished between c. 440 and 430 B.C.,[58] and who is presumed to have visited Athens during that time.[59] If so, he may have been yet another philosopher who was associated in the popular mind with Pericles.

Strepsiades is told (247–248) that the gods are not in favor in the Phrontistery, but that he can if he wishes learn there the true nature of matters divine (250–251). "By Zeus," the dramatic analogue of "the Olympian" replies (251), "that is just the thing, if it can be done." Strepsiades is made to don a wreath (255–256: Pericles is said to have introduced the custom of granting wreaths to distinguished citizens; Val. Max. 2.6.5) for his initiation, as a result of which he will become a subtle speaker (with wordplay on "fine flour" [260, 262]—alluding to Pericles' involvement with the grain supply; cf. Schol. *Acharnians* 548). Socrates' solemn prayer, for all that it is to nonexistent deities, again recalls Pericles' practice of praying before business (*Per.* 8.6): perhaps another case of deliberate role-reversal. Another such reversal may be the initiation of Strepsiades into the religion of the Clouds (250–509), which has been seen as the parody of an initiation into a Mystery cult.[60] Such initiation was widely believed in antiquity to be a means of ensuring a happy fate after death,[61] but the question of the applicability of the rite to Socrates'

55. Thuc. 1.114. There may have been a topical joke as well; cf. Mattingly 1966, 201; 1992, 135: "There was some military intervention by Athens against Euboea in 424/3 B.C., which Philochorus recorded—and he is a good, reliable source for this period of Athenian history."
56. *Per.* 10.3–4, 21.1, 31.1, 32.6–33.2; *Plut. Fab.* 30.1.
57. Cf. Dover 1968, 125–126.
58. Kirk, Raven, and Schofield 1983, 434; cf. Green 1979, 24–25.
59. *OCD*² 347–348, s.n. Diogenes (1).
60. E.g., Byl 1980; Edmunds 1985, 216.
61. Richardson 1974, 310–311.

known teachings has given rise to much debate.[62] If, however, the literal introduction of the dead Pericles' spirit into the atmosphere above his funeral pyre, rather than the teachings of the live Socrates, is the main point of Aristophanes' conceit, the initiation scene can perhaps be more easily understood. In addition, the man who probably saw to the restoration both of the shrine at Eleusis[63] and quite possibly of the Eleusinion in the Agora[64] might plausibly be thought of as having been a well-known initiate.[65]

Strepsiades is afraid of what Socrates is going to do to him. Indeed, "Strepsiades is rather easily frightened (cf. 267–268, 293–295, 481, 497, 506–509),"[66] and "is something of a coward."[67] For all that Pericles had been "brave and adventurous" earlier in life (*Per.* 7.3), his later years had been characterized by a certain caution in military affairs,[68] a caution that led to "many songs and offensive jests [being] written about him, speaking of him as a coward" (*Per.* 33.7–8); perhaps this was one of the "offensive jests."

Socrates brings on the chorus of Clouds, whose voices are accompanied by thunder. Comic writers likened Pericles' manner of speech to "thunder" and "lightning";[69] and if Pericles really did lie behind the character of Strepsiades, then it is amusing to have the latter fart back at the thunderclouds and to need a crap in the bargain (293–295). The Clouds are responsible for *inter alia* dithyrambic music and poetry (333–339); Pericles had had the Odeum built to house musical competitions, of which he was the judge (*Per.* 13.10–11). And given the Alcibiadean purpose that may underlie *Clouds,* it may be relevant to note, with Lowell Edmunds, that at 362–363, Socrates is addressed in terms that are repeated by Plato in the *Symposium* (221b), where he puts them in the mouth of Alcibiades.[70] It will probably have been amusing, too, to see a Periclean Strepsiades persuaded that Olympian Zeus does not exist, and that it is the Clouds rather than "pissing Zeus" who bring

62. E.g., Adkins 1970; Hawtrey 1976.

63. *Per.* 13.7; Stadter 1989, 169–170.

64. Francis and Vickers 1988, 163.

65. Aristotle describes a conversation with Lampon in which Pericles is as yet uninitiated (*Rh.* 3.1419a), but the date is uncertain; Plutarch records another discussion between Pericles and Lampon before 443 (*Per.* 6).

66. Sommerstein 1982, 174.

67. Dover 1968, 162.

68. *Per.* 18.1, 22.2, 33.5. Their "caution" will have been one of the reasons why Plutarch coupled the *Lives* of Pericles and Q. Fabius Maximus (the latter was called *átolmon* ["daring nothing, cowardly"]: Plut. *Marc.* 9.4).

69. *Per.* 8.4 (though dependent on *Acharnians* 531: Stadter 1989, 104).

70. Edmunds 1987b.

about rain (365–374). "Does Zeus make the Clouds move?" asks Strepsiades. "No, thunder is the product of a *Dînos* ('Vortex')," replies Socrates (380). Whereupon Strepsiades observes that Vortex is king in Zeus' place (380–381). The idea of "the noetic substance starting a vortex" originated with Anaxagoras,[71] Pericles' adviser; there may be an allusion being made here, and the talk of Strepsiades' digestive processes may thus be another "offensive jest" aimed at "the Olympian."

Frontinus' story (*Str.* 1.11.10) about Pericles allaying the panic of his men by knocking two stones together in order to explain the underlying mechanism of thunderbolts bears directly upon the scene where Strepsiades is taught about thunder and lightning. Pericles' action here is in keeping with what we know of his interest in natural philosophy, and the explanation corresponds with Anaxagoras' view that thunder came about as the result of a "collision of the clouds" (Diog. Laert. 2.9). Pericles in Frontinus' story is practically minded and not in the least superstitious or credulous. Aristophanes' Strepsiades is the very opposite, and is reluctant to believe at first in Socrates' explanation that clouds make a noise when they collide with each other (383–384). "Come now, who is expected to believe that?" is his reaction (385). Aristophanes seems to have taken a known position of a historical figure and, for the sake of a laugh, turned it on its head: the "Hermogenes principle" in action (cf. Hermog. *Meth.* 34). Pericles' actual experiences, by contrast, are alluded to when Strepsiades misinterprets (481) Socrates' talk of *mēkhanàs kainás* (479–480: "new devices") as a reference to "siege engines" (also known as *mēkhanaí*)[72]; Pericles owed his victory over the Samians to his skill at conducting siege warfare (*Per.* 27.3).

MEASURES OF GRAIN AND MUSICAL MEASURES

There is a discussion of meter and rhythm at 636–654, and as usual Strepsiades gets hold of the wrong end of the stick, and thinks that Socrates is referring to measures of grain rather than musical measures. At 650–651, Socrates tells Strepsiades that it is chic to know which rhythm is "enoplian" and which is "dactylic." These are terms we otherwise hear about in Plato's *Republic* (400b), when Socrates cites Damon's book on meter. This was the Damon

71. Kirk, Raven, and Schofield 1983, 445, cf. 364–365, 372–373.
72. Green 1979, 19.

said to have been "a sophist . . . who used the name of music to conceal this accomplishment from the world, but who really trained Pericles for his political contests just as a trainer prepares an athlete for the games" (Pl. *Resp.* 400b). Plato's Socrates also cites Damon as saying that changes in musical fashions are always accompanied by changes in the order of the state (Pl. *Resp.* 424c). Not only is it implied in *Clouds* that Pericles had kept dangerous philosophical company (the evidence suggests both that Damon suggested the idea for payment for juries to Pericles and that he was ostracized),[73] but Strepsiades' remarks about corn measures and the grain trade in general (*patrôiōn alphítōn* ["paternal flour supply"; 106]; *tálphit'* ["flour"; 176]; *alphitamoiboû* ["flour-dealer"; 640]; *tálphita* ["the flour"; 648]; *dialphitôsō* ["fill with flour"; 669]; *tálphita* [788]) also recall the *stoà alphitópōlis* ("flour-market"), a building at the Piraeus "which Pericles erected, [and] in which the city's corn supply was kept" (Schol. *Acharnians* 548).

BEDBUGS, THE PLAGUE, AND THUCYDIDES

The scene in which Socrates puts Strepsiades to bed (694–745) is a parody of one suffering from the plague; at least there are many parallels between Aristophanes' lines and what we know from Thucydides.[74] The bedbugs are described as Corinthians; wordplay (on *kóresi* [699]) apart, there may be a connection with the fact that it was believed that the plague was introduced by the Peloponnesians (Thuc. 2.48.2). The bugs are said to be devouring Strepsiades' ribs (711): one of the symptoms of the plague was that it quickly reached the chest (Thuc. 2.49.3). Line 713 is usually taken to read *toùs órkheis exélkousin* ("they are dragging out my testicles"). The plausible suggestion has, however, been made[75] that (the differently accented) *exelkoûsin* ("ulcerate") should be read instead. If so, there may be a connection with the report that the plague caused *hélkōsis* ("ulceration").[76] Against this possibility, however, is the fact that Thucydides' ulceration applied to the colon, not the testicles; but this may in turn be outweighed by the undoubted distress the

73. Arist. *Ath. Pol.* 27.4, with Rhodes' note.
74. Vickers 1991; 1993.
75. By Blaydes 1890, 94, 411 (following Reiske).
76. Thuc. 2.49.6; and cf. the *helkúdria* ("little plague-sores" on the Periclean Demus' shins at *Knights* 907.

plague did cause to the extremities (Thuc. 2.49.8). The Ravenna and Marcian manuscripts invert lines 712 and 713, and thus give the symptoms in the order in which they are presented by Thucydides, a fact that bears witness to the fundamental soundness of the Ravenna codex. At 712 we learn that the bed-bugs are draining Strepsiades' spirit: another plague symptom was severe diarrhea (Thuc. 2.49.6). At 714 the bugs are said to be digging through Strepsiades' arse (*kaì tòn prōktòn diorúttousin*): in its final stages, the plague would "descend to the bowels" (Thuc. 2.49.6). Strepsiades then claims that the bugs will kill him (715: *kaì m' apoloûsin*): according to Thucydides, "most" died of exhaustion at this stage (Thuc. 2.49.6).

Socrates tells Strepsiades not to feel hurt too much (716). "How can I not do so," replies Strepsiades, "when I have lost my money?" (718). Pericles had been fined between fifteen and fifty talents for his failure to take Epidaurus in the closing months of his life (*Per.* 35.4). "When I have lost my complexion," Strepsiades continues, "when I have lost my life" (719; Pericles was dead), "and when I have lost my shoes" (the stock joke of *Clouds* pokes fun at Socrates' cobbler fixation). "In addition to these evils, I sing on guard duty" (721; perhaps references both to the Odeum [literally Song Hall] built under Pericles' direction [*Per.* 13.9–10] and to the Periclean policy of retreating within the city walls [Thuc. 2.13]). "And I shall soon be lost altogether" (722). The punch line of this Pythonesque little scene comes (at 734) when Socrates asks what Strepsiades has managed to get hold of: "Nothing except *tò péos en têi dexiái* ('my cock in my right hand')." Aristophanes has already (710–715) made five or six apparent references to the plague. This is evidently another one, which recalls Thucydides' final symptom: "Even if a person got over the worst, the plague would often . . . attack the privy parts . . . and some escaped with the loss of these" (2.49.8). We might envisage Strepsiades detaching and brandishing the large leather phallus with which comic actors were equipped.

THUCYDIDES AND ARISTOPHANES

This is all very distasteful, but the chances of these parallels being coincidental, in a play performed before an audience that had either witnessed or experienced similar symptoms but a few years earlier, are remote. For all that Thucydides had experienced the symptoms himself, these lines reinforce the view tentatively expressed earlier, namely, that Thucydides in exile may have made use of Aristophanes as a handy means of recalling significant historical events.[77] Not only did the scene provide a useful checklist, but it even informed the tone of Thucydides' account. It was Pericles' preference for natural rather than supernatural explanations of physical phenomena that Aristophanes was lampooning. Thucydides is similarly concerned to attribute the plague to natural rather than divine causes.[78]

If these lines do relate to Pericles, then Thucydides would have been well aware of the fact. His account of plague symptoms will have been a discreet ("emphatic") way of describing the sufferings of a Pericles who had "exhibited many varieties of symptoms" (*Per.* 38) but whose memory he wished to honor.[79] Thucydides would have been aware, too, that Alcibiades lay behind the character of Pheidippides, and such an awareness would go a long way toward explaining a puzzling expression in the first of the two long speeches Thucydides puts into Alcibiades' mouth. According to a scholiast, the phrase *storésomen tò phrónēma* ("lay low the pride [of the Peloponnesians]") is one of the most unpleasant (*sklērótaton*) metaphors used by Thucydides, and it was an expression *kat' Alkibiádēn* (Schol. Thuc. 6.18.4). No one seems to have asked why the expression was considered to be so unpleasant,[80] but we may now have the makings of answer.

According to Aeschines Socraticus (fr. 5 Dittmar), Alcibiades' own *phrónēma* was "overblown," and contemporaries will have been well aware of the fact. But if Thucydides actually did make use of *Clouds,* he will have known the lines (1381–1382) where Pheidippides is reminded of his childish speech disorder, and the pun on *brûn/plún.* It is more than likely that Thucydides used Alcibiades as an informant when preparing his history,[81] and it is clear that Thucydides knew such details of Alcibiades' mode of speech as the frequent use of initial *kaì,* of paratactic constructions, and of the potential opta-

77. Westlake (1968) lists several correspondences between Thucydides and Aristophanes: Cleon described as *pithanótatos* (Thuc. 3.36.6) and abusing the Knights *xunōmótas légōn pithanótata* (*Knights* 628–629) (8 n. 5, cf. 82); Thucydides' treatment of Nicias' superstition (7.50.4) in the context of *Knights* 32–34 (11 n. 5); Thucydides describing Hyperbolus (8.73.3) "in language worthy of, and perhaps even influenced by, Aristophanes" (13 n. 1, citing *mokhthērós* [*Knights* 1304] and *ponēría* [*Clouds* 1066; cf. *Peace* 684]); Thucydides' admiration of Phormio matched by Aristophanes' "warm approval" (58). The similar usage of *ponôn pausómetha* at Ar. *Knights* and Thuc. 5.16.1, noted by Boegehold (1982), may be another possible case of Thucydidean dependence on Aristophanes.

78. Cf. Marshall 1990, esp. 169.

79. For Marshall (1990, 165), "much pro-Periclean sentiment [in Thucydides] takes the form of implicit suggestion."

80. The authors of *HCT* do not even quote the relevant part of the scholion.

81. Cf. Brunt 1952; Bloedow 1972.

tive.[82] It is possible, too, that a writer who was not averse to using puns[83] may have included an expression that was Alcibiadean to the extent that it used *lambda*-engendered wordplay. It was, as we have already had occasion to note, Thucydides' practice to imitate the manner of speech of his speakers (Hermog. *Meth.* 31). Lambdacized, the "unpleasant" phrase might have sounded like *Peloponnēsíōn te stolésomen tò plúnēma* ("and let us get the bath ready for the Peloponnesians").[84] If so, Thucydides may have been alluding both to Alcibiades' speech defect and to his love of bathing (Plut. *Mor.* 235a), as well as to the fact that the Peloponnesians, or at least the Spartans, were unenthusiastic bathers[85] and in consequence were notoriously dirty (cf. *Birds* 1282, and Chapter 8). Small wonder that the scholiast winced.

82. Tompkins 1972.
83. J. E. Powell 1937, 103; Shimron 1989, 71.
84. And note that the preceding three words, *poiṓmetha tòn ploûn* ("let us make the voyage"), may also play on the expression *plúnon poieîn tina*, literally "to make a wash" for someone, and metaphorically "to abuse," "give someone a dressing" (LSJ s.vv. *plúnos, plúnō* II).
85. Xen. *Lac.* 2.4; Plut. *Lyc.* 16.12; *Mor.* 237b.

PERICLES, ALCIBIADES, AND
THE GENERATION GAP
Aristophanes' *Clouds* II

Martin Ostwald has noted that "both in the *Clouds* and the *Wasps,* father and son affect allegiance to different social classes" and observes: "Whether this reflects a common situation in Athens or whether it is merely a comic device to highlight the generation gap we cannot tell."[1] If, however, the thesis of the previous chapter is valid, namely, that Pericles and Alcibiades underlie the main characters of *Clouds,* then it becomes a relatively simple matter to solve the problem to which Ostwald has drawn attention.[2] Allegiance to different social classes on the part of Strepsiades and Pheidippides will have reflected the ways in which their historical analogues were perceived by contemporaries. Although Pericles was well born, Aristophanes assimilates his Periclean character to the social class with which Pericles deliberately chose to be associated. Alcibiades was less inclined than his guardian to adopt a democratic facade, and Aristophanes exploits to the full his true social position and his tastes for the pastimes of the aristocracy, in particular chariot-racing.

There is a good deal of pointed satire aimed at Alcibiades when Socrates eventually gives up on Strepsiades (789–790), and the Clouds suggest that if he has a son he should be sent to school instead (795–796). The characterization of Strepsiades' son is given in terms that apply to Alcibiades. Pheidip-

1. Ostwald 1986, 235. For a thorough discussion of "the generation gap," see Strauss 1993. See, too, Vickers 1993; Handley 1993.
2. For *Wasps,* see Chapter 7.

pides is *kalós te kagathós* ("a gentleman"; 797); this was the kind of thing Pericles would have liked to say—or hear said—about his ward. Pheidippides is unwilling to go to school (798); an eyewitness source declared Alcibiades to have been *apaídeutos* ("uneducated"; Antisth. fr. 30 Caizzi *ap.* Ath. 12.534c). Pheidippides is physically attractive (799: *eusōmateî*); it was said of Alcibiades that his "physical beauty . . . was equally fascinating when he was a boy, a youth and a man."[3] Pheidippides is also lusty (799: *sphrigâi*); Alcibiades' lustiness was notorious. Pheidippides is said to be descended from "a high-plumed race of women, the house of Coesyra" (800); Alcibiades' pedigree was identical (*Alc.* 1.1).

There may be a disparaging allusion to Pericles' interest in natural phenomena[4] when Strepsiades swears *mà tên Homíkhlēn* ("by Mist") as he throws Pheidippides out of the house, and tells him to go and live off his rich Alcmaeonid relatives—in Megacles' mansion (814–815). The latter is apparently adorned with columns, and it is interesting to note that Callias, the rich brother-in-law whose fortune Alcibiades was accused of attempting to acquire by force (*Alc.* 8.4; [Andoc.] 4.13–15), possessed such a house (Pl. *Prt.* 314e, 315c)—perhaps, in that he was a grandson of Megacles, the very house Aristophanes had in mind.

The Alcibiadean resonances continue when Pheidippides enters the Phrontistery (816). His first words, *ti khrêma páskheis* ("what is the matter with you?"), if lambdacized would produce *ti klêma páskheis* ("what shoe is bothering you?")—if so, another reference to Socrates' favorite shoemaking topos (see Chapter 2). Pheidippides is called a *paidárion* ("young boy"; 821); Alcibiades' relative youth was to be still a political issue in 415 B.C., when Nicias made it one of the grounds for refusing him command of the Sicilian expedition (Thuc. 6.12–13).[5]

STRONG AND WEAK

But let us go forward to the encounter (889–1114) between the Stronger (*tòn kreíttona*) and Weaker (*tòn hêttona*) Arguments, which not only is a debate

3. *Alc.* 1.4; cf. 16.4; Pl. *Symp.* 216c–219e; *Prt.* 309a; [Pl.] *Alc.* 1.113b, 123a; Ath. 12.534c; Ael. *VH* 12.14, 14.46c.
4. Cf. Schol. *Clouds* 252 (where *kapnós* ["smoke"], *skiás* ["shadows"], and *nephélas* ["clouds"] are said to indicate worthlessness). Cf. 330 and Schol.
5. Cf. Develin 1985.

across the generation gap akin to those between Strepsiades and Pheidippi-des,[6] but also recalls a conversation between Pericles and Alcibiades reported by Xenophon (*Mem.* 1.2.40–46), where Alcibiades speaks of force and law-lessness: "Is it not when the stronger (*ho kreíttōn*) obliges the weaker (*tòn héttō*), not by persuasion but by force (*biasámenos*) to do what he pleases?"[7] Moreover, Strepsiades' injunction at 887–888, that Pheidippides should be able to argue against *pánta tà díkaia* ("every kind of justice"), strongly recalls the way Callicles argues that might is right in Plato's *Gorgias* (482c–486d), es-pecially the observation that "justice consists in the stronger (*tòn kreíttō*) rul-ing over and having more than the weaker (*toû héttonos*)" (483d; cf. 484c). Indeed, if Callicles is a "puppet,"[8] then Alcibiades is an obvious model.[9] The debate between the Stronger and Weaker Arguments in *Clouds* is usually felt to be an uncomfortable disruption between the slapstick scenes involv-ing Strepsiades and Pheidippides earlier and later in the play. *Clouds* is some-how felt to be broken-backed and inconsequential. If, however, by invoking the principle of polymorphic characterization, we can see the Stronger Argu-ment again standing for Pericles, and the Weaker for Alcibiades, continuity is preserved.

The validity of this hypothesis can be tested by comparing the values for which the Weaker Argument appears to stand (using a list drawn up by K. J. Dover)[10] with what we know, or at least with what was said, about Alcibi-ades. In nearly every case there is a parallel:

1. *Neglect of physical condition and consequent enfeeblement.* Alcibiades' son once said that "although in natural gifts and in strength of body he was second to none, [the elder Alcibiades] disdained gymnastic contests (*gumnikoùs agônas*) . . . but turned to the breeding of horses" (Isoc. 16.33). The younger Alcibiades presumably thought it necessary to stress his father's physical fitness, since many would naturally have assumed that absence from traditional keep-fit classes would inevitably induce enfeeblement.

6. On which see Ostwald 1986, 235.

7. Xenophon goes to great lengths accurately to characterize Alcibiades, beginning his speech with a potential optative (41: *ékhois án me didáxai*), and making frequent use of paratactic con-structions and of initial *kaí;* cf. Tompkins 1972. *Bía* is also a play on Alci*bia*des and occurs five times in thirteen lines of text.

8. Havelock 1957, 248.

9. See Apelt 1912; 1922; Vickers 1994.

10. Dover 1968, lix.

2. *Warm baths.* Alcibiades was fond of bathing, as is shown by the comments made about him at Sparta (Plut. *Mor.* 235a), where it was thought he bathed in too much water (although, it being Sparta, the water was cold).

3. *Too much warm clothing.* The reference is to *en himatíoisi . . . entetulíkhthai* ("to be wrapped up in cloaks") at 987. Alcibiades appears to have owned many such garments; twenty-two of his *himátia* were sold off in 414 B.C.[11]

4. *Innovations in music.* Although we know of no direct connection between Alcibiades and musical innovations as such, he must have been on friendly terms with Euripides (who was sympathetic to new ideas in music), in that he employed him to write a victory ode in 416 B.C.[12] Alcibiades is also said to have brought about a change in fashion with regard to *aulos*-playing at symposia. Since he considered that it both distorted the mouth and inhibited conversation, the *aulos* ceased to be a fashionable instrument in polite society (*Alc.* 2.5–7).

5. *The ability to talk and argue.* "[Alcibiades] relied upon nothing so much as on his eloquence for making himself popular and influential. His rhetorical powers are borne witness to by the comic dramatists [as here?]; and the greatest of orators, Demosthenes, in his speech against Meidias, speaks of Alcibiades as being most eloquent, besides his other charms. If we are to believe Theophrastus . . . Alcibiades excelled all men of his time in readiness of invention and resource" (Theophr. 134 W *ap. Alc.* 10.3; cf. Isoc. 16.21).

6. *Disbelief in, and cynical exploitation of, inherited beliefs.* "[Alcibiades] carried a shield not emblazoned with the ancestral bearings of his family, but with an Eros wielding a thunderbolt. . . . The leading men of Athens viewed his conduct with disgust and apprehension."[13] Elsewhere we learn that "returning from Olympia [Alcibiades] dedicated at Athens two paintings by Aglaophon; one of these showed figures representing the Olympian and Pythian festivals placing crowns on his head,

---

11. Pritchett 1956, 167, 190–210; 1961, 23.

12. Bowra 1960, 68–79; cf. Chapter 9.

13. *Alc.* 16.1–2; cf. Ath. 12.534e (where we learn that the Eros was golden); Blanckenhagen 1964. There was a representation of Alcibiades in the Portico of Octavia at Rome showing him as Eros wielding a thunderbolt: Pliny *HN* 36.28. The possibility that Alcibiades' shield may only have existed on the stage (Russell 1966, 45; Littmann 1970, 267–268) does not provide grounds for ignoring this testimony, rather the opposite: such a conceit would have expressed the essential public image of the man.

and on the other was the seated figure of Nemea with Alcibiades on her lap" (Satyr. 24 *ap.* Ath. 12.534d). This must be the picture concerning which Plutarch says "all men eagerly crowded to see; but older men were vexed at these things, thinking them only fit for tyrants, and considering them to be open violations of the laws" (*Alc.* 16.4–5). It was thus natural that in 415 B.C. the story should have been put around that Alcibiades was involved in both the profanation of the Mysteries and the mutilation of the Herms (although he was probably in fact only guilty of the former offense).[14]

7. *Moral nihilism, especially sexual indulgence.* Nowhere was the argument of moral nihilism put more succinctly than by Alcibiades' accuser in c. 416 B.C.: "Were I faced with the task of describing at length [Alcibiades'] career as an adulterer, as a stealer of the wives of others, as a perpetrator of lawless acts in general, the time at my disposal would be all too short."[15]

Disregard of the convention that children should be seen and not heard is the last item on Dover's list. We have no direct evidence with regard to Alcibiades on this particular issue, but we may safely speculate that he was an unwholesome brat.[16] There are, though, other features mentioned during the debate that bear upon Alcibiades. At 890 and 915, the Stronger Argument accuses his opponent of being *thrasús* ("brazen"); we hear of the Athenians, at the time of the ostracism of Hyperbolus, fearing Alcibiades' *thrásos* ("reckless daring"; Plut. *Nic.* 11.2). The mutual recrimination at 908–909, where the Stronger Argument is called a *tuphogérōn* ("silly old man," perhaps playing on *tumbogérōn ["aged tomb-person"][17] as well as *tumbogélōn [ridiculous tomb-person]), and the Weaker Argument is called a "shameless pathic," well reflects Pericles' mortal status and Alcibiades' public image. At 910 (cf. 969), the Weaker Argument is accused of being a *bōmolókhos* ("clown"); *bōmolokhía* ("horseplay") was a charge justly laid against Alcibiades (*Alc.* 40.3). At 911 (and cf. 994), the charge is that the Weaker Argument is a *patraloías* ("father-

14. *Alc.* 20.5; Dem. 21.147; cf. Thuc. 6.28.1–2. Osborne (1985, 73 n. 97) notes, "How limited is the overlap between those named in connection with the mutilation and those named in connection with the profanation."

15. [Andoc.] 4.10; cf. Lib. *Decl.* 15.49 (6.144.15).

16. The relationship between childhood speech impairment and emotional disorders, which often results in "destructiveness [and] temper tantrums" (Baker and Cantwell 1982, 291–292), may be relevant to Alcibiades' childhood development.

17. LSJ s.v. *tuphogérōn.*

beater"); although Alcibiades almost certainly did not beat his adoptive father, he did beat "as a joke" Hipponicus, the man who was later to become his father-in-law.[18] The mention of "more than ten thousand staters" at 1041 recalls Alcibiades' anonymous gift of a thousand darics (also known as staters; e.g., Thuc. 8.28.4; Hdt. 7.28.2) to test his wife's virtue (Ath. 12.534c; see Chapter 5), and the expressed determination to win the contest (1042) recollects Alcibiades' "extremely strong desire to win."[19] At 1056–1057, the Weaker Argument cites Homer describing Nestor (and others) as an *agorētḗs* ("public speaker"); Alcibiades was fond of Homer (*Alc.* 7.1–3), believed himself to be descended from Nestor,[20] and was already a public speaker of note and a frequent visitor to the Agora.[21]

Aristophanes also uses characteristic mannerisms of speech to help make the point that the Weaker Argument represents Alcibiades. The Weaker Argument's two long speeches (1036–1045 and 1068–1082) both begin with *kaí* (*kaì mén* and *kâit'*), both have sentences beginning with *kaí* halfway through (at 1041 and 1074), and both have last lines (and sentences) beginning *kaítoi*. Line 1074, moreover, ends with a potential optative. Alcibiades as reported by Thucydides uses very few abstract expressions; *anágkē* ("necessity") and *anagkaîon* ("necessary") between them account for two-thirds.[22] Hence, perhaps, *tês phúseōs anágkas* ("needs of nature") at 1075, describing illicit lovemaking, but doubtless parodying views concerning *nómos* and *phúsis* of the kind put forward by "Callicles" (Pl. *Grg.* 482c–486d),[23] who is also fond of the word *anágkē*.[24] Lambdacism, as ever, produces double meanings. For example, at 920, the Weaker Argument tells the Stronger that he is repulsively *aiskhrôs* ("ugly"); lambdacized, this would play on *Aiskhuleîos* ("Aeschylean") — which is very much in keeping with the attack on old-fashioned cultural values.[25]

18. *Alc.* 8.1; and see this book passim. For father-beating as an especially heinous crime, see N. R. E. Fisher 1992, 456 n. 12.

19. *Alc.* 2.1; cf. Thuc. 5.43.2, and Chapter 6 (on *Knights* 615).

20. Via Alcmaeon: Paus. 2.18.7.

21. Cf. the description of the Alcibiadean Sausage-seller as *ex agoras* ("from the Agora") at *Knights* 181.

22. Tompkins 1972, 189–190. It would be significant, too, perhaps, that *anágkē* and *anagkaîon* come at the beginning of each of Alcibiades' speeches at Thuc. 6.16.1 and 6.89.1, were it not for the fact that *anágkē* plays such an important role in Thucydides in any case: Ostwald 1988.

23. On the likelihood that Alcibiades lies behind the characterization of "Callicles," see Apelt 1912; 1922; Vickers 1994.

24. *Anagkasthênai*: Pl. *Grg.* 482d; *anagkázetai*: 483a; *anágkē*: 484c.

25. Cf. Chapter 6 (on *Knights* 1321).

But if the Weaker Argument expresses his ideas in the guise of a recognizable individual who has already appeared in *Clouds* in another character, may not the same perhaps be true of the Stronger Argument? Just as Alcibiades underlies both Pheidippides and the Weaker Argument, may not Pericles lie behind both Strepsiades and the Stronger Argument? Thus to personalize the generation gap would be an effective means of emphasizing the contrast between the old ways and the new. Xenophon's report of a conversation between Pericles and Alcibiades (Xen. *Mem.* 1.2.40–46; see Chapter 2) may thus have had its basis in a knowing reading of *Clouds* as much as in historical fact, and a lambdacizing reference to Aeschylus at 920 may thus have been an allusion to Pericles' liking for old-time poetry in general and to his patronage of Aeschylus in particular.[26]

The relevance of the mention of Telephus at 922 is said not to be clear,[27] but we shall see in Chapter 4[28] why the character in Euripides' play might have been as displeasing to Pericles as he apparently is to the Stronger Argument. One of Pericles' major concerns, namely the nourishment of Athens' citizens, is referred to at 926–927. Pericles' eyes had suffered, it seems, as a consequence of the plague, and Pericles was also said to have possessed a *kéntron* ("sting"; Eup. *PCG* 102.7), which may be why the Weaker Argument threatens to sting the Stronger Argument's eyes at 946–947.[29]

But the real meat is to be found in the Stronger Argument's speech at 961–983. If it relates to Pericles, it does so by exploiting the Hermogenes principle (Hermog. *Meth.* 34), for (as L. B. Carter has briefly noted[30]) lines 961–972 extol traditional Spartan values. This is something that Pericles, who was notorious for his hatred of Sparta (*Per.* 21.1, 31.1), would never of course have done, but to make a Periclean figure do so on the comic stage might well have been funny. It is in any case worth spelling out the Spartan references with which these lines are replete (and which commentators have

26. Pericles had been *choregus* for the *Persae* in 472 B.C.: Broadhead 1960, 2.

27. Sommerstein 1982, 206.

28. In a discussion of *Acharnians* 432ff.

29. Cf. the Dercetes scene in *Acharnians* (Chapter 5). Other possible references to Periclean eyesight in *Clouds* include: "I would rather have lost my eye with a stone [rather than 'the way I did,' perhaps]" (24); and on the potential significance of "stone," see the discussion of *Wasps* 280 in Chapter 7; and "Surely you see them, unless you have pus in your eyes like cucumbers (*lēmâis kolokúntais*)" (327). This both recalls Pericles' dictum about Aegina, "Pus (*lēmē*) in the eye of the Piraeus" (*Per.* 8.7, trans. Stadter 1989, 108), and the shape of his head, especially if Hermipp. *PCG* 69 applied to him: *tèn kephalèn hósēn ékhei. hósēn kolokúntēn* ("What a head he has. Like a cucumber").

30. Carter 1986, 46. For a useful account of everyday life at Sparta, see Powell 1988, 224–240.

overlooked). The archaic educational system to which the Stronger Argument looks back with nostalgia is characterized by silent boys who walk naked, though the snow might fall as thick as barley flakes. This has distinct echoes in what we know of the *agōgē*, the strict educational regime that all Spartan males had to undergo.[31] Spartan boys were taught by long periods of silent listening (Plut. *Lyc.* 19.2); from their twelfth year they did not wear a tunic, but had one garment that they wore all the year round;[32] barley was considered the staple diet of the Spartans (cf. Plut. *Cleom.* 16.7). The songs that Spartan youths learnt were "such as rouse men's blood and stir them to deeds of prowess, written in plain unaffected language" (Plut. *Lyc.* 21.1; cf. *Mor.* 238a), which is what we have in "Pallas, the terrible sacker of cities" and "A far-reaching shout" at 967. *Bóama* ("shout") is, in this context, reminiscent of the way the Spartans conducted their elections to office: the candidates would parade in silence before the voters, the intensity of whose shouts would be recorded by invigilators in tents nearby.[33] The tune the boys sing is one handed down by their fathers (968): the Spartans were famous for their conservatism in music (cf. Ath. 14.632f). Phrynis, whose musical novelties are condemned at 970–971, supposedly once had two extra—and unconventional—strings on his lyre cut off by a Spartan ephor (Plut. *Agis* 10; *Mor.* 84a, 220c) (he had, however, won the first of the musical competitions in Pericles' Music Hall, at which Pericles has been a judge).[34] The blows that would be handed out to offenders (972) recall Spartan educational practice.[35]

Aristophanes often appears to make fun of Pericles' criticism of Sophocles' pederastic tastes: one of his "very few recorded sayings" (*Per.* 8.7) was a rebuke to the playwright (who had cast lustful looks at a young cup-bearer) that "a general ought to keep not only his hands clean, but his eyes."[36] Aristophanes may be doing so again at lines 973–980 with their homoerotic undertone, but in a way that echoes similar sentiments expressed by Lycurgus, the semilegendary Spartan lawmaker. Lycurgus considered it a disgraceful thing if "any man showed that his affections were fixed on the bodily attractions

31. See, in particular, Xen. *Lac.* and Plut. *Lyc.*; cf. Cartledge 1987, 23ff.; Powell 1988.
32. Xen. *Lac.* 2.4; Plut. *Lyc.* 16.11; *Mor.* 237b.
33. Thuc. 1.87.2; Plut. *Lyc.* 26.3–5. Aristotle (*Pol.* 1271a10) thought it "excessively childish."
34. Schol. *Clouds* 971 (in 446, if *árkhontos Kallíou* [archon in 456] is emended to *árkhontos Kallimáchou*); cf. *RE* 20/1 (1941), 926, s.v. "Phrynis."
35. E.g., Xen. *Lac.* 6.6.3; Plut. *Lyc.* 17.5; Hyg. *Fab.* 261. The Spartan cloak was known as the *tríbōn* (Plut. *Cleom.* 16.7), and there may be allusions to this in *epetríbeto* (972) and *paidotríbou* (973); cf. the similar wordplay at *Peace* 8, 12, 16, 27 (Chapter 8).
36. *Per.* 8.7; Cic. *Off.* 1.40; Val. Max. 4.3 ext.1. For Sophocles' proclivities, see Ion *FGrH* 392 F 6 *ap.* Ath. 13.603e–604e.

of a youth," and legislated that lovers should refrain from intimate relations with boys (Xen. *Lac.* 2.13; Plut. *Mor.* 237b–c). In describing how boys used to smooth down sand on which they had sat so that their lovers would not see the impression of their privates, Aristophanes would seem to be imputing a certain hypocrisy to the Spartans, bearing out Xenophon's admission that "such a state of things [i.e., homosexual chastity] is disbelieved by some" (Xen. *Lac.* 2.14).[37] True modesty was one of the virtues Lycurgus hoped to inculcate in Spartan youths. Apart from preserving silence, young men had to "keep their hands under their dress . . . not to look round in any direction, and keep their eyes before their feet" (Xen. *Lac.* 3.4). The Stronger Argument's salacious description of bashfulness is in keeping with this, and his assertion that boys did not anoint themselves below the waist (977) recalls the fact that Spartan youths did not anoint themselves at all.[38]

Boys of old are said never to have snatched the *kephálaion* ("head") of a *raphanîdos* ("radish"; 981), or to have seized their elders' "dill" or "celery" while dining. This is a complex image that may refer in part to Spartan youths having to steal food,[39] to Spartan respect for older persons (e.g., Just. *Epit.* 3.3; Plut. *Mor.* 237c–d), to the supposedly aphrodisiac content of the radish (Schol. *Clouds* 981), to pubic hair,[40] to Pericles' pointy cranium, as well as to the fact that the variety of radish in question was a long pointed vegetable that was used on occasion to punish adulterers[41] when it was thrust up their fundament. The sense at 983 is in any case decidedly obscene. The whole passage will doubtless have been intended as an ironic commentary on Pericles' boast that Athens was the "school of Hellas" (Thuc. 2.41.1).[42] Pericles' old-fashioned attitudes are made to appear even more conservative by casting them in the guise of the immutable customs of Sparta; Thucydides' Pericles, by contrast, pays tribute to the flexibility of the Athenians (Thuc. 2.41.1).

What Aristophanes seems to be doing throughout his representation of the Stronger Argument is to attribute to him extremely exaggerated, and frequently Spartan, versions of known positions of Pericles. Once again, K. J. Dover conveniently provides a useful checklist of the values the Stronger Argument stands for, against which this hypothesis might be tested.

37. Cf. Cartledge 1987, 29 on Spartan pederasty.
38. Plut. *Lyc.* 16.12: *aleimmátōn ápeiroi;* cf. *Mor.* 237b.
39. Xen. *Lac.* 2.5–7; *An.* 4.6.14–15; Plut. *Lyc.* 16.6; *Mor.* 237e–f.
40. For *sélinon* ("celery") with this meaning, see Henderson 1975, 144.
41. Cf. *raphanidōthêi* at 1083.
42. Cf. Carter 1986, 46.

1. *Encouragement of physical hardiness and physical training with consequent health and strength.* Thucydides makes his Pericles say that "whereas [the Spartans] from early youth are always undergoing laborious exercises which are to make them brave, we live at ease" (Thuc. 2.39.1). Aristophanes makes the Stronger Argument defend Spartan, as opposed to Athenian, ways.

2. *Traditional music and poetry.* Apart from sponsoring Aeschylus' *Persians*,[43] Pericles had "used his influence to pass a decree for establishing a musical competition at the Panathenaic festival; and being himself chosen judge, laid down rules as to how the candidates were to sing, and play the *aulos* or the *cithara*" (*Per.* 13.11), which perhaps bespeaks a certain conservatism of taste. Phrynis had won the first of these competitions, but what may have been revolutionary in the middle decades of the fifth century will have seemed old-fashioned in the 420s B.C. The traditional musical values, on the virtues of which the Stronger Argument dwells, are in any case Dorian rather than Athenian.

3. *No encouragement to criticize mythology on moral or aesthetic grounds.* The specific reference is to 904–906, where the Weaker Argument asks, "If Justice (*Díkē*) exists, how is it that Zeus has not been destroyed for having imprisoned his father?" It is not difficult to perceive Periclean resonances here. According to Plutarch, Pericles' life was characterized by *dikaiosúnē* ("justice"; *Per.* 2.5), and Pericles' Olympian nickname was a commonplace.

4. *Encouragement of justice and chastity, physical modesty, sensitive self-respect, and respect for parents.* Pericles' reputation for *dikaiosúnē* is again relevant here, and the precise, Spartan nature of the modesty has already been discussed. The passage regarding self-respect (992) follows an injunction not to go near the Agora or bath-houses—both of which must have been much-frequented by Pericles himself,[44] as well as by Alcibiades. Pheidippides is urged to be "ashamed of what is shameful" (*toîs aiskhroîs aiskhúnesthai*), and not to "misbehave towards his parents" or do anything else that is shameful (*aiskhrón*: 995). *Aiskhrón* was a fre-

---

43. Broadhead 1960, 2.

44. Pericles in the Agora is a matter of historical record: e.g., *Per.* 7.5; his frequent bathing might be inferred from [Luc.] *Am.* 39, 42, 44 (cf. Baldwin 1993, 142: "A wash first thing in the morning after a night of amatory frolics is something of a standard motif"), and from his having suffered from the plague (on the special bathing requirements of those who suffered from "maladies de la peau," see Ginouvès 1962, 370 n. 2, 371–373). Spartans bathed infrequently, if at all.

quent word on Pericles' lips, at least on those of Thucydides' Pericles,[45] and if the characterization of Pheidippides included Pericles' physical sons, we might recall both that Pericles and Xanthippus were estranged for a long time,[46] and that Alcibiades himself had once run away from Pericles' home in shameful circumstances (*Alc.* 3.1).

5. *Insistence that boys should be "seen and not heard" in the presence of their elders, give up their seats, allow their elders to eat first at a meal, and walk in an orderly fashion in the streets.* The behavior that the Stronger Argument enjoins is, as was noted above, not simply redolent of old-fashioned values, but of manners more likely to be encountered in Sparta than in Attica. We can well imagine, however, that the young Alcibiades had disobeyed all these rules of etiquette.

METASTREPSIADES

The Weaker Argument eventually wins the debate (1102–1104) and takes Pheidippides as his pupil (1105–1110). He promises to return him to his father as a skilled sophist. When he has returned home, Pheidippides gives Strepsiades a few lessons, so that the latter is able to argue with the Creditor (1214–1302) as though he were his son. As Dover puts it: "Although Strepsiades had proved a hopelessly forgetful pupil, and the whole point of giving Pheidippides sophistic training was that Pheidippides should do his arguing for him, it is actually Strepsiades himself who carries off these scenes — confusedly (1247ff., 1278ff.) and with recourse to insolence (1237f., 1260ff.) and violence (1296ff.), but with his memory considerably improved."[47] In fact, it appears that the lesson has been so successful that Strepsiades — during this scene at least — has turned into Alcibiades.

Such a transformation should not be unfamiliar to students of Aristophanes. In *Frogs* (494–533), for example, Xanthias and Dionysus slip in and out of each other's costume and character.[48] In the context of *Clouds,* Eric Handley has well observed that the "capacity for transformation" available in

45. Tompkins 1972, 189.

46. Doubtless on account of Xanthippus' cohabitation with one Archestratus, a man who "plied a trade similar to that of the women in the cheaper brothels": Antisth. 34 Caizzi *ap.* Ath. 5.220d.

47. Dover 1968, 238–239.

48. Cf. Bobrick 1991, 74: "the reversal of roles typical of an Aristophanic play."

Athenian comedy, where "the relation between the world of realism and the world of image is not constant throughout a play, or indeed throughout the presentation of a character," makes it possible "to accommodate exchanges of role across the generation gap in a way which more realistic comedy finds it harder to manage."[49] Relevant anecdotal facts are that insolence and violence were Alcibiades' stock-in-trade, whether insulting his future father-in-law (*Alc.* 8.1) or killing a servant with a club (*Alc.* 3.1).[50] In 416 B.C. he was to purloin a friend's chariot team (worth eight talents) to race it himself at Olympia, and the ensuing litigation was to run for decades.[51]

The transformation is so complete that Strepsiades actually speaks like Alcibiades. At least his lines are susceptible of the same kind of *rho*- and *lambda*-induced double meanings as were those of Pheidippides and the Weaker Argument. A lambdacizing Strepsiades would, for example, have said *toû klḗmatos* ("what shoe [have you come about]?") at 1223,[52] and thus would have repeated one of the running jokes of the play (cf. *Clouds* 719, 816). This also serves to announce not only that Strepsiades speaks like Alcibiades, but also that he has swallowed whole the teachings of the Aristophanic Socrates.

Another possible example of Alcibiadean lambdacism is to be found at 1235ff. When Strepsiades avows (1235) that he would pay three obols for the privilege of swearing, there may be a reminder that Pericles underlies the various levels of characterization, for three obols was the current payment for jury service, a payment instituted by Pericles (at the rate of two obols) on the advice of one of his favorite sophists, Damon the musician. Strepsiades' next couple of lines appear to take up this allusion, since *halsín* ("salt"; 1237) and *khōrḗsetai* ("contains"; 1238) produce plays on *ársin* ("raising of the foot in beating time") and *khōleúsetai* ("limp"), words that relate to metrics and rhythm (cf. *khōlíambos* ["a lame iambic"]). In the *Republic,* Plato makes Socrates mention Damon as having "spoken of an iambic" (400b), and says that "in some cases [Damon] appeared to praise or censure the movement of the foot quite as much as the rhythm" (400c). Music was important in any Greek society, but especially so in Periclean Athens,[53] and this conceit neatly combines several of Pericles' concerns.

When the Creditor returns, Strepsiades asks whether perhaps it was one of the deities of *Karkínou* ("Carcinus") who gave tongue (1260–1261). If, when

49. Handley 1993, 427.
50. Physical violence was in fact very much the exception in classical Athens: Herman (1994).
51. [Andoc.] 4.20–21; Isoc. 16.1; Diod. 13.74.3; *Alc.* 12.3–5; cf. Ostwald 1986, 311.
52. For *toû khrḗmatos;* ("about what?").
53. See Wallace 1993, 142, on "music's capacity to change or disturb the state."

spoken in an Alcibiadean manner, this played on *khálkinou* ("of bronze"), there may be an allusion to something Socrates is supposed to have said about "Pericles or one of our great speakers," who "if anyone challenges the least particular of their speech, they go on ringing on in a long harangue, like brazen pots (*khalkeîa*), which when they are struck continue to sound unless someone puts their hand on them" (Pl. *Prt.* 329a). If so, it was ironic to put these words in Strepsiades' mouth. The Creditor also raises the question of *khrémata* ("money"; 1267); if Strepsiades answered *tà poîa taûta klémath'*; ("what shoes are those?"), he would be taking up the Socratic shoe theme once more.

It will have been noted that only one Creditor is in question in this reading of the play. While this may appear to do violence to the way the relevant scene is viewed by most scholars today, it is in harmony with the text of the Ravenna manuscript, which speaks of a single *Daneistés*. Since this person appears to make contradictory requests of Strepsiades, referring on his first visit to "the twelve minas that you borrowed" (1224), and on his second to "the money your son borrowed" (1268), it was felt necessary to duplicate Creditors, and some even assimilated them with the Pasias and Amynias mentioned at 21 and 30–31.[54] If, however, Strepsiades had in the eyes of the audience taken on the personality of Pheidippides, then the apparent contradiction disappears. On this view, at 1223–1224, the Creditor will have heard (but did not necessarily see) a Strepsiades speaking like Pheidippides, and consequently will have taken him for the lambdacizing Pheidippides; by 1268, however, he believes himself to be speaking to Strepsiades. Such an explanation would also remove the need to postulate four major speaking actors in the scene, a situation that would have been a remarkable departure from the norm.

FATHER-BEATING

The main theme of the next scene is the beating of Strepsiades by Pheidippides and the latter's justification of his action. If this bears any relation to Alcibiades, it must refer to his propensity to fisticuffs in general, and his beating up of his father-in-law in particular, dead by the time *Clouds* was performed.[55] But Aristophanes' conceit does not depend upon Hipponicus' being alive:

54. See Dover 1968, xxix–xxxii, for an exposition of the problem.
55. He fell at Delium in 424 (*Alc.* 8.3).

Alcibiades' hubristic action is merely transferred from a dead father-in-law to a dead foster-father. At 1313–1318 and 1345–1350, the Chorus epitomize Pheidippides in terms that it would be difficult not to take for a contemporary estimate of Alcibiades (skillful in winning an argument even when he was wrong; bold and arrogant). Pheidippides is said by Strepsiades (who has ceased to lambdacize on a regular basis, and who has reverted to type) to have refused to sing a song by Simonides at a party, since in his view such things were antiquated (1356–1357). He also states that Simonides was a bad poet (1362). Then Strepsiades relates how he proposed a song by Aeschylus, a poet with a particular Periclean association.[56] Pheidippides' reply (1366–1367) is quoted verbatim (and hence no doubt with lambdacism included); if so, it will have been reported as: "I believe Aeschylus to have been *plōtón* ('floating')[57] among poets—full of noise, confused, a ranter and a **klēmopoión* ('shoemaker')."[58] This not only brings in what has become a standard joke, but may also allude to Aeschylus' journeys (by sea) to Sicily, and to his introduction of the high boot, or *cothurnus,* to the tragic stage.[59]

Then, Strepsiades is allegedly scandalized at a Euripidean plot concerning a brother who made love to his sister (1371–1372), but there may be other resonances being set up here. For if Athenian gossip is to be believed—and even if it is not, the point remains—Pericles is said to have taken as the price of Cimon's restoration the privilege of lying with his sister Elpinice (Antisth. 35 Ciazzi *ap.* Ath. 13.589f.), a lady who was said by Eupolis to have slept with Cimon (Plut. *Cim.* 15). Alcibiades, too, was, rightly or wrongly, accused of incestuous relations with his sister (Antisth. fr. 29a, Ciazzi *ap.* Ath. 5.220c). If this gossip has reached us, we can be sure that it was known to Aristophanes' audience, and it is quite possible that he was playing on that here.

Pheidippides' attack upon his father and the sophistry he employs to justify his action was a vivid way of making the point that Socrates and his ilk were largely responsible for teaching the young to despise their parents, a charge that was still being made three decades later, when Xenophon reports Polycrates' accusation that "Socrates taught children to show contempt for their parents."[60] Strepsiades' submission and his address to old men in the audience (1437–1439) is an ironic commentary on the situation. But it is only

56. Broadhead 1960, 2.
57. For *prôton* ("first"); see Chapter 2 for Thucydides' similar lampoon of Alcibiades at 6.89.1, in the opening line of his speech to the Spartans.
58. For *krēmnopoión* ("speaking crags").
59. *Anecd. Bekk.* 2.746; Philostr. *VS* 1.9.1; *VA* 5.9, 6.10; Hor. *Ars P.* 278–280; *Suda* s.v. *Aískhulos.*
60. Xen. *Mem.* 1.2.49, cf. 51.

when Pheidippides proposes to extend the beating to his mother that the worm turns and Strepsiades at last digs in his heels. The "mother" in the context of the family whose affairs are examined in such detail in *Clouds* would be Aspasia, of whom it was widely believed that Pericles went to war with the Samians "at [her] request," and "in order to please her" (*Per.* 25.1–2), and whom Pericles loved to the extent that he never went in or out of his house without kissing her in an amorous fashion.[61] Pericles is supposed to have come to her aid when she—like some philosophers—was attacked in the courts; he is said to have shed tears in public and to have made a personal appeal to the jury.[62] Aspasia, it seems, was herself given to fisticuffs; at least the Socrates of the *Menexenus* jokingly speaks of being nearly beaten up by her (Pl. *Menex.* 236c). It is thus clear why Strepsiades puts his wife's interests before those of the new learning (and the fact that Aspasia had been part of the movement[63] makes for a certain irony).

Strepsiades' renewed faith in Zeus and justice (1468ff.)[64] is thoroughly in keeping with Pericles' traditional persona, and *patrôion* ("paternal") at 1468–1469 recalls Pericles' quasipaternal relationship vis-à-vis Alcibiades.[65] So, too, is his invocation (1478) to Hermes (a deity who appears in "Periclean" mode in *Peace;* see Chapter 8), as well as his suggestion that he might "bring a prosecution" by laying an indictment against the malefactors (Pericles had had to defend himself in several such actions). But *Clouds* is replete with Periclean— and Alcibiadean—allusions. Socrates, though not unimportant, is not central to *Clouds;* he is simply the bladder with which the licensed fool hits, and hits again, his principal target. Since Pericles is dead, the target must be Al-

61. Antisth. 35 Caizzi *ap. Per.* 24.9: *espázeto . . . metà toû kataphileîn;* on which, see Podlecki 1987, 60: "A pun is being perpetrated on her name which etymologically ought to mean 'Loved' or 'Kissable'," and cf. Maehly 1853, 225. There may be plays on "Aspasia" in *Clouds* when Strepsiades comments on his wife's weaving: *espátha* ("weave closely"; 53); *spathâis* (55; cf. *eríon* ["wool"] at 50: Milesian wool was by far the most famous in antiquity, Ath. 12.519b; Clytus *FGrH* 490 F2 *ap.* Ath. 12.540d; Eub. *PCG* 89 *ap.* Ath. 12.553b; Amphis *PCG* 27 *ap.* Ath. 15.691a; Verg. *G.* 3.306, 4.334), and when Socrates greets Strepsiades at the door of the Phrontistery (1145) with *Strepsiádēn aspázomai* ("I greet you warmly, Strepsiades"). For anecdotes concerning the historical Socrates' association with Aspasia, see, e.g., Ath. 5.219c–e, 220c.

62. *Per.* 32.1.5; and even if the story has its origins in a comic conceit (see Wallace 1993, 131–132, 148, for references), it will have reflected a popular view of Pericles' devotion.

63. Busolt 1893–1904, 3/1:510–513.

64. Cf. Macleod 1983, 51.

65. Dover (1968, 264) suspects that *patrôios* "could be interpreted as 'whose province is the relationship between fathers and children'"; Sommerstein (1982, 230–231) understands the title to mean "protector of the sanctity of fatherhood."

cibiades. Small wonder that Plato's Socrates denies any connection between the Aristophanic Socrates and the real one (Pl. *Ap.* 19b–c), or that the scholiast considered mistaken those who thought that Aristophanes composed *Clouds* "out of hostility towards Socrates" (Schol. *Clouds* 96).

Pace Dover, it is all too easy to understand "why [*Clouds*] fared so badly."[66] Alcibiades, who was surely in the audience, would have been very angry, not so much on account of what had been said about Socrates, but because of what had been implied about himself and his real and adoptive families, and about the danger that his extravagance, his violence, and his sophistry presented to Athens. The statement in the plot summary (*Arg.* 5 Coulon) that "Socrates' lovers . . . especially those in the circle around Alcibiades" prevented Aristophanes from winning the dramatic prize deserves respect. Judgment in dramatic competitions was not in the hands of the audience, but rested with a panel of ten judges, and we might well speculate that these were afraid of what might happen to them if they gave the prize to Aristophanes.[67] From a spoilt brat, Alcibiades had developed into a thug.[68] It is possible that Socrates had attempted to temper the worst excesses, but he, like Pericles, must take some of the blame for having created a monster. Aristophanes' *Clouds* was written with wit, and no little courage; it was perhaps unfortunate for Athens that the judges were less courageous.

It is now possible to see why Plato might have given a copy of *Clouds* to Dionysius (I or II) of Syracuse in order to teach him about Athenian government. Aristophanes' insight into the education and shortcomings of two leaders of Athens against both of whom charges of tyranny were made,[69] will have been a highly appropriate primer to have given to the tyrannical ruler of Athens' old enemy. If, moreover, Plato accompanied his gift with a copy of the *Gorgias,* a work with suitably Sicilian associations, and one in which Socrates is made to distance himself from Alcibiades,[70] he would stand ab-

66. Dover 1972, 119; cf. 1968b, lvii: "It is tempting to wonder why *Nu.* came third out of three when it was first performed. . . ."
67. Alcibiades once beat up a rival *choregus* "before the audience and judges," [Andoc.] 4.20–21; *Alc.* 16.5; Dem. 21.147. Cf. the passivity *di'Alkibiadēn* ("on account of Alcibiades") of the *grammateus* and the *archon* when Alcibiades went to the Record Office in order to expunge with his wetted finger an indictment against Hegemon of Thasos (Ath. 9.407c).
68. And not a truly intelligent individual either: Bloedow 1992.
69. E.g., Cratin. *PCG* 258 *ap. Per.* 7.1; *Per.* 12.2, 16.1 (Pericles, on whom see Davie 1982, 33 n. 25); Thuc. 6.15.2–4 (Alcibiades).
70. See Vickers 1994.

solved from any charge of sullying Socrates' reputation. But whether or not this occurred, it can no longer be maintained that "in the *Clouds*, Aristophanes . . . turned aside from politics,"[71] or that the play "is in no sense serious or didactic."[72]

71. A. B. West 1924, 220.
72. Fisher 1984, v.

PERICLES ON THE PNYX
Aristophanes' *Acharnians* I

Aristophanes' *Acharnians* was performed at the Lenaean festival in the early spring of 425 B.C., nearly two years before *Clouds*. The hero is one Dicaeopolis, an individual apparently devoted to food and sex, and who only wants to lead a peaceful life. Today he is usually taken to be the archetypal Aristophanic comic hero, intended to be no one in particular,[1] but from time to time the suggestion is made that he might be a mask for some historical individual.[2] To ask the question "Who is Dicaeopolis?" at all is, of course, to open the floodgates of allegory. But just as the character of Strepsiades appeared to be based on that of Pericles, so, too, does that of Dicaeopolis. Strepsiades' name seemed designed to recall stories of Periclean cruelty toward the Samians (and it is interesting to note that Dicaeopolis is made to claim early in *Acharnians* [15] — i.e., when the characterization is still being developed — that he was "subjected to torture" [*diestráphēn*]). Dicaeopolis' name also has a rich Periclean content. "Dicaeopolis" may allude in part to the Olympian nickname (*Per.* 8.3): *Díkē* ("justice") was a concept closely linked with Zeus,[3] and *díkaion* ("just") is a word that occurs in the mouth of Thucydides' Pericles.[4] The quality of *dikaiosúnē* ("righteousness" or "jus-

1. Edmunds 1980, 25, citing Bruns 1896, 149.
2. E.g., Eupolis, the playwright: Bowie 1988, 183–185; Aristophanes himself: Bailey 1936; Sutton 1988; cf. Olson 1990.
3. E.g., *Clouds* 902; Lloyd-Jones 1983; Ostwald 1986, 143–144.
4. Cf. Tompkins 1972, 189.

tice") was one that Plutarch—and doubtless many others—believed to have characterized Pericles' public life (*Per.* 2.5). The *-polis* component of the hero's name, moreover, may refer to the Athenian Acropolis, which was "called simply *pólis*,"[5] and which Pericles adorned with buildings "of immense size and unequalled in beauty and grace" (*Per.* 13.1). Most interesting of all, *dikaiópolis* was an epithet applied by Pindar (*Pyth.* 8.22) to Aegina, an island that Pericles is on record as having loathed intensely (he once described Aegina as "the pus in the eye of the Piraeus").[6] For Pericles to appear before the audience as, in effect, "Mr. Aegina" would have been diverting.

Dicaeopolis' selfish preoccupation with food and sex—the principal theme of *Acharnians*—both parody and parallel two things for which Pericles was famous. The Athenian grain supply was never far from his mind,[7] nor were women; as we have already noted—and shall do again—"Pericles was much given to *aphrodísia*" (Clearch. *ap.* Ath. 13.589d). And Acharnians were very much to the fore during the closing years of Pericles' life. It was Pericles' policy (and one that the Athenians still continued to respect in 425 B.C.) to remain within the city walls during the Spartans' annual raids to destroy the crops. These raids had caused particular damage to Acharnae, which was the largest of the Attic demes as well as the base of the Spartans' activities in 431 B.C. It was the Acharnians who made vociferous representations to Pericles to go out to meet the Spartans in the field, but their views were overlooked. Pericles avoided calling a meeting of the Assembly, "many of his friends besought him to attack, many of his enemies threatened and abused him." This is where we hear about the "many songs and offensive jests" written about him, "speaking of him as a coward and one who was betraying the city to its enemies" (*Per.* 33.7). Plutarch's *Life* is full of references to Pericles having been attacked by "comic poets,"[8] and the plot summary of Cratinus' *Dionysalexandros* suggests that whole plays, rather than a few lines here and there, might be devoted to criticism of aspects of Pericles' control of Athenian politics.[9] *Acharnians* is another such play; in it, fun is poked at Pericles' musical, military, diplomatic, and administrative activities. In death, as in life, it seems that Pericles was lampooned; and to make matters worse, jokes are made about the way he died, of the after-effects of the plague (although none is

5. LSJ s.v. *pólis;* cf. Neil 1901, 42–43; and cf. Dicaeopolis' lament, "*ô pólis pólis*," in line 27.
6. *Per.* 8.7, trans. Stadter 1989, 108; cf. *Per.* 29.5; Telecl. *PCG* 46 *ap. Per.* 34.2.
7. Garnsey 1988, 123–133; cf. Strauss 1989, 283: "What petroleum is to the modern world, grain was to the ancient Mediterranean—and then some."
8. On some of the dramatic criticism of Pericles, see Schwarze 1971; Rosen (1988b), 49–58.
9. See Appendix A, and *POxy.* 663, 44–48; *CGFP* 70; Cratin. *Dionysalexandros* i, *PCG*.

quite as nasty as the bedbug scene in *Clouds*). *Acharnians* is aimed at the man who had, in the eyes of many of his surviving contemporaries, made life miserable for the Athenians during the previous few years. That Aristophanes lampooned Pericles successfully in *Acharnians* is clear from the fact that the play won first prize.

PERICLES THE ACCOUNTANT

The web of words that Aristophanes weaves in Dicaeopolis' opening soliloquy (1–42) plays on a miscellany of Periclean themes. Pericles on stage is shown in the setting in which the historical Pericles was most frequently seen by the Athenians, namely on the Pnyx,[10] the meeting place of the Assembly. Dicaeopolis has been "tortured" and practically died (*apéthanon*)[11] having to hear the excesses of contemporary musicians. Aeschylus is Dicaeopolis' favorite (10). Pericles was the impresario of our earliest extant Aeschylean play[12] and had also established a musical festival at which he was himself a judge (*Per.* 13.11).

Dicaeopolis complains (23) that the Council members are late in attending to their civic duties; *he* was always first to arrive at the Assembly. Pericles displayed a similarly single-minded devotion to civic duty, for "he was never seen in any street except that which led to the Agora and the Bouleuterion" (*Per.* 7.5).[13] Dicaeopolis describes in vivid detail how he passes the time: "I groan, I yawn, I stretch, I fart (30–31), I am at a loss as to what to do, I write, I pluck my pubic hairs,[14] I *logízomai* ('do my accounts')." Pericles' public demeanor, by contrast, was restrained to an extraordinary degree: not only did he develop "a lofty style of oratory far removed from vulgarity and low buffoonery" (*Per.* 5.1), "he habitually spoke without gestures, keeping his hand within his garment" (Plut. *Mor.* 800c). If he is lampooning Pericles, Aristophanes is here employing the "Hermogenes principle" (Hermog. *Meth.* 34): making the audience laugh by means of an image diametrically opposed to what was being represented (but only doing so once the characterization

10. On the possible Periclean origins of which, see Thompson 1982; Hansen 1987, 12, 141; Francis and Vickers 1988.

11. Cf. the references to Strepsiades' mortality in *Clouds,* Chapter 1 above.

12. Broadhead 1960, 2.

13. Philocleon displays a similar trait: *Wasps* 268–269.

14. Henderson 1975, 58.

has been established). Dicaeopolis' civic zeal may also fall into this category in view of Pericles' reluctance to hold an Assembly at all in 431 B.C.

Like Dicaeopolis, Pericles was "at a loss as to what to do," and notoriously so during the later 430s B.C., when he was *lógon apaitoúmenos* ("called upon to given an account") of public funds, "much of which he had spent for his own purposes."[15] So anxious was he that he fell ill. Diodorus preserves an anecdote that may be relevant in the context of Dicaeopolis' accountancy:

> While he was worried over the matter, Alcibiades . . . though still a youth, provided him with a means of explaining how he had used the money. Seeing that his uncle was troubled, he asked him the reason. When Pericles said that he was being asked to explain how he had used the money and "How can I give an account (*apodoúnai . . . lógon*) to the citizens," Alcibiades replied that he should be looking for a way not how to give an account, but how not to give an account. As a result, Pericles, accepting the boy's reply, looked for a way in which he could involve the Athenians in a great war; for in this way he supposed that the city would be beset by so much disturbance, distraction, and fear that he would be able to escape an exact accounting of the funds.[16]

Though it would be unwise to stress the historicity of Diodorus' anecdote, it belongs to a well-known genre of explanations for the Peloponnesian War, all of which have as a common factor some base motive on Pericles' part. And whether or not it is simply gossip, it contains an expression (*apodoúnai lógon* ["give an account"]) that recalls the terminology of Dicaeopolis' *logízomai* ("I do my accounts"; 31), which may in turn have been included to enhance the comic image of the dead statesman. By contrast, Thucydides' statement (2.50.1) that the plague of 430–428 B.C. was *kreísson lógou* ("beyond calculation") was a knowing and subtle means of suggesting that the plague could not be foreseen, "so that Pericles can be forgiven for not taking it into account."[17]

Dicaeopolis proposes (37–39) to disrupt the Assembly if necessary, in order to raise the issue of peace—perhaps a deliberately ironic contrast to Pericles' refusal to allow the Assembly to meet at all (Thuc. 2.22). Dicaeopolis is prepared to "shout, interrupt and hurl abuse at the speakers"; again, this is the antithesis of Pericles' own behavior, but not without a possible Periclean resonance. For in addition to his "haughty spirit and lofty style of oratory,"

---

15. Diod. 12.38.2; cf. *Per.* 32.3; Val. Max. 3.1 ext. 1.
16. Diod. 12.38.2–3; cf. Stadter 1989, 301.
17. Cf. Marshall 1990, 169.

Pericles also possessed "an imperturbable gravity of countenance, and a calmness of demeanor and appearance which no incident could disturb as he was speaking" (*Per.* 5.1). If there is a Periclean reference in the competition for the *proedría* ("front-row seat" or "authority") at line 42, it may be a reflection of the struggle for power and influence that had broken out after Pericles' death, a struggle that was to be incisively analyzed by Aristophanes in *Knights* the following year (see Chapter 6).

PARODY OF THE *PERSIANS*

Dicaeopolis wants to assist an ambassador to make a private peace with the Spartans (46–58), as it was rumored Pericles had once done when he negotiated the Thirty Years' Peace in the 440s B.C. (*Per.* 23.1–2). Dicaeopolis' action may in addition be an ironic commentary on Pericles' refusal in 430 B.C. to send heralds to Sparta to discuss peace (Thuc. 2.64.6; cf. 65.2). Meanwhile, however, ambassadors have come from the Great King of Persia (61). Dicaeopolis declares that he is fed up with ambassadors, their peacocks, and all their impostures (63); Pericles had a friend, a former ambassador, who owned peacocks that he was said "to give to the ladies who granted their favours to Pericles."[18]

The first ambassador has been away, on his own admission, for eleven years, drawing expenses at the rate of two drachmas a day (equivalent to a total of more than one and a third talents, nearly thirty-five kilos of silver). An embassy sent out in 437/36 B.C. (in the archonship of Euthymenes; cf. 67) would not only have left Athens a long time ago, but would certainly have gone under the auspices of Pericles, who would doubtless have taken an interest in whatever rate of expenses was set.[19] Dicaeopolis' disgust at the great size of the amount (67) needs to be considered together with the cupidity of his own ambassador a few lines earlier; if Pericles was in Aristophanes' mind, there is an implication here of both maladministration and hypocrisy. The deceptions practiced by ambassadors is a constant theme in this scene, and

18. *Com. Adesp.* 59 *CAF* 3.410 *ap. Per.* 13.15. On Pyrilampes' embassy (to Persia), see Badian 1993, 20, 192 n. 29.

19. It was during the archonship of Euthymenes that Pericles' friend Hagnon (on whom see Chapter 10) founded Amphipolis on the Strymon. He is described as *arkhaióploutos* at Cratin. *PCG* 171, and the suggestion has been made that this did not mean "of ancient wealth," but "rich from office holding": Goossens 1935, 410–412; cf. Rhodes 1981, 354.

the criticisms — ironically — all come from Dicaeopolis (62–63, 75–76, 86–87, 90, 109, 114).

While the ambassador to Persia has been away, Dicaeopolis claims to have been *parà tèn épalxin* ("on the parapet"; 72), where Thucydides' Pericles (2.13.6) spoke of the city's hoplites serving: those who manned the walls (*tôn par' épalxin*). Dicaeopolis is told that the barbarians regard as real men (or "successful politicians")[20] only those who can eat and drink great amounts (78); his reply is that in Athens the same position of honor is occupied by gigolos and sodomites. Pericles' ward, the politically ambitious Alcibiades, qualified in both these categories (cf. Diog. Laert. 4, 49; *Acharnians* 716), as much in 425 B.C. as during Pericles' lifetime, and allusion may be being made to this here.

The arrival of the Persian ambassador, Pseudartabas (94–99), provides the opportunity for yet more implications of deception and gullibility, an allusion to the grain supply, as well as some gross imputations of unnatural vice.[21] Not only does "Pseudartabas" mean "False Artabas" or "Lying Artabas," but the name plays on *artábē*,[22] an official Persian grain measure roughly equivalent to the Attic *médimnos*.[23] And not only will the King's Eye have been given a large eye, but like most male characters in Old Comedy he will have been equipped with a large phallus. Dicaeopolis' remarks at 95–97 surely refer to it. "Why do you look like a *naúphrakton* ('warship')?" Dicaeopolis asks; *-phraktos* or *-pharktos* means "defended, strengthened, armed,"[24] but the only armament on a fighting ship of the period was a projecting beak of metal in front.[25] Dicaeopolis continues: "Are you on the lookout for a *neōsoikon* ('shipshed')?" (96), which must be (though commentators have overlooked the possibility) a crude analogue for a sexual orifice, as presumably is the leather lining around the edge of Pseudartabas' *ophthalmòn kátō* ("nether eye"; 97), that is, his anus.

Talk of shipsheds also recalls the fact that the Piraeus was extensively re-

20. Sommerstein 1980, 161.
21. Cf. Henderson 1975, 58: "Dicaeopolis' obscenities serve to cut through the disguises of the various corrupt envoys who appear before the Assembly and who represent the maddening depravity of wartime Athenian politics. These exposures all involve references to unnatural sex, namely the risible varieties of homosexuality."
22. Cf. Schmitt (1984, 464), who misses (no, actually dismisses) the pun.
23. Hdt. 1.192.2–3; cf. Hsch. *artábē: métron Mēdikòn sítou, Attikòs médimnos. Artábē* must relate to OP *arta-* "law/justice": Kent 1953, 170.
24. LSJ s.v. *phrássō*.
25. Cf. *Birds* 1256, "*stúomai triémbolon,* to stand as gigantically erect as three ships' beaks": Henderson 1975, 164. For extant metal beaks, see Steffig and Casson 1991 (thanks are due to William Murray for this reference).

modeled under Pericles, the shipsheds alone costing "not less than a thousand talents" according to Isocrates (7.66). It is also interesting to note that an extraordinary meeting of the *Boulê* had been held in the shipsheds at the Piraeus in the first prytany of 426/25 B.C., a few months before *Acharnians* was performed.[26] But the really important point, which has not been noticed hitherto, is that the pseudo-stately entrance of Pseudartabas parodies the tragic entrance of the ghost of Darius in Aeschylus' *Persians*.

The phraseology of the Persian scene in *Acharnians* is also reminiscent of Aeschylus' *Persians*. For example, *naúpharktos* is first attested in Darius' lamentation at the end of Aeschylus' *Persians; Iáōn naúpharktos* ("war fleet of the Greeks") is the expression used (Aesch. *Pers.* 951). Elsewhere in the same scene (979), the chorus of aged Persians sing of a *pistòn . . . ophthalmón* ("faithful eye").[27] A true, as opposed to a false, Artabas appears in *Persians* (317) in the person of the Bactrian who fell at Salamis.[28] It is possible, moreover, that Aeschylus' play was performed with the tent of Xerxes in the background,[29] the memory of which will have been kept fresh in the mind of the Athenian public in the shape of Pericles' Concert Hall, "said to have been built in imitation of the king of Persia's tent" (*Per.* 13.9–11), and whose pointed roof was somewhat cruelly compared by Cratinus to Pericles' misshapen skull (Cratin. *PCG* 73 *ap. Per.* 13.10). If *Persians* was indeed in Aristophanes' mind here, then the images of mock grandeur will have served as a foil to the raggedness of Euripides' *Telephus* later in the play.

Dicaeopolis has already specifically mentioned Aeschylus as his special enthusiasm at line 10, and his expletive *ô Kranaà pólis* at 75 is said by a scholiast to be typically Aeschylean. And though much of the Persian imagery of *Acharnians* 64ff. may — or may not — owe something to Herodotus,[30] certain words and turns of phrase almost certainly owe much to Aeschylus' Persian play. It is true that *basileús* ("king") and *mégas* ("great") in the Ambassador's opening statement at *Acharnians* 65 are words to be expected in the context of Athenian relations with the Persian crown, and the fact that the one occurs eleven times and the other fifteen times in *Persians* has no necessary significance; but *epémpsath'* at the beginning of 65 is a word that occurs throughout *Persians* — nine times, including the last line of all. Then, *ep' Euthuménous árkhontos* at 67 may play on *hup' euthúmou phrenós* at *Persians* 372,

26. *IG* I³.61; Rhodes 1981, 545–546; and see Chapter 5.

27. On *pistós* as an Achaemenid marker, see Bacon 1961, 67–68; Francis 1980, 58 n. 27; 1992.

28. Cf. Schmitt 1984, 464; Brixhe 1988, 114.

29. As suggested by Broneer 1944; cf., among others, Gall 1977; 1979; and Francis 1980 (where the objections of Taplin [1978, 458] are more than adequately met).

30. Fornara 1971, 27; Francis 1992.

and the three-line account of the vehicles in which the embassy luxuriously traveled recall, and will have been intended to recall, the *skēnaîs trokhēlátois* ("wheeled tents") at *Persians* 1000–1001 as much as the wagons described by Herodotus at 7.41. *Apollúmenoi* ("[we were] dying") is used ironically at 71, but *apóllumi* and *óllumi* ("destroy") are employed literally in *Persians* on some fifteen occasions. *Persians* was first performed in 472 B.C., with Pericles as the victorious *choregus*. It was certainly performed again in Sicily in 471–469 B.C. (Schol. *Frogs* 1028). A. Dieterich is perhaps correct in his assumption that the play was frequently repeated,[31] and if it were performed again at Athens during Pericles' lifetime, he will doubtless have been the *choregus* on those occasions as well.

Darius and his interlocutors in the *Persians* did not speak Persian, still less broken Greek, but this is what Pseudartabas does, with the Athenian ambassador treacherously translating. *Iartamàn éxarxas pisónastra* is the reading of line 100 in the Ravenna codex: Persian-sounding gibberish is perhaps the best explanation.[32] The Athenian ambassador translates this as, "He says that the king will send you *khrusíon* ('gold')" (102, cf. 103). Pseudartabas declares that the *khaunóprōkt'* ("wide-arsed") Greeks will not get any *khrûso* ("gold"). There may be a topical reference in *khaunóprōkt'* (104 and 106) to the revolt of Caunus, an event that seems to have occurred "in the early twenties."[33] At 114, Dicaeopolis receives confirmation that the Athenian ambassador has been deceitful, and is horrified that Pseudartabas is to be entertained in the Prytaneum.[34] The implication at 126 that guests in the Prytaneum are rogues

31. *RE* i (1894) 1075 (Dieterich): "Das Stück ist später naturlich auch wieder in Athen aufgeführt."
32. Schmitt (1984, 471) cites with approval M. L. West 1968, 6 ("Aristophanes is only collecting noises"), but notes that the noises in question are characteristically Persian. Morenilla-Talens (1989) demonstrates how this works: "Ein Kauderwelsch von Lauten und Lautsequenzen, die 'ausländisch' klingen" (176). The noises are not simply gibberish, as Brixhe 1988. For attempts at literal interpretations, see Dover 1963; Brandenstein 1964; Francis 1980; 1992.
33. Badian 1993, 35. Caunus also figured in the Samian campaign in 440 B.C.: Thuc. 1.116.3.
34. Where, by contrast with the luxury enjoyed by the Athenian ambassador to Persia, he will be entertained from public-issue pottery vessels (cf. Thompson and Wycherley 1972, 89; Rotroff and Oakley 1992, for the kind of thing). The Persian king only served wine in clay vessels to those he wished to insult: Ctesias *FGrH* 688 F 40 *ap.* Ath. 11.464a. On a related topic, the Athenian ambassador says at 73 that he and his companions drank from "*hualínōn* ('crystal') and gold cups." *Hualínōn* is often translated "glass," on the mistaken grounds that glass was then a more valuable commodity than rock crystal (e.g., Becker 1874, 145; Daumas 1985, 293–294; Sommerstein 1980, 161). Rock crystal is, however, intrinsically valuable, whereas glass is only made from sand. The finds of rock crystal in palace sites suggest that it was much rarer than glass (e.g., von Saldern 1966, 627; E. Schmidt 1957, 91, pl. 65, nos. 7–11; Rova 1987

and impostors will probably not have been intended to put Pericles in a good light either, especially if it really was the case that he moved the decree granting the privilege of dining there.[35] But although Pericles did not enjoy perpetual dining rights himself (cf. *Knights* 283), he had presumably eaten in the Tholos whenever he held office.

THE RAIN OF THE PHALLUS

The Thracian scene (134–172), too, is full of potentially Periclean material. A Thracian prince, Sadocus, had been made an Athenian citizen in 431 B.C. in the hope that Sitalces would provide troops to help the Athenians in Chalcidice (Thuc. 2.29). Sadocus would have been enrolled in the citizen lists in Thrace, and a party of officials sent out to perform the ceremony. Such deputations were known as *théōroi,* (e.g., *Dem.* 19.128), and it is surely the case, as was seen long ago [36] (but not since), that the central figure in the Thracian scene is a *théōros,* and not the individual Theorus attested elsewhere in Aristophanes. The anonymity of the *présbus* in the Persian scene might suggest as much. If so, this may provide evidence for a Periclean origin of the theoric fund,[37] which "contained whatever surplus money there might be in Athens, on which the state would have to depend for any non-routine expenditure" [38] — in other words, a slush fund. The enrollment of a Thracian prince as an Athenian citizen would count as "non-routine expenditure" by any standards, and we might safely speculate that any of Pericles' friends who went on this particular *theōría* did not return home poor men; [39] hence perhaps the humor inherent in Dicaeopolis' condemnation of the *théōros* as an *alazōn* ("cheat"; 135), who had pulled in vast expenses during his five-

[on crystal]; and von Saldern 1966; Barag 1985, 57–59 [on glass]). On the relative value of glass and semiprecious hard stones, see Saldern 1991, and cf. Pliny *HN* 36.198: "The most highly valued glass is colorless and transparent, as closely as possible resembling rock crystal."

35. Wade-Gery 1932–1933, 123–125, on *IG* I³ 131.

36. Merry 1880, *ad* 134.

37. Cf. Rhodes 1981, 514: "Aristophanes and others are suspiciously silent on the theoric fund both in the late fifth century and in the 390's." Stadter (1989, 116–117) believes that the theoric fund was introduced in the fourth century. For further possible evidence in Aristophanes, see Chapter 8 below.

38. Rhodes 1981, 515.

39. See n. 19 above, on the possibility that Hagnon came home from Amphipolis a wealthy man.

year absence. Various kinds of payment for the performance of civic duties are said to have been introduced during Pericles' administration of Athenian affairs.[40]

There may also be a play on *apátē* ("deceit"), and a suggestion that Sadocus has had the wool pulled over his eyes in the reference (146) to the Apatouria, the festival at which new citizens — such as Sadocus — were admitted to membership of their phratries. For the Athenians had indeed deceived Sitalces. In 429 B.C. they had promised him an Athenian fleet to help him in his expansionist ambitions in Thrace and Macedonia. But "the fleet which the Athenians promised never arrived; for not believing that Sitalces would come, they only sent gifts and envoys to him" (Thuc. 2.101.1).[41]

It has not been observed hitherto that Sitalces was an Odrysian, but that the *théōros* has brought Odomantians (155), enemies both of Sitalces and of Athens (Thuc. 2.101.3). It is either the case that the *théōros* stands accused of incompetence, having made a serious diplomatic error, or that to have on stage Thracians who were enemies of the Athenians' allies, would enable gross lampoons to be made without fear of a diplomatic backlash. Dicaeopolis is astounded at the rate of pay that is being demanded on the Odomantians' behalf by the *théōros* (160); two drachmas a day was high.[42] He puts in a word for the *thranítēs leṓs, ho sōsípolis* ("the top-flight oarsmen who save our city"; 162). The expression sounds sententious in Greek, but was probably meant to be. If there is a Periclean reference here, it may be to the rowers in the Athenian fleet, on whom Pericles relied for his political support, and whose victory at Salamis established the basis for the political clout of which Pericles was still the beneficiary.[43] Though it may well be true that Aristophanes through Dicaeopolis was "trying to help the Athenians by opening their eyes to the tricks and braggatries of the ambassadors,"[44] it is unlikely that he did so with a view to revealing Dicaeopolis as an "unselfish patriot,"[45] but rather the very opposite.

The Odomantians are boisterous and crude. Dicaeopolis is affronted by whatever it is they do to him, complains to the Prytaneis, forbids any discus-

---

40. Arist. *Ath. Pol.* 27.3; *Per.* 9.1; cf. 9.3 (payment for jury service; on which see Sealey 1956, 242; Ostwald 1986, 182–183; Badian 1993, 13) and 12.5 (expenses for military service).

41. On the whole affair, see Badian 1993, 181–185.

42. Rhodes 1981, 306. It was as much as soldiers serving at Potidaea received, but that sum was to pay for a servant as well as the hoplite: Thuc. 3.17.4.

43. Cf. Vickers 1990a, 239–242.

44. MacDowell 1983, 147–148.

45. Ibid., 147.

sion about pay for the Thracians, and manages to persuade the authorities that he has received a *diosēmía* ("sign from Zeus") in the form of a *ranís* ("drop of rain" or "drop of semen"; 171);[46] if the latter, then from the horny Thracians (cf. 158, 161), whose male members, like that of Pseudartabas in the preceding scene, will have been a prominent feature. One of the reasons for Pericles' "Olympian" nickname was that he "adorned his oratory with illustrations drawn from physical science" (*Per.* 8.1–3); the "sign from Zeus" may refer to such an illustration.

ACHARNIANS

After the Assembly is over (173), Dicaeopolis encounters his own ambassador on the run from some old men "from Acharnae" (177), who are furious with him because they have got wind of Dicaeopolis' private treaty with the Spartans. They have called him *miarōtate* ("polluted") (182); if this was aimed at Pericles, the reference may be to the pollution attendant upon the Alcmaeonid curse, resurrected by the family's enemies whenever political advantage could be gained by doing so — most recently in 432 B.C., when ambassadors came to Athens from Sparta requesting that the Athenians drive out "the curse of the goddess" in the hope that they might "discredit [Pericles] with the citizens and make them believe that his misfortune was to a certain extent the cause of the war" (Thuc. 1.126.2, 1.127). The Acharnians complain that a treaty is being made when their vines have been cut down (182–183). If Pericles is in question, Acharnians are the appropriate foil for Dicaeopolis, for Acharnae had suffered more than any other Attic deme during the first years of the war, and its inhabitants, cooped up in Athens, were vociferous in bringing the fact to Pericles' attention. It was at Acharnae that the Spartan Archidamus lingered, hoping that "the Athenians, who were now flourishing in youth and numbers and prepared for war as they had never been before, would perhaps meet them in the field rather than allow their lands to be ravaged" (Thuc. 2.20.2). Rather than fight, Pericles had "shut the gates of Athens, placed sufficient forces to ensure the safety of the city at all points, and calmly carried out his own policy, taking little heed of the grumblings of the discontented" (*Per.* 33.6). Thucydides describes at length the great annoyance of the Acharnians:

46. Cf. *Anth. Pal.* 10.45.

[The Acharnians,] who in their own estimation were no small part of the Athenian state, seeing their land ravaged, strongly insisted that they should go out and fight . . . the people were furious with Pericles, and, forgetting all his previous warnings, they abused him for not leading them to battle, as their general should, and laid all their miseries to his charge. But he, seeing that they were overcome by the irritation of the moment and inclined to evil counsels, and confident that he was right in refusing to go out, would not summon an assembly or meeting of any kind, lest, coming together more in anger than in prudence, they might take some false step. He maintained a strict watch over the city, and sought to contain the irritation as best he could. (Thuc. 2.21.2–22.1)

"Let [the Acharnians] shout," says Dicaeopolis (186) — an insensitive and selfish response to the Acharnians' complaints, and one that throws little credit on Pericles if he does underlie Dicaeopolis. "Do you have the treaties?" (186), Dicaeopolis asks. He then samples the treaties. The five-year treaty (188) smacks too much of naval activity (Pericles' favored theatre of war; e.g., Thuc. 1.143.4, 2.62.1–2), the ten-year treaty (191) of the allies being ground down (an accusation made against Pericles by his opponents; *Per.* 21.2–3), but the thirty-year treaty (194) is just right. Not only does it recall the Thirty Years' Peace with Sparta, negotiated when Pericles was general in the 440s B.C. (*Per.* 22–23), but it tastes of ambrosia and nectar (196), the food — appropriately enough, perhaps, in view of Pericles' nickname — of the Olympians. Best of all, Dicaeopolis can wash his hands of the Acharnians (200).

When the Chorus of Acharnian charcoal-burners arrive (204), looking high and low for their quarry, they lament the fact that they are so old, but do so in terms that recall the secondary meaning of *ánthrax* ("charcoal") in Greek.[47] When they were young, they could carry a load of charcoal, and they could run after Phayllus (215, with a pun on *phallós*); now, however, they are too decrepit, but woe betide the man who has made peace with the enemy. They will not rest until "like a *skhoînos* ('reed')" (230) they "pierce [the enemy] in revenge: sharp, painful, up to the hilt," so that the Acharnians' vines may never be trampled again. If Aristophanes had Pericles in mind here, the image is an interesting one, for *skhoînos* (like *skhoiníon* at 22[48]) may play

47. Not only does it mean "hot coals" but also "indicates the cunt inflamed by coitus and poked by a (phallic) stoker": Henderson 1975, 177.
48. Where the citizens flee to avoid the *skhoiníon . . . memiltōménon* ("the [little] rope covered with ruddle with which they drove loiterers out of the Agora to the Pnyx"): LSJ s.v. *miltóō*. If

on Pericles' nickname, *skhinoképhalos* ("squill-head"; Cratin. *PCG* 73). The Acharnians discover Dicaeopolis beginning a sacrifice to Dionysus. They stand aside, preserving, at least for the moment, holy silence (237–240).

THE RURAL DIONYSIA

Dicaeopolis' homely Rural Dionysia (241–279) begins with his calling (241; cf. 237): *euphēmeîte, euphēmeîte* ("avoid all unlucky words, during religious rites").[49] This may allude to the fact that "whenever Pericles ascended the *bêma* to speak, he would pray to the gods that nothing unfitted for the present occasion might fall from his lips."[50] But before examining Dicaeopolis' procession and sacrifice to Dionysus[51] in detail, it will be necessary to list a few apparently random facts. Pericles' relationship with Aspasia is well known, but it was said of him that he lay with many others, and most notoriously with his own daughter-in-law, the wife of Xanthippus.[52] Pericles' amours must have come to an end with the plague, for he was attacked "not acutely or continuously, as in most cases, but in a slow and wasting fashion, exhibiting many varieties of symptoms, and gradually undermining his strength" (*Per.* 38). We have already seen in the discussion of the bedbug scene in *Clouds* how the strength of plague victims might be undermined: "If a person got over the worst, the disorder would often attack the privy parts . . . and some escaped with the loss of these" (Thuc. 2.49.8). The focal point of Dicaeopolis' procession is a large ritual phallus.

At 242, Dicaeopolis makes his daughter, the *kanēphóros* ("basket bearer"), walk in front, and enjoins the slave Xanthias to hold the phallus erect behind her. "Put down your *kanoûn* ('basket'), dear, so that we can get started," he says to his daughter, who then (245–246) asks Mother to "pass [her] the *etnérusin* ('ladle') so that [she] can pour *étnos* ('sauce') over an *elatéros* ('cake')." It has been suggested that *étnos* here has the force of "female secreta,"[53] and the basket (242, 244, 260) that Dicaeopolis tells his daughter to carry daintily

---

memiltōménon in turn plays on Miletus, the hometown of Aspasia (*Per.* 24.3), a double entendre on "they flee the be-Miletused squillet" would have been full of contemporary reference.
49. LSJ s.v. *euphēméō.*
50. *Per.* 8.6; cf. p. 34 above (on Strepsiades' prayer before he enters the Phrontistery).
51. A democratic god (and Pericles was nothing if not democratic, at least outwardly: *Per.* 7.3).
52. Stesimbr. *FGrH* 107 F 19b *ap. Per.* 13.16; F 11 *ap.* 36.6.
53. Henderson 1975, 145.

(253) by extension probably signifies her sexual organs. But rather than being a phallus,[54] the ladle is perhaps a device to impute complicity between mother and daughter, and if there is any reference to the Periclean household, to the widely held belief that Aspasia's influence there was less than proper.[55]

How blest his daughter's husband will be (254–256), opines Dicaeopolis, as Xanthippus, Pericles' daughter-in-law's husband, most certainly was not. According to Stesimbrotus, "Xanthippus put about the scandal about his father and his own wife" (Stesimbr. *FGrH* 107 F 11 *ap. Per.* 36.6). Nor could Xanthippus bear his father's *akribeían* ("stinginess"; *Per.* 36.2), and if Pericles is in question in *Acharnians,* we may perhaps see in Dicaeopolis' caution that his daughter take care of her valuables (257–258) a reference to the statesman's penny-pinching ways, which were not at all to the liking of the womenfolk of his household (*Per.* 16.5).

The daughter goes first in the procession, then come two slaves holding erect the phallus behind her (260), followed by Dicaeopolis singing a hymn to the phallus, in which he states that six years have passed since he addressed it (266). Counting inclusively, it will have been six years since Pericles' "strength was undermined." Moreover, the mode of congress implied by the order of the procession had a well-known Alcmaeonid precedent in Peisistratus' abuse of the daughter of Megacles (Hdt. 1.61.1),[56] and if the slave Xanthias "stands for" Xanthippus, there is a degree of hypocrisy implied in the fact that he actually wields the phallus.[57]

To those in the audience who held Pericles responsible for the sufferings they had experienced during the war (and there will have been many such, judging by asides made by Thucydides and Plutarch), it would have been very satisfying to see Pericles getting his comeuppance in this ludicrous but highly meaningful procession, implying that "Pericles has no testicles at all." And the play is full of Periclean allusions that are frequently of an unworthy nature. Still in the Rural Dionysia scene, Mother is told to go up on the roof and watch (262). If Aspasia is intended, we can only assume that she is set up as a *voyeuse,* and can only speculate as to what she may have seen if the charges laid against her were true that she had "harbored free-born ladies, with whom Pericles carried on intrigues" (*Per.* 32.1). That she *is* intended is likely from

54. Ibid.

55. *Acharnians* 527; cf. *Per.* 32.1; Ath. 13.569f–570a.

56. There may be an echo, too, of the Peisistratid Hipparchus' insult to Harmodius' sister, "invited to come and carry a sacred basket in a procession," but then rejected: Thuc. 6.56.1. Pericles was compared by contemporaries with Peisistratus; even his voice was said to be the same: *Per.* 7.1.

57. Cf. the possible pun on *xanthízete* at *Acharnians* 1047, p. 93 below.

Dicaeopolis' command *próba* ("get going"; also 262) when the procession starts, which plays on *próbata* ("sheep"), and thus to Aspasia's remarkably quick marriage to the *probatopṓlēs* ("sheepseller") Lysicles immediately after Pericles' death (*Per.* 24.6).[58]

PERICLES THE HEADMAN

The Acharnians watch the preparations for Dicaeopolis' ridiculous procession (242–262) and listen to his song (263–279), but when they hear the reference to peace, they rush him, threatening to stone him and calling him *miarà kephalḗ* ("accursèd head"). The Alcmaeonid curse was—as we have already seen—something of a liability for Pericles,[59] and the peculiar shape of his head was a regular source of amusement for comic writers. As late as 411 B.C., Eupolis described his Pericles as "the *kephálaion* ('headman') of those below" (Eup. *PCG* 115 *ap. Per.* 3.7). Dicaeopolis' head is mentioned frequently in the rest of the play (318, 439, 486, 585, 833), and the fact may be more than coincidental.

The dialogue between the Acharnians and Dicaeopolis may, moreover, reflect the rancorous encounters Thucydides implies occurred in 431 B.C. As might well be expected, the Acharnians are virulently anti-Spartan, and are outraged at Dicaeopolis' peace treaty. They appear to rake up the Spartans' brutal destruction of Plataea two years earlier when they assert that the Spartans stand by "neither *bōmós* ('altar'), nor *pístis* ('trust'), nor *hórkos* ('oath')" (308). The Spartan Pausanias had dedicated the Altar of Zeus Eleutherios at Plataea after the battle in 479 B.C. (Thuc. 2.71.2; cf. Plut. *Arist.* 21), and "all the allies," Spartans included, had sworn an oath to protect Plataea thenceforth (Thuc. 2.71.2). Thucydides made the Plataeans "appeal to the oaths which your fathers swore" when they remonstrated with the Spartans before their city was uprooted in 427 B.C. (Thuc. 3.59.2).[60] Once again, we may perhaps see the seeds of Thucydides' own invention in Aristophanes. The point the Acharnians make is, however, lost on Dicaeopolis—understandably if he stands for Pericles, since Pericles had died a couple of years before Plataea was destroyed. Dicaeopolis instead proceeds to justify the Spartans' actions.

58. Cf. Stadter's suggestion (1989, 237) that the cohabitation may have begun during Pericles' lifetime (and see Appendix A). Sheep imagery, apparently at Pericles' expense, is a constant motif in Aristophanes: see especially *Peace* 929–930, 935–960, 1018, 1122–1124, and *Birds* 673.
59. Cf. Thuc. 1.126–127; and Williams 1952.
60. Cf. Vickers (1995).

To show how much confidence Dicaeopolis has in his own rhetorical gifts, he undertakes (318) to place his head on an *epixénon* ("chopping-board") — the conceit is a literal rendition of a rhetorical formula in *Telephus* (Eur. *TGF* fr. 706). If it was Pericles' onion-like head that was really in question,[61] it might have been diverting to see it, like a vegetable, ready to be chopped up if the argument went against him. And the image is not simply diverting, but highly disrespectful to the memory of the statesman. The Acharnians are still angry and unwilling to listen and, perhaps somewhat ironically, threaten him with death (325). After further altercation, Dicaeopolis repeats his offer to lay his head on a chopping-board (355). "Go and get your chopping-board, then," reply the Acharnians (359), and Dicaeopolis duly produces one. The chopping-board is referred to yet again at 365 and 366, and one can only deduce that the image was an amusing one.

Dicaeopolis begins his speech by promising not to hide behind a shield (368). This may be an allusion to Pericles' policy of staying within the city and not going out to fight against the Spartan invaders, a policy that had led to the unpleasantness between him and the demesmen of Acharnae (Thuc. 2.21–22), not to mention the composition of "many songs and offensive jests" (*Per.* 33.7). Dicaeopolis promises to speak on behalf of the Spartans (369), but since Pericles was notoriously, indeed excessively, anti-Spartan, this is probably another example of the "Hermogenes principle" (Hermog. *Meth.* 34). Dicaeopolis says that "country folk like to hear themselves and their city praised by some con-man, right or wrong; this way they are unwittingly sold down the river" (371–374). To our eyes, this is an unusual summation of Periclean oratory — if that is what it is; but it is one with which Pericles' enemies may have agreed.[62] Dicaeopolis also knows the ways of jurymen (375–376); so, too, did Pericles, not least because he had instituted the practice of paying jurors. At 377 Dicaeopolis briefly switches his persona to that of Aristophanes, a move best described by Douglass Parker as "that sort of half-allegory which is this poet's stock in trade."[63] The Acharnians object to what they consider to be delaying tactics. Dicaeopolis might just as well be wearing a "cap of Hades" (390), not only a garment that made one invisible, but if the personality of Pericles is at stake, one with a certain ironic topicality.[64]

61. Cf. Bacon 1626, §445: "a squill (which is like a great Onion)."

62. Cf. Thucydides son of Milesias on the power of Pericles' eloquence: "When I throw him in wrestling, he beats me by proving that he was never down, and making the spectators believe him" (*Per.* 8.5).

63. Parker 1961, 115; cf. Hubbard 1991, 46.

64. Cf. the surprise of the Periclean Strepsiades at *Clouds* 268 that he has left home without even a cap.

If Dicaeopolis is to succeed in his petition to the Acharnians, he has to dress in as impoverished manner as he can. To do this, he decides to borrow some rags from Euripides, a poet as famous for employing badly costumed actors as Aeschylus was for creating visions of great splendor. And perhaps this is the main purpose of the parody of Euripides' *Telephus,* which occupies the next scene: to provide a contrast with the magnificence of Aeschylus' *Persians,* parodied earlier. Another may be to make more jokes at Pericles' expense.

The rags Dicaeopolis wants are those worn by Telephus, but the clothes are not enough: he wants the distinctive Mysian hat as well. This is described as a *pilídion* ("a little *pîlos*"; 439) — a kind of hat that comes up in a point;[65] a terracotta group representing Telephus and Orestes "shows a very pointed *pîlos* on the head of the Phrygian king."[66] Donning a pointed hat (which Dicaeopolis expressly wants to put on his "head": 439) would merely have drawn attention to any schinocephaly rather than hidden it, and this may have been another reason for Aristophanes' choice of *Telephus.* Yet another may be that *Telephus* was performed in 438 B.C., the year after the suppression of the revolt of Samos, and the year in which restraints were placed on the freedom of dramatists.[67] There may have been something in *Telephus* that displeased Pericles: perhaps Telephus' argument that it was right for the Mysians to defend themselves against Greek invaders[68] was considered to be a criticism of the Samian campaign, perhaps there was an equation between Helen of Troy and Aspasia,[69] or perhaps there were Spartan overtones in the Telephus myth.[70] For any — or all — of these reasons, it would have been amusing to find a way of putting Pericles in the title role. Dicaeopolis gives as

65. Vocotopoulou 1980.

66. Stone 1984, 199.

67. Schol. *Acharnians* 67; cf. Halliwell 1991, 59: "The decree [of Morychides (440/39 B.C.)], if authentic, was prompted by the immediate political sensitivities aroused by the Samian War." For other possible reasons, see Harriott 1982; MacDowell 1983, 149; Foley 1988.

68. Handley and Rea 1957, 18–39.

69. Pericles compared the siege of Samos to that of Troy (Ion *FGrH* 392 F 16 *ap. Per.* 28.7); Eupolis described Aspasia as Helen (Eup. *PCG* 267). The Trojan aspects of *Telephus* are well brought out by Heath (1987b).

70. Demaratus, the Spartan king who aided Xerxes, was rewarded with territory around Pergamum: specifically the cities of Teuthrania and Halisarna (Xen. *Hell.* 3.1.6; cf. *An.* 2.1.3 and 7.8.17). Cf. Strabo 13.69: after saying where Teuthrania was and why it was so called, he goes on to tell at some length Euripides' story (acknowledged as such) of Auge and Telephus.

reasons why he wants the hat that "I must be who I am, and yet not seem to be so" (441), and "The audience must know me for who I am, but the Chorus must be hoodwinked . . ." (442–443). The repetition of motifs in Aristophanes is a sure clue that some point or other is being made insistently, but there is enough in the dressing-up scene to permit the conclusion that Dicaeopolis is dressed not only as Telephus, but as Pericles as well.

Whatever Aristophanes may have felt about Euripides, the criticisms of the playwright, placed in the mouth of Dicaeopolis as they are, or in the stage "business" in which he is involved, point to a reflection of Pericles' theatrical tastes. Pericles' attested sponsorship of Aeschylus (which can be paralleled in *Acharnians* by Dicaeopolis' liking for the poet) and his strong views on music (cf. *Per.* 13.11) probably allow us to regard Dicaeopolis' low opinion of Euripides as similar to his. Euripides' plays were, indeed, rarely successful,[71] and it was probably a good ploy on the part of Aristophanes (himself desirous of winning a prize) to attack him.

As he leaves the playwright's house, Dicaeopolis addresses his *thúmos* ("spirit"; 480, 483) and his *kardía* ("heart"; 485, 488). Together with the references to a heart attack near the beginning of the play (12), and to Dicaeopolis' *psukhḗ* ("soul") at 357 and 393, these may perhaps be read as intimations of mortality, as well as an allusion to the plague.[72] At 486 Dicaeopolis puts his *kephalḗn* ("head") on the block, ironically—if he "is" Pericles—ready to die if his arguments fail to impress his audience.

71. "He won first prize on only 4 out of 22 occasions": Collard 1981, 1.
72. Which "attacked the heart": Thuc. 2.49.3.

CHAPTER 5

PERICLES IN THE AGORA
Aristophanes' *Acharnians* II

Let us take stock at this stage, and consider whether the characteristics possessed by Dicaeopolis could belong to someone other than Pericles, or could simply be generic. These characteristics include early arrival at the Pnyx, admiration for Aeschylus, concern over his accounts, the enmity of the Acharnians, the possession of an "accursèd head," antipathy toward Euripides, and a deep interest in sex. Only early arrival at the Assembly and active dislike of Euripides are not actually attested for Pericles, but they may be legitimately inferred from what we otherwise know of the statesman: his single-minded devotion to politics and his interest in conventional musical standards. These characteristics could of course have been chosen at random, without being intended to apply to anyone in particular; but if such were the case, it is difficult to see why some features were chosen that possess a distinct Periclean resonance. To maintain, moreover, that they include well-known characteristics of Aristophanic heroes is to beg the question.

This is not to say that Dicaeopolis is "always" Pericles, for at 497ff., Aristophanes adopts his "half-allegory" mode in order to slip into the role of his protagonist, though not without Periclean touches. We must not assume, however, that what is said necessarily represents Aristophanes' personal point of view,[1] since many of the themes Dicaeopolis introduces are central to the development of the play. Dicaeopolis speaks favorably of metics (508); Peri-

---

1. *Pace* MacDowell (1983).

cles had encouraged their settlement at Athens.[2] Dicaeopolis expresses his hatred of the Spartans (509); Pericles did not like Lacedaemon.[3] Dicaeopolis hopes that the Spartans are devastated by another earthquake (510–511); Pericles owed much to the earthquake of 464 B.C., in that Cimon's difficulties that ensued from his attempts to assist the Spartans on that occasion had led to the establishment of the Ephialtic/Periclean democracy (e.g., Plut. *Cim.* 17.3). The reference to Taenarus (510) may relate to the way in which the Curse of Taenarus was thrown back by the Athenians at the Spartans when they raised the issue of Pericles' ancestral pollution (Thuc. 1.128). Dicaeopolis has also suffered from the Spartans' depredations (512); Pericles had promised to give his estate to the city if it was not damaged (Thuc. 2.13.1; *Per.* 33.3). We do not hear of this happening, and damage may thus be reasonably inferred.

This much one might have expected the historical Pericles to have said, but Dicaeopolis' denunciation of the scum who put into effect the terms of the Megarian decree (which Pericles had moved)[4] is ironic if spoken by a Periclean character. The catalogue of Megarian products (520–521), however, is given in such a way as to suggest that Megara's staples were sexual, and thus resumes what is one of the principal themes of the play.[5] Dicaeopolis' brief catalogue of Megarian delights leads immediately to an account of the kidnapping of the Megarian prostitute Simaetha by some young Athenian bloods (524–525), and of the retaliatory capture by Megarians of two of Aspasia's charges. The outbreak of the Peloponnesian War is attributed to a quarrel over three ladies of light virtue: an implicit nod, perhaps, in the direction of the Trojan War,[6] which broke out over one. In the context of the play, the incident serves to underline the theme of Periclean lasciviousness. And it does seem that Aristophanes is speaking again, for Dicaeopolis refers to Pericles in the third person at 530–534, describing how "the Olympian" lightened and thundered and embroiled Greece with his harsh anti-Megarian

2. E.g., Cephalus of Syracuse (Plut. *Mor.* 835c; cf. Lamb 1930, ix), or the craftsmen for building projects (*Per.* 12.5–6).

3. E.g., *Per.* 10.4, 21.1, 31.1.

4. Meiggs 1972, 202–203. Cornford (1907, 248) made the interesting suggestion that the fact the Alcmaeonid curse had its origin in the sacrilegious murder of Megarians may have lain behind Pericles' almost irrational attitude toward Megara.

5. E.g., *síkuon* ("cucumber" or "phallus") (cf. Henderson 1975, 125 n. 94 on *Anth. Pal.* 12.197.3); *lagódion* ("little hare" or "cunt") (cf. Henderson 1975, 144); *khoirídion* ("piggie" or "girl's cunt") (cf. Henderson 1975, 131); *khóndrous hálas* ("lumps of salt" or "salty breasts").

6. There may be an additional reference to Herodotus' treatment of the Trojan theme: Forrest 1963 (though MacDowell [1983, 151] disagrees); cf. Badian 1993, 230.

legislation. The Spartans made repeated requests for the repeal of the decrees, but without success (535–538).[7]

Dicaeopolis then explains the Spartans' military response in apparently dispassionate terms, describing what the Athenian reaction to an individual Spartan's raid on an insignificant island in the Athenian empire and the subsequent confiscation and public sale of the booty at Sparta[8] would be (541–554). Dicaeopolis' ability to see the Spartan point of view would have been greatly aided by his Telephan disguise (Telephus' home at Pergamum was currently ruled by a dynasty of Spartan origin; see p. 75, n. 70). The image he ostensibly creates is of the bustle in the Piraeus as preparations are made for a mighty fleet to go to sea, but once again several things are being said at once.

Would the Athenians take a Spartan attack on even the most insignificant part of the Athenian empire lying down? Not at all (541–543). They would immediately launch 300 ships, and there would be a good deal of associated preparatory activity, which is described at some length. The account culminates with what has been accurately summed up as "a farewell supper ending in a row,"[9] but a good deal else has gone on beforehand. There is a reference, for example, to crowded stoas and the measuring of corn (548). The reference is, so a Scholion informs us, to the *stoà alphitópōlis* ("flour-market"), a building at the Piraeus that, as we have already seen, Pericles had erected (Schol. *Acharnians* 548, and see Chapter 4). The dockyard referred to at the beginning of the next set of nautical images (552) will have been in the harbor at the Piraeus, also developed under Pericles (Isoc. 7.66). The dockyard rings with the sound of oarspars[10] being planed; of the banging of *túlon* (553: "dowel pins"), a word capable of a double meaning;[11] of the boring of holes for oars; of flutes; of *keleustôn* ("boatswains," with a likely play on *kélēs* ["yacht" or "horse"]);[12] of trilling; and finally, of *surigmátōn* (554: "hissing in derision"; cf. Xen. *Symp.* 6.5). The image is one of a sexual encounter whose promise is greater than the performance.

The quotation from *Telephus* at 556 has tended to distract commentators

7. *Metastapheíē* ("change" or "twist"; 537) may not simply be a reference to the Spartan ambassador's suggestion that Pericles should make the panel bearing the Megarian decree face the wall (*strépson eísō*) (Lewis 1977, 49 n. 157), but also to Pericles' cruel treatment of the Samians; cf. Duris *FGrH* 76 F 67 *ap. Per.* 28.2–3; and Chapters 1 and 2.

8. Rogers 1910a, 82.

9. Graves 1905, 90.

10. Cf. "the oar as penis": Henderson 1975, 49.

11. Cf. ibid., 19 n. 70.

12. In the context of sex with the woman on top: cf. ibid., 164–165.

from the last five words in the line: *noûs ár' hēmîn ouk éni* ("then we have no Mind at all"), spoken as Dicaeopolis places his head on the chopping block.[13] *Noûs* ("Mind") was central to the teaching of Anaxagoras,[14] a close friend of Pericles (Plut. *Them.* 2.5), and a philosopher whom he greatly admired and who deeply influenced him (*Per.* 5.1; [Dem.] 61.45). "Anaxagoras was called Nous by the men of that day," Plutarch tells us,[15] but his influence on Pericles was displeasing to enough members of the Athenian public to cause him to be prosecuted (probably between 438 and 436 B.C.), and Pericles to "fear lest Anaxagoras be convicted, and to send him out of the city before his trial commenced" (*Per.* 32.6).[16] Plato, moreover, makes "philosophic jokes on *voῦs à propos* of Anaxagoras."[17]

DIVIDE AND RULE

Dicaeopolis' speech has the effect of splitting the charcoal-burners into two opposing camps, some violently disagreeing with him, others finding merit in what he says. One group still finds him accursed, the other asserts that what he says is perfectly acceptable. They come to blows, but the anti-Dicaeopolis party calls upon their fellow demesman Lamachus to come to its aid (566–571). The historical Lamachus will have known Pericles well, having served under him on the expedition to the Black Sea in 436 B.C., but will doubtless have been among the Acharnians who in 431 B.C. "strongly insisted that they should go out and fight" (Thuc. 2.21.3)[18]; he thus provides the perfect foil for Dicaeopolis, if the latter stands for Pericles. Not being "rich" or "powerful," but instead notoriously poor (Plut. *Nic.* 15; and see the Introduction), he could be lampooned under his own name without fear of reprisal. At even the sound of a struggle, Lamachus rushes forward to fight (572–574), much to the amused horror of Dicaeopolis (575). When Lamachus asks him to re-

13. Sommerstein 1980, 89.

14. Kirk, Raven, and Schofield 1983, 362–365.

15. *Per.* 4.6; Pl. *Phd.* 97b–d; cf. Stadter 1989, 74.

16. For the date, see Mansfeld 1979–1980.

17. Brock 1990, 44, citing Pl. *Hp. Ma.* 283a; *Phd.* 97b.

18. See, too, the inscriptions relating to a cult of Ares (the war god) and Athena Areia at Acharnae: Robert 1938, 293–296, esp. 294: "Les documents rélatifs au culte d'Arès sont rares. Nous constatons que ce dieu était honoré spécialement par les Acharniens." Lamachus' bellicosity doubtless lay behind his subsequent characterization as Heracles in *Birds:* see the Introduction.

peat what he has just said, Dicaeopolis claims not to remember (580) and says that he is giddy at seeing the Gorgon on Lamachus' shield (581–582). Forgetfulness was one of the side effects of the plague, as we have already seen (see Chapter 2). Dicaeopolis' "giddiness" may be an imputation of cowardice, as is his request to have the shield emblem turned away from him. The latter comes into the "offensive jest" category, "speaking of [Pericles] as a coward" (*Per.* 33.7).[19]

Dicaeopolis' use of one of the ostrich plumes from the crest on Lamachus' helmet as an aid to vomiting (584–589)[20] enrages Lamachus to the extent that he—ironically perhaps—threatens to kill Dicaeopolis. Dicaeopolis' invitation to Lamachus to "skin his cock" is indeed a demeaning suggestion,[21] and may be another "offensive jest" aimed at what many perceived as Pericles' passivity. Dicaeopolis is then made to criticize the electoral arrangements—created under Pericles—that allowed men of modest means like Lamachus to rise to power. Dicaeopolis' lamenting the fact that the "man in the street" rarely went on highly subsidized embassies is an ironic commentary on Periclean democracy, made all the more telling by Lamachus' interjections, in which he excuses the resultant excesses by observing that the officials in question were all elected (598, 607).[22] Lamachus then goes off, pointedly stating that he will fight the Spartans by both sea and land (620–622), while Dicaeopolis reverses the terms of the Periclean Megarian decree (623–625).

The Acharnians declare themselves to have been convinced by Dicaeopolis' arguments: he has "changed the mind of the people" with regard to his peace treaty (626–627). Pericles not only was "able to prove that oratory is the art of influencing men's minds" (Pl. *Phdr.* 271c *ap. Per.* 15.2), and was described as "the most accomplished of rhetoricians" (Pl. *Phdr.* 269e), but in 430 B.C. actually "diverted the minds" of the Athenians from their troubles (Thuc. 2.65.1). If there is a reference to Pericles here, it may be that the debate between Dicaeopolis and the Acharnians represents a parody of the persuasive methods of a Pericles upon whose lips Persuasion was said to sit (Eup. *PCG* 102.5 *ap.* Schol. *Acharnians* 530).

19. Forde (1989) notes in the context of Pericles' Funeral Speech that his "virtual failure to mention courage as one of the virtues of the Athenian character is quite striking."
20. Is there an allusion here to *hupó sukophantôn tíllesthai* ("be plucked by sycophants"), a phenomenon mentioned at *Birds* 285?
21. Sommerstein 1980, 185; cf. Henderson 1975, 209.
22. The relationship between the historical Lamachus and Pericles is perhaps reflected in Dicaeopolis' addressing Lamachus and his like as *neanías* (601: "young men"). Pericles, born c. 498/94 B.C. (Stadter 1989, 64), could have been as much as thirty years older than Lamachus, first heard of as general in 436 B.C. (Develin 1989, 94).

At 703–718 the Chorus appear to recall how Pericles' principal political adversary, Thucydides son of Milesias, was sent into exile and hounded on his return ten years later. It was Thucydides' rivalry with Pericles that had led to the division of the Athenian body politic into two factions (*Per.* 11.1–3). Thucydides' party had protested about the vast expenditure on public building, a move that had backfired in that Pericles was given a free hand to build what he liked, and that Thucydides was ostracized (*Per.* 14). It seems that Thucydides on his return was prosecuted between 432 and 426 B.C. by one Euathlus (mentioned at 710),[23] a man who — like Pericles — was a friend of Protagoras (e.g., Diog. Laert. 9.54), and who, if the prosecution took place before Pericles' death, was perhaps a political ally of Pericles.

The passage ends with a plea that old men should be prosecuted by people of their own age, and similarly the young. The youthful advocate they specifically mention is Alcibiades, Pericles' adoptive son, who is mentioned at 716 in the same breath as "a garrulous pathic,"[24] an implicit (or "emphatic") character sketch that can have thrown little credit on the man who was entrusted with his education (*Alc.* 1.2; cf. Pl. *Prt.* 320a).

MEGARIAN MATTERS

Dicaeopolis emerges from his house (719) and immediately sets up the boundary-stones of his little agora. His words, *hóroi mèn agorâs eisin hoíde tês emês* ("these are the boundary-stones of my agora"), strongly recall the terminology of early boundary-stones from the Athenian Agora: *hóros eimì tês agorâs* ("I am the boundary-stone of the Agora").[25] And if *Acharnians* was intended to lampoon Pericles, then this graphic image must bear some relation to the arrangements in the Agora in his time. Aristophanes' words could, of course, simply mean that any well-equipped agora would have boundary-stones of the kind that survive in the archaeological record; but if the recent redating (from the early 450s to 418/17 B.C.)[26] of *IG* I³ 11, an inscription bear-

23. MacDowell 1971, 255.

24. Cf. Henderson 1975, 213.

25. Agora I 5510 and 7039; Thompson and Wycherley 1972, pl. 64a–b; Francis and Vickers 1988, 164; Lalonde 1991, 27, pl. 2 (H 25 and H 26).

26. *IG* I³ 11; Chambers, Gallucci, and Spanos 1990; Tréheux 1991, 469, no. 228; Mattingly 1992; Henry 1992 (who disagrees); cf. Mattingly 1993; Chambers 1993, 1994; Vickers 1996. The treaty between Athens and Segesta described in it has regularly been used to underpin an influential view of Athenian foreign policy (ML 80–82, no. 37; Meiggs 1972, 100–101).

ing supposedly "early" features such as the three-barred *sigma* and tailed *rho,* is correct, then it should involve a later date for the Agora boundary-stones (as indeed had already been argued before *IG* I³ 11 was firmly fixed).[27] One of the stones is stratigraphically associated with the earliest period of the canonical Agora (from North to South: the Royal Stoa, the Record Office, the Old Bouleuterion, the Tholos, the Boundary-Stones, and the Heliaia). It is tempting to view this development as Periclean.[28]

Dicaeopolis appoints three *agoranómoi* ("stewards of the market") to oversee the conduct of his agora (723).[29] Dicaeopolis' stewards are said to be made of leather from *Leprôn,* perhaps the site of a tannery outside Athens (Schol. ad loc.), and if there is a pun on *lépein* ("to skin"),[30] a reference to the demagogue Cleon, a tanner by trade and already mentioned by name earlier in the play (6), may be intended.[31] Dicaeopolis then returns to his house to get a stele so that he can set up the terms of the truce.

A Megarian arrives with his two daughters (729ff.). He greets the market from which he has been excluded for so long. He describes himself as "wretched," as well he might given what the Megarians had had to contend with during the previous few years. Not only had they suffered on account of the Megarian decree, but in 431 b.c. Pericles had invaded the territory with what Thucydides describes as "the largest army which the Athenians ever had in one place." They ravaged the Megarians' territory before retiring, "repeated the invasion, sometimes with cavalry, sometimes with the whole Athenian army, [twice (Thuc. 4.66.10)] every year during the war until Nisaea was taken [in 424 b.c.]" (Thuc. 2.31). Small wonder the Megarian threesome is starving.

There is little to be gained in dwelling on every obscenity in the Megarian scene. Henderson has deftly analyzed most of them. He summarizes 729–835 as follows:

The Megarian wants to sell his two small girls as piggies. His scheme is Megarian (738) not only because it is deceitful but because *khoîros* was a slang term for the youthful female member. Aristophanes bases the entire scene around this play on words. . . . Dicaeopolis realizes at least

27. Francis and Vickers 1988.
28. Cf. Francis and Vickers 1988; Shear (1993) does not appear to be aware of the ramifications of the redating of *IG* I³ 11, which I discussed in a lecture at the American School of Classical Studies in Athens in 1990. See, too, Mattingly 1991.
29. On the institution of *agoranómoi,* see Rhodes 1981, 575–576.
30. Cf. Holden 1902, 73.
31. On Cleon's possible involvement in the embellishment of the Agora, see Chapter 6.

as early as 781 that the Megarian's sack contains girls and not piggies, but perseveres in a discussion of piggie-sacrifice, which in its ambiguity could mean either eating or fornicating. The ambiguity is continued as Dicaeopolis offers to feed the piggies, who will "eat anything you give them": Dicaeopolis' offerings are double entendres referring to the male member, which the girls will "eat" (797ff.).[32]

There is, however, more to the encounter than this, namely, a commentary both on Pericles' policies toward Megara and on his sexual practices. Dicaeopolis comes out of his house to greet his Megarian visitors. He asks how things are back home, and is told that "we *diapeinâmes* ('we are having a starving bout') by the fire" (751). Everyone has noted the pun on *diapínomen* ("we drink"), but the possible connection between "by the fire" and the fact that the Megarians' property was subject to periodic burning (cf. Thuc. 4.66.1) has been overlooked. Dicaeopolis replies, "That's nice, if there is an *aulós* around" (752), which may be an allusion to the sound of an army marching, as Greek armies did, to the sound of the *aulós*,[33] a reed instrument whose noise must have struck terror into the heart of many a Megarian in recent years.

Dicaeopolis is interested in the price of *sîtos* ("corn"; 758); Pericles' interest in the corn supply (see Chapters 2 and 4) might be relevant. The piggies are fit for sacrifice at the Mysteries (764); Pericles had overseen the restoration of the shrine where the Mysteries were celebrated (*Per.* 13.7).[34] The piggies' diet is discussed at 801ff. "Will they eat *erebínthous* ('chickpeas')?" asks Dicaeopolis.[35] The *Phibáleōs iskhádas* ("dried Phibalian figs") at 802 for once perhaps refer to the male rather than the female member,[36] since there is a possible play on *Phibáleōs* and *phléps* ("penis"); the exceptional usage may be a reflection of the state of Pericles' equipment after the plague. Dicaeopolis is curious to know what breed the piggies are. "Tragasian," he decides (808). There is obviously a pun on *trágein* ("eat"),[37] but there may have been more comic "business" than immediately meets the eye in that Tragia was the island off

32. Henderson 1975, 60 (cf. 131). The notes in Sommerstein 1980, ad loc., are also very much to the point, as is Parker's translation (1961).

33. Cf. the "enoplic" measure: Ath. 1.16a.

34. The Eleusinion in the Athenian Agora may also have been built under Pericles: Francis and Vickers 1988; see, too, *IG* I^3 50, which records building "c. 435," probably at the Eleusinion *en ástei*.

35. Cf. Henderson 1975, 119: "*erebínthos,* chickpea, is the erect member: *Ach.* 801 [etc.]."

36. Cf. Henderson 1975, 118.

37. Cf. Sommerstein 1980, 196.

the coast of Samos where Pericles won an impressive naval victory in 440 B.C. (Thuc. 1.116).

The arrival of a Sycophant (818), or informer on contraband goods, puts a temporary stop to the deal being hatched between Dicaeopolis and the Megarian. The latter calls Dicaeopolis by name—twice (823): ironic perhaps, if the political subtext concerns Pericles, for a Megarian to make his address to "one strict in public faith";[38] ironic, too, that he should complain to the dramatic analogue of the source of all his country's recent woes that he is being informed against, and amusing that Dicaeopolis should rush to the defense. He gets the better of the Sycophant by pointing out his lack of a *thruallídos* ("wick"; 826), probably his lack of a leather phallus of the kind most comic actors wore.[39] If so, it is possible that the Sycophant—as well as the Megarian[40]—are also set up as comic analogues of Pericles. Thus to personalize yet another of the notorious consequences of Pericles' policies would be amusing; to show three such personalizations "polymorphically" could have been very funny indeed.

Dicaeopolis wishes the Megarian *khaîre póll'* ("goodbye" [literally, "rejoice greatly"]; 832). The unfortunate man objects that rejoicing is alien to him and his fellow Megarians. Then Dicaeopolis asks (833) whether what he is doing counts as *polupragmosúnē* ("meddlesomeness"). This is a phenomenon the practice of which Thucydides makes an Athenian speaker in 415 B.C. admit was a characteristic of his countrymen,[41] and although "meddlesomeness" was very much an understatement if it concerned Pericles' activities in the Megarid, it is a very significant word if the law of Thurii restricting dramatic ridicule to "adulterers and *polupragmónes*" (Plut. *Mor.* 519b) reflected Athenian practice.[42] Pericles qualified for dramatic ridicule on both counts, and it is Pericles whom Aristophanes seems to have in mind, making Dicaeopolis draw special attention to him, in the first instance by mentioning

38. LSJ s.v. *Dikaiópolis.*
39. As suggested by Ruck (1975, 34).
40. Cf. 809–810, where the Megarian father says that he managed to get one of the figs (*iskhádas* ["female member"; Henderson 1975, 118]) for himself; not so much a gloss on Megarian hunger as an "offensive jest" directed at Pericles' relationship with his daughter-in-law (cf. 834–835, with Henderson 1975, 113; Stesimbr. *FGrH* 107 F 19b *ap. Per.* 13.16; F 11 *ap. Per.* 36.6). The Megarian also uses characteristically "Periclean" words: e.g., *ánous* (736: "unwise") and *makhaná* (738: "device"). On Pericles and *noûs,* see Chapter 5 (on *Acharnians* 556); on Pericles and *mēkhanaí* ("seige engines"), see Chapter 2 (on *Clouds* 481). See further p. 129 below.
41. Thuc. 6.87.3; cf. Neil 1901, 208; Hornblower 1991, 115 (on Thuc. 1.70.8).
42. Cf. Henderson 1990; and Chapter 1.

polupragmosúnē at all, and second by saying "on my own head be it" (833): a pointed remark, if the head in question was that of Pericles.

THE SIGNIFICANCE OF PROPER NAMES

Aristophanes' use of proper names may be even more significant than has hitherto been thought.[43] Sometimes they are included simply to make a topical joke, but more frequently the names of well-known individuals seem to be used in order to make implications by means of "emphasis" regarding the principal targets (who, rather than those who are actually named, should properly be regarded as the *kōmōidouménoi* ["those who are lampooned"]). The use of apposite proper names is one way in which this was achieved. The ode sung by the Chorus at *Acharnians* 836–859 is full of such "emphatic" nomenclature. Their song is superficially laudatory of Dicaeopolis, but any possible Periclean echoes are far from favorable.

The imagery is complex, and the wit biting, in that the names of real people have been chosen with a view to creating an invidious character sketch of Pericles himself. "Ctesias" (839) — "Property-holder" — would imply that Pericles' stewardship of Athens' finances was aimed at lining his own pocket. "Prepis" would be a poke at Pericles' having claimed to stand for *tò prépon* ("what is seemly"),[44] or to the frequency of the word *prépein* in the works of Damon,[45] a philosopher who made a deep impression on Pericles.[46] "Cleonymus" (844) — "One whose name is fame" — elsewhere epitomized as a glutton and as one who threw his shield away,[47] would be an invidious counterpart to "Far-famed" Pericles, parodied as a glutton in *Acharnians* and the subject of "offensive jests" on account of his reluctance to go out and fight the Spartans. "Hyperbolus" (846) — "Excessive" — would imply that the claim to *eutéleia* ("restraint") that Thucydides puts into Pericles' mouth (2.40.1) was intended to restore the balance. "Cratinus" (849) — "Aristocratic" — may allude to Pericles' noble descent ("on both sides"; *Per.* 3.1; cf. Diod. 12.38.2). "Artemon" (850) was the name of an eye-salve (Gal. 12.780).

43. Cf. Olson 1992.
44. According to Tompkins (1972, 189), Pericles is the only speaker among Nicias, Alcibiades, Pericles, Cleon, and Hermocrates to use the word *prépon* in Thucydides (at 1.144.2, 2.36.1; cf. 2.36.4).
45. See Wallace 1991, 38, 45–46, 53.
46. *Per.* 4.1; Pl. *Alc.* 1.118c; Arist. *Ath. Pol.* 27.4; Wallace 1991, 50.
47. See, up to a point, Storey 1989.

Pericles' plague-induced eye problems are a constant theme; the Dercetes scene (at 1018–1036) is typical. "Pauson" (854) — "Delayer" — may be a commentary on Pericles' delaying tactics in 431 B.C. "Lysistratos in the Agora," the "disgrace of Cholargus" (855), perhaps encapsulate a view that saw Pericles as having loosened the dogs of war, and as being a disgrace to his deme (in fact, Cholargus; *Per.* 3.1). If this is indeed the case, then Aristophanes' satire can be seen to be allusive, even allegorical. Nowhere is Pericles "mentioned by name," and although some of the references to known individuals were doubtless wounding (to them), the people in question are but the secondary targets of Aristophanes' wit.

Aristophanes' technique here (and elsewhere) is akin to that involved in Theophrastus' Slanderer's derogatory genealogy of someone who had come up in the world. At first he was the son of Sosias (a servile name), but he became the son of Sosistratus in the army, and when he had been entered in the citizen roll, he was the son of Sosidemus (Theophr. *Char.* 28.2). Aristophanes uses the names of real people to make similar, programmatic points. Aristotle (*Poet.* 1451b) happily calls such names *tukhónta onómata.*

THEBAN TRADE

The thought of the eels mentioned at the end of the list of the delicacies[48] described by the next visitor to Dicaeopolis' mart excites him no end (881–882), and when the Theban produces one (apostrophized in phraseology reminiscent of Aeschylus,[49] the playwright with whom Pericles had been associated), Dicaeopolis speaks to it not simply as a long-lost friend, but in a way that recalls the imagery of the phallus procession at 263–279, where Dicaeopolis addressed an erect male member six years after Pericles' "strength was undermined" as a result of the plague (see Chapter 4). There may be other than culinary reasons for the nostalgic nature of Dicaeopolis' language,[50] and this seems to be confirmed when at 888 Dicaeopolis bids his servants to bring out the *eskháran* ("coals" or "the lips of the female pudenda"; Schol. *Knights* 1286). Dicaeopolis' children come out of the house at this point, thus providing the occasion and the opportunity for repeating the fact that he has been

48. See Henderson 1975, 20, 45, 143, 168, 205 on the double entendres in the commodities listed.
49. Rau 1967, 187.
50. Cf. Sommerstein 1980, 201.

longing for an "eel" for six years. Dicaeopolis ends his speech by hoping that he may never be parted from the eel even *thanṓn* ("in death"; 893). If this relates to Pericles, it will be another allusion to his special situation: both to his "loss of strength," and to the fact that he was already dead.

The conversation then moves to the possibility of barter between Athens and Boeotia. Dicaeopolis offers two commodities of which the Athenians have a surplus, namely, Phalerian sprats (or prostitutes)[51] and pottery (901–902). Sycophants, the self-righteous informers, are, however, eventually chosen for export. The Sycophant of lines 818–828 happens to reappear at that very moment and threatens to denounce the Theban's contraband (910ff.). He is especially put out that the Theban is illegally importing *thruallídas* ("wicks"; 916), and maintains that a single wick could set the Athenian dockyard on fire. That *thruallís* may be a word also meaning phallus[52] is suggested by the Sycophant's speech (920–924), full of elaborate metaphors for sexual intercourse. A Boeotian might place a lighted wick on the back of a cockroach, and send it into the dockyard by a drain, having waited for a strong north wind. Once the fire has taken hold of the ships, they would be immediately ablaze.

A wick on a cockroach is an extraordinarily mean image of an inflamed phallus, especially when coupled with the exaggerated image of female genitalia as a dockyard drain.[53] The dockyards were, as we have seen, built by Pericles (see Chapter 4), and the Piraeus was redesigned as part of the same building program. Hippodamus of Miletus, who later took part in the foundation of Thurii in 443 B.C., is attributed with the planning of the scheme (Arist. *Pol.* 1267b22), and the main agora of the port was called the Hippodamia after him. "A likely site [for the agora] is in the center of the town north of the middle harbor Zea,"[54] where the shipsheds were. Good drainage was an important feature of the possibly Periclean developments in the Agora of Athens itself,[55] and we may assume that similar arrangements were made at the Piraeus. Did the *Boulḗ*, in an extraordinary meeting in the shipsheds at the Piraeus only a few months before *Acharnians* (*IG* I³ 61; see Chapter 4), discuss fire hazards, one wonders? Whether or not it did, Aristophanes' image may be a none-too-complimentary summary of some of Pericles' achieve-

---

51. There may be an additional play on *phallós* in *Phalērikás* (901).

52. Cf. Ruck 1975, 34.

53. But cf. Pl. *Phdr.* 255c, where desire is compared to liquid flowing into the body via an irrigation trench.

54. Wycherley 1978, 263–264, fig. 77.

55. Francis and Vickers 1988.

ments and tastes, as well perhaps as an allusion to his having "blown the war into a flame" (cf. *Per.* 32.6).

The Sycophant, the lowest form of existence within Athens' body politic, is then baled up like a pot, similarly disregarded in the eyes of the ancients.[56] The worthlessness of the new export item is dwelt upon in terms that can have cast little credit on Periclean legal institutions (and if, as is possible, the aphallic Sycophant was another representation of Pericles himself, the satire will have been the more telling). The vessel sounds as though it was cracked in the firing, it will be a "mortar for pounding lawsuits," a "lampholder" for throwing light on those who have to give an account of how they performed their administrative duties, and "a cup for mixing up trouble" (936–939). Lawsuits had proliferated under Pericles. "Lampholder" may relate to Anaxagoras' remark to Pericles to the effect that "those who want to use a lamp supply it with oil" (*Per.* 16.9), a principle that Pericles had certainly put into practice with regard to payment for public service. Public officials, too, had attempted to "throw light" on how Pericles had spent the money entrusted to him, and Pericles' difficulties in producing his accounts provided the occasion for comment in the opening scene of *Acharnians* (see Chapter 4).

ATHENA PARTHENOS

When the Boeotian departs, a request comes from Lamachus for some of the meat (960–962), but Dicaeopolis cannot remember who Lamachus is. This is perhaps another example of the plague-induced forgetfulness joke. When Dicaeopolis learns about Lamachus, he is told in a way that recalls the image of Athena Parthenos, a statue whose construction by Pheidias had involved Pericles in a good deal of trouble, social and otherwise (*Per.* 13.14, 31.2–5). Like Aristophanes' Lamachus, Pheidias' Athena had a Gorgon at the center of her shield (not to mention the one on her aegis). Like Lamachus, too, she had a *treîs kataskíous lóphous* (965: "a shade-giving triple crest on her helmet").[57] There is, moreover, another possible reference to a Periclean monument in the *-ski-* element of *kataskíous*, in that the Skias, the "official name"[58] of the Tholos, the dining room of the Prytaneis and another of the buildings

---

56. Cf. Vickers 1985; Gill 1988; Vickers and Gill 1994. For a different view, see Boardman 1988.
57. Leipen 1971.
58. Thompson and Wycherley 1972, 41 n. 95; S. G. Miller 1978, 56–57.

that housed the institutions of the Periclean democracy,[59] was also where public officials dined at public expense. This will perhaps explain why Lamachus is apparently so free with his money (960–962), offering a total of four drachmas for Dicaeopolis' comestibles. The historical Lamachus was said to be a poor man (*Alc.* 21.9; Plut. *Nic.* 15.1), although such poverty will have been relative.[60] Perhaps he was perceived as a person who was only able to eat well at official feasts and who had been free with public money while doing so.

Dicaeopolis is praised by the Chorus as *tòn phrónimon ándra* (971: "the man of wisdom"), *tòn hupérsophon* ("extra-wise"). If Pericles is intended, the reference will doubtless be to his well-known philosophical dealings with the likes of Pythoclides and Damon, Protagoras, Zeno, Anaxagoras, and Aspasia.[61] The Chorus resolve to renounce War (977–987) before singing lines (988–989) that once more appear to bear upon the Periclean subtext of *Acharnians*. Dicaeopolis *megála . . . phroneî* (988: is "extremely haughty"); *megalophrosúnē* was attributed to Pericles in his heyday (*Per.* 14.2 [in the 440s]). The Chorus invoke *Diallagē* ("Reconciliation"), and their rhapsodic address (989–999) "contains a striking series of sexual double entendres based upon agricultural terminology." [62] Dicaeopolis continues the theme at 1003–1007, where he orders his servants to cook *tà lagôia* ("hare's flesh" [or "pussies"]),[63] using erotic metaphors of heat and cookery.[64] The roasting proceeds apace, with Dicaeopolis enjoining his servants to *huposkaleúein* ("poke [the fire] from underneath"), thus "providing an additional obscene touch by the use of the prefix." [65] The scene is eventually interrupted by the arrival of Dercetes, sobbing.

DERCETES AND PERICLES

Before we examine the next scene closely, it will be as well to recall another by-product of the plague, of which Pericles "exhibited many varieties of symptoms" (*Per.* 38), namely, "redness and inflammation of the eyes" if not

59. Thompson and Wycherley 1972, 41–46; Thompson 1982; 1988; Francis and Vickers 1988.
60. Cf. J. K. Davies 1971; 1984.
61. A *sophístria* ("bluestocking"), in addition to her other gifts: Schol. *Ach.* 527. On Pericles' philosophical interests in general, see Chapter 2.
62. Henderson 1975, 61.
63. Cf. ibid., 144.
64. Cf. ibid., 47–48, 143.
65. Ibid., 168.

their actual "loss" (Thuc. 2.49.2, 8). Also relevant here is that Pericles had suffered the loss of his two legitimate sons in the plague. Plutarch describes the circumstances:

> [According to Stesimbrotus, Pericles] and his son remained irreconcilable enemies until Xanthippus' death, which happened during the plague, by an attack of that disorder. At the same time Pericles lost his sister and most of his relations, especially those who supported his policy. Yet he would not yield, nor abate his firmness and constancy of spirit because of these afflictions, but was not observed to weep or mourn, or attend the funeral of any of his relations, until he lost Paralus, the last of his legitimate offspring. Crushed by this blow, he tried in vain to keep up his grand air of indifference, and when carrying a wreath to lay upon the corpse he was so overpowered by his feelings, that he burst into a passion of tears and sobs, which he had never done before in his whole life. (*Per.* 36.6–9)

Elsewhere, we learn that immediately after his sons' deaths within five days of each other, Pericles is said to have borne his sorrows so well that he addressed the Athenian people, inspiring them to war, wearing a garland and dressed in white.[66]

Dercetes (apparently a real name),[67] dressed as a country farmer, announces himself as a *kakodaímōn* ("a man accursed"; 1019) and begs for a bit of Dicaeopolis' peace, if only five years' worth. The reason for his sorrow is that he has lost his two oxen, stolen from Phyle by the Boeotians. Dicaeopolis asks (1024) why Dercetes is wearing white, having lost his oxen. It seems that his garment was regularly soiled when the oxen were around (1025–1026). "What do you want now?" enquires Dicaeopolis. Dercetes replies that he has lost both his eyes weeping for his two oxen, and says that if Dicaeopolis cares at all for Dercetes of Phyle, he will anoint his eyes with peace immediately.

The resonances are moving and made with a sure touch. The "two oxen" may stand for Pericles' two lost sons; Dercetes' impaired vision (his name means "Looker") may be an analogue for any ophthalmia or worse suffered by Pericles during the plague; Dercetes' white garment may allude to Pericles' apparel in the Assembly after his sons' death;[68] Dercetes' constant weeping

---

66. Protag. 9 DK⁶ *ap.* Plut. *Mor.* 118e–f; Val. Max. 5.10 ext. 1; Ael. *VH* 9.6.

67. Cf. MacDowell 1983, 159.

68. Consider, too, Pericles' deathbed boast that "no Athenian ever wore black because of me" (*Per.* 38.4).

may correspond to Pericles' passionate sobs at the funeral of Paralus; and the manure from the oxen that—while they were still around—soiled his clothes may be a reference to the difficulties Xanthippus and Paralus created for their father when they were still alive (*Per.* 36.2–5; Antisth. 34 Caizzi *ap.* Ath. 5.220d). If so, the Dercetes scene may be another example of polymorphic characterization, with Dercetes reflecting further facets of Pericles' public image.

"Phyle" (the word also means "tribe"), in truth a township on the Boeotian border, may allude to the problems, ultimately self-induced, that Pericles had had in persuading the Athenians to allow his illegitimate son to be enrolled as citizen (*Per.* 37.2–5). New citizens were enrolled in *dêmoi* ("demes," "villages," or "wards") in the first instance;[69] hence, perhaps, the choice of the word *dēmosieúōn* in line 1030 (where, however, it means "running a public health service"). Dercetes then asks, "How am I going to *komísōmai* ('bring back') my oxen?" (1031), but perhaps with the secondary meaning, "How am I going to 'carry [the bodies of]' my oxen [sons?] 'out to burial'?"[70] Dicaeopolis cruelly tells Dercetes to "cry off" and consult an apparently well-known medical practitioner (1032). Dercetes' rejection by Dicaeopolis was presumably intended to enhance the impression of total egocentricity with which that character is imbued; it recalls, moreover, the "coldness" with which Thucydides' Pericles consoled the relatives of the dead in the Funeral Speech of 431 B.C.[71]

FAMINE AND PLAGUE

The Chorus remark upon Dicaeopolis' selfishness (1037–1039), and then we find our hero talking about the things he likes most: food and sex. At least the double meanings are such as to allow the second as well as the first. There is, however, an extremely bitter subtext. The Chorus claim that Dicaeopolis will *apokteneîs limôi* ("kill [them and their neighbors] by starving") with the *knísēi* ("smell") of roast meat, *láskōn*—if he "shouts" or "shrieks" such things (1044–1046). There may be a play on *limós* and *loimós* ("plague"), and a deliberate allusion to a recent confusion of the words at Athens. When the plague had struck, the Athenians had, according to Thucydides,

---

69. On the fundamental importance of the demes in the workings of Athenian democracy, see Osborne 1990.

70. LSJ s.v. *komízō* II.1.

71. Gomme in *HCT* 2.143 (on 2.45.2).

called to mind a verse which the elder men among them declared to have been current long ago: "A Dorian war will come and a plague (*loimós*) with it." There was a dispute about the precise expression; some said that *limós,* a famine, and not *loimós,* a plague, was the original word. Nevertheless, as might have been expected, for men's memories reflected their sufferings, the argument in favor of *loimós* prevailed at the time. (Thuc. 2.54.2–3)

If Aristophanes is indeed alluding to the plague, the "smell of roast meat" may refer to the funeral pyres Thucydides describes so graphically:

Many . . . because the deaths in their households had been so frequent, made no scruple of using the burial place of others. When one man had raised a funeral pyre, others would come, and throwing on their dead first, set fire to it; or when some other corpse was already burning, before they could be stopped would throw their own dead upon it and depart. (Thuc. 2.52.4)

"Shrieking" would have been an understandable accompaniment to such desperate scenes. If he has Pericles in mind, Aristophanes seems to be implying that despite the personal tragedies that had beset him, Pericles had behaved, in the eyes of many, in a selfish manner during Athens' most terrible hour.[72] As if to rub the point home, he makes Dicaeopolis say in the last words in the scene: "Bake these and *xanthízete* ('brown them') well" (1047). If this is a pun on Xanthippus, it is a harrowing one, for the cooking stove has momentarily become a funeral pyre.

DRAFT-DODGING

The next arrivals (1048–1068) have come from a wedding, a Best Man (or a servant)[73] and a Bridesmaid. They bring a present of meat sent by the bridegroom from the wedding feast. Dicaeopolis thanks him, "whoever he is." If Dicaeopolis' forgetfulness is a reflection of one of the effects the plague had on Pericles, then we might take his uncertainty to be a hint that someone close to Pericles is intended. There are indications in the scene that follows that Alcibiades, Pericles' ward, may be the individual in question.

72. Cf. Macleod 1983, 50, on the way the Chorus, while "they congratulate Dicaeopolis, comment on his selfishness" at 1017 and 1037–1039.
73. Olson 1992, 310.

The bridegroom has requested a *kúathon* ("ladleful") of peace so that he need not serve in the army, but can stay at home and screw (1052–1053). *Kúathon* carries a connotation of a "black eye," for "cold metal ladles were applied to bruises."[74] Alcibiades had once hit, as a joke, Hipponicus—the man who was to become his father-in-law (*Alc.* 8.1–3). "Everyone in the city cried out at his indecent and arrogant behavior," Alcibiades made an abject apology, and the two became friendly to the extent that Alcibiades later married Hipponicus' daughter Hipparete. Dicaeopolis refuses the bridegroom's present, saying that he would not accept it for a thousand drachmas (1055). There may be an echo here of the story about Alcibiades' anonymous gift to his wife of a thousand gold staters (Ath. 12.534c). The difference in metals may be put down to the fact that the silver-rich Athenians were "simple in their tastes," according to Thucydides' Pericles (Thuc. 2.40.1).[75]

The Bridesmaid has a private message for Dicaeopolis from the bride; she wants to know how she can get her husband's cock to stay at home (1060). "Hipparete was a quiet and loving wife," Plutarch tells us, "but was so insulted by her husband's carrying-on with prostitutes foreign or Athenian" that she eventually went to live with her brother (*Alc.* 8.4). If Aristophanes' conceit does reflect the Alcibiadean *ménage,* a bit of peace was clearly required, and Dicaeopolis willingly gives her some of his store, giving her instructions as to how to use it: "If there is talk of mobilization, [the bride] should anoint her husband's cock [with the potion] at night." It may be relevant to note that Alcibiades was last heard of in the field in 432 B.C. (Isoc. 16.29; Pl. *Symp.* 220e), but not again until 424 B.C., the year after *Acharnians;* if Aristophanes was attacking him here, the insinuation that he was not pulling his weight may have been effective.[76]

THE SELFISH HERO

The beginning of the next scene (1069ff.) sees Lamachus summoned to mobilize and go on guard duty against a possible Boeotian attack during an im-

---

74. Arist. [*Pr.*] 890b7; cf. *Lysistrata* 444; LSJ s.v. *kúathos.*
75. On the implicit contrast with Persia, see Vickers 1990b.
76. If a case can be made for the "bridegroom" here reflecting Alcibiades, then we have a *terminus ante quem* of spring 425 B.C. for his marriage to Hipparete, daughter of Hipponicus. An earlier tradition placed the event before Delium in 424 B.C. ([Andoc.] 4.14; Isoc. 16.31), and a later one after the battle, in which Hipponicus fell (*Alc.* 8.3).

minent public holiday. He resents having to miss out on the feast (as, perhaps, the impecunious historical Lamachus might have done). Dicaeopolis ridicules him, but is himself summoned to attend a banquet given by the priest of Dionysus. Both of Dicaeopolis' pleasures, food and sex, are to be provided for. The two men then make parallel preparations for their respective engagements. Lamachus' language is martial, Dicaeopolis' redolent of the delights of the table and the bed. Few, if any, new themes are introduced; Aristophanes' object seems to be to suggest that Dicaeopolis, and by extension Pericles, had stayed at home enjoying physical pleasures while more conscientious citizens wanted to fight. In mitigation, however, it is quite possible that Dicaeopolis' gluttony is an example of the Hermogenes principle; the Pericles of our sources is a relatively austere individual, careful with his money and not given to party-going.

Dicaeopolis' final entry on stage is in the company of a pair of dancing girls (1198ff.), and what had for the most part been expressed by double entendres now becomes explicit. The play ends with the selfish hero, his companions, and the Chorus (who confidently sing a victory song) departing to enjoy the hospitality of the theatrical authorities (1224ff.). Food and sex, the themes that have subliminally permeated the play, are thus made manifest at its close.

What is the point of *Acharnians?* Why should it have been interesting to bring Pericles back to life on stage to be ridiculed? Clearly, nothing that was said could have changed Pericles' own mind, but the 420s B.C. are notoriously the period in which other politicians — Cleon, Nicias, and later Alcibiades — fought over Pericles' political testament.[77] Many of Pericles' policies were still in operation — staying within the city walls during Spartan invasions, the Megarian decree, and the consequent proliferation of sycophants: criticism of these policies and institutions might lead to reflection, and possibly change. It was also a period in which the grain supply became increasingly problematic.[78] Aristophanes may also have chosen a topic that was less controversial than that of his previous play, *Babylonians,* which had been outspoken on the subject of the Athenians' treatment of their allies.[79]

It was already known from ancient literary sources that Pericles came in for criticism,[80] but it is interesting to discover that such criticism apparently

77. Connor 1971.
78. Garnsey 1988, 128–133.
79. Forrest 1975, 27.
80. Schwarze 1971.

continued after his death. Some themes—caution tending to cowardice, womanizing, building projects, payment for public service, sponsorship of Aeschylus, the distinctive shape of Pericles' head, and the loss of his sons in the plague—were known already; others are new. As in *Clouds*, these include forgetfulness, eye trouble, and the way in which it was thought Pericles' strength was undermined as a consequence of the plague.

There are, moreover, instances in *Acharnians* of matters that are also discussed by Thucydides, and sometimes in remarkably similar fashion: the debate between Dicaeopolis and the Chorus of Acharnians, which closely resembles that between Pericles and his Acharnian critics; Pericles' coldness toward bereaved relatives; the political effects of the Alcmaeonid curse; the intricacies of Thracian politics; details of the plague; the destruction of Plataea by the Spartans; and the ravaging of Megara by the Athenians. Of course, both writers were recording the same events, and some kind of correspondence is to be expected. It is tempting, however, in the light of this evidence and that of *Clouds* 694–745, to consider the possibility that Thucydides (in exile from 424 B.C.) may have used Aristophanes' plays as an aide-mémoire for the composition of his history.

PERICLES, THE TYPHOON,
AND THE HURRICANE
Aristophanes' *Knights*

Aristophanes' *Knights* was performed at the next celebration of the Lenaean festival, early in 424 B.C., and, like *Acharnians,* it won first prize. Much had happened during the intervening year. The course of the war with Sparta and its Peloponnesian allies had changed in Athens' favor. The turning point had been the capture of 292 Spartan hoplites on the island of Sphacteria opposite Pylos in the southwestern Peloponnese in the summer of 425 B.C. This had been achieved under the command of Cleon, an individual whose historical reputation has suffered as a consequence of the intense dislike in which he was held by our principal informants, Aristophanes and Thucydides.[1] Cleon was, in 424 B.C., assuredly the principal heir to Pericles' position in the state, but a challenger was emerging in the person of Pericles' ward Alcibiades. It will be argued here that the ensuing struggle is the principal theme of *Knights,* and that Aristophanes puts across an equally jaundiced view of both contenders for Pericles' mantle.

The opening scene of the play presents two slaves who are, rightly, taken by nearly everyone[2] to be lightly disguised versions of two of the foremost generals of the day: Demosthenes, the architect of the victory at Sphacteria,

1. See Woodhead 1960; Ostwald 1986, 205–224; Hornblower 1991, 423. For the suggestion that the feud between Aristophanes and Cleon owed something to the iambographic tradition of "a fiction of hostility," see Rosen 1988b, 63.

2. E.g., Neil 1901; Rogers 1910b; A. B. West 1924; Sommerstein 1981; the arguments against the identification advanced by Dover (1967) do not carry conviction.

and Nicias, who had been attacked by Cleon in the Assembly and had yielded his command to him (Thuc. 4.27–28; Plut. *Nic.* 7.2–5). Nor can there be any doubt that Cleon underlies the person of Paphlagon, the steward of the household of Demus. Demus was once characterized by J. W. Donaldson as "the Athenian John Bull," and *Knights* as a whole "an allegorical caricature of the broadest kind,"[3] which is fine so far as it goes; but the surprising thing is that the most prominent character in the play (who speaks nearly one-third of the lines[4]) has been allowed to remain a figure without any apparent basis in a known individual. If the Sausage-seller was an allegorical caricature like the others, however, the model may well have been a prominent personality.

WHO IS THE SAUSAGE-SELLER?

Aristophanes in fact provides ample clues as to the identity of the Sausage-seller, and it is surprising that they have not been picked up before. At 128–145, the slave usually identified as Demosthenes describes Athens' recent political history in terms of a progression from a *stuppeiopōlēs* (129: "hemp-monger"), via a *probatopōlēs* (132: "sheepdealer"), to a *bursopōlēs* (136: "tanner"). Scholars agree that the "hemp-monger" is Eucrates, who may have been general in 432/31 B.C.;[5] that the "sheepdealer" is Lysicles, who was the "first man at Athens" (*Per.* 24.6) until his death in 428/27 B.C.;[6] and that the "tanner" alludes to Cleon. These lines thus give an accurate history in microcosm of Athenian history in the half-dozen years before the performance of *Knights* in 424 B.C., and we might well suppose that the next "seller" in the list, namely, the *allantopōlēs* (143–144: "Sausage-seller"), himself fresh on the scene, represented someone making his debut in Athenian politics.

If so, the most likely candidate is Alcibiades, who had been in the public eye for some time.[7] It is true that Thucydides does not introduce him until

3. Donaldson 1860, 183.

4. A rough count, accurate to within a line or two: Sausage-seller, 418; Chorus, 421; Paphlagon, 233; Demus, 144. There are 1408 lines in *Knights*.

5. Develin 1989, 102; Gilbert (1877, 126) makes the interesting suggestion that Aristophanes' Eucrates was general in the plague year 430/29 B.C., but was eclipsed when Pericles returned, briefly, to power.

6. Thuc. 3.19.2; hence *krateîn* ("rule") at 134, which is what the sheepdealer is supposed to have done until he perished. (But see Podlecki [1987, 59], who thinks a general rather than a specific point is being made—on the grounds, however, that the Sausage-seller is "clearly fictitious.")

7. The only discussion of the possible identity of the Sausage-seller known to me is Solomos

420/19 B.C. (Thuc. 5.43), but he may well have had dramatic reasons for keeping him out of his narrative until then.[8] Already in 432 B.C., Alcibiades' *axiōma* ("fame") had been enough to cause Socrates to waive his claim to an award of valor that was more properly his,[9] and there were those who claimed that Alcibiades both instigated (Diod. 12.38.2–3) and brought about[10] the Peloponnesian War. Whatever the truth of these allegations, it is certain that Alcibiades was coming to the fore as a politician by 424 B.C. Plutarch states that *éti meirákion ōn* ("when still immature") "Alcibiades plunged into political life, and at once surpassed most of the statesmen of his age" (*Alc.* 13.1), and seems to place his emergence shortly after Sphacteria (425 B.C.): "About this time Alcibiades began to gain credit in Athens as a public speaker" (Plut. *Nic.* 9.1).[11] Thucydides (5.43) mentions his activities on behalf of the Spartan captives in Athens, and Alcibiades was probably also, in 425 B.C., one of the *táktai* entrusted with the reassessment of the tribute of Athens' subject allies ([Andoc.] 4.11).[12] "His rhetorical powers [were] borne witness to by comic writers" (*Alc.* 10.4), and many stories were told about his childhood and youth.[13] Alcibiades was to play a crucial role in Athenian history in the last quarter of the fifth century. Libanius' observation concerning the central role of Alcibiades in the comedies of Aristophanes and Eupolis (Lib. fr. 50β [11.644.5–7]) has been neglected by critics, but it is one that — as we shall

1974, 97 (who considers Alcibiades, only to dismiss him as being an unlikely candidate for "the comic poet's vision of the State's saviour").

8. Cf. Cornford 1907, 191–192; Forde 1989, 72.

9. Pl. *Symp.* 220e; *Alc.* 7.5; cf. Vickers 1995.

10. According to Schol. *Acharnians* 524–525, Alcibiades was involved in the kidnapping of Simaetha from Megara.

11. Cf. Ellis 1989, 24: "Alcibiades began his active political career . . . around 425 . . . but there can be little doubt that he had aspirations, from an early age, to rise to a position of leadership" (citing [Pl.] *Alc.* 1, the dramatic date of which is 432 B.C.); Hatzfeld (1951, 69) places "[la] première manifestation de l'activité politique d'Alcibiade" in 425 B.C.

12. Cf. Hatzfeld 1951, 68–69; Ostwald 1986, 293; Ellis 1989, 24. There used to be a tendency to place Alcibiades' emergence into politics in the late 420s B.C.: e.g., Vischer [1843] 1877, 104; Hertzberg 1853, 18 (after the death of Cleon [422 B.C.]); Stallbaum 1861, 59–60; Grote 1870, 6:312: "not long before the peace of Nikias"; Toepffer 1894, 1519 (after Cleon's death); (Bloedow [1991a, 61; cf. 1990] speaks of Alcibiades' entry into "high politics" in 420; *Knights* deals with his prior entry into "low politics"). Grote shows his reasoning at 6:310: "At the age of thirty-one or thirty-two, the earliest at which it was permitted to look forward to an ascendent position in public life, Alkibiades came forward." But the reservations felt by many of his contemporaries about Alcibiades stemmed from the fact that he was precocious, and seeking political advancement before it was customary to do so (Develin 1985).

13. See especially the early chapters of Plutarch's *Life*.

see — is of fundamental importance for the understanding of Aristophanes' plays from *Knights* onward.

Notable among the stories told of Alcibiades were tales of sexual excess. Diogenes Laertius (4.49) puts them in a nutshell: "When he was a young boy [Alcibiades] lured husbands away from their wives, but when he was a young man he lured wives away from their husbands." Already in *Acharnians* (716), Aristophanes had strongly implied that Alcibiades was *eurúprōktos* ("debauched"; see Chapter 5); a specific example in the anecdotal tradition is the story of how, as a boy, he had run away from home to the house of one of his lovers, Democrates. His uncle wanted to offer a reward for Alcibiades' safe return, but "Pericles forbade it, saying that, if he was dead, he would only be found one day sooner because of it, while if he was safe, he would be disgraced for life" (*Alc.* 3.1). Pericles' reaction clearly shows what his ward had been up to, and to show Alcibiades as an *allantopōlēs,* or "Dick-seller,"[14] was an accurate, if invidious, characterization. The name will thus have been a "speaking" one, with Aristophanes making fun of Alcibiades' sexual activities, the stories of which put anything said about Pericles in the shade. Alcibiades has rightly been called "the very embodiment of the Athenian phallic ideal."[15]

Another reason why it might be profitable to think of Alcibiades in *Knights* is that the language of the Sausage-seller includes many of Alcibiades' linguistic mannerisms: his frequent use of initial *kaí* ("and"), of paratactic constructions, and of the potential optative.[16] In addition, the Sausage-seller's lines are susceptible of double meanings that result from a confusion of *lambda* and *rho.*

ALCIBIADES THE SAUSAGE-SELLER

When the Sausage-seller makes his entrance, he is addressed by Demosthenes in the most ingratiating terms (147–149). Nicias makes his excuses and departs. Given the real-life rivalry that existed between Alcibiades and Nicias (*Alc.* 13; Plut. *Nic.* 11; Thuc. 6.12–13), this is perhaps not surprising (and their

14. See Hermon. 84.17, where *allâs* ("sausage") probably means "penis"; cf. Henderson 1975, 20; Rosen 1988a, 38–39; Aman and Sardo 1983, 23; Hubbard 1991, 68. Ingrid Rowland kindly draws attention in this context to Bessie Smith's "I Want a Hot Dog on My Roll."
15. Keuls 1985, 384; cf. Strauss 1990, 122.
16. Tompkins 1972; cf. Cogan 1981, 99 (writing of Alcibiades in Thucydides): "We can have no doubt . . . that this is truly Alcibiades speaking."

mutual antipathy will also help explain the Sausage-seller's otherwise inexplicable threat to strangle Nicias at 358, a statement that has long puzzled commentators). If, moreover, Demosthenes' subsequent account of how he envisages the outcome of the Sausage-seller's career refers to Alcibiades, it is strangely prophetic: "O blessed one, O wealthy one! / O one who is nothing today, but tomorrow immensely great! / O commander of fortunate Athens!" (157–159).

Alcibiades was born into very favorable circumstances, and his fortune was large by Athenian standards.[17] He was just starting his political career in 424 B.C., but he was to achieve immense power and influence, albeit in highly unorthodox ways. The sure way to political power at Athens, as Pericles had shown, was to be elected general. Although Alcibiades was not to be elected to this high office until the spring of 420 B.C.,[18] *Knights* 159 may be an indication that an Alcibiadean generalship was already a foreseeable issue in 424 B.C.[19]

Demosthenes, having pointed at the audience, asks the Sausage-seller (163) whether he can *horâis* ("see") *tàs stíkhas* ("the serried ranks") of the *laôn* ("assembled host").[20] The epic language may be an allusion to Alcibiades' attested taste for Homer (*Alc.* 7.1–3), and *horâis* a means to make the Sausage-seller say *holô* in his reply (cf. *Wasps* 47); the joke is apparently repeated at 171, when the Sausage-seller says even more emphatically *kathorô* — or perhaps *katholô* ("I see them clearly"). A series of institutions of which the Sausage-seller will become leader then follows: "the Agora, the Harbors, and the Pnyx." These are all, as we have seen, references to Periclean administrative activity, in that several buildings in the Agora were probably begun early in Pericles' period of influence;[21] in that Pericles was responsible for major building works at the Piraeus;[22] and in that if the Pnyx was not actually created during Pericles' administration,[23] it was certainly the scene of much of his political activity. If Alcibiades does underlie the Sausage-seller, Demosthenes' implication is that Alcibiades will inherit Pericles' mantle.

The promise comes with a warning, however, to the audience, for Aristophanes' Demosthenes also believes that the emergent politician will "trample

17. One hundred talents is the figure of which we hear: Lys. 19.52.

18. Develin 1989, 142.

19. An unpublished inscription mentioned by Develin (1989, 429) suggests that Alcibiades was already of an age to be a general in 422/21 B.C.; cf. Develin 1985.

20. Sommerstein 1981, 27.

21. Thompson 1982; Francis and Vickers 1988.

22. Isoc. 7.66; Schol. *Acharnians* 5; and see Chapters 4 and 5 above.

23. Thompson 1982; Hansen 1987, 12, 141.

upon the Council, humble the generals, put people in fetters, put them in prison, and fornicate in the Prytaneum" (166–167). Again, if Alcibiades was the real target of these remarks, Aristophanes knew his man, and foresaw the way in which he would manipulate Athenian politics. Alcibiades had already imprisoned the painter Agatharchus in his house (*Alc.* 16.5),[24] and the allusion to young politicians who bait their elders at *Acharnians* 680ff. has been seen as a likely reference to Alcibiades.[25] Aristophanes' lines are reminiscent of the situation described by Plutarch (although *he* may well have been in Aristophanes' debt): "Those who played on [Alcibiades'] vanity and love of distinction induced him to embark on *megalopragmosúnēn* ('vast projects') before he was ripe for them, assuring him that as soon as he began to take a leading part in politics, he would not only eclipse all the rest of the generals and demagogues, but would even surpass Pericles in power and renown" (*Alc.* 6.4). The Sausage-seller is next invited to stand on a table and look down upon all the islands *en kúklōi* ("in a circle"; 170). If Pericles' political estate is still in question, the Cyclades around Delos, still the notional center of the Athenian empire,[26] may have been intended. Demosthenes then asks the Sausage-seller to cast his right eye toward Caria and his left to Carthage (174). Both these territories were objects of Athenian imperial ambitions. Lysicles had died in Caria in 428/27 B.C.,[27] and Alcibiades in particular is known to have stirred up enthusiasm for military adventures in the western Mediterranean:

> Even during the lifetime of Pericles, the Athenians had a hankering after Sicily, and after his death they attempted to gain possession of it, by sending troops to the assistance of those cities which were oppressed by the Syracusans, and thus laying the foundations for a greater expeditionary force. It was, however, Alcibiades who fanned their desires into a flame, and who persuaded them to abandon these half-hearted attempts, to proceed with a great force to the island, and to endeavor to subdue it. He raised great expectations among the people, but his own aspirations were far more extensive; for he regarded the conquest of Sicily not merely as an end, but as a stepping-stone to greater things.

24. Cf. Dem. 21.147. Plutarch appears to include this event among Alcibiades' "youthful escapades."
25. Cf. Laistner 1957, 118 n. 1.
26. And the scene of a ritual purification in 425, after which the Delian festival was revived: Meiggs 1972, 300–301.
27. Thuc. 3.19.2; Develin 1989, 123.

While Nicias was dissuading the people from the attempt, on the ground that it would be a difficult matter to capture the city of Syracuse, . . . Alcibiades was dreaming of Carthage and Libya; and after these were gained, he meditated the conquest of Italy and the Peloponnese, regarding Sicily as little more than a convenient magazine and place of arms. He greatly excited the younger Athenians by his vast designs, and they listened eagerly to the marvelous stories of the old who had served in that country; so that many of them would sit in the gymnasia and stoas, drawing sketches of the shape of the island of Sicily, and of the position of Libya and Carthage.[28]

Plutarch's account applies more particularly to the mid-teens of the fifth century, but some of what he says, especially the possible role of Sicily as a stepping-stone to North Africa, may be relevant here.

Athenian involvement with Sicily had been slow getting under way,[29] but in 427 B.C., an alliance had been made with Leontinoi,[30] and expeditionary forces were present in the island in 426 and 425 B.C.[31] It is against this background that exaggerated talk in 424 B.C. of the conquest of Carthage should perhaps be viewed. The Temptation of the Sausage-seller in *Knights,* moreover, is remarkably similar to an account of Alcibiades' ambitions given centuries later by Libanius (*Apologia Socratis* 138 [5.92.10–13]): "[Alcibiades] turned his eyes towards Ionia; he saw a great island, he stretched out his hand towards Sicily, he wanted Italy, and he hoped to gain Libya."

"I shall indeed be blest, if I *diastraphēsomai,*" replies the Sausage-seller (175). The scholia explain this as either "have my eyes distorted" or "have my neck twisted." If the latter, there may be a reference to the way in which Alcibiades "walked with his neck awry, i.e. with an affected air."[32] Demosthenes then tells the Sausage-seller that "all that [the islands of the Athenian empire] is yours *pérnatai* (176: 'to be sold for a bribe'),"[33] and again there may be a topical, and Alcibiadean, allusion in that it was said that when Alcibiades was *táktēs* in 425 B.C., he extorted bribes from Athens' allies: "Chosen as a member of a board of ten to perform the task, he virtually doubled

---

28. *Alc.* 17.1–4; cf. *Per.* 20.4; Thuc. 6.90.2. See, too, *Knights* 1303, where Hyperbolus' Carthaginian ambitions are mentioned.
29. Mattingly 1969, 211–220.
30. Chambers, Gallucci, and Spanos 1990, 52.
31. Thuc. 2.65.10, 3.115.2, 4.2.2, cf. 4.65.3; Westlake 1960, 391; Mattingly 1969, 211.
32. LSJ s.v. *klasaukheneúetai;* cf. Archipp. *PCG* 45 *ap. Alc.* 1.8.
33. LSJ s.v. *pérnēmi* II.

the tribute of each member of the alliance, while by showing himself threatening and influential (*méga dunámenon*), he made the public revenue a source of private gain" ([Andoc.] 4.11).

Demosthenes' oracle states that the Sausage-seller will become an *anèr mégistos* ("a very great man indeed"; 178). The stress laid on greatness (*hupérmegas* [158], *megálōs* [172], and *mégistos* [178]) perhaps recalls Alcibiades' youthful *megalopragmosúnē* ("vast projects"; *Alc.* 6.4), as well perhaps as that *méga dunámenon* of the Andocidean orator.[34] Plato makes Socrates mock Alcibiades in similar fashion; in a passage in the *Republic* (494c–d) that "contains a clear allusion to the career of Alcibiades and his relations with Socrates,"[35] he describes a "citizen of a great city, who is rich and noble (*ploûsiòs te kaì gennaîos*), good-looking and tall (*eueidês kaì mégas*). Will he not be full of boundless aspirations, and fancy himself able to manage the affairs of Greeks and barbarians, and in the thought of this he will dilate and elevate himself in the fullness of vain pomp and senseless pride?"

The connotations of *anér* at 178 are subtle. Not only does it mean a "man" as opposed to "boy," but it was a title of honor: "gentleman" as opposed to "person." This is by way of explaining the Sausage-seller's ambiguous question in response: "Tell me, how on earth can a Sausage-seller become a gentleman?" or, if the secondary meaning of sausage has been correctly interpreted, "How can a Dick-seller become a gentleman?" If substantiated, a charge of selling one's body for sexual purposes led at Athens to disqualification from certain civic privileges,[36] and consequently to automatic exclusion from the class of "gentlemen." Aristophanes is implying that Alcibiades qualified for such disqualification.

Demosthenes' reply explains how the Sausage-seller will become great: because he is *ponērós* ("a rogue"), *kax agorâs* ("from the Agora"), and *thrasús* ("bold"; 181). There is no lack of ancient witness to Alcibiades' roguery (e.g., [Lys.] 14; [Andoc.] 4), and his boldness was proverbial (e.g. *Alc.* 18.1 [rashness]; Pliny *HN* 34.12 [bravery]). "From the Agora" is not out of character if it referred to him, for all that *agoraîos* carried connotations of vulgarity.[37] It may be a further imputation that he sold his body,[38] or an allusion to his pre-

34. See, too, the *megálōn . . . pragmátōn* ("great career") in the fragment of a *Life of Alcibiades*, *POxy.* 411, 20–22 (on which see further Gallo 1975, 1:107–121).

35. C. C. W. Taylor 1976, 64.

36. D. Cohen 1987, 9; 1991, 171–202; Wallace 1993, 152: "The Athenians publicly and officially refused to allow those who sold their bodies for sex to participate in city administration."

37. LSJ s.v. *agoraîos* II. See, too, Connor 1971, 154–155; Ostwald 1986, 214–215. The Sausage-seller's name, Agoracritus (which is only revealed at 1257), must carry a similar connotation.

38. Cf. 1242, where the imputation is made more explicitly.

cocious intervention in Athenian politics, or both. The Sausage-seller's reply, that he is not worthy (*ouk axiô* [182]; cf. *áxion* [183]) of greatness, recalls Alcibiades' *axíōma,* which had once helped him win a prize of honor, as well as the *axíōma* of his ancestors, to which Thucydides (5.43.2) attributed Alcibiades' early success in politics.[39] The word is also used in the fragmentary *Life* of Alcibiades to describe one of the reasons why he was suspected of being "ambitious of a great career" (*POxy.* 411, 18–19).[40]

Demosthenes expresses the hope that the Sausage-seller does not come *ek kalôn . . . kagathôn* ("of respectable stock"; 185). Alcibiades did of course come from a highly respectable family, but his close family connection with Pericles may lie behind the Sausage-seller's "By the gods, no! Nothing but *ponērôn* ('bad' or 'cowardly') stock" (185–186). We have already seen how Pericles' memory was tarnished with the charge of cowardice; moreover, the Alcmaeonid curse (which Alcibiades shared, since his mother was an Alcmaeonid; *Alc.* 1.1) might be held to diminish the family's respectability. This, however, is supposedly a positive advantage in political life (187)—with perhaps the implication that such disadvantages never held Pericles back.

The Sausage-seller then volunteers the fact that he is badly educated (188); Antisthenes actually called Alcibiades *apaídeutos* ("uneducated"; Antisth. fr. 30 Caizzi *ap.* Ath. 12.534c). The same point was made about the Alcibiadean Pheidippides in *Clouds* (798): "He does not want to learn." Alcibiades' education was indeed a singular one, and must have been beset with difficulties.[41] The expression used—*oudè mousikèn epístamai,* literally "I do not understand music"—may in addition be an allusion to the revolution in musical fashion that Alcibiades had wrought by refusing to learn to play the *aulós* (*Alc.* 2.5–7). There may be a hint of this in Demosthenes' reply: "Demagoguery does not need a *mousikoû* ('educated' [literally, 'musical']) man, or someone who is good at *trópous* ('musical modes')" (191–192). What it did need, apparently, was "someone who is completely uneducated and loutish." Despite Alcibiades' social advantages, he could reasonably be held to fit these categories, and it is probably the case that Aristophanes was emphasizing here the negative side of Alcibiades' upbringing and behavior, and the points he possessed in common with Cleon, the other target of *Knights.*

39. Cf. the high esteem (*axiōmati*) in which Alcibiades was held by the Athenian citizenry, and the way in which at Olympia in 416 B.C. he ordered everything in a style worthy (*axiōs*) of his victory (Thuc. 6.16.2).

40. Rawlings (1981, 115) notes that the use of the word *axiōmatos* at Thuc. 8.73.3 is a reminder of Alcibiades; cf. Vickers 1995a.

41. Pericles had put Alcibiades' education in the hands of Zopyrus, a Thracian slave of whom we do not receive good reports (Plut. *Lyc.* 15, citing Plato).

After the discussion of oracles (195–210), the Sausage-seller refers to his potential authority in terms that recall Plutarch's phraseology regarding Pericles and Alcibiades; he is "amazed how [he] is able to *epitropeúein*" (212: "act as guardian over the people"), rather as Pericles had acted as guardian over Alcibiades.[42] Demosthenes tells the Sausage-seller to carry on as he does already, couching his advice in terms that describe both the manufacture and the sale of sausages, but that, if Alcibiades was intended, have a clear bearing upon the way he was developing his political career. "Stir and make mincemeat of their affairs, and always win over the people by coaxing them with a concoction of catch phrases," suggests Demosthenes (214–216). Aristophanes showed Alcibiades coining neologisms as early as *Banqueters* (427 B.C.), of which only fragments survive (Ar. *PCG* 205.6–7). The Sausage-seller has everything else necessary for success in political life (218): he has a *phōnḕ miará* ("a polluted voice"), he is *gégonas kakôs* ("badly born"), and he is *agóraios* ("a vulgar fellow"). Though these epithets may have been oblique shots at Cleon, they would not have gone wholly astray where Alcibiades was concerned, although in his case it was his birth that was polluted and his voice that was bad.

WHO ARE THE KNIGHTS?

Alcibiades had probably enrolled himself in the Athenian cavalry by 424 B.C. He was an infantryman at Potidaea in 432 B.C. (*Alc.* 7.3–4), and whether or not the lampoon of his wedding at *Acharnians* 1048–1068 caused him to re-enlist (see Chapter 5), we find him on horseback at the battle of Delium a few months after the performance of *Knights*.[43] Judging by a case brought decades later against Alcibiades' son ([Lys.] 15), it was a highly irregular matter to change regiments in this way, and so Alcibiades' action will not have gone unnoticed. And if Alcibiades does underlie the personality of the Sausage-seller, there may be a topical allusion in the choice of horsemen as a prominent feature of Aristophanes' play.[44] And they *are* prominent, having — like the Sausage-seller — one-third of the total number of lines.[45] They are said to hate Cleon (226), who immediately appears on the stage to be recognized by

42. Cf. *epitropeúein* at *Alc.* 1.2.

43. *Alc.* 7.6; Pl. *Symp.* 221a; and see below, on *Knights* 1369–1371.

44. Such a connection would remove the "inconsistency in the paradoxical alliance between the sausage-seller and the knights": Brock 1986, 20; cf. Landfester 1967, 44.

45. See n. 4 above.

all in the person of the Paphlagonian, despite the fact that the wardrobe manager refused to provide a mask bearing his features[46]—the corollary of which is that there probably were recognizable masks of Nicias and Demosthenes,[47] as well as of Alcibiades and, when necessary, of Pericles.

When Paphlagon emerges (235), he immediately swears an oath by the Twelve Gods. "Is there a reason for the oath?" R. A. Neil once asked.[48] The excavations in the Athenian Agora revealed the site of the Altar of the Twelve Gods, together with evidence for building activity there in the "last third of the fifth century."[49] If Cleon had been responsible in the 420s B.C. for a refurbishment of what Pindar had once called "the fragrant navel of the city" (fr. 75 Snell), this would both serve to identify Paphlagon and provide a reason for an otherwise unmotivated departure from the regular pattern of expletives.

Paphlagon is very concerned about what he calls a conspiracy (*xunómnuton*) against the state, picking up what may be a political idea implicit in the *xun-* compound at 222 (words beginning with *xun-* seem often to have carried a special significance in the later fifth century, namely, allusion to the political clubs to which many aristocratic Athenians belonged).[50] He runs a preposterous argument about treason (237–238) before rounding on Demosthenes and the Sausage-seller, threatening them with death (239). The Sausage-seller is frightened, and begins to run away (240), before he is halted by Demosthenes, who appeals to his nobility and begs him not to betray the cause (241–242). The appeal works, and the Sausage-seller pulls himself together and addresses (242–246) the approaching cavalry in imperious terms.

The Ravenna manuscript gives lines 242–246 to the Sausage-seller, but most editors assume that they are a continuation of Demosthenes' speech.[51] The lines in question do, however, enable Aristophanes to show Alcibiades throwing his weight around, giving orders to two of the hipparchs,[52] one of them probably Simon, the respected author of a book on horsemanship, and the dedicator of a bronze statue of a horse at the Eleusinion in the Athenian

46. Sommerstein 1981, 154–155, has a very sensible note.
47. *Pace* Dover (1967).
48. Neil 1901, 37.
49. Crosby 1949, 98; Thompson and Wycherley 1972, 132–134; Francis and Vickers 1988, 143; Gadbery 1992, 459–460.
50. Aurenche 1974, 40–41; Ostwald 1986, 537–550. Cf. *xunōmotôn* at 257 and *xunepíkeisth'* at 266.
51. Gilbert Murray, in his annotated copy of Neil 1901 (now in the Ashmolean Library, Oxford), gives the lines to the Sausage-seller.
52. Schol. *Knights* 242; Develin (1989, 130) expresses doubt as to whether they were real hipparchs.

Agora (Xen. *Eq.* 1.1), and the other probably the Panaetius who had political connections with Alcibiades.[53]

Several characters in *Acharnians,* Dicaeopolis, the Megarian, the Sycophant, and Dercetes, may have gone into a composite parody of Pericles, exemplifying the principle of polymorphic characterization. In *Knights,* the chorus of cavalrymen seem to contribute to Aristophanes' picture of Alcibiades. If he had indeed recently joined the Athenian cavalry, it would have been appropriate, amusing, and satirically effective to imply that Alcibiades' new comrades-in-arms had been totally subsumed in his personality. At all events, the Chorus in *Knights* appear to share Alcibiades' speech mannerisms, and their lines are full of *lambda-* and *rho-*generated puns. These once again permit more violent attacks on Cleon than might have otherwise been politic. Suitably "hidden," it would not have been possible for anyone, even — especially — Cleon himself, to have claimed that such attacks had been made.[54] There was a well-founded enmity between the Athenian cavalry (the "Knights") and Cleon: at some time before the performance of *Acharnians,* Cleon had been forced to pay a fine of five talents as the result of a campaign conducted by the Knights.[55] The degree to which Alcibiades may have been an enemy of Cleon's in 424 B.C. is more problematic. Ostwald speaks of Alcibiades' "vocal support of Cleon's financial policy," which is possible, given that Alcibiades may have become a *táktēs* with Cleon's help and that they shared an anti-Spartan stance.[56] Alcibiades' attested transfer to the cavalry may, however, have marked a change of policy on his part. The cavalry were in any case a brigade with more social cachet than the hoplites.[57]

The Chorus' first song (247–254) is eight lines long, but *kaí* occurs fourteen times, twice at the beginning of a sentence. Even as the text stands, the Knights' invective against Cleon is outspoken, but it is enriched with the aid of double entendres, the most noteworthy of which is at 258, where if Charybdis were pronounced "Chalybdis," the result would be a pun on the Chalybes, a well-known Paphlagonian tribe. Similarly, *hōs d'alazōn* ("What a

---

53. Ostwald 1986, 538–541, citing Dover in *HCT* 4.283.

54. Cf. Czeslaw Milosz's description of the ways in which poets in postwar Poland went to some lengths to make it dangerous for those who had noticed their covert subversion to bring charges. One story involves a poet complaining that the only flaw in the otherwise perfect city of Moscow was the all-pervasive smell of oranges. To denounce this would simply draw attention to the fact that oranges were notoriously unavailable (Milosz 1953; Ahl 1984, 186).

55. *Acharnians* 6–7; Theopomp. *FGrH* 115 F 94 *ap.* Schol. *ad loc.* For what can be known of this business, see Ostwald 1986, 204–205.

56. Ostwald 1986, 293.

57. Cf. Spence 1993.

charlatan!")[58] at 269 may have played on *hōs d'arázōn* ("What a snarler!"). Then there is an apparent reference to Pylos, the scene of Cleon's unexpected victory over the Spartans in 425 B.C., at line 277, where it is stated that if the Sausage-seller outdoes Paphlagon in shamelessness, then the *puramoûs* ("cake"), lambdacized *pulamoûs* ("Pylos-cake"), will belong to the Knights.[59] In other words, Cleon's right to the glory consequent on the victory at Pylos is being challenged.

Alcibiades once bought a very fine hound for seventy minae, and proceeded to dock its tail, to universal disapproval. When his friends told him how sorry everyone was for the dog, Alcibiades replied, "Then what I want has come about. I want the Athenians to talk about this, rather than that they should say something worse about me" (*Alc.* 9). Aristophanes seems to allude to this in the threat that the Sausage-seller makes to Paphlagon/Cleon at 289: "*kunokopēsō* ('I will dog-cut') you with regard to your back" is what the word (unique in Greek) appears to say, and the notion of tail-docking is emphasized by *hupotemoûmai* ("I will cut away from below") at 291.[60] There is another possible allusion to Alcibiades' hound's tail later in the play (1031–1032), when Paphlagon has set himself up as a dog, which the Sausage-seller promptly compares to a Cerberus "wagging its tail."

George Forrest once came close to an interpretation of the *Knights* similar to that expounded here. He believed that the theme of the pseudo-Xenophontic *Ath. Pol.* "is typical of the kind of political thinking in which [young sophisticated aristocrats] indulged," and observed that "its theme is very close to that of the *Knights.* . . . Callicles in Plato's *Gorgias,* Alcibiades in real life, are typical of the class. These young men were not oligarchs in the 420s B.C.; rather the reverse for, as the Ps. Xen. points out, oligarchy was not practical politics. They learned instead to beat Cleon at his own game, to become Sausage-sellers."[61] This is what Aristophanes does with Alcibiades, the most prominent representative of his generation, and an individual whose linguistic idiosyncrasies were such that the playwright was able to exploit them in order to make a far more penetrating attack on Cleon than the one we thought we knew.

58. Cf. MacDowell 1990, 289: "I conclude that an ἀλαζών in Old Comedy is a man who holds an official position or professes expertise which, he claims, makes him superior to other men; he exploits it, normally in speech, to obtain profit, power, or reputation; but what he says is actually false or useless. 'Charlatan' is probably the best English translation."

59. Pylos and "Pylos-cake" are in fact constant themes elsewhere in *Knights;* cf. A. B. West 1924, 219, on lines 54–56, 392, 745, 1201.

60. Cf. Rosen 1988b, 70, on threats of physical violence in invective contexts.

61. Forrest 1963, 11; on "Callicles" as Alcibiades, see Vickers 1994.

That Aristophanes had Alcibiades in mind receives confirmation in a passage in the *parabasis* at *Knights* 511, where the Chorus praise Aristophanes for having taken on *two* targets, rather than one: *tòn Tuphô . . . kaì tḕn eriṓlēn* ("the Typhoon *and* the hurricane"). The Typhoon must be Cleon, but commentators are probably wrong to take the hurricane as referring to him as well. The word employed, *eriṓlē*, occurs again at *Wasps* 1148, where there is a pun on *érion* and *óllunai* ("wool" and "destroy") at the end of a long passage on exotic cloaks of wool (*eríōn*; 1147). As will be argued in Chapter 7, it is not too difficult in that context to see an allusion to an Alcibiades who owned a multiplicity of such garments,[62] who wore a purple cloak "which he trailed through the Agora" (*Alc.* 16.1), and who used to wear a "Milesian mantle" (*Alc.* 23.4) — the woollen garment par excellence. If the pun had an Alcibiadean point in 422 B.C., it could easily have had one in 424 B.C. If so, Alcibiades will have shared with Cleon the criticism that Aristophanes heaped on the new class of demagogues.[63] The plot of *Knights* is not therefore "narrow and trivial,"[64] based solely on Aristophanes' personal enmity toward Cleon. It has a much broader scope, and there is indeed much more "at work in the play than the venting of spleen against Cleon."[65]

MORE ALCIBIADEAN RESONANCES

The Sausage-seller's account to the Knights of his speech before the Athenian Council (624–682), in which he brags that he persuaded the councillors to vote against a peace treaty, recalls the fact that Alcibiades "from the very outset had opposed the peace [with the Spartans], but ineffectually at first" (Plut. *Nic.* 10.3).[66] The Sausage-seller claims (615) to have been like Nicobulus, and to have been "victorious in the council." The "speaking name" (for all that it may have belonged to someone else) and the action both bring to mind Alcibiades' predominant characteristic according to Plutarch — *tò philónikon iskhurótaton . . . kaì tò philóprōton* ("his extremely strong desire to win and to

---

62. Pritchett 1956, 167, 190–210; 1961, 23; cf. Lewis 1966.
63. Lind (1991, 253) is not alone in believing Cleon to be the sole target.
64. Rosen 1988b, 64 n. 15.
65. Ibid., 66.
66. The Spartans had dealt through Nicias and Laches rather than the youthful Alcibiades (Thuc. 5.43.2), and the first fruit of such negotiations was the treaty of 423 B.C., moved by Laches (Thuc. 4.118.11), and to which Nicias was a signatory (Thuc. 4.119.2).

come first"), a trait that was apparent from his earliest youth (*Alc.* 2.1; cf. Thuc. 5.43.2). The Knights' reference to the Sausage-seller as *neanikótatos* (611), usually taken to mean "vigorous,"[67] may in fact have been intended to be taken literally ("extremely young"), and thus be an allusion to Alcibiades' precociousness in politics; it was his *neótēta* ("youth") that had caused the Spartans to overlook Alcibiades in the peace negotiations of the later 420s B.C., despite the long-standing relations his family had had with Sparta, and the attentions he paid to the Spartan prisoners from Sphacteria.[68]

The speech itself is full of possible Alcibiadean allusions. The first two-thirds is full of initial *kaí*s, many of them egocentric (*kaì mén,* 624; *kágōg',* 632; *kagó, kâita,* 640; *kagó,* 647; *kágōg',* 658; *kâith',* 665), and they occur at a rate that is directly comparable with those in Thucydides' Alcibiadean speeches.[69] The actions described by the Sausage-seller as he begins his address to the Council are characterized by horseplay (cf. 1194). Not only did Plutarch criticize Alcibiades for stooping to *bōmolokhía* to gain the favor of the lower classes (*Alc.* 40.3), but he records that his very first public act (a voluntary subscription to the state) was "cheered and applauded by the people"; and when he accidentally let slip a quail concealed beneath his cloak, "the Athenians cheered all the more" (*Alc.* 10.1–2). Back in *Knights,* the audience listened to the Sausage-seller open-mouthed (*ekekhḗnesan;* 651); although the expression occurs quite frequently in Aristophanes, it is tempting to think that Lucian may have had access to an account of Alcibiadean oratory when he flattered a patron by saying of his son that "whenever he comes forward to speak in public, the entire city listens to him open-mouthed (*kekhēnótes*), just as they say the Athenians of old were affected by the son of Cleinias" (Lucian 24.11).

The Sausage-seller's invocation to his special deities to give him "boldness, an inventive tongue, and a shameless voice" (636–637) recalls the fact that "Alcibiades relied upon nothing so much as on his eloquence for making himself popular and influential" (*Alc.* 10.4). According to Theophrastus, Alcibiades "excelled all men of his time in readiness of invention and resource" when it came to public speaking (Theophr. 134 W. *ap. Alc.* 10.4). Alcibiades' boldness was well known; he is said to have been "by far the most outstanding citizen in daring."[70] Shamelessness was Alcibiades' especial forte.

---

67. LSJ s.v. *neanikós.*
68. Thuc. 5.43.2; cf. Plut. *Mor.* 345a on Alcibiades' *neanieúmata* ("youthful excesses").
69. At a rate of 7 initial *kaí*'s in 22 sentences; cf. the 14 initial *kaí*'s in 44 sentences of Thuc. 6.89–92 (Tompkins 1972, 206).
70. Diod. 13.37.2 (*tolmâi polá proékhōn*); cf. *Alc.* 44.2 (*thrasútatos*).

Talk of sodomy or the like at 640–641[71] may well have brought to mind Alcibiades' youthful reputation as a pathic, already imputed by Aristophanes in the year before *Knights*.[72] But the contents of the package the Sausage-seller offers the Assembly are redolent of Alcibiades' current tastes, for the "sprats" and "anchovies" (645, 649, 662, 666, and 678) are double entendres for "prostitutes."[73] Alcibiades had married Hipparete daughter of Hipponicus by 425 B.C. (see Chapter 5), and had caused her, and was probably still causing her, considerable distress by consorting with prostitutes, "both foreign and Athenian." Hipparete left home to live with her brother, but Alcibiades took no notice and continued his debauchery. His wife eventually went in person to deliver a letter of separation to the archon, but was seized by Alcibiades in the Agora and taken home with him (*Alc.* 8.4–5). It is uncertain precisely when these events took place, but there are likely indications of Hipparete's disquiet already in 425 B.C.,[74] and the nature of Alcibiades' unfaithfulness must have been common knowledge.

The competition with Paphlagon over who could offer the most animals for sacrifice (652–662), a competition that the Sausage-seller wins, recalls Alcibiades' taste for animal slaughter, on record for 416 B.C., when he single-handedly sacrificed all the offerings at Olympia (Ath. 1.3e),[75] but doubtless a trait already a matter for gossip in 424 B.C.[76] The Sausage-seller's speech, moreover, is also full of lambdacizing wordplay; a few examples: *anékragon* ("shouted"; 642 and 670; cf. 674) when spoken *kat' Alkibiádēn* produces *anéklagon* ("barked"); *rḗmasin* ("words"; 653) produces *lḗmasin* ("arrogance");

71. Cf. Hubbard 1991, 67–68.

72. *Acharnians* 716. The "fart on the right" (639) is the comic equivalent of "thunder on the right," regarded as a highly favorable omen (Xen. *Cyr.* 7.1.3); cf. the supposed homophony of *pordḗ* ("fart") and *brontḗ* ("thunder") at *Clouds* 394. The image here may be to show Alcibiades receiving the meanest imaginable equivalent of the kind of omen appropriate to the "Olympian."

73. Hyp. 28 Blass² *ap.* Ath. 13.586b: *hetairôn eponumíai hai aphúai* ("sprats are what prostitutes are called"); whatever the precise meaning of *trikhídōn* ("anchovies") may be at *Acharnians* 551, it is clear that "garlands, anchovies, flute-girls and black eyes" suggest more than simply a plate of fish; cf. Sommerstein 1980, 183. That there is some such explanation is confirmed by the Sausage-seller's report that his audience "stood erect" (666: *hestēkótes*) on account of the "sprats."

74. See Chapter 5 on *Acharnians* 1060.

75. The sacrificial animals were presented by either the Chians or the Cyzicenes (the sources differ). Whichever it was, it is reasonable to suppose that the donors knew Alcibiades' tastes in advance.

76. At an unknown date, Alcibiades successfully proposed a decree providing for monthly sacrifices at the Temple of Heracles at Cynosarges: Ath. 6.234d–e.

and "coriander (*koríanna*) and onions" (676–677) generates *kolíanna*, playing on *kóla:* hence "tripe and onions": appropriate for a dealer in offal.

PERICLEAN RESONANCES

There is much more of an Alcibiadean nature in *Knights,* but this should be sufficient to nail the Sausage-seller down as a parody of Alcibiades. It is important to establish this, for the way the Sausage-seller addresses Demus at 725 as *ô patér* ("Father") and at 1215 as *ô pappídion* ("Daddikins") suggests that Demus may be based on the historical figure of Pericles. Fatherhood was Pericles' perceived relationship to Alcibiades,[77] and we may perhaps think of Demus as another of Aristophanes' Periclean characters. Though there were many politicians besides Pericles who identified themselves with the interests of the *dêmos,*[78] Demus in *Knights* shares too many of the features of Pericles for anyone else to lie behind the political aspect of the characterization. When Demus first comes on the stage (728) soon after the middle of the play, he asks who is making such a noise at his door, and why do they not go away? If this was intended to recall the story of the rough fellow (*bdelurós*) who once conducted a one-man demonstration outside Pericles' door until well into the night (*Per.* 5.2), it will not have put either Paphlagon or the Sausage-seller in a favorable light. Then Demus complains (729) that his visitors have destroyed his *eiresíōnē* ("wreath"), an object that is usually taken to be an otherwise unmotivated "harvest wreath" (unlikely in a play performed in the early spring). If, however, a "funerary wreath" was intended — a usage that is also attested[79] — then we may have a suggestion that Demus has returned from the dead.

There is not, however, a precise one-to-one correspondence in *Knights* between Pericles and Demus, for the latter also frequently personifies the Athenian people in 424 B.C. There may be another reason for the name of Demus as well, and one associated with an anecdote that brought together both Alcibiades and Pericles: namely, the occasion when the boy Alcibiades ran away from home to the house of his lover, Democrates, and Pericles chose not to announce the fact publicly, lest it harm Alcibiades' reputation (*Alc.* 3.1). It is possible that this event was used as the basis for the plot of *Knights,*

77. Cf. Loraux 1981, 467; Strauss 1990, 122.
78. Connor 1971; for Pericles and democracy, see, e.g., *Per.* 7.3, 14, 15.1–2, 17.1, 23.1.
79. Cf. the use of *eiresíōnē* at *IG* III.1337; Alciphron 3.37 [2.35]; Eup. *PCG* 131.

that the idea for Demus' name came in part from that of Democrates, and that the competition between Paphlagon and the Sausage-seller for Demos' favors (they describe themselves respectively as *erastés* ["lover"] and *anterastés* ["rival in love"] at 732 and 733; cf. 1163) was an unedifying comment on Alcibiades' youthful escapade. Moreover, the Sausage-seller's accusation at 737–740 that Demus is "like the boys who have lovers: you do not accept respectable ones, but give yourself to lampsellers, and cobblers and shoemakers and tanners" is ironic. The primary targets are Hyperbolus and Cleon, but one of Alcibiades' lovers had been Anytus, a tanner (albeit a very rich one indeed),[80] and another was in the habit of drawing illustrations from the world of the cobbler and shoemaker (Xen. *Mem.* 1.2.37 [Socrates]; and see Chapter 2). Thucydides' Pericles, on the other hand, maintained that Athenians should become lovers (*erastaí*) of their city (or its power),[81] whereas Plato (or a contemporary) makes Socrates express the fear that Alcibiades might become a *démerastés* ("lover of the *dêmos*"), and thus be corrupted ([Pl.] *Alc.* 1.132a). Pericles' well-known disapproval of Sophocles' pederasty would have added to the piquancy of the conceit,[82] as would the fact that Alcibiades is on record as having been enamored of Demus son of Pyrilampes.[83]

Demus' question, when he asks (732) who the Sausage-seller is, may be an example of the kind of forgetfulness that afflicted Strepsiades and Dicaeopolis (see Chapters 2 and 5), for to suggest that Pericles had forgotten who Alcibiades was would have been an effective way of recalling one of the statesman's post-plague handicaps. According to the Sausage-seller (753), Demus is the *andrôn . . . dexiótatos* ("cleverest of men") within his domestic circle, words that recall the occasion when Alcibiades told Pericles that he wished that he had conversed with him in the days when he was *deinótatos* ("the most skillful") at conducting an argument (Xen. *Mem.* 1.2.46). When, however, Demus sits—like Dicaeopolis—on the rock of the Pnyx, he is described by the Sausage-seller (755) as *kékhēnen hósper empodízōn iskhádas* ("gawp[ing] like one who chews dried figs").[84] The expression has caused much puzzlement among commentators,[85] but if we allow for Alcibiadean

80. *Alc.* 4.5–6; J. K. Davies 1971, 40–41. Whenever Socrates spoke to Anytus, he used images of leather and tannery: Cf. Dio Chrys. 55.22.

81. Thuc. 2.43.1; cf. Forde 1989, 30–43, on the concept of Eros in Thucydides.

82. *Per.* 8.8; Cic. *Off.* 1.40; Val. Max. 4.3 ext. 1. See Chapter 2, and the discussion of *Knights* 1384–1386 below.

83. Pl. *Grg.* 481d, where there is a play on the Athenian *dêmos* and Demus' name.

84. Following Sommerstein 1981, 81. For the many alternative suggestions, see Neil 1901, 107.

85. "The simile is unexplained . . . obscure even to the Alexandrians": Neil 1901, 107.

lambdacization (with *hôsper* pronounced *hôspel*), we get an expression that is gross, but entirely in character, and one for which there is an Aristophanic parallel, namely, *kékhēnen hôsper lampadízōn iskhádas* ("he gawps like one who applies a lamp to a cunt").[86] Aristophanes was subsequently to use precisely this unusual means of depilation as the basis for a knockabout scene at *Thesmophoriazusae* 238–248,[87] and lamps are elsewhere associated with Periclean figures in Aristophanes (see Chapters 2 and 7).

There is probably a certain irony in the way in which Aristophanes makes Paphlagon/Cleon express his devotion to Demus/Pericles at 767, 773, and 820–821, for Cleon was one of Pericles' most bitter enemies in the later 430s B.C.: "Cleon, too, attacked [Pericles], using the anger which the citizens felt against him to advance his own personal popularity" (*Per.* 33.8). Plutarch also quotes some lines of Hermippus (*PCG* 47.1 *ap. Per.* 33.8), in which Cleon's bravery is contrasted with the cowardice of "the King of the Satyrs" (Pericles), who is unwilling to wield his spear. Hermippus, it may be relevant to note, is said to have been the prosecutor of Aspasia.[88] Aspasia is probably in Aristophanes' line of sight when Paphlagon asserts that he has been the best servant of the Athenian people after "Lysicles, Cynna, and Salabaccho," for — as we have seen — Lysicles became Aspasia's husband after Pericles' death. If there is a further reference to the Aspasian ménage in the names of the two prostitutes, they could be the women seized from Aspasia's house (Schol. *Acharnians* 524–525), a rape that Aristophanes suggested (*Acharnians* 523–529) led to the imposition of the Megarian Decree and consequently to the outbreak of the Peloponnesian War.

At 904–910, there are several allusions to Periclean matters. Paphlagon offers Demus a bowl of *misthoû* ("state pay") for doing nothing (905), recalling perhaps Pericles' institution of payment for public service. The Sausage-seller offers him ointment to rub on the *helkúdria* ("little plague sores")[89] on his shins (907), doubtless one of the "varieties of symptoms" that Pericles himself exhibited (*Per.* 38). The Sausage-seller also offers Demus something with which to wipe his *ophthalmídiō* ("little eyes"; 909). Pericles' eyes were, as we have seen, a motif in both *Acharnians* and *Clouds* (see Chapters 3 and 5); "redness and inflammation," if not the actual loss of the eyes, was another symptom of the plague (Thuc. 2.49.2, 49.8).

86. Cf. Henderson 1975, 134.
87. For a full discussion, with pictures, of the technique involved, see Descoeudres 1981.
88. *Per.* 32.1; but cf. Wallace 1993, 131, 148 (on the possible theatrical origin of Hermippus' charges).
89. Thuc. 2.49.5. Cf. *kulíkhnion* (906). The Sausage-seller is employing what has been called the "wheedle" use of "child-to-adult coaxing": Ferguson 1977, 231.

ORACLES

The discussion of oracles at 1011–1099 is full of Periclean imagery. Demus' favorite oracle, that he will become an "eagle in the clouds" at 1013, recalls Pericles' supposed Olympian status (*Per.* 39.2; cf. Cratin. *PCG* 258 *ap.* 3.5, 13.10), the eagle being Zeus' favorite bird (Hom. *Il.* 24.310; cf. Pind. *Pyth.* 1.6). The woman bearing a lion at 1037 brings to mind the well-known omen relating to Pericles' birth (when his mother dreamt that she would be delivered of a lion),[90] and Demus' supposed ignorance of the story may be another example of plague-induced forgetfulness.

The reference to Diopeithes (1085) is relevant in a Periclean context in that he was the person who attacked Anaxagoras in the courts as a way of getting at Pericles (*Per.* 32.2).[91] There seems to be a further allusion to (Zeus') eagle at 1087, as well as to Pericles' alleged pretensions to monarchy.[92] At 1091 (in *plout **hugíeian***), there may be a glance in the direction of the miraculous incident during the construction of the Propylaea that resulted in the erection by Pericles of a statue of Athena Hygieia (*Per.* 13.13). If Demus' references to bathing at 1061 and 1091 (cf. 50) have a Periclean reference, it may be that the allusion is to the ancient practice of bathing after — "immediately" after, according to our source — sexual intercourse ([Luc.] *Am.* 39, 42, 44), and hence to Pericles' attested liking for *aphrodísia* (Clearch. *FHG* 2.314 *ap.* Ath. 13.589d). Pericles had a skeptical attitude toward omens,[93] and to make Demus gleefully accept the oracles of Glanis may be another example of the Hermogenes principle in operation.[94]

At the end of the oracle scene, Demus states that he will hand over the reins of the Pnyx to either Paphlagon or the Sausage-seller, to whichever of them renders him better service (1107–1109) — an appropriate image if what is really at stake is Pericles' political testament. They compete in bringing Demus delicacies, and the level of farcical humor is increased by the exploitation of Alcibiades' speech mannerism. The hare's meat scene at 1192–1204 pro-

90. Hdt. 6.131.2; cf. Schwarze 1971, 159.
91. Cf. Ostwald 1986, 196–198.
92. *Basileúeis;* cf. *Per.* 9.1, 11.1, esp. 15.1 (*basilikḗn . . . politeían*).
93. Cf. the discussion of the ram's skull with a single horn at *Per.* 6.2, and Anaxagora's skeptical dissection of it.
94. Cf. the stories relating to Pericles' lack of superstition: *Per.* 6.1–2, 35.2, 38.2; Frontin. *Str.* 1.11.10.

vides a good example of this. Paphlagon/Cleon boasts that he has hare's meat (*lagôia*) to give to Demus, while the Sausage-seller does not. He in turn asks, "Oh dear, where can I get hare's meat from?" and calls upon his soul to come up with something *bōmolókhon* ("clownish") — and hence typically Alcibiadean — to help save the situation. *Lagôia* in any case means "pussy" as well as "hare's meat," but on Alcibiadean lips would also play on the presumably somewhat cruder *ragás* ("crack").[95] Either way, such dainties would have been considered fitting offerings for a Periclean figure, given Pericles' attested tastes. This interpretation of the scene is confirmed at line 1204, when the Sausage-seller[96] states *egò d' ôptēsa ge,* not simply "I cooked them," but "I aroused them."[97]

The Sausage-seller eventually wins the argument, and proceeds to refine Demus. The metaphor he employs is one that can mean either boiling down meat or refining gold in the fire.[98] At 1321, he announces that he has rendered him *kalòn ex aiskhroû* ("handsome instead of ugly"), perhaps with a play on *kalòn ex Aiskhuleíou* ("handsome instead of Aeschylean"). If so, he is perhaps referring to a taste for the dramatic poet for whom Pericles had acted as *choregus,* but in any case he uses a word, *aiskhrón,* that was frequently employed by Thucydides' Pericles.[99] The new Demus is referred to as *ho kleinòs Dêmos* ("the famous Demus"; 1328); if a deliberate allusion to Alcibiades' patronymic *ho Kleiníou* ("the son of Cleinias"), this is an indication that Demus is now to be thought of as being in the Sausage-seller's pocket, and that consequently Pericles' mantle has fallen on Alcibiades' shoulders.

Aristophanes treats the Sausage-seller/Alcibiades as roughly as he did Paphlagon/Cleon, but does so with wit and subtlety, employing all the resources of Alcibiades' speech mannerisms to achieve his end. Nor does he cease to make fun of Pericles, making cruel use of the infirmities with which he was afflicted in his declining months. At 1326, Demus appears in his finery, through a stage version of the Propylaea,[100] the monumental entrance to the Acropolis, a building erected during Pericles' conduct of Athenian affairs. The Chorus address Demus as "king of the Greeks" (1333), recalling Pericles' supposed monarchical tendencies (*Per.* 15.1). Demus then makes his entrance,

95. LSJ s.v. *ragás* III: = rima, *gunaikeía phúsis* ["female sexual organ"], Gloss.
96. According to the manuscripts; cf. Neil 1901, 159.
97. Cf. Henderson 1975, 178: "*optân,* to heat up and thus excite . . . a very popular term . . . for sexual incendiarism."
98. *Aphépsēsas* (1321): cf. *ápephthos* ("refined") at Theog. 449 and Hdt. 1.50.
99. Tompkins 1972, 189.
100. Cf. Loraux 1981, 454.

and asks what he was like before he was refined (1339) — perhaps another allusion to loss of memory due to the plague.

One of the things Demus is said to have done is to open up his ears like a *skiádeion* ("sunshade"; 1348), a possible allusion to the *Skiás* in the Athenian Agora; see Chapter 5). "Was I that *anóetos* ('without *noûs*' or 'silly')?" Demus asks at 1349; *Noûs* ("Mind") was the nickname of Anaxagoras, Pericles' teacher and protégé (*Per.* 4.6).[101] Talk of *misthós* ("pay for office"; 1352, 1367) again recalls Periclean practice, but when Demus states that rowers should be paid as soon as they put in to port (1367), it may be an ironic commentary on what actually happened in Pericles' day.

Demus' statement that henceforth "no hoplite whose name is entered in a list shall be hurriedly transferred to another list, but shall be enrolled where he was first listed" (1369–1371) may well be a pointed allusion to Alcibiades' perhaps recent change of regiment (see Chapter 5), and the promulgation of a rule to forbid access to the Agora to anyone whose beard was not grown, an allusion to Alcibiades' precocious political career.[102] Similarly, the newfangled language that "young men use in the perfume market" (1375–1380) recalls the kind of jargon with which Alcibiades was associated in Aristophanes' *Banqueters* (Ar. *PCG* 205).

When the Sausage-seller proposes that Demus should have a boy complete with testicles (items that Pericles may have lost as the result of the plague) to bugger when he felt like it (1384–1386), Demus states that the good old days are back again. If this relates to Pericles, it must be an ironic allusion to his condemnation of Sophocles' pederasty many years earlier:[103] the Hermogenes principle again. Women, however, were Pericles' real interest, and two of them are produced for Demus' pleasure — personifications of the terms of a "thirty years' peace": another allusion to the "good old days" in that Pericles had brought about such a peace in the 440s B.C. (*Per.* 23.1). As for Paphlagon, he will have the Sausage-seller's old trade, which he will ply *epì taîs púlais* ("at the gates"; 1398), a significant contrast with Pylos, the scene of Cleon's recent triumph, in that "the gates" were where Athens' more disreputable trades were practiced, namely, pottery and prostitution.[104]

---

101. The themes of "sunshade" and Anaxagoras are used again in the context of *Birds* 1494–1551.

102. On which see Develin 1985. It *may* be relevant that extant portraits of Alcibiades show him clean-shaven (R. R. R. Smith 1990; 1991, 148–150, fig. 4) — although these are much later.

103. See Chapter 1 and the discussion of *Knights* 737–740 above.

104. Cf. Hsch. s.vv. *Kerameikós: tópos Athénesin éntha hoi pórnoi proestékesan* ("The Ceramicus: where the rent-boys ply their trade") and *Demíaisi púlais . . . pròs gàr autás phasin hestánai tàs*

The play ends with Demus/Pericles inviting the Sausage-seller/Alcibiades to occupy the place in the Prytaneum that Paphlagon/Cleon occupied: if Cleon had formerly worn the mantle of Pericles (for all that Pericles never had perpetual dining-rites in the Prytaneum), he is made to relinquish it to Alcibiades.[105] Cleon is to become *pharmakós* ("scapegoat"; 1405), the lowest form of Athenian political life imaginable. Aristophanes carries his campaign against the Boardmanesque figure of Cleon to the very end of the play, in making Demus suggest that Paphlagon should practice his trade where those whom he has outraged, namely *hoi xénoi* ("the foreigners"; 1408), can see him, presumably somewhere outside the city, ostracized and in exile.[106] We cannot fail to notice, however, that "Demos has been restored and rejuvenated by someone who is merely the old Paphlagonian writ large."[107]

Knights remains of course an attack on Cleon, but if the reading presented here is correct, then the "rich, aristocratic, and powerful" Alcibiades should be considered to be another victim of Aristophanes' humor. In taking on two potentially violent adversaries—the Hurricane as well as the Typhoon—Aristophanes took full advantage of the freedom of speech that was granted by convention, if not by law, to comic dramatists; but "emphasis," allegory, and lambdacizing wordplay enabled him to be even more critical of his targets than a superficial reading of the text would suggest. For all that Alcibiades comes out on top in the competition with Cleon, he scarcely emerges from the comparison with great credit: his boyhood entanglements, which Pericles had had the foresight to conceal lest his ward be deprived of citizen rights, are held up to both ridicule and scrutiny. The lampooning of Alcibiades' corrupt practices, of his grand ideas for overseas conquests, and of his probably opportunistic enrollment in the Athenian cavalry can scarcely have been intended to enhance his reputation.

As for Pericles, his role is somewhat more honorable than in *Acharnians*. In *Knights,* he stands for "good government" in contrast with the abuses Cleon perpetrated, and in contrast with those it was feared Alcibiades might commit. Pericles' building program, his fondness for Aeschylus, his plague

---

pórnas ("The Demian gate . . . where prostitutes are said to work"). For male prostitution as an escape from the world of the potter, cf. Just. *Epit.* 22.1.

105. Cf. Gomme 1962, 111: "[Pericles'] inheritance fell into the hands of Kleon and Alkibiades."
106. On this view, there is no "startling inconsistency in the plot" in the finale of *Knights; pace* Bennett and Tyrrell (1990, 235).
107. Macleod 1983, 50.

symptoms, his liking for women—all recurrent motifs in *Acharnians*—are to be found again in *Knights,* but although the Periclean imagery can at times be somewhat unpleasant, it is rarely as gross as that of *Acharnians* (or as it was again to be in *Clouds*). There is, however, a strong implication that Demus was "partly to blame for the decline of standards in Athenian politics";[108] if so, it is a charge laid against Pericles.

108. Brock 1986, 26.

CHAPTER 7

PERICLES, ALCIBIADES, THE LAW COURTS, AND THE SYMPOSIUM
Aristophanes' *Wasps*

Wasps was performed early in 422 B.C., in the year after the performance of *Clouds,* at the Lenaean festival, where it won second prize. The play incorporates two of the dramatic devices that Aristophanes used in *Clouds.* There, thanks to polymorphic characterization, it was possible to keep the main vehicles for Aristophanes' satire on stage all the time; whether in the guise of Strepsiades and Pheidippides or of the Stronger and Weaker Arguments, Pericles and the younger members of his household, and especially Alcibiades, are present throughout. In *Wasps,* Pericles and Alcibiades are again the recognizable pegs upon which Aristophanes hangs his humorous sallies at the contemporary scene, and the same dramatic techniques are employed. The legal institutions Pericles had established were now being abused by Cleon (whose allegorical analogue figures large in *Wasps*), and Alcibiades was not only a force to be reckoned with, but was probably now of an age to take a full part in politics.[1]

---

1. New epigraphical evidence (an unpublished inscription described by Develin 1989, 429) reveals Alcibiades proposing legislation in 422/21 B.C., which may indicate that he was already thirty years old. *Clouds* 862 (with its reference to a six-year-old Pheidippides) perhaps therefore indicates the age at which Alcibiades entered Pericles' guardianship after the death of Cleinias in 447 B.C. Counting inclusively, this also would make Alcibiades thirty in 422 B.C.

In the opening scene of *Wasps,* the slaves Sosias and Xanthias respectively embody Periclean and Alcibiadean characteristics; then Philocleon and Bdelycleon are based upon Pericles and his ward; and, just as the chorus of cavalrymen in *Knights* reinforced the characterization of Alcibiades as the Sausage-seller, so the chorus of elderly jurors in *Wasps* serve as additional personifications of a Pericles who was later to be described by Eupolis as a speaker who "left his sting behind in his hearers,"[2] and by Plutarch as "stung by the populace" as an old man (*Per.* 36.1).[3] The dialogue between the Chorus leader and his slave boy (who also "comes forward" as Alcibiades) thus enables, by means of polymorphic characterization, the Periclean and Alcibiadean imagery to continue unbroken.

The other technique employed in *Clouds* that Aristophanes uses again in *Wasps* is role transformation. In Chapter 3, we saw how Strepsiades adopted the persona of Pheidippides, the "Periclean" taking on many of the characteristics of the "Alcibiadean" figure. Toward the end of the *Wasps,* the main characters again reverse roles for humorous effect. This occurs when Philocleon, who has throughout the play exemplified Pericles' practice of never attending a symposium (*Per.* 7.5–6), begins to behave (and speak) like a party-going lambdacizing Alcibiades. The play is not disjointed, as is sometimes claimed. If this hypothesis is correct, the characterization will undoubtedly have been indicated by means of masks. The language of the text plays allusively on the experiences and tastes of the historical individuals on whom the characters are based, but the audience will have been primed already as to what to expect.

THE SLAVE SCENE

At the beginning of *Wasps,* the two slaves Sosias and Xanthias are on night duty, guarding the house in which Bdelycleon is holding captive his father Philocleon. Sosias arouses Xanthias, who seems to have been asleep. Both slaves' names will have been taken from the existing pool of servile nomenclature, but chosen with a view to making "emphatic" commentaries on the perceived roles in real life of their models. Sosias' name (from *sōisein,* "to

---

2. Eup. *PCG* 102; cf. Lane 1966, 44, on the Liverpudlian expression "Got a gob like a bee's bum": "said of a sarcastic person; one given to making biting or stinging remarks."

3. Plutarch, at least, may have been influenced by *Wasps:* Stadter 1989, 325.

save"), with its emphasis on safety and caution, well reflects a Periclean policy that attracted criticism in public debate and satire on the comic stage. Xanthias' name will have played upon Alcibiades' de facto filial relationship to Pericles, the son of one Xanthippus and the father of another.

The imprisonment of Bdelycleon's father under the pretense that he is mad probably has some bearing upon the charge made against Socrates that he "taught children to show contempt for their parents, persuading his followers that he rendered them wiser than their fathers, and observing that a son was allowed by the law to confine his father on convicting him of being deranged, using that circumstance as an argument that it was lawful for the more ignorant to be confined by the wiser" (Xen. *Mem.* 1.2.49, cf. 51). This passage occurs in Xenophon's *Memorabilia,* very soon after an account of the discussion between Alcibiades and Pericles on the nature of law, which, if it recorded an actual conversation, prefigured the debate between the Stronger and Weaker Arguments in *Clouds,* but if it was fictitious, may well indicate that Xenophon, like Thucydides, may have used Aristophanes as an aide-mémoire. But whether or not this was the case, the similarity of Aristophanes' conceit in *Wasps* to what Xenophon says about Socrates probably implies that Aristophanes is continuing the attack on Socratic positions begun in *Clouds* in the preceding year — or rather, is continuing the attack on Alcibiades that had been thwarted by the adverse judgment *Clouds* had received.[4] Alcibiades had also caused a scandal by holding an artist prisoner in his house (*Alc.* 16.5).

Sosias tells Xanthias that he runs the risk of being soundly beaten, for a monster (*knōdalon;* 4) lies within. If there is a pun on *kóndulon* ("fist") here, the allusion will be to Alcibiades' beating up of his future father-in-law, already lampooned by Aristophanes in *Acharnians* and *Clouds* (see Chapters 2–5). Xanthias' response, that he wants to "banish dull care" (5: *apomermērísai*),[5] incorporates an exotic word "not otherwise found in prose, comedy, or tragedy,"[6] but which is both the kind of highfalutin word Alcibiades was accused of using in the *Banqueters*[7] and one that may incorporate an obscene pun, if **-mēlísai* (= -*mērísai* lambdacized) relates to *mêla* ("a girl's breasts").[8] Sosias, too, has erotic images passing before his eyes, as befits a character based on a "Pericles much given to *aphrodísia*" (Clearch. *FHG*

---

4. Cf. the way in which Cleon's prosecution of Aristophanes for *Babylonians* (427) supposedly rankled: *Acharnians* 377–382.

5. Sommerstein 1983, 5.

6. Ibid., 152.

7. *Apobúsetai:* Ar. *PCG* 205.6–7.

8. LSJ s.v. *mêlon* (B) II.1.

2.314 *ap.* Ath. 13.589d), for *kórain* (7) means "girls" as well as "the pupils of the eye."[9]

Sosias says that he is possessed by a "sleepiness from Sabazius" (9). This was a Thraco-Phrygian deity who was regularly shown carrying a thunderbolt and accompanied by an eagle, and whose cult was associated with that of Zeus.[10] Sabazius also had a psychopompic role.[11] The image is thus appropriate for a comic character based on the "Olympian," whose soul had been led from earth a few years earlier. There were reminders of Dicaeopolis' and Strepsiades' mortal status early in *Acharnians* (15) and *Clouds* (16) as well. Xanthias claims that he "tends" the same god (10). The word he employs is *boukoleîs,* not an allusion to Sabazius' "tauriform worship,"[12] for Sabazius is never shown as a bull, but rather, perhaps, an allusion to Alcibiades' attested enthusiasm for sacrificing animals.[13] *Boukoleîs* also means "cheat," which will perhaps have reflected upon Alcibiades' character.

Xanthias' dream involves an omen about an eagle flying down to the Agora and lifting up a bronze shield before dropping it, having turned into Cleonymus (15–19). The loss of a shield on the part of Cleonymus ("One whose name is fame") seems to be a joke at the expense of Pericles (the "Far-famed"), whose association with the Agora is beyond question.[14] Like earlier Cleonymus references,[15] this looks very much like an indictment of Periclean caution, or "cowardice," as some critics saw it. The eagle is the bird of Zeus, and by extension of the "Olympian." The joke is played again at 21–23, with Sosias made to repeat it in terms of a riddle told at a symposium—and Pericles' well-known avoidance of symposia seems to be the basis for the humor toward the end of *Wasps*. Then (27) Aristophanes makes a third, and even more vicious, dig at Pericles' memory by making fun of the supposed loss of his genitalia as a result of his illness in 430 B.C.: Xanthias speaks of it being

9. LSJ s.v. *kórē* III: "pupil of the eye because a little image appears therein."

10. Picard 1961; not "Dionysus" as, e.g., Starkie 1897, 99; Coulon and van Daele 1923–1930, 16; MacDowell (1971), 128–129; Sommerstein 1983, 152; likewise Dunbar 1995, 512 (on *Birds* 873–875).

11. Picard 1961, 168.

12. LSJ s.v.

13. Ath. 1.3e; cf. Chapters 6, 8, and 9 (on *Knights* 652–662, *Peace* 637–1126, and *Birds* 43 and 848–1057). Bulls for sacrifice would also be expensive: Jameson 1988.

14. *Per.* 7.5; cf. Francis and Vickers 1988.

15. *Acharnians* 88, 844; *Knights* 958, 1372; *Clouds* 353, 400, 674–675, 680. Storey (1989) sees the historical Cleonymus as a prominent demagogue active between 426 and 414 B.C. (255–256), an individual whose notorious evasion of hoplite service "was distorted either by the comedian himself or by popular gossip" (260).

a terrible thing for a man to throw away his *hópla* ("arms" or "genitals").[16] This was indeed an "offensive jest," almost as unpleasant as the bedbug scene in *Clouds* (see Chapter 2).

Sosias' dream concerns the whole body politic (29), rather than the reputation of a single individual. He dreamt he saw *próbata* ("sheep") sitting in assembly on the Pnyx being harangued by a whale (31–36; perhaps the former constituents of Lysicles the *probatopóles* ["sheepseller"] — and the successor of Pericles in Aspasia's affections — being addressed by Cleon). The whale has a set of scales on which he weighs out lumps of fat (*dēmón*), not only a pun on *dêmos* ("people"), but perhaps, too, on the name of Demus, the son of Pyrilampes, with whom the Alcibiadean Callicles in Plato's *Gorgias* (481d) was said to have had a particular friendship,[17] and who is actually mentioned by the Alcibiadean Xanthias at 98. Xanthias' anxiety for the unity of the *dêmos* (41) reflects a concern lest Cleon should interfere with Alcibiades' relationship with the populace — and perhaps with the son of Pyrilampes.

Sosias had also seen an individual called Theorus with the head of a *kórax* ("crow"; 43), and he observed Alcibiades saying to him *traulísas* ("lambdacizing"; 44): "Theolus has the head of a *kólax* ('flatterer,' 'arse-licker,' or 'creep')" (45), a term used for those who tried to curry favor with prominent persons. The reason why Alcibiades' speech defect is spelled out for once,[18] instead of being left to the actor, is that the line in question is spoken by a character who is *not* based on Alcibiades. The mention of Theorus may be not only a topical reference to the kind of unsavory individual with whom Cleon had surrounded himself, but also an allusion to the *theoría* ("slush fund") that, it was argued in Chapter 4, was created under Pericles. Whether or not this was the case, there is a likely reference to a Periclean institution in the mention of payment at the rate of two obols (52), for two obols was the rate of payment for jury service in Pericles' day, though it had risen to three by the time *Wasps* was performed (Schol. *Wasps* 88, 300).

Xanthias then begins to tell the audience the plot (54).[19] There will be nothing too grand (56: *méga*), not even "jokes stolen from Megara (57: *Megaróthen*)," perhaps recalling the prostitute whom Alcibiades and his friends had once stolen from Megara, an act that supposedly precipitated the Megarian decree and the Peloponnesian War (Schol. *Acharnians* 524–525). But if the

16. See Sommerstein 1983, 154.
17. On the equation of Callicles and Alcibiades, see Apelt 1912; 1922; and Vickers 1994.
18. Contrast Quint. *Inst.* 1.5.32.
19. *Lógon* (54); cf. *logídion* (64); there may be an "emphatic" reference here to Pericles' difficulties over presenting a *lógos* ("account") of his expenditure: Diod. 12.38.2; cf. Chapter 4.

word were spoken Alcibiades-wise, *Megalóthen* ("from the great"), it would both pick up the *méga* of the previous line and play on Alcibiades' pretensions to "greatness," already lampooned at *Knights* 158–178. Their master Bdelycleon—who is also based on Alcibiades—is in fact described as *mégas* at 68. He is sleeping on the roof, having ordered his slaves to keep watch lest his father Philocleon should try to escape.

The latter suffers from an obscure malady, a *nóson allókoton* (71), and *nósos* and its cognates frequently recur in the pathology of Philocleon's illness (71 [twice], 76, 80, 87, 114). *Allókoton* may have been a word with a peculiarly Cleonian resonance; it is used by Thucydides (who never chooses his words lightly) in order to describe the fleet sent at Cleon's urging to slaughter the inhabitants of Mytilene in 427 B.C.: they had been sent upon a *prâgma allókoton* ("an untoward errand"; Thuc. 3.49.4). It had already been used by Aristophanes at *Wasps* 47 in the context of Cleon's hanger-on, Theorus.

The list of suggestions that supposedly come from the audience as to quite what form the illness might take (*philokubía* ["a fondness for dice"], 75; *philoposía* ["a fondness for drinking"], 79; *philothusía* ["a fondness for sacrificing"], 82; or *philoxenía* ["a fondness for foreigners"], 83) corresponds to attested tastes of Alcibiades: (1) as a boy, Alcibiades was so intent on a game of dice that he refused to give way to a wagon (*Alc.* 2.3–4);[20] (2) Alcibiades' boozing was presumably already well known: Pliny was later to put him in a list of the most famous topers of all time (Pliny *HN* 14.144; cf. *Alc.* 1.8; Plut. *Mor.* 800d); (3) Alcibiades was personally to sacrifice all the offerings at Olympia in 416 B.C. (Ath. 1.3e); (4) in the aftermath of Sphacteria, Alcibiades had paid special attention to the Spartan captives in the hope that he might reactivate his family's *palaiàn proxenían* ("traditional proxeny") with the Spartans.[21]

In fact, the malady from which the old man suffers (88) is that he is a *philhēliastēs* ("lover of the Heliaia"), one of the principal legal institutions of Periclean Athens.[22] He loves jury service, and is distressed when he cannot sit in the *prótou xúlou* ("front bench") of the court (90). There may, however, be an allusive—and abusive—reference to the occasion when Pericles' Samian

20. Cf. Lys. 14.27, where Alcibiades Jr. (who took after his father in many respects) *katakubeús[e]* ("diced away") his fortune.

21. Thuc. 5.43.2; cf. 6.89.2 and Herman 1990.

22. The Heliaia may be the same as the Metiocheum (MacDowell 1971, 273–274). If so, this strengthens the connection, since Metiochus was a friend of Pericles (Plut. *Mor.* 811f.). For the historical development of the Heliaia, see Ostwald 1986, 3–83. The Rectangular Enclosure in the southwest corner of the Agora can no longer be regarded as the site of the Heliaea: See Stroud 1994.

victims were said, rightly or wrongly, to have been beaten over the head with *xúlois* ("wooden clubs"; Duris *FGrH* 76 F 67 *ap. Per.* 28.2–3). In addition, when lambdacized (on Xanthias' lips), the expression gives *plōtoû xúlou* ("floating wood"), which recalls both the navy, Pericles' favorite military sphere, and Thales' description of the earth as *plōtēn hōsper xúlon* ("floating like wood"; Arist. *Cael.* 294a30) and hence perhaps Pericles' interest in natural philosophy (see Chapter 2). The old master's *noûs* ("mind") flies all night around the water clock (93). *Noûs* was a word with close Periclean associations, being a favorite theme of Anaxagoras.[23] While the law courts and their administration will have been a major preoccupation of the real Pericles, Philocleon's emotional attachment to judicial equipment is such that if he sees the graffito *Dêmos kalós* ("Demus [son of Pyrilampes] is beautiful"), he adds *kēmós kalós* ("the funnel of the voting urn is beautiful"; 99): an implicit comparison of orifices that is fundamentally gross, and one that perversely ran counter to Pericles' attested tastes: the Hermogenes principle in operation. If the cock crows late, Xanthias says that Philocleon maintains it has been bribed with *khrḗmata* ("money"; 102). That there may be a carefully placed pun on *klḗmata* ("shoes") is suggested by Philocleon's calling for his *embádas* ("boots") at the end of the next line.[24] The whole passage dwells upon Philocleon's exaggerated sense of judicial duty in a manner that recalls Plutarch's image of Pericles' devotion to his civic tasks (e.g., *Per.* 7.5).

Philocleon's son is said to have tried various means of curbing his father's activities, and all of them play lightly and allusively upon well-known aspects of the history and public images of Pericles and Alcibiades. They include persuasion (115), bathing and purification (118), and a visit to the shrine of Asclepius at Aegina (122–123). Persuasion was said to sit upon Pericles' lips (Eup. *PCG* 102.5), and Alcibiades' persuasive gifts were well known (e.g., Isoc. 16.21). We have already seen how, for one reason or another, both Pericles and Alcibiades may have been given to overly frequent bathing (Plut. *Mor.* 235a; [Luc.] *Am.* 39, 42, 44). Their shared Alcmaeonid heritage, which included a family curse (Thuc. 1.126–127; *Per.* 33.1), laid both of them open to a perceived need for ritual purification, to which in any case those such as Pericles in the last months of his life, suffering from a chronic disease, had recourse.[25] Aegina was, however, a curious choice, in that Pericles considered Aegina to be "the pus in the eye of the Piraeus,"[26] words that may have been

---

23. See Chapters 2 and 5 on *Clouds* 380 and *Acharnians* 555.
24. See the Introduction and Chapter 3 on the similar puns at *Birds* 1658 and *Clouds* 816, 1223, and 1270.
25. Plut. *Mor.* 920b; cf. Podlecki 1987, 79.
26. *Per.* 8.7, trans. Stadter 1989, 108.

spoken in the debate in 431 B.C., as a consequence of which the inhabitants of the island were expelled.[27] Finally, the sewers through which it was feared Philocleon might escape from the house (126) could relate to a well-known feature of the Agora, namely the drainage system, for which Pericles may have been responsible,[28] as he was for the sewers in the Piraeus (see Chapter 5).

Only after this long account of attempted remedies, and of the measures taken to contain the old master, does the audience learn the names of the characters (133–136). The name of the old man[29] is Philocleon, or Cleon-lover: highly significant and amusing if Pericles does underlie the characterization, for although Cleon apparently succeeded to Pericles' position of power and influence in the state by making full use of Periclean institutions, the two men were enemies when Pericles was still alive.[30] The outrageous image will account for Sosias' insistent assurance (134) that his name really *is* Philocleon. The son's name is Bdelycleon, or Cleon-loather, and even if the Cleon-Alcibiades relationship as depicted in *Knights* (see Chapter 4) was exaggerated, it well indicates how an Alcibiadean character might be held a year or so later to "loathe" Cleon. Plutarch, moreover, uses a telling expression, *tòn bíon ebdelúttonto* ("they were disgusted with his way of life"; *Nic.* 11.2) in describing the attitude of the Athenians toward Alcibiades in the mid-teens of the fifth century B.C. While the audience were doubtless rolling in the aisles at the revelation of the names of Philocleon and Bdelycleon (133–134),[31] they were assailed with another: that of Sosias. The reasons underlying the characterization of Xanthias and Sosias have already been discussed, but if these are correct, the slaves' names coupled at 136 will have raised another big laugh.

PERICLES AT HOME

Bdelycleon issues a peremptory order for one of the slaves to slip round the back of the house. Sosias does so, and re-emerges as Philocleon — and as smoke. This is how most of the audience will have last seen Pericles — going up in smoke above his funeral pyre in 429 B.C. Upper-class Athenian funerals

27. Thuc. 2.27; cf. Burn 1948, 213.

28. Thompson and Wycherley 1972, pl. 100a; cf. Francis and Vickers 1988.

29. *Géronti* lambdacized as *gélonti* would carry overtones of "ridiculous."

30. Cleon was one of Pericles' accusers in 429: *Per.* 35.5; cf. 33.8.

31. See Olson 1992, 306–309, on the "late" naming of comic heroes: "It allows Aristophanes to establish a character or situation and then bestow a name as a final climactic joke."

took the form of cremation,[32] and we can probably envisage Pericles' obsequies as having resembled those of some prominent Indian politician today. The fact that "smoke," like "clouds," signified "worthlessness" (cf. Schol. *Clouds* 252) may also have contributed to the image.

No sooner, however, has Philocleon been introduced than the issue of *xúlou* ("wood") is raised (145). Not only may the wood of a funeral pyre be in question, but also the *xúla* ("wooden clubs") of Samos. The point is emphasized, in both the ancient and the modern senses of the word, by Bdelycleon's application of a *tēlía* ("chimney-board"; 147), followed by a *xúlon* ("wooden club"; 148), to force Philocleon's head back down the chimney. There may be some contemporary, Alcibiadean references as well: to Alcibiades' having beaten one of his servants to death with a *xúlon* ("wooden club"; *Alc.* 3.1),[33] as well as to his having beaten up the man who became his father-in-law (*Alc.* 8.1). Aristophanes' witty image brings all these allusions together. The Samian reference is then further reinforced by Bdelycleon's challenge to Philocleon to find another *mēkhanḗ* ("device"; 149) whereby to escape. It was thanks to the inventive use of *mēkhanaí* ("siege-engines") that Pericles had forced the Samians to capitulate.[34]

Bdelycleon asks what is the nature of the wood from which the smoke comes (145). "Wood of the fig," comes the reply. Not only was figwood an acrid fuel,[35] but it came from a tree with a wide range of Periclean resonance. Figs were the staple product of Megara, the city whose goods Pericles had caused to be banned in the markets of the Athenian empire.[36] We may even speculate that the name of Megara's characteristic fruit (*sûka*) gave rise to the term "sycophant" (*sukophántes*), which was applied to informers who denounced contraband and which first occurs in the 420s B.C.[37] Then, "figwood" and "figs" carried a sexual connotation,[38] and there may thus be an

---

32. E.g., Solon (whose ashes were strewn over Salamis), Plut. *Sol.* 32.4; cf. Luc. *Luct.* 21: "The Greek burnt, the Persian buried"; Vickers 1984, 95; Vickers and Gill 1994, 71–72.

33. It is interesting to note that Plutarch applies the same qualification as he does to Pericles' supposed cruelty: the information came from an ill-disposed source, so may not be reliable.

34. Ephor. *FGrH* 70 F 194 *ap. Per.* 27.3. For further references to *mēkhanaí,* see *Wasps* 365, and Chapter 2 on *Clouds* 479–481; *melíttion* ("little bee") at *Wasps* 366 may play on the name of Melissus, the Samian commander: *Per.* 26.2.

35. Cf. Theophr. *Hist. Pl.* 5.9.5. A sweet-smelling fuel such as olive wood ([Dem.] 43.71) would be employed for an aristocratic funeral; cf. Browne 1658: "the Funerall pyre consisted of sweet fuel."

36. Meiggs 1972, 201, 430–431.

37. For various conjectures as to the origin of the word, see Lofberg 1917, vii–viii; and the discussion in Ostwald 1986, 209–210.

38. Henderson 1975, 22, 118, 134–135, 200.

additional allusion to Pericles' womanizing. Bdelycleon laments the fact that he must now be called the son of *Kapníou* ("Smokey"; 151)—a play, perhaps, on *Kleiníou* ("son of Cleinias"), Alcibiades' patronymic.

Philocleon is not amused by the attention paid to him by Bdelycleon and Xanthias, for he wants to be off to the law courts (157). His intended victim has a significant name, if Philocleon is based on Pericles, for Dracontides was the man who had, in 432 B.C., proposed a decree to force Pericles to give an account of the public funds in his care.[39] The punch line of the scene in which Philocleon tries to escape beneath a donkey along the lines of Odysseus' escape from the Cyclops' cave (168–195) is *perì ónou skiás* ("about the shadow of a donkey")—not simply proverbial for "a trivial matter" (Schol. *Clouds* 252), but if Pericles is in question, perhaps a reference to the Skias, or Tholos, in the Agora,[40] as well as to Pericles' leadership of the Athenians having been compared to the management of various kinds of livestock, in particular of *ónon* ("donkeys"; Pl. *Grg.* 516a–b)—a characterization that was presumably known beyond the Socratic circle.

WASPISHNESS

Philocleon's friends and fellow jurymen are said to sing songs that recall Phrynichus' *Phoenissae* (220; cf. 269); in 472 B.C., Aeschylus had begun the *Persae,* of which Pericles was the *choregus,* with a salute to that work.[41] The lamps the chorus carry (246) may be an allusion to Anaxagoras' remark to Pericles to the effect that "those who want to use a lamp supply it with oil" (*Per.* 16.9); it was a principle that Pericles had certainly followed with respect to payment for jury service. The lamp motif is repeated, and reinforced, at 249, 250, 255, and 262. It is likely that the Chorus also "come forward" as Pericles, according to the principle of polymorphic characterization. At *Clouds* 57 Strepsiades upbraided a slave for having used too thick a lamp wick, in a context where Pericles' notorious parsimony (*Per.* 16.5; 36.2) seemed to be in question. The image is repeated at 249–262, where the Chorus leader is similarly concerned over the amount of oil that is used. Moreover, the Cho-

39. *Per.* 32.3; Westlake 1968, 27; see further Frost 1964b; Ostwald 1986, 191–199; Stadter 1989, 300–301.

40. Thompson and Wycherley 1972, 41–46; Thompson 1982; Francis and Vickers 1988. See Chapters 5 and 6 on *Acharnians* 965 and *Knights* 1348.

41. Broadhead 1960, 38; MacDowell 1971, 160–161.

rus leader's pedantically scientific investigation of fungus on the lamps reminds us of Pericles' interest in natural philosophy, which he also owed to Anaxagoras (*Per.* 6.1–3).

Philocleon always used to be in front, singing lays by Phrynichus, state the Chorus, "for he is *philōidós* (270: 'fond of singing')." Pericles had been Athens' leader for many years, a link with Phrynichus was noted at line 220, and it was doubtless as a lover of singing that Pericles instituted a musical competition at the Panathenaic festival, with himself as a judge (*Per.* 13.11), and arranged for the construction of an *Ōideîon* ("Song Hall") next to the Theatre of Dionysus (*Per.* 13.9–11). Like *philhēliastḗs* at 88, *philōidós* plays "emphatically" on a building with Periclean associations.

The Chorus may make some allusions to the plague at 277 and 284, although it is impossible to say whether Philocleon's having "suffer[ed] from swellings in the groin" (277: *boubōniôiē*) relates to the pathology of the epidemic of 431 B.C.; if it does, it can be added to the list of symptoms noted by Thucydides. His having been "ill of a fever" (284: *puréttōn,* cf. 813) does, however, correspond to one of Thucydides' symptoms.[42] Philocleon's severity is described (278) in the same terms as the smoke as which he emerges at 146: *drimútatos* ("extremely bitter" or "acrid"); *drimútēs* ("acerbity") was a word applied to the wit of Aspasia (Lucian *Imag.* 17), at whose urging—or so it was said—the Samian campaign was undertaken.[43] There is in any case a specific reference to the events at Samos in 440 at 282–283.[44]

The boy who is the Chorus leader's interlocutor not only speaks on behalf of the other servants, but also is characterized as Alcibiades. He addresses the Chorus leader as "Father," or the like, five times (248 [twice], 290, 304: *patér;* 297–298: *pappía*), and treats him as a doddering old fool; the situation may parody the relationship between Alcibiades and the very old Pericles, when "Alcibiades and other friends" persuaded Pericles to take up public life again after his trial and impeachment in 430/29 B.C. (*Per.* 37.1). The discussion over how to trim the lamp perhaps reflects the different public images of the two individuals. The Chorus leader wants to use a "twig"—a deft allusion to Pericles' real or imaginary way with "wood"—whereas the boy actually uses his finger—analogous to Alcibiades' readiness to resort to fisticuffs.

The language the boy is made to employ bears out an identification with Alcibiades. In the *Banqueters,* Alcibiades had been mentioned by name as us-

---

42. *Thérmai iskhuraí:* Thuc. 2.49.2; cf. Appendix B.
43. *Per.* 24.2, 25.1. Cf. Stadter 1989, 233: "It is in fact not unlikely that Aspasia had some role in Pericles' decision."
44. And cf. n. 34 above on 365–366.

ing the affected word *apobúsetai* ("stop up"; Ar. *PCG* 205.6–7). The succes-
sive *tòn lúkhnon probúson* (249) and *tòn lúkhnon probúsein* ("trim the lamp";
250) play on this, and culminate in the boy's *aposbésantes toùs lúkhnous* ("ex-
tinguish the lamps"; 255), which not only puns on the Alcibiadean expression, but also deflates it. *Kondúlois* ("knuckles"; 254) recalls Alcibiades' ill
treatment of his future father-in-law (picking up the point made by "finger"
at 251), and the *astragáloi* ("dice" [or "*knuckle*-bones"])[45] that the Chorus
leader offers the boy at 295–296, the dice on which Alcibiades is said to have
been so keen (*Alc.* 2.3–4; cf. *Wasps* 75). *Pace* Dover, Aristophanes' wit is
nothing if not sophisticated, a fact that tells us much about his audience
(which at the Lenaea will have consisted entirely of Athenians).

The interchange at 297–303 when the boy asks for *iskhádas* ("figs" [or
"cunts"])[46] instead of dice, and the Chorus leader remonstrates with him,
includes language that neatly encapsulates Pericles' tastes and political career.
"Figs" refer "emphatically" to both *aphrodísia* and Megara. The *álphita*
("grain"), *xúla* ("wood"), and *ópson* ("food"), for which the Chorus leader has
to pay from his *mistharíou* ("jury fee"), recall several Periclean phenomena.
Two obols was the jury pay in Pericles' day; it had been increased to three by
Cleon in 425 B.C.[47] *Tríton* (301) neatly plays on this: the commodities listed
each cost "one-third" of the pay, whereas in normal parlance, "one-third"
would be a third of a drachma, or two obols. The grain supply was another of
Pericles' concerns (Schol. *Acharnians* 548; and see Chapters 2, 4, and 5), and
"wood" perhaps relates to the Samian campaign. The list may also be an
ironic commentary on the Great King's gift to Themistocles of three cities to
provide "bread, wine, and *ópson*" (Thuc. 1.138.5).[48] If so, Periclean parsimony
is being contrasted with Persian splendor.

TEARS, MONARCHY, COWARDICE, AND ADULTERY

This book is not a commentary on Aristophanes. Its purpose is simply to
suggest that Pericles and Alcibiades may have informed many of Aristophanes' characters. This is why the role of Cleon in *Wasps* is not dwelt upon here.
In addition, to note every parallel between the plays and the anecdotal tradi-

45. Cf. LSJ s.v. *astrágalos*.
46. Henderson 1975, 134.
47. Schol. *Wasps* 88, 300; Ostwald 1986, 220, 222, 223.
48. The precise meaning of *ópson* is uncertain: Badian 1993, 193.

tion relating to Pericles and Alcibiades would make this work even more repetitive than it already is. There are, however, some further general points that tend to confirm an identification between Philocleon and Pericles; these might be summarized under the headings: tears, Pericles' nickname, his alleged cowardice, and his adultery. On two public occasions, Pericles' normally austere reserve was overwhelmed by his emotions to the extent that he wept openly. Apart from his "passion of tears and sobs" at the funeral of his last legitimate child (*Per.* 36.9), Pericles is said to have "shed tears" so effectively on Aspasia's behalf when she was charged with impiety that she was acquitted[49] (and if that particular story "only" has its origins in a scene from comedy,[50] so much the better in the present context). Bdelycleon's prayer that his father should burst into tears when defendants supplicate him (882), and the tears that Philocleon actually sheds when weeping puppies are lined up in front of him (978–979, cf. 983), are, like the Dercetes scene in *Acharnians* (see Chapter 5), likely allusions to Periclean tearfulness. Moreover, a combination of stories of Periclean tears and cruelty probably underlie Philocleon's claim to his slaves that they are men whom he has taught to weep at four measures to the choinix (440).

Comic writers called Pericles "the Olympian," and Aristophanes elsewhere draws attention to his *brontân* ("thundering") and *astráptein* ("lightning").[51] There are several allusions to Philocleon's "Olympian" status in *Wasps,* most notably at 620–627: "Do I not wield great power, in no way less than that of Zeus—in that the same things are said of Zeus and me? If, for example, we make a noise, every passer-by says, "How the court *brontâi* ('is thundering'), O Zeus the king. And if I *astrápsō* ('make lightning'), the rich and the very grand catch their breath and beshit themselves." Then, at 653, Philocleon significantly misinterprets Bdelycleon's invocation to Zeus as an address to himself.

Pericles' natural caution (*Per.* 18.1), and his reluctance to face the Peloponnesian and Boeotian hoplites who invaded Attica in 431 B.C., gave rise to a good deal of discontent, and made him the butt of many jokes, as we now have seen. Philocleon's cowardly nature has been noted in the past with a certain puzzlement.[52] In his youth, Philocleon was able to run away while on campaign with impunity, but "now there are *xùn hóplois ándres hoplîtai* ('fully armed men') drawn up to keep a watch on the passes" (359–361). We

49. Aeschin. *ap. Per.* 32.5; cf. Ath. 13.589e; cf. Ostwald 1986, 194–195.
50. As has often been argued: see Wallace 1993 for bibliography; and Podlecki 1987, 107.
51. *Acharnians* 531; cf. *Com. Adesp.* 10 *CAF* 3.399 *ap. Per.* 8.4.
52. E.g., Dover 1972, 126–127.

have no reason to believe that Pericles' early military career was other than creditable (e.g., *Per.* 7.2), but his caution toward the end of his life may have given rise to the implication that it was not (cf. Chapters 4 and 5). Philocleon's description of his present predicament is exaggerated if it refers to the action on stage, but is a fair assessment of Pericles' view of the thousands of hoplites who had threatened Athens in 431 B.C. (*Per.* 33.5). There may be further implied criticism of Pericles' general unwillingness to embark on a campaign at 1163, where Philocleon objects to putting on a Laconian slipper, lest his foot land on enemy soil (although the primary allusion is perhaps to Pericles' long-standing dislike of the Spartans).[53]

Philocleon's sexual urges are made to parallel those of Pericles, and there are many more offensive jests in this vein. An obscene note certainly pervades the trial of household equipment,[54] but it is the fact that the equipment is supposedly in the house of Pericles and Aspasia that makes the scene really funny. We hear of "the comic poets" charging Pericles "with great profligacy" (*Com. Adesp.* 59 *CAF* 3.410 *ap. Per.* 13.15). *Acharnians* was one such case, and *Wasps* would appear to be another, since there are many apparent references to Pericles' liking for female company. The passage at 605–612, in which Philocleon describes how pleasant it is to come home with his pay from the law courts, is a case in point. Not only had Pericles instituted such payment (*Per.* 9.3; Arist. *Ath. Pol.* 24.3), but the language and situations play on the anecdotal tradition relating to his domestic situation. Everyone *aspázōntai* ("kisses") Philocleon on account of the money (607); there is a pun on "Aspasia" here, as well as a commentary upon Pericles' homecomings ("Pericles never went in or out of his house during the day without kissing Aspasia in an amorous fashion [*espázeto . . . metà toû kataphileîn*]"; *Per.* 24.9). His daughter tongue-kisses him to get his wages out of his mouth (609); such incestuous behavior recalls Pericles' supposed relationship with his daughter-in-law,[55] as well as the fact that there was a widespread feeling on the part of his womenfolk that he was something of a skinflint, that he was not a *dapsilès khorēgós* — "not exactly an impresario" — when it came to money matters (*Per.* 16.5).[56] Philocleon's *gúnaion* ("little wife") presents her puff-pastries

53. *Per.* 10.3–4, 21.1, 31.1, 32.6–33.2; Plut. *Fab.* 30.1.

54. J. G. Griffith 1988, 31–35.

55. Stesimbr. *FGrH* 107 F 19b *ap. Per.* 13.16; F 11 *ap. Per.* 36.6. Cf. Dover's characterization of Philocleon as the kind of man who would spend "his evenings running his hand up his daughter's skirt": 1972, 127.

56. Pericles had of course actually been a producer on at least one occasion, but it is difficult to imagine that the *Persae* was mounted in a cheese-paring fashion, which was presumably the

(*phustèn mâzan;* surely with a play on *mâzan* ["cake"] and *mazón* ["breast"]), which she invites him to nibble (610).

Pericles was very prone to love affairs, as Clearchus noted (*FHG* 2.314 *ap.* Ath. 13.589d). Not for nothing was he called "king of the satyrs" by Hermippus (*PCG* 47.1 *ap. Per.* 33.8). The stories told about him included the charge that he got Pheidias to arrange assignations with respectable ladies who visited the Acropolis to look at work in progress; that Pyrilampes would bribe with peacocks women who granted their favors to Pericles; that Pericles developed a passion for the wife of Menippus, his friend and colleague (*Com. Adesp.* 59 *CAF* 3.410 *ap. Per.* 13.15–16); that Pericles was once in love with Chrysilla of Corinth, daughter of Teleas (Telecl. *PCG* 47 *ap.* Ath. 10.436f); that Aspasia gave hospitality to respectable women with whom Pericles had affairs (*Per.* 32.1); that Pericles took as the price of Cimon's restoration the privilege of lying with Elpinice (Antisth. 35 Caizzi *ap.* Ath. 13.589f); and worst of all, that Pericles lay with his own daughter-in-law, the wife of Xanthippus.[57]

PERICLES AT THE SYMPOSIUM

His womanizing apart, Pericles' life was characterized by austerity and restraint. This was a matter of deliberate policy, for he feared lest he might be suspected of tyrannical ambitions. He consequently

> altered his mode of life; was never seen in any street except that which led to the Agora and the Bouleuterion, and declined all invitations to dinner, and all similar social gatherings, to such an extent that during the whole of his political life he never dined with one of his friends except when his first cousin Euryptolemus was married. On this occasion he sat at the table till the libations were poured, upon which he at once got up and went away. For solemnity is wont to unbend at festive gatherings, and a majestic demeanor is hard to keep up when one is in company.[58]

---

basis of his womenfolk's complaints. Cf. Thuc. 2.40.1 for a view of Periclean canniness with regard to wealth and ostentation.

57. Stesimbr. *FGrH* 107 F 19b *ap. Per.* 13.16; F 11 *ap. Per.* 36.6.

58. *Per.* 7.5–6; cf. Aristides (3.17), on Pericles' "providing no avenue of approach for flatterers."

In other words, Pericles had never, in all the years he was in politics, attended a symposium, the drinking-party that regularly took place after the eating was over, and the libations were poured.[59] One of the principal strands of *Wasps* is to make Philocleon attend a symposium. So unaccustomed is he to sympotic practice that he has to be taught how to behave elegantly at a party. We can probably take it that Philocleon's trial run (1208–1264) showed him to be gauche in the extreme.[60] He is persuaded to sing *skólia* ("party songs"; 1222); an apt image, given that Pericles was said to have set up *nómous hósper skólia* ("laws like party songs").[61] Philocleon is so out of his depth that he wonders whether he is at a dream banquet (1218)—another apt image, given Pericles' attested interest in oneiromancy (*Per.* 13.13; Pliny *HN* 22.44).

Once again, Hermogenes' account (*Meth.* 34) of the techniques employed by the writers of Old Comedy[62] comes to mind in the context of Philocleon's party-going. It is as though Aristophanes has taken Pericles' most treasured principle and exaggerated its opposite, just as in *Clouds* he poked fun at his spirit of scientific enquiry, and in both *Knights* and *Clouds* he made Pericles' outspoken criticism of Sophocles' pederasty the occasion for unworthy imputations. Thus, when Philocleon finally arrives at an upper-class symposium,[63] he is reported to have been the *hubristótatos* (1303: "most outrageous") person there. We learn of his behavior in a kind of "messenger speech" delivered by Xanthias (1299–1325). Philocleon tells all kinds of irrelevant jokes (1320–1321; cf. 1399–1400), prancing and literally farting around (1305). Pericles' usual demeanor was the very opposite: disinclined to unbend at a party (*Per.* 7.5–6), and restrained to a degree (*Per.* 5.1; Plut. *Mor.* 800c).

Philocleon has in fact taken on many of the characteristics we generally associate with the young Alcibiades: reckless drunkenness, buffoonery, and irresponsible hooliganism; it is the kind of "exchange of roles across the generation gap"[64] we saw at the end of *Clouds,* when Strepsiades appeared to adopt Pheidippidean traits. This seems to have been the main thrust of Aristophanes' play, perhaps implying that just as Pericles might be perceived as having been more or less directly responsible for the political excesses that occurred

59. E.g., Pl. *Symp.* 176a; Xen. *Symp.* 2.1; O. Murray 1990a.

60. Cf. Henderson 1975, 80–81.

61. *Acharnians* 532. On *nómoi,* see further Ostwald 1986, 129–136.

62. Cf. G. Murray 1933, 86.

63. On the social status of the participants at the symposium at *Wasps* 1299ff., see MacDowell 1971, 303; Storey 1985; Carter 1986, 65–69.

64. Handley 1993, 428.

after his death, so he might also be held responsible for the excesses of his tyrannically disposed (cf. 417, 486–502)[65] de facto son.

It is not so much that Bdelycleon ceases to matter in *Wasps*[66] as that the comic inversion results in his Alcibiadean persona being both ethically and linguistically subsumed in the character of Philocleon. Thus at 1385–1386, where Philocleon strikes Bdelycleon in a drunken fit, we are perhaps to imagine Alcibiades getting his own medicine in a comic reversal of what we might almost call the "father-beating convention," and Philocleon's dancing and prancing at 1485–1496 are typically Alcibiadean rather than Periclean activities. Indeed, Bdelycleon's increasingly stuffy attitude[67] and the almost parental protectiveness he displays toward his wayward father (1418–1420) may imply that the Alcibiadean character is metamorphosed into a Periclean one. The Chorus's hymn of praise for Philocleon (1450–1473), for all its irony,[68] suggests as much. Philocleon, meanwhile, tells stories about chariots (1427), heads (1428), a jar (*ekhînos:* 1436, 1437),[69] and *Noûs* (1440), themes that concern either Alcibiades or Pericles.

The degree to which later writers such as Plutarch were dependent, especially for anecdotes, upon the comic tradition is extremely difficult to determine. But the exercise conducted in this book has one advantage in that the possibility of a later anecdote concerning a specific individual having its origin in drama can be used in arguments regarding the presence of that individual at all in dramatic contexts. Though it is unlikely that Plutarch derived his thumbnail sketch of Pericles never being "seen in any street except that which led to the Agora and the Bouleuterion, and declin[ing] all invitations to dinner, and all similar social gatherings" from a knowing reading of the political allegory of *Wasps* or a similar play, the sentence does contain the essence of the plot of *Wasps:* the first two-thirds of the play make fun of the civic responsibilities Pericles took so seriously, and the last third consists of an imaginative picture of what might have happened had Pericles freed himself from his inhibitions in the way in which his wayward ward did so frequently. Alternatively, *Wasps* documents a rapid transition from exaggerated *polupragmosúnē* to excessive *apragmosúnē*. Although it is no longer necessary

---

65. Especially if Thucydides was right to see the Athenian empire already a tyranny under Pericles: 2.63.2; cf. Meiggs 1972, 379. See, too, Seager 1967.

66. *Pace* Sommerstein (1983, xviii).

67. E.g., his disapproving comments on wine at 1392–1393.

68. Cf. Macleod 1983, 50.

69. Cf. LSJ s.v.: "vase in which the notes of evidence were sealed up by the *diaitētai,* in cases of appeal."

to argue for the unity of the plot of *Wasps*,[70] or even to acknowledge the question "What is the ending doing there, anyway?"[71] it is interesting to see such a tightly knit arrangement apparently based so closely on Pericles' day-to-day existence.

Pericles and Cleon were rivals during Pericles' lifetime, but we can nevertheless detect a certain continuity of both domestic and foreign policy between the one and the other. It has been noted that Thucydides (who may owe much to Aristophanes, as we have seen throughout this book), goes out of his way to "draw attention to the affinity between the policies of Pericles and Cleon."[72] This may explain why the Periclean Philocleon bears a name apparently favorable to the new demagogue, whereas since Alcibiades' political ambitions were probably impeded by Cleon — and almost certainly so since his enrollment in the cavalry — Bdelycleon bears a name that carried the opposite meaning. Jurors were the mainstay of both Pericles' and Cleon's political platforms. If it really was the case that "the elderly poor, who accounted for a high proportion of Athenian jurors, were among Cleon's most faithful supporters"[73] (the evidence comes entirely from *Wasps* and is therefore not wholly trustworthy), this may account for the way in which Philocleon is represented as having different social affinities from those of his sophisticated son. Like the allegorical characterization of Strepsiades and Pheidippides in *Clouds,* to show Philocleon and Bdelycleon "affecting allegiance to different social classes" was a very clever, and trenchant, "comic device to highlight the generation gap."[74] Such a reading would also remove the "fundamental inconsistency" between Philocleon's sentimental bond with the chorus of jurors and his apparent status as "the retired head of a relatively opulent household" with "access . . . to circles of considerable influence in the state."[75] Although Pericles was very well born indeed, Aristophanes assimilates his Periclean characters, Dicaeopolis, Strepsiades, and Philocleon included, to the social class with which Pericles deliberately chose to be associated. In Aristophanes' next extant play, *Peace,* we thus find Pericles appropriately cast in the guise of a low-life god.

70. See MacDowell 1971, 7 n. 1; Heath 1987a, 48–49.
71. D. Parker 1962, 2.
72. Westlake 1968, 65; cf. Gomme 1962, 107–108; Romilly 1963, 171; Connor 1971.
73. Sommerstein 1983, 164.
74. Ostwald 1986, 235.
75. Konstan 1985, 37.

ALCIBIADES AND PERICLES
ON OLYMPUS
Aristophanes' *Peace*

Aristophanes' *Peace* was performed in Athens at the City Dionysia of 421 B.C. (at which it won second prize), shortly before the ratification of the treaty between Athens and Sparta, which was known from the start as the Peace of Nicias. *Peace* is very much concerned with these developments, and takes the form of a patriotic appeal to an Alcibiades who was bitterly opposed to talk of peace to change his view. To this end, Aristophanes uses various characters to reflect different aspects of Alcibiades' personality, notably Trygaeus, who is slowly transformed into an increasingly more responsible and civic-minded individual. By 421 B.C., Alcibiades was of an age to be elected to public office,[1] which may account for the reference to a "would-be general" at 450[2] and may also explain why Trygaeus is shown as an older man, rather than as the young tearaway who had been the object of much criticism in earlier plays. Alcibiades' presence on the political stage was a fact that had to be accepted, but there was a hope that his excesses might be curbed. In the event, Aristophanes' appeal to Alcibiades to drop his opposition to the Peace of Nicias

1. Cf. Develin 1989, 429. In fact, Alcibiades was not to be elected general until the spring of 420 B.C.: ibid., 142–148 (he was to hold the post for the next five years).
2. Hatzfeld 1951, 83. Line 451 (which mentions a "slave preparing to run away") may allude to the time when Socrates, being so enamored of Alcibiades, "hunted him down like a runaway slave" (*Alc.* 6.1); cf. Pl. *Symp.* 216b, where Alcibiades "déguerpit comme l'esclave en fuite" (Loraux 1981, 321).

failed. Personal spite against its architect seems to have been the main reason for Alcibiades' reluctance to collaborate with an arrangement that, if Aristophanes' analysis was correct, offered a hope of real peace after more than a decade of wasteful warfare.

The plays produced together with *Peace* at the City Dionysia of 421 B.C. were Eupolis' *Kolakes* ("Flatterers") and Leucon's *Phrateres* ("Clansmen"). Both seem to have had a basis in contemporary politics. *Phrateres* was apparently aimed at the demagogue Hyperbolus (*CAF* 1.704.1), a politician who, interestingly enough, shared with Alcibiades the distinction of having had his individual mode of speech lampooned on the comic stage (Pl. Com. *PCG* 183), whereas *Kolakes* dealt with both Callias, Alcibiades' brother-in-law,[3] and Alcibiades himself (Eup. *PCG* 171). It will be argued in this chapter that *Peace* is every bit as political a work as these seem to have been, and every bit as political as the other plays of Aristophanes discussed so far.

ALCIBIADES AND TRYGAEUS

The information Aristophanes provides about Trygaeus' estate at Athmonia (190) is of fundamental importance in establishing a link with Alcibiades, since *epikarpía Athmonoî* ("crops from Athmonia") appear in a significant position on an inscription listing the possessions of those who were convicted of impiety in 414 B.C.[4] The inscription is lacunose, but the place where the relevant lines occur makes it likely that the estate in question belonged to Alcibiades.[5] Trygaeus' name in any case evokes both vinosity and garrulousness. *Trúx* (genitive, *trugós*) means "new, raw wine,"[6] and Alcibiades was not abstemious in this respect (Pliny *HN* 14.144; cf. *Alc.* 1.8; Plut. *Mor.* 800d). Trygaeus' name also puns on *trṓgōn* ("turtledove"), and it may even have contributed to the dung-beetle conceit in the opening scene of *Peace,* for the proverb "more talkative than a turtledove" had its origin in the fact that "the turtledove not only never stops speaking through its mouth, but they say that it utters much through its hinder parts also" (Ael. *NA* 12.10, citing Men. *CAF* 416).

---

3. Schol. *Birds* 282; Ath. 5.218c (cf. *PCG* 5.380–381).
4. ML 79, lines 22–23; Pritchett 1953, 241.
5. Cf. the photograph in Pritchett 1953, pl. 68. The late David Lewis gave very helpful advice on this point.
6. LSJ s.v.

Trygaeus also shares Alcibiades' speech mannerism, pronouncing *rho* as *lambda* (*Wasps* 44–48; *Alc.* 1.6–7). He claims not only to be a vine-dresser (190) but also to be *oud' erastès pragmátōn* (191: "no lover of disputes"). Spoken in Alcibiadean fashion, this would play on *oud' elastès plēgmátōn* ("no striker of blows"),[7] which is an ironic but appropriate description if Alcibiades was indeed in Aristophanes' mind, given his attested physical attacks on one of his servants (*Alc.* 3.1), on a rival *choregus* ([Andoc.] 4.20–21; *Alc* 16.5),[8] on a schoolmaster (*Alc.* 7.1), and upon his future father-in-law (*Alc.* 8.1).

It might, however, be argued with some justice that our *Peace* could not be about Alcibiades because *he* was notoriously young,[9] whereas Trygaeus is described as an "old" man, a *gérōn* (860), a *presbútēs* (856–857), albeit one who is turned "young" again later in the play (861). It may be, though, that Aristophanes was drawing attention to Alcibiades' precocious insistence on the privileges of senior citizenship, for which he had recently qualified. Alcibiades' tender age was a current issue in 421 B.C.,[10] as is clear from Thucydides' very first reference to him, in an account that also places him in the war party opposed to the Peace of Nicias.

> Foremost among them was Alcibiades the son of Cleinias, a man who would have been thought young in any other city, but was influential by reason of his high descent: he sincerely preferred the Argive alliance, but at the same time he took part against the Lacedaemonians from temper, and because his pride was touched. For they had not consulted him, but had negotiated the peace through Nicias and Laches, despising his youth, and disregarding an ancient connection with his family, who had been their *proxenoi;* a connection which his grandfather had renounced, and he, by the attention which he had paid to the captives from Sphacteria, had hoped to have renewed. Piqued at the small respect which was shown to all his claims . . . he declared that the Lacedaemonians were not to be trusted.[11]

If, however, *Peace* really is (as will be argued here) couched in the form of a patriotic appeal to Alcibiades to put his youthful excesses behind him, this would explain Trygaeus' relative maturity.

7. Cf. *plagá,* the Doric form of *plēgé* ("blow"): LSJ s.v.
8. Probably before 415 B.C. (see the date [whether real or dramatic] for [Andoc.] 4 proposed by Raubitschek [1948]), and perhaps even before 421 B.C.
9. As late as 415 B.C., Nicias was still apparently dwelling on Alcibiades' youth: Thuc. 6.12–13.
10. Cf. Develin 1985, on precociousness.
11. Thuc. 5.43; cf. 6.89; *Alc.* 14.1–2; *POxy.* 411, 105–106.

Alcibiades' traditional family ties with Sparta were reinforced by his Spartan name (Thuc. 8.6), and by his having had Spartan nannies (*Alc.* 1.3 [Amycla]; Schol. Pl. *Alc.* 1.121d [Lanice]). At the time of the performance of *Peace,* he was attempting to renew the *proxenía* with Sparta that his grandfather had enjoyed.[12] And it is Alcibiades' earlier philo-Laconism, of which we also hear in Plutarch (*Alc.* 14.1), that seems to be parodied in the opening lines of *Peace.* The Spartan way of life was characterized as *tèn mâzan kaì tríbōna* ("barley bread and Spartan cloak"; Plut. *Cleom.* 16.7). The repetition of *mâzan* in lines 1, 3, and 4, for all that the cake was made of excrement, will have reminded the audience of the Spartans' staple diet of barley bread. If *tríbe* ("knead"; 8), *tetrimménēs* ("kneaded"; 12), *tríb'* (16), and *trípsas* (27) were deliberate puns, they will have recalled the name of the Spartans' simple dress.[13] The Spartans were notorious for their lack of cleanliness (cf. *Birds* 1282), and the material that the slaves are kneading will surely have led to a state of *rupokondulía* ("having dirty knuckles"), a condition with which they were supposed to be beset (Pl. Com. *PCG* 132; Ar. *PCG* 736). Indeed, we may well suppose that the slaves are Spartans, for if "repetition for the sake of emphasis is . . . recorded as a leading characteristic of [the Laconian] style, adding to its pungency,"[14] we have examples of such repetition in the first two words of the play (*Aîr' aîre:* 1) and ten lines later (*hetéran hetéran:* 11).

Moreover, the deities mentioned by the slaves — Zeus Kataibates,[15] Apollo, Aphrodite, and the Graces — were all venerated at Sparta.[16] Zeus Skataibates (cf. *Diòs kataibátou,* 42) would, as most agree, have produced an additional scatalogical resonance. Irrespective of any possible Alcibiadean reference, the scene would have been a joke at the Spartan enemy's expense, some of whom may well have been in the audience. But if Alcibiades was indeed in Aristophanes' sights, there may be yet more layers of meaning. The *téras* (42) must be, as H. Usener saw,[17] the "thunderbolt" of Zeus. Alcibi-

---

12. Thuc. 5.43.2; cf. Bloedow 1991a, 52.

13. Cf. the pun on the laconizing Socrates' *tribōn* at *Clouds* 870 (Chapter 2).

14. Francis 1991–1993, 203.

15. Usener (1905) suggested that the cult of Zeus Kataibates (well known at the Spartan colony of Tarentum: Ath. 12.522d–f) was the same as that of Zeus Kappotas, near Gythium (Paus. 3.22.1); cf. Cook 1914–1940, 942.

16. Wide 1893, 63–96 (Apollo), 136–146 (Aphrodite), 210–214 (Charites); cf. Guarducci 1984.

17. Usener 1905, 13.

ades had attracted criticism for having put aside his ancestral shield emblem and adopted an Eros wielding a (Zeus') thunderbolt instead (*Alc.* 16.1; Ath. 12.534e). Aristophanes then neatly indicates[18] that the beetle is intended to be Cleon. In political terms, Trygaeus' ride on the back of the dung beetle may symbolize Alcibiades' replacement of Cleon as the representative of the war party, just as his adoption of a thunderbolt-wielding Eros as a shield emblem may have been a witty claim to the political mantle of the Olympian. The journey to Olympus itself, moreover, may allegorize Alcibiades' political ambitions (to achieve the same status as his guardian) in a similar fashion.

Trygaeus' first words (62–63) are susceptible of meaningful lambdacization: "O Zeus, why on earth are you enduring [if *draseíeis* plays on *tlaseíeis*] our *león* ('people')?" There may be a punning reference here to the Spartan Leon, of whom we hear later as one of the Spartan ambassadors sent to Athens in 420 B.C., the year after the performance of *Peace.* He was one of three "who were thought likely to be acceptable at Athens" (Thuc. 5.44.3), which perhaps suggests that he had been to the city before, and had engaged in high-level negotiations with the authorities. If so, he may have been one of the Spartan envoys who had paid Alcibiades "small respect . . . despising his youth" and thus contributed to his "pique." Just as Alcibiades' pique lay behind his resistance to the Peace of Nicias, his antipathy to the peacemakers on both sides seems to provide the background to the plot of Aristophanes' *Peace.*

CHARIOT-RACING AND PHILOSOPHY

Alcibiades' speech was also characterized by the frequent use of the potential optative.[19] The slave's next quotation of his master (*pôs án pot' aphikoímēn àn euthú toû Diós;* [68: "How on earth might one go right up to Zeus?"]) is just such a usage. The beetle is treated by Trygaeus as a racehorse—another of Alcibiades' passions, as we saw in the discussion of *Clouds.* The beetle is from Etna, not simply the home of large beetles, but in its day a city famous for chariot-racing (Pind. *Pyth.* 1, *Nem.* 1, 9; Bacchyl. 20c.7). "Why do you *meteōrokopeîs* ('prate about high things')?" asks one of the slaves (92). The terminology recalls a description of the new learning that had become fashion-

---

18. See the Introduction. Rosen (1984) has some persuasive arguments to explain why an Ionian makes the point.
19. Tompkins 1972, 214.

able at Athens during the previous couple of decades, and which was, as we have seen, lampooned in *Clouds* (Chapters 2 and 3). Trygaeus declares that he is going to "fly over all the Greeks" (93), which may be a perception on the part of Aristophanes of incipient tyranny.[20] Trygaeus will devise a new enterprise (*tólmēma néon palamēsámenos;* 94). *Tólmēma* was a word that Thucydides was later to use in his allegorical character sketch of Alcibiades,[21] whereas *palamēsámenos* may stand for what has been called, in only a slightly different context, "the special skills of sophistry,"[22] with, however, violent overtones.

HERMES AND PERICLES

Pericles in *Peace* underlies the figure of Hermes, a deity who "led the souls of the dead down to Hades," who was "essentially the god of simple people," and who was "used by Zeus to run his errands."[23] Hermes would thus be appropriate for the characterization on stage of one who had been dead for seven years, and who in life had depended for his political support upon the humbler members of Athenian society. Pericles had, however, been known as "the Olympian": to present him in the guise of Zeus' messenger was unflattering. It is Hermes who opens the door when Trygaeus eventually arrives on the threshold of *tền oikían tền toû Diós* (178: "the house of Zeus"), having asked, "Who is within the doors of Zeus?" To have shown Pericles as the Olympian deity himself might perhaps have been impious, but to show him as a servant was appropriately demeaning. The audience, however, will have been led to believe that they were about to see "Zeus" (cf. 68, 77, 104, 161, 178, 179), and if they expected to see a Periclean character, Hermes would have been an unexpected, but amusingly fitting, substitute for the Olympian.

The initial dialogue between Trygaeus and Hermes is redolent with pollution imagery, suitably enough if the two figures are based on individuals who, like Alcibiades and Pericles, were afflicted with the Alcmaeonid curse. Both individuals, moreover, might also have been held to be subject to the *miasma*

---

20. Cf. the slave's address, *ô déspot' ánax* ("O lord and master"), at *Peace* 90. If it points up Alcibiades' tyrannical inclinations, this would explain Trygaeus' insistence (91) that the slave be silent.

21. Thuc. 6.54.1; cf. Vickers 1995a.

22. Blumenthal 1983, 64.

23. Guthrie 1950, 90–91.

attendant on those who indulged in sexual excess.[24] This would explain the emphasis (in the modern sense) on pollution in the exchange, which begins *ō miaré*[25] ("O polluted one"; 182)—and continues in similar vein (183–184). Trygaeus asserts that his very name is polluted to a degree (185); so is his family (186), and so is his father (187). In view of the way in which Alcibiades' stage fathers to date have been evocations of Pericles, it seems likely that a similar implication is being made here, and made the more amusing because it is being said to another analogue of the dead statesman. (If this sounds complicated, it is, but any complexity is to be attributed to Aristophanes.) "What have you come for?" asks Hermes at 192. Trygaeus ostensibly says that he has come to give Hermes some meat: *tà kréa tautí soi phérōn;* lambdacized, however, this would play on *tà kléa,* with a pun on the *kléos* ("renown") element of the name Pericles. At 193 Trygaeus calls Hermes *glískhrōn* ("niggardly"); if this is a reference to Pericles, then it is to his penny-pinching ways, which contributed much to Aristophanes' characterization of Strepsiades and Philocleon.[26]

The gods have left, but the language used by Hermes to describe their departure (*exōikisménoi* [197], *exōikísanto* [203]) recalls the expressions Thucydides uses (*exoikísantes*) for the forcible evacuation from their homes by Pericles of Euboeans of Histiaea in 445 B.C. (Thuc. 1.114.3), and for the relocation (*exōikéthē*), also by Pericles, of many inhabitants of Attica at the beginning of the Peloponnesian War (Thuc. 2.17.1). The establishment of War in their former dwelling (205: *hin' êsan autoí, tòn Pólemon katóikisan*), moreover, is reminiscent in its phraseology of Thucydides' description of the occupation by refugees of the sacred Pelasgian precinct. This had occurred in contravention of both a curse and the Delphic oracle, but "under sudden pressure of necessity." "The occupation came about *dià tòn pólemon* ('on account of the war')," says Thucydides, "and the oracle without mentioning the war foresaw that the place would be inhabited (*katoikisthēsómenon*) someday for no good" (Thuc. 2.17.2). Such parallels both support an equation between Hermes and Pericles and may also be further evidence for Thucydides' use of Aristophanes as an aide-mémoire.

There are other possible Periclean references to be found at 201–202, where Hermes says that he guards (*tērô*) the gods' *skeuária* ("little things"), their *khutrídia* ("little buckets"), their *sanídia* ("little boards"), and their *am-*

24. R. Parker 1983, 94–100.

25. According to all manuscripts. *Miaré* is unaccountably emended to *bdeluré* in most modern texts.

26. See Chapters 2, 3, and 7; and cf. *glískhra* used in a Periclean context by Plutarch: *Per.* 36.2.

phoreídia ("little amphoras"). *Tērô* smacks of the guard duty that was a prominent feature of life in wartime Athens (Thuc. 2.13.7 [*etēreîto*], cf. 2.22.1, 2.24.1), whereas *sanídes* were a notorious part of the lore surrounding Pericles: he was said to have bound the Samian captives to such objects in the Agora at Miletus in 439 B.C. (Duris *FGrH* 76 F 67 *ap. Per.* 28.2). The use of diminutives ending in *-ion,* moreover, recalls their frequent use in contexts involving those other evocations of Pericles, namely, Dicaeopolis,[27] the Megarian,[28] and the Sycophant[29] in *Acharnians,* Strepsiades[30] and the Stronger Argument[31] in *Clouds,* and Philocleon[32] and the Chorus of Jurymen[33] in *Wasps.* They are used either by figures who are characterized as Pericles, or by others who are trying to wheedle something out of one of them.[34] In a detailed study of Greek diminutives in *-ion,* W. Petersen found the earliest uses to be *pódion,* in a play of Epicharmus (Epich. 57 Kaibel), who died c. 440 B.C., and the *boúdion* of Hermippus (*CAF* 35.2), Pericles' contemporary.[35] He wondered why there was a "sudden productivity" and "rapid spread" of the word form:[36] could it be that these developments occurred because Aristophanes evoked a characteristic aspect of Pericles' language—the equivalent of his lampooning the speech mannerisms of an Alcibiades or Hyperbolus?

27. E.g., *skhoiníon* (*Acharnians* 22: "little rope"), *paidíoisi* (132: "children"), *Euripídion* (404: "little Euripides"), *pilídion* (439: "little pointy hat"), *skeuáriōn* (451: "little things"), *spurídion* (453: "little basket"), *kotulískion* (459: "little cup"), *khutrídion* (463: "little jar"), *spurídion* (469), *Euripídion* (475), *andrária* (517: "little men"), *khlanískia* (519: "little cloaks"), *lagóidion* (520: "little hare"), *khoirídion* (521: "piglet"), *khoiridíoisin* (806), *khoirí'* (808), *khoirídia* (812), *khoirídi'* (830).

28. E.g., *khoiríōn* (740), *rugkhía* (744: "little snouts"), *khoiríōn* (747), *khoiría* (749); *khoirídia* (834).

29. E.g., *khoirídia* (819).

30. E.g., *Pheidippídion* (*Clouds* 80: "little Pheidippides"), *oikídion* (92: "little house"), *paidíon* (132: "child"), *pragmátion* (197: "trifling matter"), *Sōkratídion* (223, 237, 746: "little Socrates"); *gnōmídiōi* (321: "little thought"), *zōmídion* (389: "bit of soup"), *gastrídiou* (392: "little stomach").

31. E.g., *pēridiou* (*Clouds* 923: "little bag"); *meirakíois* (928: "lads"); *himatíoisi* (987: "cloaks"; cf. LSJ s.v.); *meirákion* (990); *pornidíou* (997: "little whore"); *pragmatíou* (1004: "little matter").

32. E.g., *kalódion* (*Wasps* 379: "little rope"), *dikídion* (511: "little lawsuit"), *gúnaion* (610: "little wife"), *khōríon* (850: "little place").

33. E.g., *paidíon* (293: "child"), *mistharíou* (300: "small fee"), *melíttion* (366: "little bee").

34. E.g., in *Knights: Dēmídion* (726: "little Demus")—Paphlagon addressing Demus; *kulíkhnion* (906: "little jar"); *helkúdria* (907: "little sores"); *ophthalmídiō* (909: "little eyes"); *ô pappídion* (1215: "Daddikins")—the Sausage-seller speaking to Demus. In *Wasps: thulákion* (313–314: "little bag"), addressed by the Boy to the Chorus leader; *rēmatíois* (668: "little phrases"), addressed by Bdelycleon to Philocleon. In *Peace: khoirídion* (374: "piglet"); *hōrmídion* (382: "little Hermes"), Trygaeus speaking to Hermes.

35. Petersen 1910, 202–203, 218.

36. Ibid., 139.

Hermes explains why the other gods have gone away (211–219), and neatly characterizes the attitudes of the belligerents in the Peloponnesian War by quoting typical Spartan and Athenian statements. Trygaeus says of the latter (220) that "those words (*rēmátōn*) bear the stamp of our people"; lambdacized, however, there would be a play on *lḗmatōn* ("arrogance"). Trygaeus learns that War personified has hidden a statue of Peace away in a deep cavern, and that he is preparing a pestle and mortar with which to pound up the Greek states. By means of polymorphic characterization, Aristophanes effectively confronts his hero Trygaeus with the effects of Alcibiades' recent warlike policies, for War appears to share both Alcibiades' speech mannerism and his sometime laconism; in addition, he fails to achieve his stated objective of stirring up the conflict again. He may thus reflect an Alcibiades who "from the very outset opposed the peace" (Plut. *Nic.* 10.3) and did his best — but ineffectually — to ruin it. Alcibiades was later to be famous for his ability, chameleonlike, to adopt foreign ways and modes of speech; he "never found anything, good or bad, which he could not imitate to the life" (*Alc.* 23.5), and thanks to his Spartan nursery training was probably already adept at mimicking Spartan ways of speech.

War begins (236) by indulging in Laconian repetition, and if he lambdacizes, he addresses "audacious floaters (*plōtoì plōtoì plōtoì polutlḗmones*),"[37] which sounds silly, and was probably meant to. Thucydides seems to put a similar expression into Alcibiades' mouth at the beginning of his speech to the Spartans,[38] and Eupolis includes no fewer than three in a fragment that is generally taken to include a dialogue involving Alcibiades.[39] War then threatens to punch his hearers on the chin. As we have already seen, this was a well-known Alcibiadean ploy (cf. *Alc.* 3.1, 7.1, 8.1, 16.5; [Andoc.] 4.20–21), but it causes Trygaeus considerable alarm (238–241). During the next few lines, War throws into his mortar various items that carry meanings at the culinary

37. For *brotoi, brotoi, brotoi* ("mortals, mortals, mortals").

38. Thuc. 6.89.1 (a play on *prôton* ["first"] and *plōtón* ["afloat"]); Alcibiades had recently crossed from Southern Italy to the Peloponnese "in a small boat": Thuc. 6.88.9.

39. Eup. *PCG* 385 *ap.* Ath. 1.17d (preserving the manuscript readings), 3: *prôtos, prôt', 5: prôtos.* Puns involving *plōtós* would generate talk of "boozing at sea" (cf. 3: *plōt' epipínein*). In 405, Alcibiades was accused of having entrusted his command to "men who owed their influence with him to boozing and cracking seamen's jokes" (*Alc.* 36.2). The specific reference is to Antiochus, who had been Alcibiades' close friend since the mid-420s (*Alc.* 10.2).

and political levels. On the culinary level, Prasiae at 242 is a punning reference to leeks (*prása*); Megara is mentioned at 246–249 on account of one of
its staple products, garlic; Sicily (250) was famous for cheese, and Attica (252)
for honey. On the political level, Laconian Prasiae was laid waste by Pericles
in 430 (Thuc. 2.56.6); Megara also suffered at his hands (Thuc. 4.66.10);
Sicily was an island for which "the Athenians had a hankering even during the lifetime of Pericles," a hankering that Alcibiades eventually "fanned
into a flame" (*Alc.* 17.1–2); the Attic honey is said (254) to cost four obols
(*tetróbolon*). Not only was this word proverbial for "soldier's pay,"[40] but four
obols happens to have been the going daily rate for military pay at the time
Peace was performed.[41]

Alcibiades was a leading member of the Athenian faction that favored a
continuation of hostilities in 421 B.C. (Thuc. 5.43); hence, perhaps, his characterization as War in *Peace*. Trygaeus, however, appears to represent some
of the more benign and peaceful aspects of Alcibiades' nature; Trygaeus
has been said, with justice, to be "a hero more distinctly characterized than
perhaps any other personage in [Aristophanes'] works . . . shrewd, practical,
brave, and imperturbable."[42] Aristophanes may have felt that he could win
the prize by stressing the positive side of Alcibiades' character, and by making
an appeal to any desire he may have had for a return to his country estates —
at Athmonia or elsewhere — and for the delights of peace. Such an appeal
would in any case have been a patriotic one, for the Athenians "more than
any other Hellenic people" had been "accustomed to residing in the country"
(Thuc. 2.15.1), and the expression of patriotic values was a helpful means of
winning the dramatic prize.[43]

War's slave arrives, only to be thumped hard — perhaps another allusion
to Alcibiades' way with subordinates, as well as to the Spartans' way with
helots (p. 164 below). War's language also allows for meaningful lambdacism.
The slave is told to run[44] and fetch a pestle (259: *aletríbanon*), perhaps with a
pun on *Areithlíbanon* ("a device for arousing war"). The pestle is not to be
found, and the slave is told to go and get one from the Athenians. In the
event, Athens and Sparta have neither pestles nor "devices for arousing war."
War goes off to make his own, and Trygaeus asks for assistance in rescuing

40. LSJ s.v. *tetróbolon.*
41. The terms of the treaty between Athens, Argos, Mantinea, and Elis in 420 B.C. included
daily provision for hoplites, light-armed troops, and archers at the rate of three Aeginetan
obols (Thuc. 5.47.6), equivalent to four Attic obols.
42. Platnauer 1964, viii–ix.
43. Cf. Goldhill 1987.
44. On running at Sparta, see Chapter 9 on *Birds* 77, etc.

Peace. If there is a political point being made here, and if War and Trygaeus represent different aspects of Alcibiades' multifaceted character, Aristophanes may be suggesting that it is possible for Alcibiades to put his fruitless belligerence behind him and put his energies instead into fostering the peace that everyone—farmers, merchants, carpenters, artisans, metics, foreigners, and islanders (296–298)—really wants.

And this is the message of the rest of the play. Trygaeus disapproves (301–345) of the Chorus prancing around in the way in which Alcibiades in his cups was presumably wont to do. The seriousness of Trygaeus' intentions is clear from the fact that he gives Hermes a gold phiale (424–425) from which to pour *spondaí*, the libations that regularly accompanied peace treaties.[45] The deities invoked are those of peace and sex (456), and Trygaeus is made specifically to exclude the war gods Ares and Enyalius. The manner in which Trygaeus criticizes the different groups pulling on ropes and trying to extract Peace from where she is buried perhaps recalls the political situation in 421 B.C., and if Trygaeus reflects Alcibiades, his criticisms show the latter as he would have been had he changed his policy. Alcibiades had opposed the Spartans, but Trygaeus now appears to think well of their efforts to achieve peace (478); Alcibiades had "sincerely preferred the Argive alliance" (Thuc. 5.43.2), but Trygaeus threatens to strike the Argive representatives (493); Alcibiades had opposed the peace *tout court,* but Trygaeus' greeting once Peace is dragged on stage is effusive (520–538). There is less ambiguity of a political nature in Trygaeus' later speeches, though possibilities for suggestive wordplay are not overlooked.

PERICLES, SERVANTS, AND SHEEP

But what of Pericles? Hermes continues to behave in a manner in keeping with the negative view of the statesman we have seen thus far. Hermes' stated liking for gold (425) may have been an unworthy imputation based on Pericles' difficulties over the public accounts.[46] Hermes' dislike of Megara (500–502) may reflect Pericles' hatred of that city (e.g., *Per.* 30.1–2), and the suggestion that the Chorus stand closer to the sea (507), the maritime policy

---

45. Hermes' eager acceptance of the vessel (425) will be an ironic commentary on Pericles' famous incorruptibility: *Per.* 16.3.

46. With, perhaps, an ironic reference to Pericles' claim to be above bribery; cf. Thuc. 2.60.5, 2.65.8; and Harvey 1985.

that Pericles conducted. The criticism of Euripides (532–534) echoes the views of that other Periclean character, Dicaeopolis (*Acharnians* 395–479; see Chapter 4). *Noûs* ("Mind") as the active principle of the Universe was, as we have seen, a concept devised by Pericles' adviser Anaxagoras. This is why Hermes asks in the first line on his re-entry at 362 what Trygaeus *dianoeî* ("has in mind"), and why when the Chorus ask him (602) to explain whatever happened to Peace, they address him as the most *eunoústate* ("kindlyminded") of deities. At 603–648 the Chorus are told the history of the outbreak and conduct of the war in terms that, if they are supposedly spoken by a character who stands for Pericles, are ironic.

The scandal surrounding Phiedias' statue of Athena is said to have been the start of the trouble (605), but Pericles contrived the Megarian decree as a diversionary tactic (606–614); though the details of Phiedias' problems are uncertain,[47] his involvement with Pericles is beyond doubt, and Pericles' punishment of Megara has been a constant Aristophanic theme. Despite sizable bribes to the Spartan leaders (622), war broke out; the reference is either to the one-off payment of ten talents "for a necessary purpose" made by Pericles in 445 B.C., or (though the story is inherently unlikely) to an annual ten-talent bribe sent by Pericles to the chief magistrates at Sparta (Theophr. *ap. Per.* 23.2). Hermes then summarizes (632–648) the political and social changes at Athens, culminating in Cleon's leadership. Although Pericles will have known of Cleon's ambitions (cf. *Per.* 33.8), he died before the victory at Pylos. This may be why Hermes has to consult the statue of Peace[48] to be told what happened at Pylos, and the various possibilities for peace that victory had presented (661–667). Hermes also has to be brought up to date on currently active politicians (673–691) and playwrights (694–703).

Hermes' final gesture is to give away Peace's two handmaidens as a present. Opora, a personification of fruitfulness, is to go to Trygaeus, and Theoria, perhaps best translated as "Freebie" (cf. *Acharnians* 134ff.), to the Athenian *Boulé* or Council. Both these names may have a Periclean resonance. It was because Pericles could not afford to open his fields to all comers, as his predecessor Cimon had done *hópōs opōrízōsin hoi boulómenoi* ("so that anyone who wished might gather the fruit"), that he had "turned his attention to a distribution of public funds among the people" (*Per.* 9.2). This is perhaps where Theoria comes in; although she is usually taken as a personification of Spectacle,[49] it could be that the fact that she is given to the *Boulé* is a further indi-

47. Donnay 1968; Podlecki 1987, 107–108; Stadter 1989, 285–287.
48. A relative—significantly perhaps—of Pericles' Phiedias (617–618).
49. E.g., LSJ s.v. *theōría* II.

cation that the theoric fund that enabled politicians to enjoy themselves at public expense (cf. the three-day feast mentioned at 716–717) may have been a Periclean, and not a later, institution.[50]

When the action resumes after the Parabasis (and it is perhaps worth noting that the Chorus in *Peace* are generally recognized as displaying the kind of polymorphic characterization[51] and metamorphosis[52] that one would claim was to be found elsewhere in Athenian comedy), there is again a scene between Trygaeus and a Servant: not the servant of the gods, but Trygaeus' own attendant. It is not simply that the Servant was played by the same actor as Hermes,[53] or that a low-life deity requires a low-life counterpart; there are other reasons for believing that he, too, reflects aspects of Pericles. The Servant thus asks Trygaeus whether he saw anyone else wandering through the air (827–828). Only dithyrambic composers were seen (829): an appropriate answer to one who may have stood for the individual who both took a personal interest in musical competitions and built the hall in which dithyrambic competitions were held (*Per.* 13.9–11). Small wonder that the Servant is interested in what the composers were doing (830), and amusing—in view of Pericles' interest in astronomy (see Chapter 2)—for him to ask whether people became stars after they were dead. Trygaeus' instructions regarding the girls lead the Servant to say that he wouldn't give three obols for the gods if they behaved like pimps "like us mortals" (848–849); ironic if this is "the Olympian" speaking, who instituted payment for certain civic duties, the rate for which was, at the time of *Peace,* three obols.

The Servant departs and returns some lines later to report that "the girl has been bathed, . . . and the only thing that is lacking is a cock" (868–870). This may be another allusion to the "loss of strength" for which we have argued Pericles was lampooned in *Acharnians* (241–279, 889–890; cf. Chapters 4 and 5), *Knights* (1384–1386; cf. Chapter 6), *Clouds* (709–734; cf. Chapter 3),[54] and *Wasps* (27; cf. Chapter 7). The attention that the Servant pays to

50. Cf. Rhodes 1981, 514; and Chapter 4.

51. E.g., "Considerable uncertainty has been felt as to the composition of [the] chorus [of *Peace*]": Platnauer 1964, xiv; "The identity of the chorus seems oddly fluid": Sommerstein 1985, xviii.

52. E.g., "There is no really clear break at which the chorus is transformed from Greeks into Athenians": Dover 1972, 139.

53. Russo 1962, 225.

54. The reference to Theoria's bottom at 868 recalls the implications inherent in the order of the procession in Dicaeopolis' Rural Dionysia: *Acharnians* 260 (Chapter 4); cf. the Servant's outspoken praise for Theoria's bottom at 876, and Trygaeus' order that he keep away from the rump of the sacrificial animal at 1053. According to Cratinus (*PCG* 259), it was *Katapu-*

Theoria (879–880) and the knowing allusion to the Council's oven before the war (891–893) are again in keeping with the Periclean persona he seems to adopt.

Likewise, it is ironic, if Hermes "came forward" as Pericles, for the Servant to spurn the idea of little pots (a diminutive: a word form with a likely Periclean resonance) as an offering for Peace, on the grounds that such offerings might be made to a wretched little image (another diminutive) of Hermes. It would also have been highly amusing for another alter-Pericles to reject as a sacrificial animal an ox or a pig in favor of a sheep (929), since Lysicles the "sheepdealer" briefly — and amazingly quickly — succeeded to both Pericles' public and private positions with Aspasia's help.[55] If, as is suggested in Appendix A, all the talk of sheep in Cratinus' *Dionysalexandros* was part of a posthumous lampoon of Pericles that achieved its end by harping on the role of Lysicles, this may be another example of the genre. The Servant does not suggest just any kind of sheep, but uses the Ionian dialect word *ôï* (929, 930; and cf. *Iōnikón* and *Iōnikôs* at 930 and 933). The ostensible reason is to generate the joke at 933 when the Assembly shout *ôï*, but it would be surprising if no reference to Lysicles' Ionian wife and Pericles' Milesian spouse was intended.

The sheep motif in fact provides a good deal of amusement, presumably at Pericles' expense. The Athenians will become like lambs (according to the Servant at 935). Trygaeus tells the Servant to go and get a sheep (937), but he only does so after a reminder (949). There is comic business with the sheep when it does appear (960 and 1018), and the Servant eventually has to take it indoors again to be sacrificed, being told by Trygaeus to be sure to bring the thighs out so that "the *choregus* will not lose his sheep" —a possible reference to Pericles' *choregia,* which Aristophanes had lampooned in *Acharnians.*[56] When the Servant eventually emerges (1040), he brings the thighs, but says that he is going back for the *splágkhna* ("innards"). *Splágkhna* were also thought to be the seat of the emotions, including love.[57] The way in which the Servant fondles his female charges earlier in the play, and describes in detail the behavior of a potentially adulterous housewife at 979–985, recalls Pericles' amorous reputation. At 1122–1124, the Servant is eager

---

gosúnē (the personification of "anal intercourse": Stadter 1989, 241) that begat "Hera Aspasia, the bitch-faced paramour."

55. *Per.* 24.6; cf. Stadter 1989, 237.

56. See the spoof of *Persians* in *Acharnians* (Chapter 3), and cf. Pericles' not being a liberal *choregus* in the eyes of the womenfolk of his household (*Per.* 16.5).

57. Cf. LSJ s.v. *splagkhnon* II.

to rescue the skins of the sheep,[58] and again there may be a joke at Pericles' expense.

Alcibiades, it seems, was fond of sacrificing. At least, we know that he was given a "great number of sacrificial animals" by either the Chians or the Cyzicenes[59] when in 416 B.C. he came in first, second, and fourth in the chariot race at Olympia. Not only did he perform the sacrifice himself, but he also laid on a banquet for the whole assembly (Ath. 1.3e) with the Chian meat and with wine and dining equipment provided by the Lesbians. This was of course a few years after 421 B.C., but it is not difficult to imagine Alcibiades having already been given to *philothusía* (as he apparently had been since at least 424 B.C.; cf. Chapter 6). If so, we can understand why such a long scene (937–1126) is devoted to Trygaeus' sacrifice to Peace. The dialogue with Hierocles provides an excuse to recall Alcibiades' love of Homer (1189, 1196; cf. *Alc.* 7.1), his predisposition to dispense blows to those who annoyed him (1119),[60] but mostly to affirm, and reaffirm (1063, 1080, 1108),[61] by making Trygaeus express his devotion to Peace, the hope that he would change his policy with regard to the Peace of Nicias. Aristophanes has the same objective in view in the scenes with the sickle-maker (1197–1209), the arms merchant (1210–1264), and the singing boys (1265–1304): Alcibiades had, perhaps recently, been *choregus* responsible for a chorus of boys ([Andoc.] 4.20–21; *Alc.* 16.5).

Although the play ends happily, with Trygaeus marrying Opora and returning to his farm, we know that Aristophanes' patriotic appeal to Alcibiades to drop his opposition to the Peace of Nicias did not succeed. Indeed, at probably the very same festival, Euripides' virulently anti-Spartan, and Alcibiades-engendered, *Herakles* was performed.[62] Instead, Alcibiades successfully encouraged an alliance with Argos, the Spartans' traditional enemy, and the war dragged on for nearly twenty more years.

---

58. *Tōn kōidíōn* (1122) and *ta kōidia* (1124); Socrates always addressed Lysicles in terms of *kōidia* ("fleeces"): Dio Chrys. 55.22.

59. *Alc.* 12.1; [Andoc.] 4.30 (Chians); Satyr. *FHG* 3.160 *ap.* Ath. 12.534d (Cyzicenes). Cf. Prandi 1992, 286 n. 59.

60. *Alc.* 3.2, 7.1, 8.1, 16.15; [Andoc.] 4.20–21.

61. Is *tón bíon hēmîn* ("all our life") at 1108 a play on -*bia*- in Alcibiades? Cf. Henry 1974; Vickers 1989b, 279; 1994, 92–93, for other plays on *bíos* and *bía*.

62. Vickers 1995c.

CHAPTER 9

ALCIBIADES AT SPARTA
Aristophanes' *Birds* I

If the case made so far is valid, namely, that in the plays written during the 420s B.C., Aristophanes used popular images of Pericles and Alcibiades — based as much on gossip as on ascertainable fact — as the primary vehicles for plays dealing with matters of immediate concern, then the widely held view that *Birds,* written in 414 B.C., was an exercise in escapism calls for re-examination, not least because there is a long tradition, going back at least to the tenth century, that would see *Birds* as somehow related to Alcibiades' exile and the fortification of the Attic township of Decelea by his Spartan hosts (*Arg.* 1 Coulon). As was noted in the Introduction, it is no exaggeration to say that current scholarship surrounding *Birds* is firmly in the hands of those who are antipathetic to political allegory. Such a tradition descends from A. W. von Schlegel, for whom *Birds* was "merely a 'Lustspiel', full of imagination and the marvellous, with amusing touches at everything, but with no particular object."[1] This apolitical approach was reinforced by the fact that by the second half of the nineteenth century, the allegorists had apparently spun out of control. By 1879, there were no fewer than seventy-nine accounts of the *Tendenz* of the *Birds* — some political, some "escapist fantasy" — on offer.[2] The most influential allegorical interpretation of *Birds* was J. W. Süvern's 1827 study of *Birds,*[3] which is now generally dismissed, and only mentioned to be

1. Blaydes 1882, x.
2. Süss 1911, 137, citing W. Behaghel.
3. Süvern 1827; English translation: Süvern 1835.

held up as a warning to those who might be tempted to take the allegorical route.[4]

If, however, Aristophanes' first five extant plays had a rather more explicit political design than most recent students have thought, then it may be worthwhile examining some allegorical analyses to see what might be rescued. Barry R. Katz's work on the political content of the scene at *Birds* 1565–1691 was discussed in the Introduction and found to be very much on the right lines. Allegorical explanations are not in any case ruled out by what we know of the ground rules for Old Comedy, which seem to have been restricted in various ways by means of legislation a year or two before *Birds* (see the Introduction). It might thus be claimed that in failing to mention Alcibiades in his next play, Aristophanes was simply obeying the law. An obvious example in *Birds* is to be found in lines 145–147, where there is a reference to the *Salaminia,* one of the Athenian state triremes. Everyone — even the allegorical skeptics — takes this to be an allusion to the recall of Alcibiades in 415 B.C., but the procedure, *apokrúptōn mèn tò ónoma, tò dè prâgma dēlôn* ("hiding the name, but making clear the act"), in the words of the writer of one of the medieval plot summaries (*Birds, Arg.* 2 Coulon), is of wider applicability.

SÜVERN AND BRUMOY ON *BIRDS*

What was Süvern's explanation of *Birds?* Put briefly, his case was that the Chorus represent the Athenian populace, that in the characterization of Peisthetaerus, elements of Gorgias were laid over those of Alcibiades, and that the Epops was Lamachus. But Süvern's analysis is far more subtle than this, for he is even willing to grant the fundamental soundness of Schlegel's view of *Birds* as "the most innocent buffoonery or farce, touching upon all subjects, gods as well as men, but without entering deeply into any, like a fanciful fairy-tale," taking such an interpretation as "proof of the fine construction and masterly perfection of the piece."[5] Only to go so far, however, would be to overlook any "deep design" the poet may have had — of a kind apparent, according to Süvern, in *Clouds,*[6] and of a kind present, we might now add, in the other plays of Aristophanes we have from the 420s B.C.

4. Dobrov 1990, 214; Dunbar 1995, 4.
5. Süvern 1835, 2.
6. Ibid., 4–5.

Süvern's explanation has much in its favor, but it is because there are so many loose ends that it failed "to persuade posterity."[7] Any Gorgian overtones to the character of Peisthetaerus can be put down to the fact that Alcibiades came under the Sicilian sophist's spell; Plato made much the same point in setting his satirical dialogue *Gorgias* in the house of the Alcibiadean Callicles.[8] The Epops as Lamachus contains a nugget of sense, but the characterization is far more complex, as we shall see in the next chapter. Similarly, though the chorus of Birds might well display many features of the Athenian populace, they are quite specifically marked out as something else. It was, of course, forbidden "to lampoon or defame" the Athenian *dêmos* on the stage ([Xen.] *Ath. pol.* 2.18), which is why any criticism would have had to be guarded. Where Süvern was seriously wrong, however, was in dismissing any connection between the foundation of Cloudcuckooland and the fortification of Decelea in Attica by the Spartans. This possibility had been alluded to in one of the medieval plot summaries (*Birds, Arg.* 1 Coulon), and was taken for granted by many.[9] Since Decelea was not thus fortified until several months after the performance of *Birds,* the equation was (wrongly) considered by Süvern to fall down.[10]

Süvern is about as far back as most modern scholars are prepared to look. There was, however, an important study devoted to the "allegorical comedy" that Süvern's misjudgment concerning Decelea led him to reject. An important observation concerning the Spartan setting of *Birds* made in the seventeenth century by Jacques le Paulmier de Grentemesnil was taken up in 1730 by Pierre Brumoy, who developed it at considerable length.[11]

Judging by what le Paulmier actually says, he was not alone in his view that *Birds* was written not long after Alcibiades' flight into exile, when he was active at Sparta in encouraging the Lacedaemonians to fortify Decelea. His principal aim was to rebut an error in one of the medieval plot-summaries (*Arg.* 1 Coulon), namely, that *Birds* was written after, rather than before, the Athenian disaster in Sicily of 413 B.C. Some scholars had been puzzled as to why there was no reference to the disaster in the play, and Phrynichus' fine for

7. Dobrov 1990, 214.

8. On the likely nature of the *Gorgias,* see Vickers 1994. Hubbard (1991, 181) rightly sees "some truth in the general parallel" between Peisthetaerus and Gorgias. Even Whitman (1964; 172–176) believes that Aristophanes might be using the terms and ideas of Gorgias.

9. Brumoy 1730; 1780; Clodius 1767–1769, 2:240; Rötscher 1827, 73.

10. Süvern 1835, 6.

11. "M. Paulmier a trouvé avant moi cette explication de la comédie allégorique: mais il n'en dit qu'un mot": Brumoy 1780, 12:152.

having written in terms that were too poignant about the fall of Miletus in 485 B.C. was adduced as an explanation. Le Paulmier quite properly noted that since two of the plot summaries (*Arg.* 1 and 2 Coulon) clearly stated that *Birds* was performed during the archonship of Charias, that is, in 415/14 B.C., the problem did not exist. He happened to think that Aristophanes was attempting to persuade the Athenians to discontinue the Sicilian campaign "by intimating . . . by means of Cloudcuckooland . . . the disasters which the Spartans were going to inflict on Athens and Attica, if Decelea were to be fortified in their neighborhood according to Alcibiades' advice." [12] Whether or not this was Aristophanes' motivation (and we must never lose sight of the fact that his primary concern was to win the dramatic prize), le Paulmier's brief plot summary is wholly accurate.

Brumoy's *Le Théâtre des grecs* was a series of translations of Greek tragedies and comedies accompanied by commentaries. The first edition appeared in 1730, and the second (which was the only one available to me) in 1780. Brumoy's account and interpretation of the plot of *Birds* is to be found in the second half of volume 12 of the later edition. [13] Although Süvern refers to Brumoy's account, he cannot have read it very carefully, for Brumoy makes clear what the medieval plot summary does not (but which le Paulmier astutely had done), namely, that it was Alcibiades' *proposals* for Decelea, rather than the actual implementation of the plan, that Aristophanes had in mind. He begins by quoting several chapters in Plutarch's and Cornelius Nepos' lives of Alcibiades, and lays particular stress on Plutarch's remarks on Decelea: [14]

> As soon as he left Thurii, [Alcibiades] fled to the Peloponnese, where, terrified at the violence of his enemies, he determined to abandon his country, and sent to Sparta demanding a safe asylum, on the strength of a promise that he would do the Spartans more good than he had in time past done them harm. The Spartans agreed to his request, and invited him to come. On his arrival, he at once effected one important matter, by stirring up the dilatory Spartans to send Gylippus at once to Syracuse with reinforcements for that city, to destroy the Athenian army in Sicily. Next, he brought them to declare war against the Athenians themselves; while his third and most terrible blow to Athens was his causing the Spartans to fortify Decelea, which did more to ruin Athens than any other measure throughout the war.

12. Le Paulmier de Grentemesnil 1668, 750.
13. Brumoy 1780, 12:138–219.
14. *Alc.* 23.1–2; Nepos *Alc.* 4; Brumoy 1780, 12:143–151.

"All this passage is remarkable," Brumoy says, "and especially the last words, which form the basis of the comedy." His conclusion is that *Birds* was produced at the moment when "the scheme to fortify Decelea was on the point of being carried out." He does not cite Thucydides, but could usefully have done so, for he has Alcibiades outlining the scheme soon after his arrival at Sparta.[15]

Süvern rightly observes that Brumoy's interpretation would have made the chorus of birds into Spartans (*he* wanted to see them as Athenians *tout court*), but where he falters is to argue that this "is quite at variance with all the characteristics attributed to them in the piece."[16] Again, Süvern dismisses Brumoy's case too hastily, for the latter gives persuasive arguments in favor of a Spartan setting and of the Spartan status of some of the characters. Notably, Peisthetaerus is Alcibiades in exile at Sparta, afraid of the Salaminian galley (147, 1204), the ship that had come to collect him from Sicily.[17] The reference to Lepreum in Elis (149–151) recalls Alcibiades' sojourn in Elis before traveling to Sparta,[18] where there is no need of a purse ("À Sparte l'état étoit riche, non les particuliers").[19] The characterization of the Spartans as Birds is appropriate in that the Spartans were regarded by the Greeks as a race apart, on account of their rude and somewhat savage customs;[20] the simple diet of the Birds (160) recalls the sobriety of the Spartan cuisine.[21] The Birds' lack of education (470) refers to the Spartans' preference for the cultivation of the body over the mind.[22] The Hoopoe is intended for Agis, the Spartan king,[23] and the "*galanteries*" that Peisthetaerus pays to Procne are an allusion to the attentions Alcibiades paid to Timaea, Agis' queen, whom he made pregnant.[24] "You who were once kings" (466) alludes to the Spartans' traditional role as leaders of Greece until the Athenians disputed their position,[25] and the evils to which the birds are subjected — chased into temples, caught by a hundred

15. Thuc. 6.91.6. On the relative neglect of Thucydides in eighteenth-century France, see Mat-Hasquin 1981, 225. Levesque (1795) was the first influential French translation. Contrast le Paulmier de Grentemesnil 1668, who quotes Thucydides where appropriate.

16. Süvern 1835, 6.

17. Brumoy 1780, 12:159 and 201.

18. Ibid., 12:160, citing Nepos *Alc.* 4. Better, perhaps, to cite Lepreum in the context of Alcibiades' involvement in the anti-Spartan alliance of 421/20 B.C.: Thuc. 5.31, 34, 47.

19. Brumoy 1780, 12:160; cf. Thuc. 6.91.6–7.

20. Ibid., 12:155.

21. Ibid., 12:160.

22. Ibid., 12:175. Cf. Thuc. 1.84.3.

23. Brumoy 1780, 12:157.

24. Ibid., 12:184.

25. Ibid., 12:174.

kinds of stratagems, and even cooked and dressed with various sauces — are an allegorical account of the treatment meted out to the Spartans in recent years. Their liberator, however, will be Peisthetaerus, or rather, Alcibiades.[26]

The important point for Brumoy, however, is that the project to build Cloudcuckooland is the basis for what was to be the fortification of Decelea. "Fix yourselves in enemy territory" (164–170) — which is what Alcibiades had said to the Spartans.[27] Lines 187–191 make this clear:[28] if Decelea in Attica were to be fortified, it would be for them the same as Boeotia barring the Athenians' passage to Delphi. Brumoy only comes adrift toward the end of his discussion, when he wants to see the various divinities Aristophanes mentions (those in the embassy scene discussed in the Introduction) as masks for temporal powers in Greece. He is also on uncertain ground when it comes to the interpretation of the play as a whole. He admits that "l'allégorie n'est pas aisée à diviner,"[29] but he states his belief that Aristophanes clearly wants to persuade the Athenians that it is in their interest to make an honorable peace, and that they can only do so by ceding with good grace to the Spartans the primacy that they have possessed from time immemorial. Though he is mistaken here, Brumoy's observations on the way in which *Birds* is permeated with Spartan, and Decelean, imagery are largely sound, and should never have been discarded.

ALLEGORY IN *BIRDS*

The imagery of *Birds* is in fact rather more complicated than Brumoy, Süvern, Schlegel, or I[30] ever imagined it to be. It is as though Aristophanes rose to the challenge presented by the new legislation, and wrote a play that did not simply have two layers of meaning, but frequently had more.[31] It would be difficult enough to describe what is happening at the best of times, but so long as there are people — some of them able scholars — who maintain that *Birds* is about "meaninglessness," "Utopian fantasy," or even "ornithology," the task is even harder. The economy of Aristophanes' wit is such that he

26. Ibid., 12:177.
27. Ibid., 12:160.
28. Ibid., 12:164.
29. Ibid., 12:216.
30. Vickers 1989b; but see Vickers 1995b.
31. This was apparent to the author of the plot summary, *Arg.* 2 Coulon, for whom the allegory of Aristophanes' earlier plays was more transparent than that of *Birds*.

manages simultaneously to tell the tale of Peisthetaerus' exploits in the land of the Birds; to dwell upon Alcibiades' exile in Sparta; and to comment on Athenian politics past and present. The vehicles he employs to do this are, as ever, Alcibiades and — surprising as it may seem — Pericles. It is not difficult to see Peisthetaerus as an individual with strong Alcibiadean characteristics, and there is good reason to believe that the Epops was presented in the guise of a Spartan ruler, and the Chorus of Birds as Spartans. What is extraordinary is the way in which Aristophanes succeeds in additionally representing the Epops as a Pericles (who hated Lacedaemon) playing the part of a Spartan official. (But already in *Clouds,* Aristophanes had lampooned Pericles' relatively conservative positions by couching them in traditional Spartan terms; see Chapter 3.) This ambiguity extends to the Chorus, who, being nominally characterized as Spartans, are nevertheless beholden to a "Periclean" character. This enables Aristophanes to lampoon, if not actually "defame," the Athenian *dêmos* in a way that was legally off-limits. It is an extremely clever and intricate conceit.

ALCIBIADES AND PEISTHETAERUS

First of all, the hero's name. This has caused editors and commentators a good deal of unnecessary embarrassment. Rogers is one of the few to have maintained that if *all* the relevant testimonia conspire to call him *Peisthétairos,* they probably do so because that is what Aristophanes wrote.[32] The name was probably meant to be ambiguous, if not polyvalent, combining the notions of "persuasion" and "seduction." Although he had in the past won over many cities to friendship with Athens through his persuasive gifts (*lógōi peísas*),[33] Alcibiades had conspicuously failed to persuade (*ouk epeíthen*) the Messenians to join the Athenians in Sicily (Thuc. 6.50.1), and in his youth had been notoriously *peistheís* ("seduced") by his admirers (*Alc.* 3.1, 6.1). There is a pun on *hetaîroi* ("partisans") and *hetaírai* ("prostitutes") as well.[34] For not only was Alcibiades' membership of a *hetaireía* ("political club") well known,[35] but he was also notorious for consorting with prostitutes, "foreign or Athenian," at Athens in the 420s B.C. (*Alc.* 8.4), and with whoever was

32. Rogers 1906, viii–x.

33. Isoc. 16.21; and cf. Plutarch on the *pithanotēs* ("persuasiveness") of Alcibiades' speech: *Alc.* 1.6.

34. Cf. the pun on *hetairôn* and *hetairōn* at Ath. 13.571e.

35. Cf. Ostwald 1986, 537–550; Aurenche 1974; cf. Westlake (1989), 160: "Throughout his ca-

available behind the "doors of prostitutes" at which "he used to break in" at Sparta, where he was currently in exile (Ath. 13.574d).

The reference to the *Salaminia* in lines 145–147 is taken by everyone to be a "hidden" allusion to Alcibiades' recall in the previous summer. There are many more historical allusions in *Birds,* and so many of them are tied up in the characterization of Peisthetaerus that it is reasonable to assume that he effectively "is" Alcibiades, in the way that the Sausage-seller, Trygaeus, and other figures in the earlier plays "were" the son of Cleinias. Alcibiades' belligerence is well attested, as we have frequently seen. On one occasion, he thrashed the trainer of a chorus of boys ([Andoc.] 4.20–21; *Alc.* 16.5); does this lie behind the dithyrambic poet's reproach (1403) when Peisthetaerus begins to hit him, "Is this the way you treated the chorus trainer?" Peisthetaerus is in fact as free with his blows as was the historical Alcibiades.[36] By the time he strikes the poet, Peisthetaerus has already beaten up the Soothsayer (990, cf. 985), Meton (1019), the *Epískopos* (1029–1031), and the Statute-seller (1042–1043). There is even a scene with a character called a *Patraloías,* or "Father-beater" (1337–1371), which, if Alcibiades is in question, can only refer to his having hit Hipponicus before marrying his daughter Hipparete, as well as to the suspicion (voiced in the Assembly) that he wished to kill his brother-in-law in order to lay his hands on the family fortune (*Alc.* 8.4; [Andoc.] 4.13–14). The *Patraloías* is attracted to the new city by its laws (1343–1345), especially the one that allows one to strangle and bite one's father; this way he would gain a fortune (1352)—a distorted echo of Alcibiades' situation, but an echo all the same.

Pheidippides in *Clouds* "came forward" in the guise of an Alcibiades who was passionately fond of horses. In 416 B.C., Alcibiades had successfully participated in the Olympic chariot event, entering seven teams and placing first, second, and fourth. The Chians provided feed for his horses. Alcibiades himself performed the sacrifice to Olympian Zeus, and gave a feast to the whole crowd.[37] The previous time this had occurred, the victor commissioned an epinician ode from Simonides. Alcibiades commissioned such an ode from Euripides, who obsequiously (and inaccurately) stated that his patron's horses had come in first, second, and third.[38] There is much in *Birds* that would

---

reer it was [Alcibiades'] practice . . . to gather round himself a formal or informal *hetaireia* consisting of associates, including relatives, who would support him in his schemes."

36. Who, it will be recalled, is on record as having bitten a wrestling opponent (*Alc.* 2.2) and also beaten up a schoolmaster (*Alc.* 7.1), his future father-in-law (*Alc.* 8.1), and a servant (*Alc.* 3.1).

37. Ath. 1.3e; *Alc.* 11.1–3; Thuc. 6.16.2; Isoc. 16.34; Suda, s.v. *Alkibiádēs.*

38. Ath. 1.3e; *Alc.* 11.1–3; Isoc. 16.34 ("third").

seem to play upon Alcibiades' singular interests and experience, in particular in the scenes involving the priest and the poet (864–957). The Chians are singled out as especially pleasing to Peisthetaerus (879–880); Chians had been especially generous to Alcibiades at Olympia. The priest is dismissed by Peisthetaerus, who says that he alone will perform the sacrifice (894), an action that is again reminiscent of Alcibiades' conduct at Olympia.[39] The poet has long hair (911), is dressed in a thin cloak that is full of holes (915), and sings "something Simonidean" (919). Euripides, Alcibiades' hireling, had long hair,[40] was regularly lampooned for dressing his characters in ragged clothing,[41] and in composing an epinician ode for Alcibiades' Olympic victory was following in the footsteps of Simonides. The poet sings of chariot-racing in obsequious terms (924–930), comparing Peisthetaerus to Hiero of Syracuse, who refounded Catana as Aetna in 475 B.C., and whose victories in the games were hymned by Simonides, Bacchylides, and Pindar. It was at Catana that the *Salaminia* had recently called to fetch Alcibiades back to Athens (Thuc. 6.52.2–53.1). Instead of beating the poet, Peisthetaerus rewards him, albeit at someone else's expense (933–935, 946–948). This was again behavior characteristic of Alcibiades; the winning horses at Olympia belonged to someone else, although "Alcibiades took for himself the glory of the victory."[42]

The months preceding the Athenian expedition to Sicily were occupied with the various parties involved attempting to get oracles favorable to their respective positions. "The priesthood is said to have offered much opposition to the expedition. But Alcibiades had other diviners in his private service" (Plut. *Nic.* 13.1). The Soothsayer who is on stage from 959 to 991 may allude to Alcibiades' employment of such people a year or so earlier. His fee is certainly evocative of known Alcibiadean phenomena. He asks (973) for a *himátion katharón* ("a cloak free from taint or defilement") and *kainá pédila* ("newfangled shoes"). Twenty-two of Alcibiades' *himátia* were sold at auction a few months before the performance of *Birds* among the property of those who were *not* free from taint or defilement.[43] Then, Alcibiades "wore shoes of a striking pattern, which from him are called 'Alcibiades'" (Satyr. *FHG* 3.160 *ap.* Ath. 12.534c).

Peisthetaerus' appearance as indicated by Aristophanes recalls various Al-

---

39. Peisthetaerus' Alcibiadean *philothusía* ("love of performing sacrifices") is evident from the fact that he comes on stage at the beginning of the play laden with a ritual basket, a fire pot, and myrtle wreaths, all necessary for performing a sacrifice: Schol. *Birds* 43; Hubbard 1991, 161.
40. Richter 1965, 133–140, figs. 717–779.
41. E.g., *Acharnians* 410–470; *Clouds* 921; *Frogs* 842.
42. Diod. 13.3; *Alc.* 12.3; Isoc. 16. See further Vickers 1995b.
43. Pritchett 1956, 167, 190–210; 1961, 23; cf. Lewis 1966.

cibiadean characteristics. By line 806 he has been thoroughly naturalized as a Bird, and has had the hair (or rather feathers) of his head cut very short. Alcibiades at Sparta did the same (Plut. *Mor.* 52e; *Alc.* 23.3). Peisthetaerus is dressed as a swallow (1412), a bird whose twittering was called *traulós* in Greek, the same as Alcibiades' speech mannerism[44] according to which (*Wasps* 44–45) he pronounced *kórax* ("raven") as *kólax* ("flatterer"). Alcibiades had been much beset by *kólakes* (*Alc.* 6.1), and just before the departure of the fleet for Sicily, ravens had pecked the golden fruit from a sacred palm tree at Delphi (Plut. *Nic.* 13.5; cf. *Birds* 1611–1612). Much is made of these conceits in the opening scene of *Birds,* where Peisthetaerus and Euelpides (who helps to carry along the Alcibiadean idea by means of "polymorphic characterization") also make play with the double meanings stemming from a confusion between *korónē* ("she-crow") and *Kolónē*/Colone, the site of a famous Spartan brothel, "conspicuous and well known to many inhabitants of the city" (Polem. Hist. 48 Preller *ap.* Ath. 13.574d).

Peisthetaerus' new city is to be *ti méga kaì kleinón* ("something big and famous"; 810), phraseology that recalls the tendency toward *megalopragmosúnēn* ("vast projects"; *Alc.* 6.4) of an Alcibiades who was *méga dunaménon* ("threatening and influential"; [Andoc.] 4.11), and who had his eye on *megálōn . . . pragmátōn* ("a great career"; *POxy.* 411, 20–22), already lampooned by Aristophanes in *Knights;* Alcibiades' patronymic *ho Kleiníou* ("son of Cleinias/Famous"), used by itself to designate Alcibiades (e.g., *Acharnians* 716; cf. Crit. 4.1 West); and Alcibiades' descent from Megacles (cf. *Alc.* 1.1), twice ostracized (presumably because he was suspected of having designs on tyranny; *Ath. pol.* 22.5; Lys. 14.39). This in turn recalls the fears expressed on the eve of the departure of the fleet for Sicily, that Alcibiades himself was aiming at tyranny at Athens (Thuc. 6.15), a status that Peisthetaerus actually achieves in *Birds* (1708).

THE SPARTAN SETTING

Brumoy gave some of the reasons for seeing the action of *Birds* occurring at Sparta. One of these was the fact that there was no need of a purse (157) in the land of the Birds.[45] Though it is true that birds do not carry purses, it was also the case that Spartan currency consisted of iron, "so that ten minas'

44. *Wasps* 44–45; Archipp. *PCG* 48 *ap. Alc.* 1.8; see LSJ s.vv. *traulízō* and *traulós.*
45. Brumoy 1785, 12:160.

worth required a large store-room in the house, and a yoke of cattle to transport it."[46] The observation follows a statement by the Epops, who is a figure of some authority, that life among the Birds is *ouk ákharis es tḕn tribḗn* (156: "pleasant enough in the passing [of time]"). There would appear to be at least one Laconian reference here. The clue to the full significance of *tribḗn* is given by a scholiast who states that it is "a metaphor from clothes made of good material which stand wear and tear a long time" (Schol. *Clouds* 156). The clothing in question is the *tríbōn,* the short cloak that was proverbially associated with the Spartans.[47] "Strangling" (*ágkhein*) figures large in the Father-beater scene (1348, 1352); it is also an issue at 1575 and 1578, where Heracles wants to strangle Peisthetaerus. As was noted in the Introduction, strangling was the normal form of capital punishment at Sparta (Plut. *Agis* 19.6, 20.1, 20.5). In similar vein, it is worth noting that the name of the public prison at Sparta where malefactors were strangled was the *Dékhas* (Plut. *Agis* 19.6); there may be plays on this when Peisthetaerus is welcomed by the Epops and replies *dekhómetha,* "we are duly received" (646); when Peisthetaerus formally receives a golden crown and replies *dékhomai* ("I accept"; 1276); and when the birds are enjoined to welcome (*dekhésthe*) their tyrant to his opulent halls (1708) and to welcome him (*dekhésthe*) with marriage songs (1729).

Still on a violent note, blows were part not only of Alcibiades' public image, but also of that of Sparta. Helots, for example, were given a certain number of blows once a year lest they forget their unfree status (Myro *FGrH* 106 F 2 *ap.* Ath. 14.657d). The encouragement the Chorus give Peisthetaerus (1327) when he beats up the slave Manes at 1323 is perhaps to be seen in this light. Peisthetaerus' complaint, *hōs blakikôs diakoneîs* ("how sluggishly you serve!"), combines both Alcibiadean and Spartan allusions: *blakikôs* in the mouth of a Peisthetaerus who regularly pronounced *rho* as *lambda* might be understood as *brakikôs* ("clublike," with a play on *brákalon* ["club"]). Alcibiades had of course once beaten a servant to death with a club (*Alc.* 3.1). Spartan and Alcibiadean elements are intertwined at lines 1320–1321: the Graces (1320) refer (cf. 156) to major Spartan deities, whereas *Hēsukhía* ("Peace"; 1321) must refer both to the Spartan ideal of *hēsukhía* extolled by Thucydides' Archidamus,[48] and to the priestess from Clazomenae called Hesychia who was produced in 415 B.C. by the opposition to Alcibiades' war party in an attempt to stop the

46. Plut. *Lyc.* 9.2; cf. Laum 1925.
47. Cf. Dem. 54.34; Plut. *Cleom.* 16; *Lyc.* 30.2. The Graces were greatly revered at Sparta (cf. *ákharis,* 156): Wide 1893, 210–214; Plutarch wittily describes the *kháris* of Laconian speech at *Mor.* 511a.
48. Thuc. 1.83.3; cf. 1.71.1; and in general, Carter 1986, 45–46.

Sicilian campaign (Plut. *Nic.* 13.6; *Mor.* 483b). The ability to make several allusions at once is the very essence of wit, and it is a skill we may safely assume
Aristophanes to have possessed.

Still on Spartan topics, it has not been noticed before that Plato's account
of the visit paid by Hippias of Elis to Sparta touches on some of the themes
of *Birds.* Hippias was as unwelcome a visitor to Sparta as is Meton in Cloudcuckooland. Meton wants to *geōmetrêsai* ("measure out") the air (995); Hippias' Spartans did not want to hear about *geōmetría* (Pl. *Hp. Ma.* 285c). Meton's geometry is concerned with a city laid out "in the form of a star, with
straight rays flashing out in all directions" (1007–1009). Peisthetaerus warns
him that he may well be expelled, Spartan-style (1012–1013).[49] Hippias was
probably not thus expelled, being protected by his status as an ambassador,[50]
but it was "the stars and movements in the sky," a topic he knew most about,
that the Spartans could not stand.[51] What the Spartans did appreciate was
"hearing about the genealogies of heroes and men . . . and the settlements
(how cities were founded in ancient times), and in a word all ancient history"
(Pl. *Hp. Ma.* 285d [trans. Woodruff]). This is precisely what Aristophanes
gives in Peisthetaerus' persuasive history of the Birds' kingship (467–547)
and in the "ornithogony"[52] of the Parabasis, where the Birds describe their
origins from the earliest times (685–722). The *Hippias Major* has been described as "the most forthrightly comic of all the works attributed to Plato,"[53]
and both *Acharnians* and *Clouds* have been suggested as possible models.[54]
Perhaps *Birds* should be added to their number.

THE EPOPS AS EPHOR

"Who *boôn* (60: 'is shouting') for my master?" asks the Servant: an immediate Spartan reference in that it was the Spartan custom "not to knock on the

49. A reference to the *xenēlasia* ("expulsion of foreigners"), which the Spartan authorities carried out from time to time.
50. Pl. *Hp. Ma.* 283b; cf. 281a. That sophists were expelled from Sparta is clear from Chamael.
ap. Ath. 13.611a.
51. Pl. *Hp. Ma.* 285c; cf. Plut. *Agis* 11.3–5 on what it was believed the sight of a shooting star at
Sparta could bring about.
52. Henderson 1975, 83.
53. Woodruff 1982, 108. The dramatic date is "after 427 and . . . during the peace of Nicias":
Taylor 1926, 29.
54. Woodruff 1982, 100–101.

outer doors, but to *boân* ('shout') from outside."[55] The Servant is a *doûlos* ("slave"; 70), whose terms of service are summed up at 73 and 74 (*diákonon* and *diakónou;* cf. 1323: *diakoneîs*). Thucydides (or his written source)[56] used *diakoníais* and *diakonôn* in a sentence spoken by a Spartan servant (Thuc. 1.133). Sparta may have been a society in which the freeman was more of a free man than anywhere else, but it was a place where a slave was more a slave (Plut. *Lyc.* 28.11). The Servant describes how he performs the tasks his master sets him: *trékhō* ("I run"; 77, and again at 79; cf. 205). This brings the response that he must be a regular *trokhílos* ("runner-bird"; 79, cf. 80).[57] The stress laid on running is deliberate, and part of Aristophanes' Spartan scene-setting, for even the most influential Spartans carried out magistrates' orders *trékhōntes kaì mè badízontes* ("running and not walking"; Xen. *Lac.* 8.2). The most powerful magistrates at Sparta were the Ephors,[58] five annually elected Spartan officials before whom "foreign envoys to Sparta were brought . . . in the first instance,"[59] and Epops ("Hoopoe") plays on this. The word first occurs in the form *tòn époph', hós . . .* ("the hoopoe, who . . ."; 16), which puns on *éphoros. Épops* also plays on *epopsâsthai,* a word used to describe the consumption of the soup for which Sparta was famous (Plut. *Lyc.* 12.7). "Soup" is appropriately included in the Epops' diet at line 78.

The brusque and clipped language of both the Epops and his Servant recalls Plutarch's characterization of Laconian speech: "Although the speech of the Spartans seems short, yet it certainly reaches the point, and arrests the thought of the listener" (Plut. *Lyc.* 19.2).[60] "Throw wide the wood, that I may issue forth!" Rogers translates the Epops' first line (92). If we are intended to be at Sparta, this is a suitable image, for Spartan doors seem to have consisted in effect of lumps of wood. Lycurgus had enjoined that they should be made with the saw only (Plut. *Lyc.* 13.3), and Xenophon said of the doors to Agesilaus' house: "You might think they were the very doors that Aristodemus set with his own hands" (Xen. *Ages.* 8.7). Euelpides fittingly swears by Heracles on the Epops' appearance (93); Heracles was the legendary ancestor of both houses of Spartan kings (e.g., Hdt. 6.52, 7.204, 8.131), and late-fifth-century

---

55. Plut. *Mor.* 239b; cf. the Spartan system of voting by means of shouts: Thuc. 1.87.2.

56. Cf. Westlake 1989, 10; Hornblower 1991, 211. On Thucydides' careful choice of language, see, e.g., Tompkins 1972; Ostwald 1988; Badian 1993; Francis 1991–1993.

57. Sommerstein 1987, 25.

58. On the role of the ephorate, see Cartledge 1987, 125–129.

59. Andrewes 1966, 13; cf. Cartledge 1987, 128: "The competence of the Ephors in foreign affairs was comprehensive."

60. For discussions of Spartan speeches in Attic Greek, see Francis 1991–1993; Tompkins 1993.

Sparta was compared by Plutarch to the hero "with his lion-skin and club" (Plut. *Lyc.* 30.2). Other reasons for seeing the Epops as a Spartan dignitary will be discussed in the next chapter.

PEISTHETAERUS AND ALCIBIADES AT SPARTA

Alcibiades' sojourn at Sparta was notorious on two counts: for the way he influenced Spartan policy in the conduct of the war, and for his supposed seduction and impregnation of the wife of one of the Spartan kings. There are echoes of the circumstances surrounding both of these exploits in *Birds,* as Brumoy rightly saw. Peisthetaerus insists on the birds swearing an oath not to attack him (438–447); Alcibiades had been careful to extract an undertaking of immunity from the Spartans before he agreed to go to Lacedaemon (Thuc. 6.88.9). The speech that Peisthetaerus makes wins the Birds over, and they "exult" (629) in his plan. The effect is remarkably similar to that achieved by the speech Thucydides makes Alcibiades deliver to the Spartans soon after his arrival in 414 B.C. (Thuc. 6.89–92). This speech *paróxune* ("inflamed") and *exórmēse* ("aroused") the Lacedaemonians (Thuc. 6.88.10). There are similarities in detail as well. Peisthetaerus takes some time getting to the point, but when he begins to describe the new city, his language comes to resemble that of Thucydides' Alcibiades. Daniel Tompkins (who first noted that Thucydides' Alcibiades tended to begin sentences with *kaì* ["and"]) has carefully analyzed the sentences in the Thucydidean speech and observes that although they are very long, "[their] low level of subordination makes [them] easy to interpret."[61] Peisthetaerus announces his plan in a series of statements beginning with, or linked with, *kaì* (550, 551, 554, 555). Few of the sentences in his (frequently interrupted) speech are short, and some are very long indeed (e.g., 25, 26, 29, 32, 25, 37, and 31 words), and the longest comes at the end of another series of sentences beginning *kaì* (555–560). Though they all have a "low level of complexity," their length presents a marked contrast to the sentences of, for example, the Trochilos and Epops earlier in the play, which seemed to be laconic.

The Birds will provide their *rōmē* ("strength") for the construction of Cloudcuckooland, but will leave the planning to Peisthetaerus (637–638). There is, moreover, to be no *mellonikiân* ("Nicias-like hesitation"; 640).

61. Tompkins 1972, 212–213.

Again, there are close parallels in Thucydides' phraseology: the Spartans had been intending to attack Athens, but were *méllontes* ("hesitating"); they were, however, *eperrốsthēsan* ("strengthened") by the speech of Alcibiades, "when they heard all these points being urged by him who, as they thought, knew best. Accordingly they turned their thoughts to the fortification of Decelea" (Thuc. 6.93.1–2). There can be no doubt that Alcibiades' proposals—made in a public forum, and not in secret to the ephors—were quickly common gossip back at Athens.[62] The special relations that Sparta already enjoyed with the demesmen of Decelea (*HCT* 4.367) will have aided the spread of the news.

Another theme of *Birds* relates to Alcibiades' affair with Timaea, the wife of one of the Spartan kings. Plutarch suggests that the liaison began soon after Alcibiades' arrival at Sparta: "He had not been there long, before he was suspected of having sexual intercourse with Timaea, the wife of Agis" (Plut. *Ages.* 3.1–2). The historicity of the affair does not concern us;[63] the fact is that the stories were told and widely believed at Athens.[64] Duris of Samos (who claimed to be himself descended from Alcibiades; Duris *FGrH* 76 F 76 *ap. Alc.* 32.2) reported that "Alcibiades himself stated that he did not seduce Timaea out of *húbris,* but *philotimoúmenon* ('seeking after the honor') of placing his own descendants on the throne of Sparta."[65] Alcibiades' witty pun on Timaea's name (which means "highly honored") is worthy of note in the context of *Birds,* because Aristophanes puts a similar one in Peisthetaerus' mouth when he first sees the Epops' Nightingale: *ô Zeû polutímēth'* ("O greatly honored Zeus"), he exclaims (667).

That this is a reference to Timaea is clear from the buildup in the previous few lines. The Chorus call upon the Epops (658 [with Laconian repetition]). They ask him to leave the Nightingale with them, *ekbibásas* ("having brought her out") so that they can play (*paísōmen*) with her (659–660). Peisthetaerus asks him to bring her out (*ekbíbason*) from the sedge (662),[66] a request that is repeated by Euelpides (*ekbíbason;* 663). This can only be a reference to the *bíbasis,* a strenuous form of exercise in which Spartan girls jumped up and down, kicking their buttocks with their heels.[67] They presumably did this naked: the "processions, undressings, and exercises" of Spartan maidens took

62. le Paulmier de Grentemesnil (1668, 750) makes the same point.

63. For differing views: Westlake 1938, 34 (against); Hatzfeld 1951, 217–218; Schaefer 1949–1950, 295 n. 4; Cartledge 1987, 113 (for).

64. Cf. *Com. Adesp.* 3, 4, 5 (*CAF* 3.398) *ap.* Ath. 13.574d.

65. Duris *FGrH* 76 F 69 *ap.* Plut. *Ages.* 3.2; cf. *Alc.* 23.7; Ath. 12.535b.

66. *Boutómou* ("sedge") may refer to the fact that there was a *límnē* ("marshy lake") next to the royal palace at Sparta: Xen. *Lac.* 15.6.

67. Poll. 4.102; cf. *Lysistrata* 82. The exercise was also employed by women who wished to pro-

place in the sight of young men as an incentive to marriage (Plut. *Lyc.* 15.1). A major Spartan festival was the *Gymnopaidíai* (from *gumnós* ["naked"] and *paízein* ["play"]); hence perhaps the Chorus' request to "play" with the Nightingale, albeit the festival in question was for males alone.[68] That the Nightingale was naked is clear from both the Epops' injunction to *epideíknu* (666: "reveal") herself, and from Peisthetaerus' remark (668) at how soft and white she is. Not only was *epideíknumi* used by Herodotus in describing Candaules' revelation of his wife's nakedness (Hdt. 1.11.5), but it figures in an anecdote (Plut. *Mor.* 241b) relating to a Spartan mother who upbraided her cowardly sons (who had fled from a battle) by asking them whether they intended to "slink in here whence you came forth," hitching up her skirt, and *epideíxasa* ("displaying herself"). Unfortunately, the antiquity of the story is unknown. Nor do we know when the Spartan practice of "stripping young girls before guests" (Ath. 13.566e) operated; but Athenian knowledge of it may have informed Aristophanes' conceit. It seems that Alcibiades did exploit "in unsporting fashion the (to an Athenian) surprising availability of Spartan wives for extra-marital sex,"[69] and in making the Epops thus ingenuously display his wife's charms, Aristophanes draws graphic attention to Agis' cuckoldom, albeit Agis was king, not Ephor.

One of the examples adduced by Plutarch to explain why the "leading men" of Athens regarded Alcibiades' behavior as "tyrannical" was that Alcibiades had his shield "not emblazoned with the ancestral bearings of his family, but with an Eros wielding a thunderbolt" (*Alc.* 16.1; Ath. 12.534e). Eros figures large in Alcibiadean imagery, most notably in Plato's *Symposium.* If there is an Alcibiadean side to *Birds,* we might judge Aristophanes to have made good use of Alcibiades' "trademark" in the Parabasis, where Eros is made out to be the ancestor of the Birds (695–704),[70] rather as Alcibiades wished to become the ancestor of a line of Spartan kings. By the end of the play, Peisthetaerus has won a bride and himself wields Zeus' thunderbolt, but this is surely the image of Eros on the Alcibiadean shield rather than an image of omnipotence. Eros actually attends the wedding, and the description of the

---

cure an abortion (Hp. *Nat. Puer.* 13.2), and there may thus be an "emphatic" allusion to Timaea's being with child, ostensibly by Alcibiades, at the time *Birds* was performed.

68. *Paízein* may in addition reflect an Athenian view of the Spartan way of life: cf. Plut. *Arist.* 10.8 (cf. 10.9), where Spartans spend a festival in "playing and idleness" (*paízein kaì raithumeîn*); and *Birds* 1097–1098, where the Chorus sing of their daily life *sumpaízōn* ("playing") with nymphs in *koílois ántrois* ("hollow caves")—an allusion to *koílēn Lakedaímona* ("hollow Lacedaemon"; Hom. *Od.* 4.1).

69. Cartledge 1987, 113; cf. Cartledge 1981.

70. On *eros* in *Birds* in general, see Arrowsmith 1973; Dobrov 1990, 210.

love god as *amphithalḗs* (1737: "flourishing on two sides") may allude to Alcibiades' propensity for double-dealing.[71] The splendid vision of the tyrant entering his glorious mansion with his sovereign bride is full of similarly ironic touches: Peisthetaerus' approach is likened to a *pamphaḕs astḕr . . . khrusaugeî dómōi* ("brilliant star in its gold-gleaming home"; 1709–1710); the sight of a shooting star at Sparta could bring about the downfall of a king (Plut. *Agis* 11.5). The Chorus claim that thunder and lightning now belong to Peisthetaerus (1745–1754). These are not the easiest of Nature's gifts to control, and for Alcibiades to have placed a thunderbolt on his shield, for all that he was widely believed to be physically descended from Zeus and Eros,[72] was an act of the utmost *húbris*. The allegory of *Birds* is, however, infinitely more complex, subtle, and sophisticated than has been suggested in this chapter. Pericles figures large—very large—in the play, and in a manner that puts his impious foster son in a very invidious light.

71. Cf. *examphoterízonta tòn Alkibiádēn: Alc.* 25.7.
72. Via Salaminian Ajax; cf. *Alc.* 1.1.

CHAPTER 10

PERICLES AT SPARTA
Aristophanes' *Birds* II

To recapitulate: legislation passed in c. 415 B.C. forbidding the targets of comic satire to be mentioned by name caused writers for the comic stage to write in an even more oblique manner than hitherto. In *Birds,* Aristophanes was obeying the law in not mentioning Alcibiades, the individual who was otherwise on everyone's lips. Alcibiades was currently in Sparta betraying his city to the enemy, and also deceiving his hosts by seducing and getting with child the wife of one of the Spartan kings. Aristophanes alludes to these circumstances in *Birds* by allegorical means, by causing his hero Peisthetaerus (who is marked out by costume and diction as the comic equivalent of Alcibiades) to take refuge in a land that is clearly characterized as Laconia, and by having him persuade the inhabitants enthusiastically to accept his guidance — as the Spartans had recently done in the case of Alcibiades. They build a new city (in clear acknowledgment of the proposal Alcibiades had put to the Spartans to fortify Attic Decelea), and Peisthetaerus takes an interest that can only be described as erotic in the wife of their ruler (recalling Alcibiades' seduction of Timaea, the wife of Agis). Even at this level, the tyrannical tendencies of Alcibiades that had caused comment at Athens the year before *Birds* was performed are thoroughly brought out. Peisthetaerus becomes increasingly dictatorial and imperious, beating up anyone to whom he takes a dislike, generally throwing his weight around, and eventually becoming sovereign of Cloudcuckooland.

The role of the Epops as the ruler of a Spartan statelet is no less clear. His servant performs his duties "at the run," as did the ministers of Spartan Ephors. His hospitality toward Peisthetaerus, which extends to displaying his wife naked, can only be a lampoon of Alcibiades' generous reception at Sparta and of his seduction of Timaea, the wife of king Agis.

There is, however, another — Athenian — level of meaning in the characterization of the Epops, one that has much in common with the ways in which Pericles was brought onto the stage in Aristophanes' earlier extant plays. There were allusions made there to such matters as the fact that Pericles was dead, his devotion to *aphrodísia,* the peculiar shape of his head, and to various side effects of the plague, notably the loss of the genitalia with which sufferers were often said to be afflicted. There are allusions to all of these phenomena at the point where the Epops is introduced. The Epops' bedraggled plumage elicits the enquiry as to whether its condition was due to some *nósou* (104: "illness" or "plague"); the great plague had contributed to Pericles' misfortunes toward the end of his life. There is a none-too-oblique reference to the Epops' lack of a phallus when he is told, "The Twelve Gods seem to have crushed you" (95–96). The "affair of the Altar of the Twelve Gods" had occurred about the same time as the mutilation of the Herms, before the departure of the Sicilian expedition (Plut. *Nic.* 13.3–4): "An unknown man leaped upon [the Altar] all of a sudden, bestrode it, and then *apékopsen* ('cut off') his genitalia *líthōi* ('with a stone')." The groundwork for the joke — if that is what it was — is laid in the slapstick scene (56–59) when Peisthetaerus and Euelpides are knocking at the Epops' door. "Take a stone *(líthōi)* and strike *(kópson),*" one says to the other, followed by an injunction not to say *paî paî* ("boy, boy," punning on *pópoi* ["an exclamation of surprise, anger, or pain": LSJ]), but to make a more appropriate sound: *epopoî,* imitating the sound of the hoopoe. This comic "business" is not without point, and combines allusions both to the Sicilian expedition and — if there are Periclean resonances at all — to Pericles' "loss of strength."

"Death" may lie behind the statements that the Epops "was formerly a man" (75, cf. 97 and 114), before he took to the skies (like the psyche of the deceased Pericles, perhaps) and adopted the life of the Birds; that he *heúdei* (82: "is now asleep"), and that he will have to be aroused (83 and 84). "Death" itself is actually mentioned twice, "emphatically," in line 85. *Aphrodísia* are alluded to when the visitors are told that Epops has been eating *múrta* ("myrtle-berries") and *sérphous tinás* ("some gnats"); *múrta* was a "common slang term" for the female sexual organ,[1] and if there is a pun on *súrphas tinás* ("some low undergrowth"),[2] it will be one of the many double entendres relating to pubic hair based on "short foliage."[3] The slapstick outside the Epops' door includes a reference to a *kephalḗ* ("head"; 55), but if anyone in the audience was expecting a bare-headed Periclean figure to emerge, he would have been disappointed. Instead, the Epops as hoopoe has a splendid triple crest (94) of a kind that was otherwise to be seen on the head of Athena Parthenos, Pericles' major addition to Athens' sculptural inventory, which had already provided the basis for a lampoon of Lamachus in *Acharnians*.[4] If the crest were mounted on a helmet, the picture would correspond to the familiar image of a helmeted Pericles.

There are further likely references to Periclean themes and institutions in the same scene. Pericles' friend Pyrilampes owned peacocks (cf. the reference to peacocks at 102), which he was said "to give to the ladies who granted their favors to Pericles."[5] "Triremes" (mentioned at 108) represent Pericles' favorite military sphere of activity (e.g., Thuc. 2.13.2). The Heliaea (cf. *hēliastá, apēliastá* [109–110]) was a civic institution whose development was fostered by Pericles.[6] Anaxagoras, a philosopher close to Pericles (see Chapter 2), called the elements *spérmata* (cf. *speíretai . . . tò spérm'* at 110–111; Anaxag. 4 DK[6] [2.24.6]). Pericles had severe financial problems toward the end of his life, especially when he was *lógon apaitouménos* ("called upon to give an account") of public funds, "much of which he had [allegedly] spent for his own purposes";[7] the Epops is reminded that he once owed money (115–116) — as his visitors did — and that he liked to avoid paying his debts — again as his visitors did. If his visitors reflected aspects of Alcibiades, we might remember that Thucydides describes him as being in debt in 415 B.C., the year before *Birds* (Thuc. 6.15.3; cf. 6.12.2, and Chapters 2 and 3). Then the oath sworn by *toû Diòs toulumpíou* at 130 is an obvious allusion to the man who was jokingly known as the Olympian (*Per.* 39.2).

These themes (death, *aphrodísia*, a misshapen cranium, peacocks, tri-

1. Henderson 1975, 134; 1987, 174.

2. *Súrphē: phrúgana* ["undershrub"] Hsch.

3. See Henderson 1975, 135–136; for *katesthíein* ("eat") in the context of cunnilingus, see ibid., 186.

4. It was this association that made Süvern think of an equation of Lamachus with the Epops.

5. *Com. Adesp.* 59 *CAF* 3.410 *ap. Per.* 13.15. On Pyrilampes' embassy (to Persia), see Badian 1993, 20, 192 n. 29.

6. Ostwald 1986, 3–83; cf. Chapter 7.

7. Diod. 12.38.2; cf. *Per.* 32.3; Val. Max. 3.1 ext. 1.

remes, the Heliaea, Anaxagoras, money troubles, Olympian Zeus) all occur in Periclean situations in earlier plays, and it is difficult not to believe that in the characterization of the Epops in *Birds* there is an additional Periclean element. His name, Tereus (15, 46) — that of the mythical hoopoe who raped his sister-in-law and ripped her tongue out — may be an exaggerated allusion to Pericles' amorousness and supposed cruelty. The Epops "comes forward" both as a Spartan ruler and as an old-fashioned Athenian one. His name must also allude in some way to the *epopteía,* the highest grade of initiation into the Eleusinian Mysteries,[8] a status that Pericles may well have enjoyed (cf. *Per.* 13.7). *Epóptai* (those thus admitted) was also one of the titles that — according to the indictment — Alcibiades bestowed on his friends when they parodied the Mysteries in his house (*Alc.* 22.4).

ALCIBIADES AND ASPASIA

Not only was Alcibiades condemned to death for the profanation of the Mysteries, "but his property was confiscated, his name was put on a stele, and all priests and priestesses were instructed to curse him. All . . . except one . . . duly did so, turning to the west and waving red sheets."[9] Aristophanes had once shown a parody of a Mystery cult on the stage (when Strepsiades is initiated into the religion of the Clouds; *Clouds* 250–509 [cf. Chapter 2]), but 414 B.C. was not the time to repeat the experiment if he wished to win the prize before an audience that was highly sensitive on such issues. What Aristophanes does is to show Alcibiades being equally indifferent to traditional values, but in other directions altogether.

In order to make progress with the first of these strands of Aristophanes' complex web of plotting, it will be necessary to reflect for a while upon Alcibiades' unusual upbringing, and upon the nature of the gossip that surrounded the household of Pericles during the statesman's declining years and months. There may well have been no basis of truth in this gossip, but its subject matter is at the center of the unworthy imputation Aristophanes makes in *Birds,* namely, that Alcibiades may have slept with Aspasia, Pericles' consort, as well as with Agis' wife Timaea. There is no evidence that he ever

8. Richardson 1974, 310–312; cf. Keuls 1985, 388.
9. Lewis 1966, 177 and 189 ("the details of the curse are from Lys., vi, 51, but the extension to Alcibiades seems legitimate").

did so, but the way the Nightingale scene is constructed strongly suggests that Aristophanes wanted to put across the idea on stage.

Antisthenes, who actually knew Alcibiades, said that "he lay with his mother, his daughter, and his sister" (Antisth. 29a Caizzi *ap.* Ath. 5.220c), but the charge may have been derived from comedy. We have no hard information about his relations with his sister,[10] but there was a well-attested rumor that Alcibiades slept with his putative daughter.[11] The "mother" in Pericles' household will have been Aspasia, and we have seen her so addressed in *Acharnians* (245–246, 262), and invoked — albeit indirectly — toward the end of *Clouds.* There are in any case regular plays on Aspasia's name in the context of various Periclean characters, as we have seen. Alcibiades' natural mother, Deinomache, daughter of Megacles, does not appear in the anecdotal tradition.[12] A maternal role, of sorts, was played by Aspasia. It was in the house of Pericles that Alcibiades spent the years 447 to 434 B.C.; Aspasia came to Athens after 452/51 and before 441/40 B.C.,[13] and lived in the same house, a house, moreover, that Pericles never entered or left without kissing her amorously (cf. Chapter 7 on *Wasps* 607). Aspasia's association with Lysicles the "sheepdealer" on Pericles' death seems to have been lampooned by Aristophanes in *Peace* (929ff.) in 421 B.C., and earlier still by Cratinus (see Appendix A), whose *Dionysalexandros,* it has been argued, contains not only "remarks to the audience about the getting of sons,"[14] but the line, "Your wives will bear all of you babies, five-month ones and three-month ones and thirty-day ones."[15] If there is a connection, it might appear that Pericles' "loss of strength" induced Aspasia to seek solace elsewhere, perhaps even "while Pericles was still alive"[16] — though with Lysicles, not Alcibiades. The only documented connection between Aspasia and Alcibiades lies in the verses addressed to Socrates, said to have been written by Aspasia, instructing him how to win Alcibiades' affections (Ath. 5.219b–e). They are preserved in Athenaeus, who quotes them from Herodicus, a student of Crates, the Cynic philosopher who lived in Athens during the fourth and third centuries B.C.

10. Although if the hypothesis is correct that Alcibiades' mother Deinomache was the first wife of Hipponicus, Alcibiades' eventual father-in-law (Cromey 1984, 397; Podlecki 1987, 111), Hipparete may have been the half-sister of Alcibiades' half-brother.

11. Lys. p. 346 Thalheim *ap.* Ath. 12.534e–535a; 13.574d.

12. She is only mentioned at *Alc.* 1.1 (and in a verse attributed to Aspasia *ap.* Ath. 5.219c).

13. Bicknell 1982, 243–244.

14. Handley 1982, 110.

15. Trans. Handley 1982, 110.

16. Stadter 1989, 237.

Though these pieces of gossip show what kind of woman Aspasia was thought to be (and, in passing, it is worth noting that Thucydides was simply being ironic when he made his Pericles declare that "a woman should not be spoken about for good or evil"[17]), they do not bring Aspasia and Alcibiades together in any truly compromising way. There is, however, an imputation that Alcibiades did indulge in the "especially heinous" offense[18] of adultery with his de facto stepmother in the scene in *Birds* where the Epops (whom we have already seen to have been characterized both as a Spartan official and as Pericles) tells the Nightingale to display herself to Peisthetaerus and Euelpides. "How beautiful is your little bird" (667 [and cf. 662]), says Peisthetaerus, using a diminutive (frequently a marker of something Periclean [and cf. 662]).[19] Euelpides wants to get rough: "How I should like to *diamērízoim'* (669: 'spread her legs') for her"—which is harsh enough, but pronounced *diamēlízoim'* would recall Alcibiades' involvement in the slaughter and enslavement of the inhabitants of Melos. Not only did he propose the motion that the men of military age be put to death, but he actually took one of the captive slavewomen as a mistress and had a child by her, considered a scandalous business by his detractors (*Alc.* 16.5–6; [Andoc.] 4.22–23).[20] Peisthetaerus brings the conversation back to a Periclean context, saying that the Nightingale is "covered with gold like a *parthénos* (670: 'maiden')"—but with an allusion to the gold and ivory Athena Parthenos.

Euelpides wants to kiss her (671), but Peisthetaerus points out that her beak is like two spits (*obelískoin:* with a pun on the two-obol jury pay that Pericles instituted). Did Aspasia have a long nose? Euelpides wants to divest the Nightingale of her clothing, like peeling an *ōión* (673: "egg")—but surely with a pun on *óia* ("sheepskin"), alluding to Lysicles' trade. Stripping the *lémma* ("shell") from her *kephalês* ("head"), he will make love to her (674). There is an "emphatic" allusion here to Pericles' remark about Aegina being the *lémē* ("pus in the eye") of Athens, and another to Pericles' own deformity. Taken singly, these points mean little enough; there is, after all, no reason why the word "head" should inevitably mean Pericles, or "sheepskin" Lysicles.

17. Thuc. 2.45.2. Is it necessary to say any more about this passage?

18. Barrett 1964, 12 n. 1.

19. This must be the "wheedle" use of the diminutive: Ferguson 1977, 231.

20. Alcibiades' brutality with regard to Melos may be connected with that island's refusal to pay the fifteen-talent tribute demanded during the assessment of 425 (Meiggs 1972, 328), when Alcibiades was probably one of the *táktai*. Alcibiades could not have taken part in the Melian debate (although the anonymous "Athenian" arguments [Thuc. 5.85–111] must be his), because he was conspicuously elsewhere at the time: preparing to compete with seven teams of horses, at the Olympic Games.

But taken together, they add up to a formidable suggestion that Alcibiades had profaned not only the Mysteries, but also his foster father's bed. Whereas history, according to Aristotle, is "what Alcibiades did, or what was done to him," poetry (which included comedy) "consists in describing things that a person of a certain character [such as Alcibiades] would say or do probably or necessarily" (Arist. *Poet.* 9.1–4). To juxtapose Alcibiades' cuckoldry of Agis with even a fictional cuckoldry of Pericles would be an effective way of lampooning Alcibiades' *paranomía* ("utter disregard for the decencies"), which had recently been the most pressing issue facing the Athenians.

There are hints earlier in *Birds* that the Nightingale might represent Aspasia as well as Timaea (and the Nightingale's proverbial garrulity might also be relevant to the characterization).[21] The most notable indication is where the Epops remonstrates with the Chorus of Birds, who are trying to attack Peisthetaerus and Euelpides (367–368): "Why do you want to destroy and *diaspásai* (367: 'tear asunder') two men who are of the same family and tribe as my wife?" The supposed family and tribal connection is today a knotty problem in the interpretation of *Birds*.[22] The explanation may, however, lie in the results of some recent prosopographical research. P. J. Bicknell, in noting that both Aspasia's father and Alcibiades' uncle were called Axiochus (the latter a demesman of Scambonidae, as was Alcibiades), and that a third-century grave stele from the Piraeus bears the names of *Aspásios Aiskhínou Skambōnídēs,* his wife *Eúkleia,* their daughters *Sōstrátē* and *Aspasía,* and their son *Aiskhínēs Aspasíou Skambōnídēs* (*IG* II² 7379), does not believe these facts to be coincidental. In order to explain them, he suggests that when Alcibiades' grandfather (of the same name) was ostracized, probably in the spring of 460 B.C., he chose to live in Miletus, where he remarried. His new wife was the daughter of Axiochus, a Milesian aristocrat, and her younger sister was called Aspasia. When his period of ostracism came to an end, he returned to Athens in late spring 450 B.C., together with his wife, his young sons (born before Pericles' citizenship law of 451/50 B.C., and therefore legitimate) — and Aspasia. At some time between then and 441/40 B.C., Pericles met and fell in love with Aspasia. Axiochus' sons Aspasios and Axiochus eventually married. The latter called one of *his* sons Aeschines, after a relative on his wife's side. This Aeschines is the father of Aspasius son of Aeschines on the Piraeus stele.[23] In support of family arrangements along these lines, Bicknell also notes that

21. Cf. Leutsch and Schneidewin 1839, 202, and Schol. *Archarnians* 527 (on the tradition that Aspasia taught Pericles how to speak in public).

22. See, e.g., Sommerstein 1987, 220–221.

23. Bicknell 1982, 245–247; cf. M. M. Henry 1995, 10–11.

Thucydides describes, without explanation, our Alcibiades as "a friend of the leading men of Miletus" (Thuc. 8.17.2): the family connections had presumably been maintained.

Not only is this a plausible reconstruction of the known facts, but it provides a context within which Aspasia could be described as a relative and fellow tribe member of Alcibiades. She would have been the aunt of Cleinias' half-brother Axiochus, who was a member of the same deme (and a fortiori of the same tribe — Leontis) as Cleinias' son Alcibiades. She would not have been a citizen, of course, but a connection with the deme of Scambonidae will have represented the nearest she ever got to citizenship. If so, *diaspásai* (367) will have played neatly on Aspasia's name.

OTHER MANIFESTATIONS OF PERICLES

The Epops' lines are redolent with Periclean, as well as Spartan, imagery. The scene at 801–847 (today usually split between Peisthetaerus, Euelpides, and the Chorus leader) is in fact a dialogue between Peisthetaerus and the Epops. On any assessment, Euelpides becomes redundant somewhere along the line; nothing is lost (in that he and Peisthetaerus both reflect aspects of Alcibiades) if he leaves the stage at line 675, and much is gained if the dialogue across the generations can continue. The evidence of line divisions in R, taken together with hints in V,[24] suggests that the Epops comes on stage with Peisthetaerus at 801, that the discussion about Cloudcuckooland takes place between them alone, and that it is the Epops who is told to perform the list of tasks described at 837–845. It is thus the Epops, at once a Spartan official and a Pericles who greatly disliked Lacedaemon,[25] who suggests that the new city be called "Sparta" (813–814). It is the Epops, judging by the division of speakers in R,[26] who suggests that the name be taken from "the clouds and from *tôn meteórōn khōríōn* ('up in the air'), something altogether *khaûnon* ('frivolous')" (818–819). The allusions are Periclean: it was Anaxagoras who had told Pericles that thunder came about as the result of a "collision of the clouds" (Diog. Laert. 2.9; cf. Frontin. *Str.* 1.11.10), and who interested him in *meteōrologías kaì metarsioleskhías* ("grand speculations"; *Per.* 5.1; cf. Chapter 2). The revolt

24. The crucial information is V's allocation of 836 to the Epops: White and Cary 1918, 107.
25. *Per.* 10.3–4, 21.1, 31.1, 32.6–33.2; Plut. *Fab.* 30.1.
26. White and Cary 1918, 106.

of Caunus from Athens "in the early twenties,"[27] perhaps when Pericles was still alive, was the evident basis for *khauno*-based humor in *Acharnians*.[28] Then, not only does *khaûnos* mean "frivolous," but *nephélas* ("clouds") indicate worthlessness (Schol. *Clouds* 253), and *meteóron* something uncertain. "Do you want *Nephelokokkugía?*" asks Peisthetaerus at 819. "Cloudcuckooland" not only encompasses the notions of "worthlessness" and "emptyheadedness,"[29] but on the lambdacizing lips of Peisthetaerus, *Nephelokokkugía* would additionally conjure up an image that is in keeping with the erotic themes of the play: *nephro-* ("testicles"),[30] *kókkos* ("female sexual organs")[31] and perhaps *guîa* ("womb": *h Merc.* 20) add up to something along the lines of "Cockandcuntbury."

"Who will be the tutelary deity?" asks the Epops (826–827). "For whom *xanoûmen* ('shall we card the wool') for the peplos?" There is an allusion here to the huge peplos woven every four years for the Great Panathenaea,[32] doubtless one of the historical Pericles' concerns. Athena is suggested, and discarded, before the Epops describes a fighting cock, "Ares' chick" (835).[33] *Ô neottè déspota* ("O masterful chick"), responds Peisthetaerus (835), presumably employing cock-fighting jargon.[34] The Epops observes (836) that "a masterful chick" was an eminently suitable deity to live *epì petrôn* — not simply "on the rocks" but on the Athenian Acropolis, what Euripides (*Ion* 936) had called the "Cecropian rocks" (*Kekropías pétras*). There are simultaneous allusions here to Alcibiades' *neótēs* ("youth"), which had been an issue in the debate on the Sicilian expedition in 415 B.C. (Thuc. 2.18.6; cf. 2.12.2), to the perception that Alcibiades had been aiming at tyranny (cf. Thuc. 6.15.4), and to the fact that the last inhabitants of the Acropolis had been Peisistratus and his sons (Hdt. 1.59–60). Small wonder that Peisthetaerus' reaction is to order the Epops to depart and perform various menial tasks in connection with the construction of Cloudcuckooland (837); it was Agis, Timaea's husband, who was eventually to oversee the fortification of Decelea (Thuc. 7.19.1).

27. Badian 1993, 35.
28. *Acharnians* 104 and 106; cf. Chapter 4 above. Alternatively (or additionally), there may be an allusion to an event in the Samian campaign, where Caunus figured: Thuc. 1.116.3.
29. Cf. Sommerstein (1987, 250–251), who cites *Acharnians* 598 and Pl. Com. fr. 64.
30. Euphemism for *órkheis* [testicles], Philippid. 5.4 (*CAF*) 3.302.
31. *Kókkos: tò guneikeíon mórion:* Hsch.
32. Mansfield 1985; Vickers (forthcoming).
33. The Spartans sacrificed a cock to Ares whenever they won a battle in the open: Plut. *Mor.* 238f.
34. The losing cock was called the *doûlos* ("slave"): Phryn. 17 *TGF ap. Alc.* 4.3.

Peisthetaerus' orders have a Spartan flavor to them: the Epops is told [to] *para-diakónein* (838: "lend a hand"), but in the manner of a Spartan servant.[35] The rest of the passage is curiously reminiscent of what we know of Brasidas, perhaps the best known of all Spartan ephors, during his campaigns in Chalcidice. Aristophanes uses allusions to his exploits to adorn the passage where Peisthetaerus/Alcibiades begins seriously to throw his weight about. In 423 B.C. Brasidas had fortified Torone by building a new *periteíkhisma* ("city wall"; Thuc. 5.2.4). In the same year he attempted to take Potidaea, attacking by night, with a *klímax* ("ladder") placed at the point that "the guard carrying the *kódōn* ('bell') had just quitted," but was spotted before he could climb up and had to withdraw (Thuc. 4.135.1). Brasidas was to die in Amphipolis the following year (Thuc. 5.10.11). In *Birds,* the Epops is to help *toîsi teikhízousi* (838: "those who are building the walls") by fetching lime, stripping off and mixing mortar, and carrying a hod, by falling off the *klímakos* (840: "ladder"), by setting guards, by keeping the fire concealed (841), by running round *kōdōnophorôn* ("carrying a bell"), and by falling asleep there (842). "Sleep" meant "death" earlier in *Birds;*[36] the imputation here perhaps is that, like Brasidas, Agis should die away from home. "Sleep" (842) may additionally bear on the fate of the fifty Athenian hoplites who were disastrously caught asleep in the Agora at Torone by Brasidas in 424.[37] But this is merely to skim the surface of this passage. We may have a picture here of Brasidas' "personal leadership and example"[38] in joining in the building work. We certainly have an allusion to a famous Spartan institution in the injunction *tò pûr égkrupt'* ("to conceal the fire") at 841. The *Krupteía* provided a kind of paramilitary training for the future leaders of the Spartan police state.[39] Its precise functions are unknown (and Plutarch's view [*Lyc.* 28.1–5] that it existed primarily to kill helots surreptitiously may be exaggerated). Thucydides makes a similar play in speaking of *tó kruptón* ("the secrecy") of the Spartan politi-

35. Cf. Thuc. 1.133 on *diakonía.*

36. Cf. *Birds* 82, 83, 84. Does the fact that the Nightingale has to be aroused from sleep (203, 208, 209) also mean that Aspasia was dead by 414 B.C.? She probably died in Athens, but the date of her death is otherwise unknown; cf. M. M. Henry 1995, 17.

37. Thuc. 4.113.2; cf. van Leeuwen 1902, 132.

38. Westlake 1968, 163.

39. Jeanmaire 1913; Vidal-Naquet 1983, 161–164; Cartledge 1987, 31–32; Levy 1988.

cal system (Thuc. 5.68.2). "Concealment of fire" must be ironic, for Spartans were not permitted to "walk with a light . . . so that they might accustom themselves to the dark" (Plut. *Lyc.* 12.14). *Kōdōnophorôn*, moreover, may play on *kōthōnophorôn* — "carrying around *kōthōnes*," the characteristic Spartan drinking vessel, and one that was "most suitable for military service."[40] That this activity was to be performed "at the run" (cf. *perítrekhe*, 842) recalls the fact that Spartan magistrates' orders were carried out *trékhôntes kaì mè badízontes* ("running and not walking"; Xen. *Lac.* 8.2; cf. *Birds* 77–80).

In somehow equating the Epops with Brasidas, Aristophanes gets in an "emphatic" dig at Pericles via one of his associates. Not only had Brasidas been granted heroic honors by the inhabitants of Amphipolis upon his death there in 422 B.C., but he was thenceforth deemed to have been their founder.[41] The actual founder of Amphipolis had been Pericles' friend Hagnon (a co-general at Samos, who had come to Pericles' aid when prosecuted by Dracontides).[42] The Amphipolitans, however, had pulled down Hagnon's buildings and obliterated any inscriptions that related to his foundation role (Thuc. 5.11.1; cf. Diod. 12.68.2).

The dialogue across the generations is continued throughout the rest of the play by means of encounters between Peisthetaerus and such characters as the Priest (864–889), the Poet (904–953), the Oracle-monger (959–990), Meton (992–1019), the Episcopus (1021–1031, 1046–1052), the Lawseller (1035–1054), the Sire-striker (1337–1371), Cinesias (1372–1409), the Sycophant (1410–1466), Prometheus (1494–1551), and Poseidon, Heracles, and Triballus (1565–1692). Meton almost certainly represents the historical Meton, who had raised serious objections to the Sicilian expedition (Plut. *Nic.* 13.7–8; *Alc.* 17.5–6). The three gods, as was noted in the Introduction, "come forward" as Nicias, Lamachus, and Alcibiades, and reflect the debate over strategy that had taken place at Rhegium in 415 B.C. Some of the others "come forward" as Pericles once more. Notable among them are Cinesias and Prometheus, whose treatment well illustrates Aristophanes' comic technique.

---

40. Cf. Crit. *ap.* Ath. 11.483b and *Birds* 1160. At 1159, we learn that the new fortification is guarded *kúklōi* ("around"); the Spartan military camp was always built *kúklon* ("circular"): Xen. *Lac.* 12.1.

41. Thuc. 5.11.1; cf. Badian 1993, 204 n. 24.

42. Thuc. 1.117.2; *Per.* 32.4. Hagnon was later to be a signatory of the Peace of Nicias (Thuc. 5.19.2, 24.1) and was a *próboulos* in 413–411 B.C. (Lys. 12.65). His son Theramenes was to advocate the recall of Alcibiades in 411 B.C. (Diod. 13.38).

Aristophanes frequently used the names and reputations of known individuals as a means of enriching the caricatures of his principal targets, as we have seen. Cinesias, who is on stage from line 1372 to 1409, comes into this category. He was a well-known contemporary poet whose name and reputation, however, are co-opted by Aristophanes to contribute to the Periclean picture he is painting. The name Cinesias is eminently suitable for one much given to *aphrodísia,* in that *kínein* ("move") was synonymous with *bínein* ("screw").[43] It will also have recalled the event for which Pericles was widely held to be responsible, namely the Peloponnesian War, which Thucydides was to call the greatest *kínēsis* ("movement, disturbance, convulsion") ever to affect the Greeks.[44] Pericles' musical interests are also relevant: he instituted a competition at the Panathenaic festival, and arranged for the construction of the Odeum next to the Theatre of Dionysus, where "all musical contests thenceforth took place" (*Per.* 13.9–11). To equate Pericles with a living dithyrambic poet named Cinesias would have had a certain logic (cf. *Peace* 827–829). To equate Pericles with a living dithyrambic composer who had to wear a wooden chest brace[45] would have possessed a certain irony, in that Pericles had a notorious way with wood (Duris *FGrH* 76 F 67 *ap. Per.* 28.2–3), and the allusion would have been intensified on the lips of a lambdacizing Peisthetaerus, who would have greeted Cinesias not so much as *philúrinon* ("of limewood") as **philúlinon* ("lover of wood"): Aristophanes' puns are nothing if not sophisticated.[46] Cinesias makes a metrical blunder in the second verse he sings (1374),[47] a blunder that is picked up by Peisthetaerus (1379): amusing if Cinesias is indeed a lampoon of a Pericles, who "had himself chosen judges [in his musical competitions], and laid down rules as to how the candidates were to [perform]" (*Per.* 13.11).

43. Henderson 1987, 174 (citing Schol. *Lysistrata* 838). It is ironic that the title of Olympic Airways' inflight magazine is *Kínisi,* given the relationship of one of its former flight attendants with Greece's current Pericles (at the time of writing). I hope to discuss Cinesias in *Lysistrata* on another occasion.

44. Thuc. 1.1.2 (trans. Hornblower 1991, 479).

45. As apparently did the historical Cinesias, "in order not to be bent in two by his height and leanness": Ath. 12.551d.

46. At the level of slapstick, however, note *aspazómetha* (1377: "we greet"): a play on "Aspasia."

47. Ruijgh 1960, 320–321; Sommerstein 1987, 290.

Cinesias declares (1372; cf. 1383) that he is "soaring on light wings to Olympus": an appropriate image for one whose nickname was "the Olympian" (*Per.* 39.2) and whose soul—if contemporary paintings are any guide—will have been thought of by Athenians as a small winged creature.[48] Cinesias wants to become a *ligúphthoggos aēdōn* ("clear-voiced nightingale"; 1380); again appropriate if the Nightingale earlier in the play "was" Aspasia, and if Aspasia really was Pericles' teacher in rhetoric.[49] Cinesias wants to acquire wings and get *anabolás* from the clouds (1385; cf. 1386). *Anabolás* in the context of dithyrambic poetry are "preludes," and there may be ridicule here leveled against preludes written by the historical Cinesias.[50] *Anabolaí* and *anabállomai* were also used in connection with the "postponement of debts" (Isoc. 3.33; Dem. 3.9), a Periclean concern highlighted in *Acharnians* and *Clouds* (see Chapters 2–5); *anabolē̂*, moreover, is used by Thucydides' Pericles in the Funeral Speech in the context of "putting off" the evil day "in the hope, natural to poverty, that a man, though poor, may one day become rich" (Thuc. 2.42.4).

Cinesias' verses displease Peisthetaerus so that the latter beats him, recalling Alcibiades' treatment of Taureas, the trainer of a chorus of boys (*Alc.* 16.5). Peisthetaerus asks Cinesias whether he would like to stay and train a chorus of winged birds "for Leotrophides" (lit. "the son of one who has been nurtured by the *leōs* ['people']"). There was a real Leotrophides,[51] but again there is actually a play upon the name of a historical individual in order that an attack be made on a more important target, in this case Alcibiades. *He* was a member of the Leontis tribe (the name is concerned with lions), and Aristophanes was later to use the notion of *trophē̂* ("nurture") of lions in the very context of Alcibiades' upbringing (*Frogs* 1431). His tribal name "Crecopis" plays on that of Cecropis: *Krekopís* would be concerned with the bird called *kréx* ("corn-crake," perhaps), rather than Cecrops, but since Eupolis apparently used *kréx* as a synonym for *alazōn* ("charlatan"; *PCG* 461), there may be a reference to Alcibiades' own situation in 414 B.C. The Cinesias scene thus makes a neat pendant to the father-beating scene with its own peculiarly Alcibiadean references. That the historical Cinesias' father Meletus was implicated in both the profanation of the Mysteries (Andoc. 1.13) and the dese-

48. See, e.g., Charon receiving a hovering Psyche on a painted pottery *lekythos* in the Ashmolean Museum, Oxford: Vickers 1978, 51; Sourvinou-Inwood 1995, 336–337.

49. Pl. *Menex.* 235e; *Com. Adesp.* 122 *CAF* 3.431; Schol. *Acharnians* 527; Did. *ap.* Clem. Al. *Strom.* 4.122, where we also learn that Aspasia "figured large in the works of comic writers."

50. Pickard-Cambridge 1962, 44.

51. On whom, see Sommerstein 1987, 291.

cration of the herms (Andoc. 1.35; cf. 63), and that Cinesias himself was notorious for his utter disrespect for established religious practices,[52] will have added further relish.

PROMETHEUS AND PERICLES

Similarly, Peisthetaerus' encounter with Prometheus (1494–1551) shows the latter in Aristophanes' Periclean mode. Prometheus' name is clearly connected with *prométheia* ("foresight," "prudence"),[53] and it may not be wholly coincidental that Thucydides, in discussing the way in which the meaning of words changed during the 420s B.C., notes that "reckless daring was held to be loyal courage; prudent (*prométhēs*) delay was the excuse of a coward" (Thuc. 3.82.4). The latter observation can only relate to contemporary judgments made about Pericles that have been discussed at length in this book. The mythical figure of Prometheus had been punished by Zeus with a series of agonizing tortures; it will have been amusing to have seen an analogue of the "Olympian" (who had himself perhaps inflicted appalling torments on his Samian captives in 439 B.C.) trying to avoid Zeus' notice with, significantly, a *skiadeíon* (1508, cf. 1550: "parasol"). Ancient sunshades were conical,[54] and the conceit will have been another means of lampooning Pericles' pointy cranium. *Skiadeíon* is, moreover, a diminutive, and will also have played on the Tholos or Skias in the Athenian Agora, a building where Pericles will often have dined at public expense, and whose roof came to a point,[55] as well as on the Skias in the Agora at Sparta (Paus. 3.12.10), where *Birds* was in part notionally set.

Prometheus is said to have well *epinóēsas* (1511: "thought [things] out") — the word is cognate with *noûs,* Anaxagoras' prime mover, as is *eúnous* (1545), spoken by Prometheus when he says how "well disposed" he is to mankind. Anaxagorean jokes are a stock motif whenever Periclean characters are on stage. Prometheus' fear and hatred of the gods, and especially of Zeus, which is explicitly stated several times (1494, 1496–1497, 1501–1502, 1506, 1515, 1550) and is implicit throughout, not only is what might be expected of Pro-

---

52. Lysias (fr. 53 Thalheim *ap.* Ath. 12.551d–552b) called him "the most impious and lawless man in the world."

53. Cf. Rose 1959, 72.

54. M. Miller 1992.

55. Thompson and Wycherley 1972, 41 n. 95.

metheus given his experiences on the Caucasian crag, but also is a witty example of value-reversal, or the "Hermogenes principle." It shows the "Olympian" both forswearing his divine eponym, and having experienced something of the treatment supposedly meted out to his Samian captives. Prometheus' question: "What is Zeus doing? Is he clearing away the clouds or is he gathering them?" (1501–1502) may relate to the incident recorded by Frontinus when Pericles supposedly explained thunder by the action of the clouds (Frontin. *Str.* 1.11.10). The scene ends with an allusion to both Athenian and Spartan institutions: the *díphros* (1552: "stool"; cf. *diphrophórei* ["carry a *díphros*"]), the word used both for the stool carried in the Panathenaic procession (Hermipp. *PCG* 25), and for the official chair of the Spartan eponymous ephor.[56]

THE ROLE OF THE CHORUS

The Chorus in *Peace,* the immediately preceding surviving play in the Aristophanic corpus, are, as we have seen, generally regarded as "oddly fluid" with "no clear breaks" between their characterization as at times *Panhéllēnes* (302: "Greeks"), at times farmers (508), and at times Boeotians, Argives, Laconians, Megarians, and Athenians.[57] The Chorus in *Birds* are even more poecilomorphic, being at first in thrall to a Spartan official who doubles as an Athenian statesman, and then to a Laconian tyrant who realizes all the worst fears of those who foresaw the rise of an Attic tyrant. The Chorus in *Birds* at times thus represent the Spartan assembly, and at times Pericles' traditional audience. The fact, however, that the Birds are firmly characterized as Spartans to begin with means that Aristophanes always has a certain protection whenever he makes observations that might otherwise have been held to disparage the Athenian *dêmos,* something that was formally forbidden (Xen. [*Ath. pol.*] 2.18). Süvern saw elements of the Athenian populace in the Chorus—in their fickleness and gullibility, but these are heavily overlain by the Spartan features to which he was unfortunately blind. Such Spartan features are especially apparent at the end of the Epops' song, when he repetitively attracts the attention of the Chorus of birds. *Torotorotorotorotíx,* he cries in order to attract their attention (260), *kikkabaû kikkabaû* (261), followed by *torotorotoro-*

56. Plut. *Cleom.* 7.2, 10.1. I owe to Sir Kenneth Dover (*per litt.*) the idea that the ex-Aeschylean *Prometheus Vinctus* is full of specifically Periclean imagery (though he would not agree).

57. Platnauer 1964, xiv; Sommerstein 1985, xviii; Dover 1972, 139.

torolililíx (262; cf. 267: *torotíx torotíx*). It was the *torōtatos* ("most alert") of the eirens (Spartan youths aged between twenty and thirty)[58] who was to take charge of bands of boys in the absence of a Spartiate (Xen. *Lac.* 2.11).[59]

At 263–264, Euelpides cannot yet see any birds, even though he gawpingly "gazes up to the heavens" (*es tòn ouranòn blépōn*). This must allude to the periodical stargazing when "the ephors select a clear and moonless night, and in silence sit and *pròs ouranòn apoblépontes* ("watch the heavens"; Plut. *Agis* 11.4). If a shooting star was seen, the ephors would "decide that their kings have transgressed in their dealings with the gods, and suspend them from their office, until an oracle from Delphi or Olympia [came] to the aid of kings thus found guilty" (Plut. *Agis* 11.5). This would also explain the oath by Apollo in line 263.

Peisthetaerus and Euelpides speculate as to whether the first bird that comes along is a peacock (269): they leave it to the Epops to say (270). This again neatly touches upon Pericles' connection with Pyrilampes the peacock-fancier, before the Epops declares that the bird in question is *limnaîos* ("a marsh bird"): there was a *límnē* ("marshy lake") next to the royal palace at Sparta (Xen. *Lac.* 15.6) (and was the Eurotas Valley the haunt of *phoinikópteroi* ["flamingoes"; cf. 273] in the fifth century?).[60] *Phoiníkious* (272: "red"), however, neatly combines allusions to the *phoinikís* that was "the red sheet" with which those who (like Alcibiades) were found guilty of profanation were solemnly cursed,[61] and the *phoinikís* that was the "dark-red military cloak of the Spartans" (*Lysistrata* 1140; Xen. *Lac.* 11.3). By means of the "economy of wit," three ideas come neatly together.

When the Chorus of Birds finally assemble, their first cries are full of Laconian "repetition for the sake of emphasis":[62] *popopopopopopopopopoû* (for *poû* [310: "where"]), and *titititititititítína* (for *tína* [315: "what"]). Their language is laconic, even Laconian: *poí; pâi; pôs phḗs;* (319: "Where? How? What do you say?"). *Pâi* is a Laconian form, elsewhere used by Aristophanes in the mouth of Lampito in *Lysistrata*.[63] The Epops tells them that *presbúta dúo* (320: "two ambassadors")[64] have just arrived who are *leptò logistà* (318: "men of subtlest genius"). The Chorus want nothing to do with them. Again, we recall the ambassadorial journeys of the sophist Hippias of Elis (Pl. *Hp. Ma.* 283b; cf.

58. Hooker 1980, 172; Clauss 1983, 144, 150.
59. *Torúnēs* and *torúnēn* at 78 and 79 probably play on the same idea.
60. It was certainly marshy: Plut. *Lyc.* 16.14.
61. Lys. 6.51; cf. Lewis 1966, 177.
62. Francis 1991–1993, 203.
63. *Lysistrata* 171; Henderson 1987, xlviii.
64. LSJ s.v. II; cf. ibid. III: "at Sparta a political title, president."

281a), and the difficulties he encountered in gaining a hearing at Sparta (Pl. *Hp. Ma.* 285c). Despite the Epops' telling the Birds not to be afraid (323: *phobēthêis*) (and we might note the existence of a Temple of Phobos next to the *ephoreíon* at Sparta; Plut. *Cleom.* 9), the Chorus are aghast, and make serious accusations about the Epops, their *phílos* (329: "friend"), who had fed beside them (*homótropha*); Spartans fed communally in *philítia* ("dining halls").[65]

It takes some time for the Birds to accept their visitors, but when eventually they do so, it is the fact that Peisthetaerus is subtle, crafty, and scheming (429–431) that actually wins them over. The encouragement of habits of deceit and cunning was a well-known part of the Spartan educational system. Spartan boys were encouraged to "play the deceiver" (Xen. *Lac.* 2.6–8), and it has been reasonably suggested that Xen. *Cyr.* 1.27ff. reflects Spartan practice: "The man who proposes to [gain an advantage over an enemy] must be deceiving and cunning and deceitful, a thief and robber, overreaching the enemy at every point."[66]

THE PROFANATION OF THE HYACINTHIA

Not only is Peisthetaerus able to twist the leader of the Birds around his little finger (in principle, if not in detail, in the way in which Alcibiades must have persuaded the Spartan authorities to allow him to speak to the Spartan assembly), but he also persuades the Birds as a whole that they are rightfully lords of the earth, and greater than the gods. He even persuades them to declare a Holy War against the gods (556), and they invent a long pedigree (685–722) to justify their usurpation. It is important to note that this is delivered in *anapaísta* (684: "anapaestic verse") to the sound of the *aulós,* and that it concludes with the defiant declaration that the Birds are themselves the "prophetic Apollo," not least because it corresponds with what is known

---

65. Often confused with *phidítion* (derived from *pheídomai* ["be sparing"], see LSJ s.v.): *phidítion* may have been applied jokingly; Michell 1964, 282. *Homótropha* (cf. *'tráphēn,* 322) may play on the Spartan institution of *tróphimoi,* about which little is known for certain. *Xénoi tróphimoi* ("Spartan-raised foreigners") were to be prominent in the fourth century; see Cartledge 1987, 61, 253. The Birds' accusation that the Epops has broken ancient laws, and broken *hórkous* ("oaths"; 331–332), may relate to the immutability of the laws at Sparta (Hdt. 7.104.4; Xen. *Lac.* 15.7; Plut. *Mor.* 230f.) and to Spartan kings and ephors having to swear *hórkous* once a month (Plut. *Lyc.* 12).

66. Proietti 1987, 91.

about the celebration of the Hyacinthia at Sparta. "Boys . . . sing to the *aulós* . . . praising [Apollo] in *ruthmôi anapaístōi* ('anapaestic rhythm')" (Ath. 4.139e). In thus parodying the Hyacinthia (or rather, having Peisthetaerus/Alcibiades cause the Spartans/Birds to do so), Aristophanes makes the Birds behave in a wholly impious and totally un-Spartan way by employing the Hermogenes principle, in this instance taking to extremes the opposite of what the Spartans held most dear, namely respect for traditional religious practices. It is Aristophanes' oblique allusion to Alcibiades' supposed involvement in the profanation of the Mysteries,[67] paralleled by Eupolis' having shown Alcibiades in the *Baptae* participating in the sacred orgies of the Thracian deity Cotytto.[68] How serious a departure from the traditional norm this parody is becomes clear when we recall that it was the Spartans who were late for Marathon because they could not depart until the moon was full (Hdt. 6.120); it was the Spartans who delayed sending an army against Mardonius in 479 B.C. because they were celebrating the Hyacinthia;[69] it was at Sparta that permanent officials known as *Púthioi* were maintained, whose task it was to consult the oracle at Delphi whenever a decision was required by the kings or the people (Hdt. 5.57; Xen. *Lac.* 15.5). To represent the Spartans as utterly impious on the Athenian stage must be a criticism of their having given sanctuary to a person who had been subjected to the most severe religious sanctions within the legal armory of the Athenian state. Their punishment is to be placed in the thrall of Alcibiades and to have their ancestral constitution — their "alternative to tyranny"[70] — overthrown. All of this is accomplished in allegorical fashion in the finale, where the various themes — Spartan, Periclean, and Alcibiadean — are welded together by means of thunderbolt imagery. Spartan kings were priests of Zeus (Zeus *Lakedaímōn* and Zeus *Ouránios* ["of the Heavens"]); Pericles was "the Olympian"; the nuptials of Olympian Zeus and Hera, attended by Eros, are alluded to at 1731–1741. Alcibiades was said to have laid claim to an Eros wielding a thunderbolt in lieu of his ancestral shield emblem (*Alc.* 16.1; Ath. 12.534e). The resonances do not just resonate, they fulminate.

Birds is not, therefore, "about meaninglessness": it is full of meaning, but much of its significance is hidden beneath an allegorical veil. That this is so is due to the legal constraints within which writers for the Athenian comic stage had to work. In 414 B.C., it was Aristophanes' brief to write comedy not "openly, but figuratively," without mentioning anyone who was "rich,

67. For others, see *Birds* 489–491, 1553–1564, with Ruck's notes (1986).
68. Cf. Ambrosino 1986–1987, 103 n. 28.
69. Hdt. 9.7, 11; Idomeneaus *FGrH* 338 F 6 *ap.* Plut. *Arist.* 10.8–9.
70. Andrewes 1956, 66.

or aristocratic, or powerful" by name. Thomas Hubbard has well observed that "nothing focuses creative energies so much as official attempts to stifle them";[71] Aristophanes rose to the challenge, and, without mentioning Alcibiades, Pericles, Aspasia, Nicias, or Lamachus, succeeded not only in investigating what these individuals had actually done historically, but also, by "telling of events that might happen," by "describing the kind of thing that a person of a certain character would say or do" (Arist. *Poet.* 9.2–4), in imputing the most outrageous acts to some of them.

71. Hubbard 1991, 160.

CONCLUSION

One purpose of this book has been to suggest that Pericles cast a long shadow over both Athenian politics and drama after his death (another has been to illustrate Alcibiades' rising star). Nearly every detail of the day-to-day existence of Athenians in the 420s B.C. was governed by the consequences of measures Pericles had taken, and it is scarcely surprising if writers for the stage made frequent allusion to the fact. Athenians penned within their city, committed to a policy of not going out to meet the periodic Peloponnesian invasions, may well have enjoyed Aristophanes' comic revival of their dead leader in the person of Dicaeopolis; at least *Acharnians* won first prize. It might fairly be said that *Acharnians* was "about" Pericles, but two of the other five plays discussed here are more concerned with Cleon (*Knights* and *Wasps*), and all five with the rise to power of Alcibiades, Pericles' ward. This was a development that was viewed by many with increasing concern, a concern mirrored in the figures of the Sausage-seller, Pheidippides, Bdelycleon, Trygaeus, and Peisthetaerus. In *Knights, Clouds, Wasps,* and *Peace,* however, Pericles is revived in order to provide a contrast between the new values that Alcibiades personified, and those for which Pericles stood. But none of the characterizations — Demus, Strepsiades, Philocleon, Hermes, or the Servant — suggest that Pericles was without blame for the current state of affairs, or that his public policies and private neglect had not contributed to contemporary problems. His resurrection as the Epops in *Birds* served to put a shameful cast on Alcibiades' seduction of Timaea, an action that might otherwise have done Alcibiades credit in Athens in 414 B.C. Pericles' peculiarities, his tastes, and even his virtues are made the vehicles of Aristophanes' satire. Commentators have taken too literally the statement of Thucydides' Pericles that "the living have their rivals and detractors, but when a man is out of the way, the honor and goodwill he receives is unalloyed" (Thuc. 2.45.1). The ancient reality, not to mention Thucydides' awareness of it, was probably rather different.

Many questions remain outstanding. How does the case presented here change our overall assessment of Aristophanes as a poet and playwright? How does it alter our view of him as a commentator on, or participant in, Athenian politics? How should it cause us to reassess the history of the last quarter of the fifth century B.C.? What questions of stagecraft does it raise? What does it tell us about the general sophistication and level of education of an Athenian audience? What can we now learn about the relationship between drama and political oratory? The answers to such questions must await completion of a study of the rest of Aristophanes' plays. Only half of the evidence is in. The other five extant plays are written in a similar vein, with Pericles and Alcibiades still used as the pegs upon which Aristophanes hangs his comic — and fantastic — treatments of questions of current interest; politics, rather than "the role of women" or "literary criticism," is still the order of the day — just as *Clouds* is not "about" Socrates, or *Birds* "about" our feathered friends.

There has been a good deal of repetition of motifs in this book. Standard jokes involving, say, the shape of Pericles' head, his sufferings due to the plague, or the pain he had supposedly inflicted on others — or Alcibiades' speech mannerisms, his grandiose notions, and his thuggery — were run, re-run, and reworked. It was perhaps a little mischievous of Aristophanes a decade after *Birds* to begin his *Frogs* with the charge that his competitors' jokes were old, rather than his. One Alcibiadean character says to another: "Shall I tell one of the hackneyed jokes, master, the sort at which the audience forever *gelōsin* ('laugh') and/or *gerōsin* ('grow old')?" The double entendre engendered by Xanthias' traulism renders amusing a line that is otherwise bland. It also helps to explain why Dionysus comes away from a dramatic festival "more than twelvemonth older than [he] went" (18).[1] But this is to go beyond the limits of this book.

There is, however, one point that needs to be made — if somewhat prematurely — now. In order to absolve both Aristophanes and myself from a charge of being Pericleo-alcibiadizers to the exclusion of a concern with other politicians known to have been active — and lampooned on the comic stage — let me state here my belief that the eleven plays of Aristophanes we have may well have been selected at a very early stage from the forty or more

1. Trans. Rogers (1902, 5).

plays he wrote (i.e., during the first half of the fourth century B.C.) with the express purpose of illustrating the role played in Athenian politics by Pericles and Alcibiades. They were selected, and arranged, by someone who knew well what the issues were, and how Aristophanes had elucidated—or obfuscated—them. We shall probably never know the precise agency, and it would be going beyond the evidence to suggest that this collection had anything to do with the gift that Plato made to the Syracusan tyrant Dionysius, or with the discovery of a copy of Aristophanes' plays in Plato's bed after his death (Olymp. *Vit. Pl.* 5).

The fact that allegorical interpretations of Aristophanes' plays have been discouraged—even derided—for so long does little credit to classical scholarship. There is much ground to be made up, and everything to be done. We should make the attempt to escape from a mind-set of the kind recently described by Joseph Farrell:

> We are in the habit of reading ancient literature through nineteenth-century lenses. Whether this is so because our profession coalesced in that century or because all of us, classicist or not, are still, nearly a hundred years later, caught in the grip of its chief intellectual and spiritual categories, I will not attempt to say. For whatever reason, it troubles us when we cannot make our ancient texts speak to us in a voice that would have been intelligible to Arnold, Carlyle, or Mommsen.[2]

It is much more fun, though, to make the text of Aristophanes speak in a voice that would have been intelligible to Aristophanes' sophisticated audience, and it is a pity that the ability to do so should have been lost in the name of "scientific" scholarship; what some unobservant scholars have failed to recognize is that the study of the ancient world is no more a science than a man with a wooden leg is a tree.

2. Farrell 1993.

APPENDIX A
Posthumous Parody in Cratinus' *Dionysalexandros*

Cratinus' *Dionysalexandros* may be a posthumous lampoon of Pericles rather than one written and performed in the statesman's lifetime. "In the [*Dionysalexandros*] Pericles is satirized with great plausibility by means of *émphasis,* because he brought the war on the Athenians,"[1] says the plot summary. The concept of "emphasis," and its role in comedy, has been discussed in the Introduction. According to Byzantine commentators, authors of Old Comedy attacked their victims *phanerôs* ("openly"), and it was only through pressure from "the rich and the authorities, who did not want to be lampooned," that attacks made *ainigmatikōdôs* ("in riddles") became obligatory (*De comoedia* 4.12–14 [Koster]). Aristophanes stands at the transitional point between the one manner and the other, between Old and Middle Comedy. Audiences were expected to look for hidden meanings, although they were no doubt aided by portrait masks, which made identification of the protagonists an easy matter.[2]

The plot of *Dionysalexandros* is complicated: it involves a mock judgment of Paris, an abduction of Helen, a devastating attack by Achaeans, and the transformation of Dionysus into a ram, before "Alexander [Paris] appears and detects both [Helen and Dionysus], and orders them to be led away to the ships intending to hand them over to the Achaeans; but when Helen objects he takes pity on her and keeps her to be his wife, but sends off Dionysus to be handed over."[3] Many attempts have been made to elucidate the nuances of the "emphasis" of Cratinus' play. It is agreed that Dionysus "comes forward" in the character of Pericles, but there is less unanimity over whether he "becomes" Paris, or whether for Aphrodite and/or Helen we are to read Aspasia.[4] I have no firm view on these points, beyond noting that if either of them was valid, we should have examples of the kind of "polymorphic characterization" I believe to be widespread in Athenian drama.

What can confidently be said about *Dionysalexandros,* however, is that it is imbued with talk about sheep to such an extent that it is reasonable to entertain the possibility that the play is a parody of Lysicles and Aspasia as much as of Pericles. Apart from what we know, or can deduce, from the plot—that Dionysus is turned into a ram, and that Paris was a shepherd—there are lines such as: *ho d'ēlíthios hôsper próbatōn bê bê légōn badízei* ("the fool walks along saying 'baa baa' like a sheep";

1. *POxy.* 663, 44–48; *CGFP* 70; Cratin. *Dionysalexandros* i, *PCG.*
2. Sommerstein 1981, 154–155.
3. Trans. Grenfell and Hunt 1904.
4. Schwarze 1971, 4–6; Rosen 1988b, 52–53, for proposals that have been made; add Stadter 1989, lxvi n. 90. The line "in baskets I will bring salt-fish of Pontus" (Cratin. *PCG* 44 *ap.* Ath. 3.119b) may allude to Pericles' activities in the Black Sea area.

Cratin. *PCG* 45); *eneisi d' entauthoî mákhaira koúrdes, haîs keípomen tà próbata kaì toùs poiménas* ("In there we keep shears with which we do not only clip sheep but shepherds"; Cratin. *PCG* 39); *oúk, allà bólita khlōpà kaì oispótēn pateîn* ("No, but fresh cow dung and sheep droppings"; Cratin. *PCG* 43); *nakótiltos hōspereì kōdárion ephainómēn* ("I appeared shorn like a fleece"; Cratin. *PCG* 48).

Immediately after Pericles' death, Aspasia married Lysicles, a "sheepdealer." At least he is implicitly described as such by Aristophanes in *Knights* (*probatopólēs:* 132), and Socrates is supposed always to have addressed him in terms of *próbata* ("sheep") and *kóidia* ("fleeces"; Dio Chrys. 55.22). According to Aeschines Socraticus, Aspasia bore Lysicles a son, taught him (Lysicles) to speak in public (just as she had supposedly taught Pericles), and thanks to her he became a successful politician, the "first man in Athens."[5] Lysicles was a general and was killed collecting tribute in Caria in 428/27 B.C.[6] It is probably indeed the case that "stories of Lysicles' political 'primacy' and relationship with Aspasia reached Aeschines through comedy and must therefore be taken at something less than face value,"[7] but in the present context this is all to the good.

The date of *Dionysalexandros* is not fixed, but arguments have been put forward in favor of 430 and 429 B.C., on the assumption that the play was performed in the lifetime of Pericles, and that the depradations of the Achaeans were a topical allusion to the Spartan invasions of either 431 or 430 B.C.[8] Pericles died in 429 B.C., but there was another Spartan invasion in 428 (Thuc. 3.1.1), another in 427 (Thuc. 3.26.1), and yet another in 425 B.C. (Thuc. 4.2.6).[9] Eric Handley has, moreover, convincingly shown that at the very beginning of what we have of the fragmentary plot summary, there is a statement to the effect that "Hermes goes off, and they [the Chorus of satyrs] make some remarks to the audience about the getting of sons," reading *p⟨erì⟩ huôn poió⟨seōs⟩* at *POxy.* 663.8.[10] While it is true that there was the question of the legitimacy of the son of Pericles and Aspasia in 429 B.C., this is not quite the same thing; nor is Handley's tentative suggestion that there may be a reference to the gift of Athenian citizenship to Sadocus the Thracian especially convincing. There was, however, the remarkably quick marriage (or cohabitation) of Aspasia and Lysicles after Pericles' death, and the birth of a son, Poristes (*Per.* 24.7).[11] This certainly fits the

5. *Per.* 24.6; Schol. Pl. *Menex.* 235e; Call. Com. *PCG* 21.

6. Thuc. 3.19.2; Develin 1989, 123. It is interesting that Lysicles was killed by Samian exiles from Anaea (cf. Thuc. 3.32.1); was this revenge on Aspasia for her alleged part in Pericles' Samian campaign?

7. Frost 1964a, 398 n. 44.

8. Cf. Schwarze 1971, 24; Handley 1982, 115.

9. The invading force sent in 426 turned back at the Isthmus because of earthquakes in Sparta (Thuc. 3.89).

10. Handley 1982, 110.

11. Stadter (1989, 237) raises the interesting possibility that the association of Aspasia and Lysicles may have begun when Pericles was still alive.

bill, and if *POxy.* 2806, of which fragment 1.1.6–7 makes mockery of premature births ("Your wives will bear all of you babies, five-month ones and three-month ones and thirty-day ones"),[12] also belongs to *Dionysalexandros* (as Handley has proposed), then we may have both a fresh insight into the Aspasian ménage, and suitable material for the posthumous lampooning of Pericles.

12. Trans. Handley 1982, 110.

APPENDIX B
The Athenian Plague of 430–428 B.C.

There are several apparent references to the Athenian plague in Aristophanes' first six extant plays. They are usually introduced in order to cripple-tease the memory of Pericles, who was said by Plutarch to have suffered from "varied symptoms" (*Per.* 3.1). Pericles was to recover, before dying a few months later. The most extended and informative use of plague imagery in Aristophanes is to be found in the bedbug scene at *Clouds* 694–745 (discussed more fully in Chapter 2), where Strepsiades' account of what the insects are doing to him closely parallel the symptoms described rather more fully by Thucydides. The bedbugs are described as Corinthians (710); the plague was supposedly introduced by the Peloponnesians (Thuc. 2.48.2). The bugs devour Strepsiades' ribs (711); the plague quickly reached the chest (Thuc. 2.49.3). The bugs drain Strepsiades' spirit (712); another symptom of the plague was severe diarrhea (Thuc. 2.49.6). The bugs ulcerate Strepsiades' testicles (713); the plague caused ulceration, albeit to the colon.[1] The bugs dig through Strepsiades' arse (714); in its final stages, the plague would "descend to the bowels" (Thuc. 2.49.6). Then Strepsiades claims that the bugs will kill him (715); according to Thucydides, "most" died of exhaustion at this stage (Thuc. 2.49.6). Finally, Strepsiades' cock drops off (734); according to Thucydides: "even if a person got over the worst, the plague would often . . . attack the privy parts . . . and some escaped with the loss of these" (Thuc. 2.49.8). The feature that is present in Aristophanes but not in Thucydides, and which might throw new light on the pathology of the plague, is the involvement of insects.

Otherwise, most of the other allusions to the plague in Aristophanes' earlier plays elaborate upon one or another of the symptoms given in Thucydides' account. In *Acharnians* (425 B.C.), there are references to the loss of the privy parts (236–279, 802, 881–894), to forgetfulness (580, 963, 1050; cf. Thuc. 2.49.8), to eye problems (850, 1018–1036; Thuc. 2.49.2), and to the heart (12, 485, 488);[2] in *Knights* (424 B.C.), to the loss of the privy parts (1385), forgetfulness (732, 1041, 1339), ulceration (903), and eye trouble (909); in *Clouds* (423 B.C.), apart from the bedbug scene, there are references to forgetfulness (129–130, 414, 482–483, 631, 685, 854–855), and eye trouble (946–947); in *Wasps* (422 B.C.), to *nósos* ("plague"; 71 [twice], 76, 80, 87, 114), which is made the basis for an elaborate conceit, and elsewhere in the play to fever (284, 813; cf. Thuc. 2.49.2) and to *boubōniōiē* ("suffer[ing] from swollen glands"; 277). In *Birds,* the Epops' bedraggled appearance is attributed to some *nósou* (104). All these allusions are made in the context of characters who, like Strepsiades, are closely based on the historical Pericles.

1. Thuc. 2.49.6; and cf. the *helkúdria* ("little plague-sores") on the Periclean Demus' shins at *Knights* 907.
2. Where the plague settled: Thuc. 2.43.5.

This is not the place to re-examine all the theories relating to the plague, concerning which, it has been said, "more ink has been spilt in argument than there was blood shed in the Peloponnesian War."[3] All previous theories, however, are based on Thucydides' account alone. They need to be reassessed in the light of Aristophanes' evident interest in an event that had directly affected every member of his audience during the previous few years. Though there is little that is new, that little may be enough to suggest that an insect-borne disease was believed to be in question. In *Clouds* in particular, there is much talk of fleas (145–152), bedbugs (37, 694–715), and gnats (156–165). Although lice are not mentioned in that play, they were apparently a commonplace of low comedy judging by *Peace* 740, and presumably therefore of everyday life. But if lice were deemed unworthy vehicles even for Aristophanes' humor, it would explain why Thucydides fails to mention insects in his sober and dignified account of the plague.

It may well be that "modern research has been seriously misguided in its persistent attempts to identify the Great Plague of Athens,"[4] but this new evidence, if that is what it is, would tend to support the verdict of Sir William McArthur that the plague was epidemic louse-borne typhus:

> The mixed inhabitants of Athens were no strangers to the insect vector of typhus and relapsing fever, for Aristophanes says that lice were among the stalest jokes of Athenian comedy; and the conditions in the besieged city, crowded with fugitives, would soon build up . . . the concentration of contagion that causes mild typhus to assume its malignant petedical character, and grow very mortal. . . . If Thucydides had told us no more of the Plague of Athens than that it was an infectious and fatal fever, with gangrene at the extremities as an outstanding feature, that alone would suffice to label it as typhus.[5]

At least, this would appear to be the only possible explanation, were it not for the reference to *boubōniōie* ("suffer[ing] from swollen glands") at *Wasps* 277, which may open up other possibilities.

3. MacArthur 1961, 166. For bibliographical references to some of these theories, see, e.g., Longrigg 1980; 1992; Sallares 1991, 244–256; Vickers 1991, 64 n. 1.
4. Longrigg 1980, 221.
5. MacArthur 1959; 1961, 167, 173; unknown to Longrigg 1980, 1992.

BIBLIOGRAPHY

Adkins, A. W. H. 1970. "Clouds, Mysteries, Socrates and Plato." *Antichthon* 4: 13–24.

Ahl, F. 1984. "The Art of Safe Criticism in Greece and Rome." *American Journal of Philology* 105: 174–208.

———. 1985. *Metaformations: Soundplay and Wordplay in Ovid and Other Classical Poets.* Ithaca, N.Y. and London: Cornell University Press.

———. 1988. "Ars est ca(e)lare artem (Art in Puns and Anagrams Engraved)." In Culler 1988, 17–43.

———. 1991. *Sophocles Oedipus: Evidence and Self-Conviction.* Ithaca, N.Y. and London: Cornell University Press.

Aman, R., and G. Sardo. 1983. "Canadian Sexual Terms." *Maledicta* 6: 21–28.

Ambrosino, D. 1986–1987. "Aristoph. *Nub.* 46s. (Il matrimonio di Strepsiade e la democrazia ateniese)." *Museum Criticum* 21–22: 95–127.

Andrewes, A. 1956. *The Greek Tyrants.* London: Hutchinson.

———. 1966. "The Government of Classical Sparta." In *Ancient History and Its Institutions: Studies Presented to Victor Ehrenberg on His 75th Birthday,* pp. 1–20. Oxford: Blackwell.

Anon. 1959. "*Under Milk Drip* or *Now We Are Sick.*" *Oxford Medical School Gazette* 11: 13–14.

Anon. 1961. "Lady Chatterley's Liver." *Oxford Medical School Gazette* 13: 16–18.

Apelt, O. 1912. *Platonische Aufsätze.* Leipzig: Teubner.

———. 1922. *Platon Gorgias.* Leipzig: Felix Meiner.

Arnott, W. H. 1988. Review of Sommerstein 1987. *Classical Review,* n.s. 38: 211–213.

Arrowsmith, W. 1970. *The Birds by Aristophanes.* New York: New American Library.

———. 1973. "Aristophanes *Birds:* The Fantasy Politics of Eros." *Arion* 1: 119–167.

Atherton, H. M. 1974. *Political Prints in the Age of Hogarth.* Oxford: Clarendon.

Aurenche, O. 1974. *Les Groupes d'Alcibiade, de Léogoras et de Teucros: Remarques sur la vie politique athénienne en 415 avant J.C.* Paris: Belles Lettres.

Austin, C., ed. 1973. *Comicorum graecorum fragmenta in papyris reperta.* Berlin and New York: de Gruyter. [Abbreviated as *CGFP.*]

Bacon, F. 1626. *Sylva Sylvarum: or a Naturall Historie.* London: William Lee.

Bacon, H. 1961. *Barbarians in Greek Tragedy.* New Haven, Conn.: Yale University Press.

Badian, E. 1992. "Thucydides on Rendering Speeches." *Athenaeum* 80: 187–190.

———. 1993. *From Plataea to Potidaea: Studies in the History and Historiography of the Pentecontaetia.* Baltimore, Md.: The Johns Hopkins University Press.

Bailey, C. 1936. "Who Played 'Dicaeopolis'?" In *Greek Poetry and Life: Essays Presented to Gilbert Murray on His 70th Birthday,* pp. 231–240. Oxford: Clarendon.

Baker, L., and D. P. Cantwell. 1982. "Language Acquisition, Cognitive Development, and Emotional Disorder in Childhood." In *Children's Language,* edited by K. E. Nelson, pp. 286–321. Hillsdale, N.J.: Laurence Erlbaum Associates.

Baldwin, B. 1993. "What Comes Out in the Wash? Mesomedes 9.15." *Liverpool Classical Monthly* 18: 141–142.

Barag, D. 1985. *Catalogue of Western Asiatic Glass in the British Museum.* London: British Museum Publications.

Barrett, W. S. 1964. *Euripides Hippolytus.* Oxford: Clarendon.

Barron, J. P. 1980. "Bakchylides, Theseus and a Woolly Cloak." *Bulletin of the Institute of Classical Studies* 27: 1–8.

Becker, W. A. 1874. *Charicles, or Illustrations of the Private Life of the Ancient Greeks.* 4th ed. London: Longmans, Green.

Bendz, G. 1963. *Frontin Kriegslisten.* Schriften und Quellen der alten Welt 10. Berlin: Akademie-Verlag.

Bennett, L. J., and W. B. Tyrrell. 1990. "Making Sense of Aristophanes' *Knights.*" *Arethusa* 23: 235–254.

Bentley, R. 1699. *A Dissertation upon the Epistles of Phalaris with an Answer to the Objections of the Hon. Charles Boyle, Esq.* 2d ed. London: H. Mortlock and J. Hartley.

———. 1883. *Dissertation upon the Letters of Phalaris, etc.* Edited by W. Wagner. London: George Bell.

Bernal, M. 1987. *Black Athena 1: The Fabrication of Ancient Greece, 1785–1985.* London: Free Association Press.

Bicknell, P. J. 1972. *Studies in Athenian Politics and Genealogy. Historia* Einzelschrift 19. Wiesbaden: Steiner Verlag.

———. 1982. "Axiochos Alkibiadou, Aspasia and Aspasios." *L'Antiquité classique* 51: 240–250.

Biel, J. C. 1779–1780. *Novus Thesaurus philologicus; sive Lexicon in LXX et alios interpretes et scriptores apocryphos Veteris Testamenti.* 3 vols. The Hague: J. A. Bouvink.

Blake, R. 1982. *Disraeli's Grand Tour.* London: Weidenfeld and Nicolson.

Blakesley, J. W. 1854. *Herodotus.* London: Whittaker and Co.

Blanckenhagen, P. von. 1964. "The Shield of Alcibiades." In *Essays in Memory of Karl Lehmann,* edited by L. F. Sandler, 38–42. New York.

———. 1992. "Stage and Actors in Plato's *Symposium.*" *Greek, Roman and Byzantine Studies* 33: 51–68.

Blaydes, F. H. M. 1845. *Aristophanis Acharnenses.* London: Williams and Norgate.

———. 1882. *Aristophanis Aves.* Halle: Orphanotrophei Libraria.

———. 1883. *Aristophanis Pax.* Halle: Orphanotrophei Libraria.

———. 1890. *Aristophanis Nubes.* Halle: Orphanotrophei Libraria.

Bloedow, E. F. 1973. *Alcibiades Reexamined. Historia* Einzelschrift 21. Wiesbaden: Steiner Verlag.

———. 1990. "'Not the Son of Achilles, but Achilles Himself': Alcibiades' Entry on the Political Stage at Athens, 2." *Historia* 39: 1–19.

————. 1991a. "'On Nurturing Lions in the State': Alcibiades' Entry on the Political Stage in Athens." *Klio* 73: 49–65.

————. 1991b. "Alcibiades, a Review Article." *Ancient History Bulletin* 5: 17–29.

————. 1992. "Alcibiades 'Brilliant' or 'Intelligent'?" *Historia* 41: 139–157.

Bluck, R. S. 1953. "The Origin of the *Greater Alcibiades*." *Classical Quarterly*, n.s. 3: 46–52.

Blumenthal, H. J. 1983. "Aristophanes *Frogs* 1437–65: Palamedes." *Liverpool Classical Monthly* 8: 64.

Boardman, J. 1982. "Herakles, Theseus and Amazons." In D. C. Kurtz and B. Sparkes, eds., *The Eye of Greece: Studies in the Art of Athens*, 1–28. Cambridge: Cambridge University Press.

————. 1988. "Trade in Greek Decorated Pottery." *Oxford Journal of Archaeology* 7: 27–33.

Bobrick, E. 1991. "Iphigeneia Revisited: *Thesmophoriazusae* 1160–1225." *Arethusa* 24: 67–76.

Boegehold, A. L. 1982. "A Dissent at Athens *ca.* 424–421 B.C." *Greek, Roman and Byzantine Studies* 23: 147–156.

Boruchovich, V. G. 1959. "Aristophanes and Alcibiades" [in Russian]. *Acta Antiqua Academiae Scientiarum Hungaricae* 7: 329–336.

Bowie, A. M. 1987. "Ritual Stereotype and Comic Reversal: Aristophanes' *Wasps*." *Bulletin of the Institute of Classical Studies* 34: 112–125.

————. 1993. *Aristophanes: Myth, Ritual and Comedy*. Cambridge: Cambridge University Press.

Bowie, E. L. 1988. "Who Is Dicaeopolis?" *Journal of Hellenic Studies* 108: 183–185.

Bowra, C. M. 1960. "Euripides' Epinician for Alcibiades." *Historia* 9: 8–79.

————. 1961. *Greek Lyric Poetry*. Oxford: Clarendon.

Brandenstein, W. 1964. "Der persische Satz bei Aristophanes, *Akharnhês*, Vers 100." *Wiener Zeitschrift für die Kunde Süd- und Ostasiens* 6: 3–58.

Brewer, J. 1986. *The Common People and Politics, 1750–1790s*. Cambridge: Cambridge University Press.

Brillante, C. 1987. "La figura di Filocleone nel prologo delle *Vespe* di Aristofane." *Quaderni Urbinati di Cultura Classica*, n.s. 26: 3–35.

Brixhe, C. 1988. "La langue de l'étranger non grec chez Aristophane." In R. Lonis, ed., *L'Etranger dans le monde grec*, 113–138. Nancy.

Broadhead, H. D. 1960. *The Persae of Aeschylus*. Cambridge: Cambridge University Press.

Brock, R. W. 1986. "The Double Plot in Aristophanes' *Knights*." *Greek, Roman and Byzantine Studies* 27: 5–27.

————. 1990. "Plato and Comedy." In Craik 1990: 39–50.

Broneer, O. 1944. "The Tent of Xerxes and the Greek Theater." *University of California Publications in Classical Archaeology* 1: 305–311.

Browne, Sir Thomas. 1658. *Hydrotaphia, Urne Buriall*. London: Henry Brome.

Brulé, P. 1994. *Périclès: L'apogée d'Athènes*. Paris: Gallimard.

Brumoy, P. 1730. *Le Théâtre des Grecs.* 3 vols. Paris: Chez Rollin père etc.

———. 1780. *Le Théâtre des Grecs.* 2d ed. 13 vols. Paris: Cussac.

Bruns, I. 1896. *Das literarische Porträt der Griechen im fünften und vierten Jahrhundert vor Christi Geburt.* Berlin: Hertz.

Brunt, P. A. 1952. "Thucydides and Alcibiades." *Revue des études grecques* 65: 59–96.

Bryant, M. 1990. *A Dictionary of Riddles.* London: Cassell.

Burn, A. R. 1948. *Pericles and Athens.* London: Hodder and Stoughton.

Busolt, G. 1893–1904. *Griechische Geschichte.* 3 vols. in 4. Gotha.

Byl, S. 1980. "Parodie d'une initiation dans les Nuées d'Aristophane." *Revue belge de philologie* 58: 5–21.

Caizzi, F. 1966. *Antisthenis Fragmenta.* Milan: Istituto editoriale cisalpino.

Callaghan, V. W. 1990. "The Erasmus-Hercules Equation in the Emblems of Alciati." In Selig and Sears 1990, 41–57.

Cantarella, E. 1984. "Per una preistoria del castigo." In *Du châtiment dans la cité: Supplices corporels et peine de mort dans le monde antique,* 37–73. Rome: École française de Rome.

Carter, L. B. 1986. *The Quiet Athenian.* Oxford: Clarendon.

Cartledge, P. 1981. "Spartan Wives: Liberation or Licence?" *Classical Quarterly,* n.s. 31: 84–105.

———. 1987. *Agesilaos and the Crisis of Sparta.* Baltimore, Md.: The Johns Hopkins University Press.

Cartledge, P. A., and F. D. Harvey, eds. 1985. *Crux: Essays Presented to G. E. M. de Ste. Croix on His 75th Birthday.* Exeter: Imprint Academic.

Chambers, M. H. 1993. "The Archon's Name in the Athens-Egesta Alliance (IG I^3 11)." *Zeitschrift für Papyrologie und Epigraphik* 98: 171–174.

———. 1994. "Reading Illegible Greek Inscriptions: Athens and Agesta." *Thetis, Mannheimer Beiträge zur Klassischen Archäologie und Geschichte Griechenlands und Zyperns* 1: 49–52, pl. 5.

Chambers, M., R. Gallucci, and P. Spanos. 1990. "Athens' Alliance with Egesta in the Year of Antiphon." *Zeitschrift für Papyrologie und Epigraphik* 83: 38–63.

Clark, W. G. 1871. "The History of the Ravenna Manuscript of Aristophanes." *Journal of Philology* 3: 153–160.

Clauss, M. 1983. *Sparta: Eine Einführung in seine Geschichte und Zivilisation.* Munich: C. H. Beck.

Clodius, C. A. 1767–1769. *Versuche aus der Literatur und Moral.* 4 vols. Leipzig: B. C. Breitkopf.

Cobb, R. 1986. *Promenades: A Historian's Appreciation of Modern French Literature.* Oxford: Blackwell.

Cogan, M. 1981. *The Human Thing: The Speeches and Principles of Thucydides' History.* Chicago: University of Chicago Press.

Cohen, B. 1991. "Perikles' Portrait and the Riace Bronzes: New Evidence for 'Schinocephaly'." *Hesperia* 60: 465–502.

Cohen, D. 1987. "Law, Society and Homosexuality in Classical Athens." *Past and Present* 117: 3–21.

———. 1991. *Law, Sexuality and Society: The Enforcement of Morals in Classical Athens.* Cambridge: Cambridge University Press.

Collard, C. 1981. *Euripides. Greece and Rome* New Surveys in the Classics, no. 14. Oxford.

Colvin, S. 1995. "Aristophanes: Dialect and Textual Criticism." *Mnemosyne* 48: 34–47.

Connor, W. R. 1971. *The New Politicians of Fifth-Century Athens.* Princeton, N.J.: Princeton University Press.

Cook, A. B. 1914–1940. *Zeus: A Study in Ancient Religion.* 3 vols. in 5. Cambridge: Cambridge University Press.

Cornford, F. 1907. *Thucydides Mythistoricus.* London: Edward Arnold.

Coulon, V., ed., and H. Van Daele, trans. 1923–1930. *Aristophane.* Budé edition. 5 vols. Paris: Les Belles Lettres.

Craik, E. M., ed. 1990. *"'Owls to Athens': Essays on Classical Subjects Presented to Sir Kenneth Dover.* Oxford: Clarendon.

Cromey, R. D. 1984. "On Deinomache." *Historia* 33: 385–401.

Crosby, M. 1949. "The Altar of the Twelve Gods in Athens." In *Commemorative Studies in Honor of Theodore Leslie Shear,* 82–103. *Hesperia,* suppl. 8.

Culler, J. 1988. *On Puns: The Foundation of Letters.* Oxford: Blackwell.

Daumas, M. 1985. "Aristophane et les Perses." *Revue des études anciennes* 87: 289–305.

Davie, J. N. 1982. "Theseus the King in Fifth-Century Athens." *Greece and Rome,* 2d ser., 2: 25–34.

Davies, J. K. 1971. *Athenian Propertied Families, 600–300 B.C.* Oxford: Clarendon.

———. 1984. *Wealth and the Power of Wealth in Classical Athens.* Salem, N.H.: Ayer Co.

Davies, R. 1992. "Reflections from the Golden Age." In *The Greek Miracle: Classical Sculpture from the Dawn of Democracy: the Fifth Century B.C.,* edited by D. Buitron-Oliver, 69–76. Washington D.C.: National Gallery of Art.

Denniston, J. D. 1952. *Greek Prose Style.* Oxford: Clarendon.

De Quincey, T. 1857. *Collected Works.* Vol. 13. London: J. Hogg.

Descoeudres, J.-P. 1981. "Ἥδιστος δαίμων." *Antichthon* 15: 8–14.

Develin, R. 1985. "Age Qualifications for Athenian Magistrates." *Zeitschrift für Papyrologie und Epigraphik* 61: 149–159.

———. 1989. *Athenian Officials, 684–321 B.C.* Cambridge: Cambridge University Press.

Diels, H., and W. Kranz, eds. 1951–1952. *Die Fragmente der Vorsokratiker.* 6th ed. Berlin: Weidmann. [Abbreviated as DK⁶.]

Dindorf, W. 1838. *Aristophanis comoediae et deperditarum fragmenta.* Paris: A. F. Didot.

Dobrov, G. 1990. "Aristophanes' *Birds* and the Metaphor of Deferral." *Arethusa* 23: 209–233.

Dodds, E. R. 1951. *The Greeks and the Irrational.* Berkeley and Los Angeles: University of California Press.

Donaldson, J. W. 1860. *Theatre of the Greeks.* 7th ed. London: Longman and Co.

Donnay, G. 1968. "La Date du procès de Phidias." *L'Antiquité classique* 37: 19–36.

Dover, K. J. 1958. Review of Newiger 1957. *Classical Review,* n.s. 8: 235–237.

———. 1963. "Notes on Aristophanes' *Acharnians.*" *Maia* 15: 6–25.

———. 1967. "Portrait-masks in Aristophanes." In *Kōmōidotragēmata: Studia Aristophanea viri Aristophanei W.J.W. Koster in Honorem,* 16–28. Amsterdam: A. M. Hakkert.

———. 1968. *Aristophanes Clouds.* Oxford: Clarendon.

———. 1972. *Aristophanic Comedy.* Berkeley and Los Angeles: University of California Press.

———. 1978. *Greek Homosexuality.* Cambridge, Mass.: Harvard University Press.

Dracoulidès, N. N. 1967. *Psychanalyse d'Aristophane.* Paris: Éditions Universitaires.

Droysen, J. 1835. "Des Aristophanes Vögel und die Hermokopiden." *Rheinisches Museum für Philologie* 3: 161–208.

Dübner, F. 1842. *Scholia graeca in Aristophanem.* Paris: A. F. Didot.

duBois, P. 1991. *Torture and Truth.* New York: Routledge.

Dunbar, N. 1995. *Aristophanes Birds.* Oxford: Clarendon.

Edmunds, L. 1980. "Aristophanes' *Acharnians.*" *Yale Classical Studies* 26: 1–41.

———. 1985. "Aristophanes' Socrates." *Proceedings of the Boston Area Colloquium in Ancient Philosophy* 1: 209–230.

———. 1987a. *Cleon, Knights, and Aristophanes' Politics.* Lanham, Md.: University Press of America.

———. 1987b. "Il Socrate aristofaneo e l'ironia pratica." *Quaderni urbinati di cultura classica,* n.s. 26: 7–21.

Ehrenberg, V. 1954. *Sophocles and Pericles.* Oxford: Blackwell.

Elliot, R. T. 1914. *The Acharnians of Aristophanes.* Oxford: Clarendon.

Ellis, W. 1989. *Alcibiades.* London: Routledge.

Else, G. F. 1957. *Aristotle's Poetics: The Argument.* Cambridge, Mass.: Harvard University Press.

Farrell, J. 1993. "Allusions, Delusions, and Confusions: A Reply." *Electronic Antiquity* (November).

Fatouros, G., and T. Krischer. 1983. *Libanios.* Darmstadt: Wissenschaftliche Buchgesellschaft.

Ferguson, C. A. 1977. "Baby Talk as a Simplified Register." In *Talking to Children: Language Input and Acquisition,* edited by C. E. Snow and C. A. Ferguson, 209–235. Cambridge: Cambridge University Press.

Fisher, N. R. E. 1992. *Hybris: A Study in the Values of Honour and Shame in Ancient Greece.* Warminster: Aris and Phillips.

———. 1993. "Multiple Personalities and Dionysiac Festivals: Dicaeopolis in Aristophanes' *Acharnians.*" *Greece and Rome* 40: 31–47.

Fisher, R. K. 1984. *Aristophanes Clouds: Purpose and Technique.* Amsterdam: A. M. Hakkert.

Foley, H. P. 1988. "Tragedy and Politics in Aristophanes' *Acharnians.*" *Journal of Hellenic Studies* 108: 33–47.

Forde, S. 1989. *The Ambition to Rule: Alcibiades and the Politics of Imperialism in Thucydides.* Ithaca, N.Y. and London: Cornell University Press.

Fornara, C. 1971. "Evidence for the Date of Herodotus' Publication." *Journal of Hellenic Studies* 111: 25–34.

Forrest, W. G. 1963. "Aristophanes' *Acharnians.*" *Phoenix* 17: 1–12.

———. 1975. "Aristophanes and the Athenian Empire." In *The Ancient Historian and His Materials: Essays in Honour of C. E. Stevens on His Seventieth Birthday,* edited by B. Levick, 17–30. Farnborough: Gregg.

Francis, E. D. 1980. "Greeks and Persians: The Art of Hazard and Triumph." In *Ancient Persia, The Art of an Empire,* edited by D. Schmandt-Besserat, 53–86. Invited Lectures on the Middle East at the University of Texas at Austin, 4. Malibu, Calif.: Undena.

———. 1990. *Image and Idea in Fifth-Century Greece: Art and Literature after the Persian Wars.* London: Routledge.

———. 1991–1993. "Brachylogia Laconica: Spartan Speeches in Thucydides." *Bulletin of the Institute of Classical Studies* 38: 198–212.

———. 1992. "Oedipus Achaemenides." *American Journal of Philology* 113: 333–357.

Francis, E. D., and M. Vickers. 1981. "Leagros Kalos." *Proceedings of the Cambridge Philological Society* 207, n.s. 27: 97–136.

———. 1988. "The Agora Revisited: Athenian Chronology c. 500–450 B.C." *Annual of the British School at Athens* 83: 143–167.

Frost, F. J. 1964a. "Thucydides, Son of Milesias, and Athenian Politics before the War." *Historia* 13: 385–399.

———. 1964b. "Pericles and Dracontides." *Journal of Hellenic Studies* 84: 69–72.

Furley, W. D. 1989. "Andokides iv ('Against Alkibiades'): Fact or Fiction?" *Hermes* 117: 138–156.

Gadbery, L. M. 1992. "The Sanctuary of the Twelve Gods in the Athenian Agora: A Revised View." *Hesperia* 61: 447–490.

Gall, H. von. 1977. "Das persische Königszelt und die Hallenarchitektur in Iran und Griechenland." In *Festschrift für Frank Brommer,* edited by U. Höckmann and A. Krug, 119–132. Mainz: von Zabern.

———. 1979. "Das Zelt des Xerxes und seine Rolle als persicher Raumtyp in Griechenland." *Gymnasion* 86: 444–462.

Gallo, I. 1975. *Frammenti biografici da papiri.* Rome: Edizioni dell' Ateneo.

Garnsey, P. 1988. *Famine and Food Supply in the Graeco-Roman World: Responses to Risk and Crisis.* Cambridge: Cambridge University Press.

George, M. D. 1959. *English Political Caricature, 1793–1832.* Oxford: Clarendon.

Gilbert, G. 1877. *Beiträge zur innern Geschichte Athens im Zeitalter des peloponnesischen Krieges.* Leipzig: Teubner.

Gill, D. W. J. 1988. "Expressions of Wealth: Greek Art and Society." *Antiquity* 62: 735–743.

Ginouvès, R. 1962. *Balaneutiké: Recherches sur le bain dans l'antiquité grecque.* Paris: de Boccard.

Goldhill, S. 1987. "The Great Dionysia and Civic Ideology." *Journal of Hellenic Studies* 107: 58–76.

Gomme, A. W. 1962. *More Essays in Greek History and Literature.* Oxford: Clarendon.

Gomme, A. W., A. Andrewes, and K. J. Dover. 1948–1981. *A Historical Commentary on Thucydides.* 5 vols. Oxford: Clarendon. [Abbreviated as *HCT.*]

Gonick, L. 1987. *All About Athens. The Cartoon History of the Universe,* vol. 7. San Francisco: Rip Off Press.

Goossens, R. 1935. "Les 'Ploutoi' de Cratinus." *Revue des études anciennes* 37: 405–434.

Graves, C. E. 1905. *Aristophanes, The Acharnians.* Cambridge: Cambridge University Press.

Green, P. 1979. "Strepsiades, Socrates and the Abuses of Intellectualism." *Greek, Roman and Byzantine Studies* 20: 15–25.

Grenfell, B. P., and A. S. Hunt. 1904. "Argument of Cratinus' *Dionusalexandros.*" *Oxyrhynchus Papyri* 4: 69–72, no. 663.

Griffith, J. G. 1988. "The Witnesses at the Trial of the Dog Labes in Aristophanes' *Wasps.*" In *Festinat Senex: Essays in Greek and Latin Literature and Archaeology.* Oxford: Oxbow.

Griffith, R. H. 1945. "The *Dunciad.*" *Philological Quarterly* 24: 155–157.

Grote, G. 1870. *A History of Greece.* New ed. 12 vols. London: John Murray.

Guarducci, M. 1984. "I culti della Laconia." In *Problemi di Storia e Cultura Spartana,* edited by E. Lanzillotta, 87–106. Università di Macerata, Pubblicazioni della Facoltà di Lettere e Filosofia, 20. Rome: G. Bretschneider.

Guthrie, W. K. C. 1950. *The Greeks and Their Gods.* London: Methuen.

———. 1969. *A History of Greek Philosophy.* Cambridge: Cambridge University Press.

Hall, H. G. 1984. *Comedy in Context: Essays on Molière.* Jackson, Miss.: University Press of Mississippi.

Halliwell, S. 1990. "The Sounds of the Voice in Old Comedy." In Craik 1990: 69–79.

———. 1991. "Comic Satire and Freedom of Speech in Classical Athens." *Journal of Hellenic Studies* 111: 48–70.

Hammond, N. G. L., and H. H. Scullard. 1970. *The Oxford Classical Dictionary.* 2d ed. Oxford: Clarendon. [Abbreviated as *OCD².*]

Handley, E. W. 1982. "*POxy.* 2806: A fragment of Cratinus?" *Bulletin of the Institute of Classical Studies* 29: 109–117.

———. 1993. "Aristophanes and the Generation Gap." In *Tragedy, Comedy and the*

Polis: Papers from the Greek Drama Conference, Nottingham 18–20 July 1990 edited by A. H. Sommerstein, 417–430. Bari: Levante editori.

Handley, E. W., and J. Rea. 1957. *The* Telephus *of Euripides. Bulletin of the Institute of Classical Studies,* suppl. 5.

Hansen, M. H. 1987. *The Athenian Assembly in the Age of Demosthenes.* Oxford: Blackwell.

Harriott, R. M. 1982. "The Function of the Euripides Scene in Aristophanes' *Acharnians.*" *Greece and Rome* 29: 35–41.

———. 1986. *Aristophanes, Poet and Dramatist.* London: Croom Helm.

Harvey, F. D. 1985. "Dona Ferentes: Some Aspects of Bribery in Greek Politics." In Cartledge and Harvey 1985: 76–117.

Hatzfeld, J. 1951. *Alcibiade: Étude sur l'histoire d'Athènes à la fin du Vᵉ siècle.* 2d ed. Paris: Presses Universitaires de France.

Havelock, E. A. 1957. *The Liberal Temper in Greek Politics.* London: Jonathan Cape.

———. 1972. "The Socratic Self as It Is Parodied in Aristophanes' *Clouds.*" *Yale Classical Studies* 22: 1–18.

Hawtrey, R. S. W. 1976. "Plato, Socrates and the Mysteries: A Note." *Antichthon* 10: 22–24.

Heath, M. 1987a. *Political Comedy in Aristophanes. Hypomnemata* 87. Göttingen: Vandenbroeck and Ruprecht.

———. 1987b. "Euripides *Telephus.*" *Classical Quarterly* 37: 272–280.

Heckscher, W. S. 1967. "The Genesis of Iconology." In *Stil und Überlieferung in der Kunst des Abendlandes: Akten des 21. Internationalen Kongresses für Kunstgeschichte,* 3: 239–262.

Heckscher, W. S., A. B. Sherman, and S. Ferguson. 1984. *Emblem Books in the Princeton University Library: A Short-Title Catalogue.* Princeton, N.J.: Princeton University Library.

Henderson, J. 1975. *The Maculate Muse: Obscene Language in Attic Comedy.* New Haven, Conn.: Yale University Press.

———. 1987. *Aristophanes Lysistrata.* Oxford: Clarendon.

———. 1990. "The Demos and Comic Competition." In *Nothing to Do with Dionysus: Social Meanings of Greek Drama,* edited by J. Winkler and F. Zeitlin, 271–313. Princeton, N.J.: Princeton University Press.

———. 1993. "Problems in Greek Literary History: The Case of Aristophanes *Clouds.*" In Rosen and Farrell 1993: 591–601.

Henry, A. S. 1974. "Bios in Sophocles' Philoctetes." *Classical Review* 24: 3–4.

———. 1992. "Through a Laser Beam Darkly: Space Age Technology and the Egesta Decree *IG* i³ 11." *Zeitschrift für Papyrologie und Epigraphik* 91: 137–146.

Henry, M. M. 1995. *Prisoner of History: Aspasia of Miletus and Her Biographical Tradition.* New York: Oxford University Press.

Herman, G. 1990. "Treaties and Alliances in the World of Thucydides." *Proceedings of the Cambridge Philological Society* 216: 83–102.

———. 1994. "How Violent Was Athenian Society?" In Hornblower and Osborne 1994: 99–117.

Hertzberg, G. F. 1853. *Alkibiades: Der Staatsmann und Feldherr*. Halle: C. E. M. Pfeffer.

Hock, R. F. 1976. "Simon the Shoemaker as an Ideal Cynic." *Greek, Roman and Byzantine Studies* 17: 41–53.

Holden, H. A. 1902. *Onomasticon Aristophaneum*. 2d ed. Cambridge: Cambridge University Press.

Holwerda, D. 1977. *Scholia vetera in Nubes*. Groningen: Bouma's Boekhuis.

Hooker, J. T. 1980. *The Ancient Spartans*. London: J. M. Dent.

Hopkins, K. 1993. "Novel Evidence for Roman Slavery." *Past and Present* 138: 3–27.

Hornblower, S. 1987. *Thucydides*. London: Duckworth.

———. 1991. *A Commentary on Thucydides*. Vol. 1. Oxford: Clarendon.

Hornblower, S., and R. Osborne, eds. 1994. *Ritual, Finance, Politics: Athenian Democratic Accounts Presented to David Lewis*. Oxford: Clarendon.

Hubbard, T. K. 1991. *The Mask of Comedy: Aristophanes and the Intertextual Parabasis*. Ithaca, N.Y. and London: Cornell University Press.

Hunter, V. 1990. "Gossip and the Politics of Reputation in Classical Athens." *Phoenix* 44: 299–325.

Hussey, E. 1985. "Thucydidean History and Democritean Theory." In Cartledge and Harvey 1985: 118–138.

Hutchinson, P. 1983. *Games Authors Play*. London: Methuen.

Immerwahr, H. 1990. *Attic Script: A Survey*. Oxford: Clarendon.

Jacoby, F., ed. 1923–1958. *Fragmente der griechischen Historiker*. Berlin: Weidmann; and Leiden: E. J. Brill. [Abbreviated as *FGrH*.]

Jameson, M. H. 1988. "Sacrifice and Animal Husbandry in Classical Greece." In *Pastoral Economies in Classical Antiquity*, ed. C. R. Whitaker, 87–119. Cambridge Philological Society Supplement 14.

Janko, R. 1984. *Aristotle on Comedy: Towards a Reconstruction of Poetics II*. London: Duckworth.

Jeanmaire, H. 1913. "La Kryptie lacédémonienne." *Revue des études grecques* 26: 121–150.

Kagan, D. 1990. *Pericles of Athens and the Birth of Democracy*. New York: Simon and Schuster.

Kassel, R., and C. Austin, eds. 1983–. *Poetae Comici Graeci*. Berlin and New York: de Gruyter. [Abbreviated as *PCG*.]

Katz, B. R. 1976. "The *Birds* of Aristophanes and Politics." *Athenaeum*, n.s. 54: 353–381.

Kaufmann, T. D. 1987. "The Allegories and Their Meaning." In Rasponi and Tanzi 1987: 89–108.

———. 1990. "Arcimboldo's Serious Jokes: 'Mysterious but Long Meaning'." In Selig and Sears 1990, 59–86.

Kent, R. G. 1953. *Old Persian: Grammar, Texts, Lexicon.* New Haven, Conn.: American Oriental Society.

Keramopoullos, A. D. 1923. *Ho apotumpanismos.* Athens.

Keuls, E. C. 1985. *The Reign of the Phallus: Sexual Politics in Ancient Athens.* New York: Harper and Row.

Kirk, G. S., J. E. Raven, and M. Schofield. 1983. *The Presocratic Philosophers: A Critical History with a Selection of Texts.* 2d ed. Cambridge: Cambridge University Press.

Kirchner, J. 1901–1903. *Prosopographia Attica.* Berlin: G. Reimer.

Köchly, H. 1857. *Über die Vögel des Aristophanes.* Zurich: Zürcher and Furrer.

Kock, T., ed. 1880–1888. *Comicorum Atticorum Fragmenta.* 3 vols. Leipzig: Teubner. [Abbreviated as *CAF.*]

Konstan, D. 1985. "The Politics of Aristophanes' *Wasps.*" *Transactions of the American Philological Association* 115: 27–46.

———. 1990. "A City in the Air: Aristophanes' *Birds.*" *Arethusa* 23: 183–207.

Koster, W. J. W. 1975. *Scholia in Aristophanem.* Vol. 1a. *Prolegomena de Comoedia.* Groningen: Bouma's Boekhuis.

Kraus, W. 1985. "Aristophanes' politische Komödien: *Die Acharner/Die Ritter.*" *Sitzungsbericht der Akademie der Wissenschaften in Wien, Philosophisch-historische Klasse* 453.

Laistner, M. L. W. 1957. *A History of the Greek World from 479 to 323 B.C.* 3d ed. London: Methuen.

Lalonde, G. V. 1991. *Horoi. The Athenian Agora* 19, 1–51. Princeton, N.J.: Princeton University Press.

Lamb, W. R. M. 1930. *Lysias.* London: Heinemann.

Landfester, M. 1967. *Die Ritter des Aristophanes.* Amsterdam: B. R. Gruner.

Lane, L. 1966. *The ABZ of Scouse: How to Talk Proper in Liverpool.* Vol. 2. Liverpool.

Lang, M. L. 1978. *Socrates in the Agora.* Princeton, N.J.: Princeton University Press.

Laschitzer, S. 1888. "Die Genealogie des Kaisers Maximilian I." *Jahrbuch der Kunsthistorischen Sammlungen des Allerhöchsten Kaiserhauses* 7: 1–200.

Latte, K. 1966. *Hesychii Alexandrini Lexicon.* Vol. 2. Copenhagen: E. Munksgaard.

Laum, B. 1925. *Das Eisengelt der Spartaner.* Braunsberg: Verlag der Staatlichen Akademie.

van Leeuwen, J. 1898. *Aristophanis Nubes.* Leiden: A. W. Sijthoff.

———. 1902. *Aristophanis Aves.* Leiden: A. W. Sijthoff.

———. 1908. *Prolegomena ad Aristophanem.* Leiden: A. W. Sijthoff.

Lefkowitz, M. 1981. *The Lives of the Greek Poets.* London: Duckworth.

Leipen, N. 1971. *Athena Parthenos: A Reconstruction.* Toronto: Royal Ontario Museum.

von Leutsch, E. L., and F. G. Schneidewin. 1839. *Corpus Paroemiographorum Graecorum.* Göttingen: Vandenbroeck and Ruprecht.

Levesque, P.-Ch. 1795. *Histoire de Thucydide, fils d'Olorus, traduite du grec.* Paris.

Levi, M. A. 1967. *Quattro studi spartani e altri scritti di storia greca.* Milan: Istituto Editoriale Cisalpino.

Levy, E. 1988. "Métèques et droit de résidence." In *L'Étranger dans le monde grec,* ed. R. Lonis, 245–252. Nancy: Presses Universitaires de Nancy.

Lewis, D. M. 1966. "After the Profanation of the Mysteries." In *Ancient History and Its Institutions: Studies Presented to Victor Ehrenberg on His 75th Birthday,* 177–191. Oxford: Blackwell.

———. 1977. *Sparta and Persia.* Leiden: Brill.

Liddell, H. G., R. Scott, and H. S. Jones. 1968. *A Greek-English Lexicon.* 9th ed., with supplement. Oxford: Clarendon. [Abbreviated as LSJ.]

Lind, H. 1991. *Der Gerber Kleon in den "Rittern" des Aristophanes: Studien zur Demagogenkomödie.* Frankfurt: P. Lang.

Lintott, A. 1982. *Violence, Civil Strife and Revolution in the Classical City.* London: Croom Helm.

Littman, R. J. 1969. "A New Date for Leotychidas." *Phoenix* 23: 267–277.

———. 1970. "The Loves of Alcibiades." *Transactions of the American Philological Association* 101: 263–276.

Lloyd-Jones, H. 1982. *Classical Survivals: The Classics in the Modern World.* London: Duckworth.

———. 1983. *The Justice of Zeus.* 2d ed. Berkeley and Los Angeles: University of California Press.

Lloyd-Jones, H., and N. G. Wilson. 1990. *Sophoclis Fabulae.* Oxford: Clarendon.

Lofberg, J. O. 1917. *Sycophancy in Athens.* Menasha, Wis.: Collegiate Press.

Longrigg, J. 1980. "The Great Plague of Athens." *History of Science* 18: 209–225.

———. 1992. "Epidemics, Ideas and Classical Athenian Society." In *Epidemics and Ideas: Essays on the Historical Perception of Pestilence,* edited by T. Ranger and P. Slack. Cambridge: Cambridge University Press.

Loraux, N. 1981. *L'Invention d'Athènes: Histoire de l'oraison funèbre dans la "cité classique."* Paris: Mouton.

MacArthur, W. P. 1959. "The Medical Identification of Some Pestilences of the Past." *Transactions of the Royal Society of Tropical Medicine and Hygiene* 53: 423–439.

———. 1961. "The Medical Identification of Some Pestilences of the Past." *Oxford Medical School Gazette* 13: 166–173.

MacDougall, H. A. 1982. *Racial Myth in English History: Trojans, Teutons and Anglo-Saxons.* Montreal: Harvest House.

MacDowell, D. M. 1971. *Aristophanes Wasps.* Oxford: Clarendon.

———. 1983. "The Nature of Aristophanes' *Akharnians.*" *Greece and Rome* 30: 143–161.

———. 1990. "The Meaning of *alazōn.*" In Craik 1990: 287–292.

Macleod, C. W. 1982. "Politics and the *Oresteia.*" *Journal of Hellenic Studies* 102: 124–144. (= Macleod 1983, 20–40.)

———. 1983. *Collected Essays.* Oxford: Clarendon.

Maehly, H. 1853. "De Aspasia Milesia commentariolus." *Philologus* 8: 213–230.

Mahood, M. M. 1957. *Shakespeare's Wordplay.* London: Routledge.

Maidment, K. J. 1941. *Minor Attic Orators.* Vol. 1. London: Heinemann.

Mansfeld, J. 1979–1980. "The Date of Anaxagoras' Athenian Period and the Date of His Trial," parts 1 and 2. *Mnemosyne*, 4th ser. 22: 39–69; 23: 17–95.

Mansfield, J. M. 1985. "The Robe of Athena and the Panathenaic Peplos." Diss., University of California-Berkeley.

Marcus, S. 1966. *The Other Victorians*. London: Weidenfeld and Nicolson.

Marshall, M. 1990. "Pericles and the Plague." In Craik 1990: 163–170.

Mat-Hasquin, M. 1981. *Voltaire et l'antiquité grecque*. Oxford: Voltaire Foundation.

Mattingly, H. B. 1966. "Periclean Imperialism." In *Ancient History and Its Institutions: Studies Presented to Victor Ehrenberg on His 75th Birthday*, 193–223. Oxford: Blackwell.

———. 1969. "Athens and the Western Greeks: c. 500–413 B.C." In *La circolazione della moneta ateniese in Sicilia e in Magna Grecia; Atti del I convegno del Centro internazionale di 1967*, 201–221. Rome: Istituto italiana di numismatica.

———. 1991. "The Practice of Ostracism at Athens." *Antichthon* 25: 1–26.

———. 1992. "Epigraphy and the Athenian Empire." *Historia* 41: 129–138.

———. 1993. "New Light on the Athenian Standards Decree (ATL II, D 14)." *Klio* 75: 99–102.

Meiggs, R. 1972. *The Athenian Empire*. Oxford: Clarendon.

Meiggs, R., and D. M. Lewis. 1969. *A Selection of Greek Historical Inscriptions*. Oxford: Clarendon. [Abbreviated as ML.]

Meineke, A., ed. 1839–1857. *Fragmenta Comicorum Graecorum*. 5 vols. Berlin: G. Reimer. [Abbreviated as *FCG*.]

Merry, W. W. 1880. *Aristophanes, The Acharnians*. Oxford: Clarendon.

———. 1904. *Aristophanes, The Birds*. 4th ed. Oxford: Clarendon.

Michell, H. 1964. *Sparta*. Cambridge: Cambridge University Press.

Miller, M. 1992. "The Parasol: An Oriental Status-Symbol in Late Archaic and Classical Athens." *Journal of Hellenic Studies* 112: 91–105.

Miller, S. G. 1978. *The Prytaneion: Its Function and Architectural Form*. Berkeley and Los Angeles: University of California Press.

Millett, P. 1991. *Lending and Borrowing in Ancient Athens*. Cambridge: Cambridge University Press.

Milosz, C. 1953. *The Captive Mind*. London: Secker and Warburg.

Mitford, W. 1829. *The History of Greece*. New ed. 8 vols. London: T. Cadell.

Montuori, M. 1974. *Socrate: Fisiologia di un mito*. Florence: Sansoni.

———. 1981. *Socrates, the Physiology of a Myth*. Amsterdam: J. C. Gieben.

Moorton, R. F. 1988. "Aristophanes on Alcibiades." *Greek, Roman and Byzantine Studies* 29: 345–359.

Morenilla-Talens, C. 1989. "Die Charakterisierung der Ausländer durch lautliche Ausdrucksmittel in den *Persern* des Aischylos sowie den *Acharnern* und *Vögeln* des Aristophanes." *Indogermanische Forschungen* 94: 158–176.

Müller, C. 1841–1870. *Fragmenta Historiarum Graecorum*. Paris: A. F. Didot. [Abbreviated as *FHG*.]

Murray, G. 1933. *Aristophanes, a Study*. Oxford: Clarendon.

Murray, O., ed. 1990a. *Sympotica: A Symposium on the Symposium.* Oxford: Clarendon.

———. 1990b. "The Affair of the Mysteries: Democracy and the Drinking Group." In Murray 1990a: 149–161.

Nauck, A. 1889. *Tragicorum Graecorum Fragmenta.* 2d ed. Leipzig: Teubner. [Abbreviated as *TGF.*]

Neil, R. A. 1901. *The Knights of Aristophanes.* Cambridge: Cambridge University Press.

Newiger, H.-J. 1957. *Metapher und Allegorie: Studien zu Aristophanes. Zetemata* 16. Munich: Beck.

———. 1983. "Gedanken zu Aristophanes 'Vögeln'." In *Aretḗs mnḗmē: Aphiérōma eis mnḗmēn toû Kōnstantínou I. Bourbérē,* 47–57. Studies and Researches 35. Athens: Greek Anthropological Society.

Norman, A. F. 1960. "The Book Trade in Fourth-Century Antioch." *Journal of Hellenic Studies* 80: 122–126.

———. 1965. *Libanius' Autobiography (Oration 1).* Hull: University Publications.

Norwood, G. 1931. *Greek Comedy.* London: Methuen.

Nussbaum, M. 1980. "Aristophanes and Socrates on Learning Practical Wisdom." *Yale Classical Studies* 26: 43–97.

Ober, J. 1989. *Mass and Elite in Democratic Athens.* Princeton, N.J.: Princeton University Press.

Olson, S. D. 1990. "Dicaeopolis and Aristophanes in *Acharnians." Liverpool Classical Monthly* 15: 31–32.

———. 1992. "Names and Naming in Aristophanic Comedy." *Classical Quarterly* 42: 304–319.

O'Neill, Y. V. 1980. *Speech and Speech Disorders in Western Thought before 1600.* Westport, Ct. and London: Greenwood.

O'Regan, D. E. 1992. *Rhetoric, Comedy and the Violence of Language in Aristophanes' Clouds.* New York: Oxford University Press.

Osborne, R. 1985. "The Erection and Mutilation of the Hermai." *Proceedings of the Cambridge Philological Society* 31: 47–53.

———. 1990. "The *Demos* and Its Divisions in Classical Athens." In *The Greek City from Homer to Alexander,* edited by O. Murray and S. Price, 265–293. Oxford: Clarendon.

Ostwald, M. 1986. *From Popular Sovereignty to the Sovereignty of Law: Law, Society and Politics in Fifth-Century Athens.* Berkeley and Los Angeles: University of California Press.

———. 1988. ΑΝΑΓΚΗ *in Thucydides.* American Classical Studies 18. Atlanta: Scholars Press.

Panagl, O. 1983. *"Pheidippides:* Etymologische Überlegungen zu einem aristophanischen Personennamen." In *Festschrift für Robert Muth,* edited by P. Händel and W. Meid, 297–306. Innsbruck: Arnoe.

Parker, D. 1961. *The Acharnians by Aristophanes.* Ann Arbor, Mich.: University of Michigan Press.

———. 1962. *Aristophanes, The Wasps*. Ann Arbor, Mich.: University of Michigan Press.

Parker, R. 1983. *Miasma, Pollution and Purification in Early Greek Religion*. Oxford: Clarendon.

Pascal, R. 1973. *From Naturalism to Expressionism: German Literature and Society, 1880–1918*. London: Weidenfeld and Nicolson.

Paully, A., G. Wissowa, and W. Kroll. 1894–1980. *Real-Encyclopädie der klassischen Altertumswissenschaft*. Stuttgart: Alfred Druckenmüller. [Abbreviated as *RE*.]

le Paulmier de Grentemesnil, J. 1668. *Exercitationes in optimos fere auctores Graecos*. Leiden.

Petersen, W. 1910. *Greek Diminutives in -ιον: A Study in Semantics*. Weimar: R. Wagner.

Pfeiffer, R. 1976. *History of Classical Scholarship from 1300 to 1850*. Oxford: Clarendon.

Picard, C. 1961. "Sabazios, dieu thraco-phrygien: Expansion et aspects nouveaux de son culte." *Revue archéologique*: 129–176.

Pickard-Cambridge, A. W. 1962. *Dithyramb, Tragedy and Comedy*. Revised by T. B. L. Webster. Oxford: Clarendon.

———. 1968. *The Dramatic Festivals of Athens*. Revised by J. Gould and D. M. Lewis. Oxford: Clarendon.

Platnauer, M. 1964. *Aristophanes Peace*. Oxford: Clarendon.

———. 1987. *Plutarch: Life of Pericles*. Bristol: Bristol Classical Press.

Pope, M. 1986. "Athenian Festival Judges — Seven, Five, or However Many." *Classical Quarterly* 36: 322–326.

———. 1989. "Upon the Country — Juries and the Principle of Random Selection." *Social Science Information* 28, no. 2: 265–289.

Powell, A. 1988. *Athens and Sparta: Constructing Greek Political and Social History from 478 B.C.* London: Routledge.

Powell, J. E. 1937. "Puns in Herodotus." *Classical Review* 51: 103.

Prandi, L. 1992. "Introduzione." In *Plutarcho, Vite parallele, Coriolano/Alcibiade*, 255–317. Milan: Rizzoli.

Pritchett, W. K. 1953. "The Attic Stelai." *Hesperia* 22: 225–299.

———. 1956. "Attic Stelai, Part II." *Hesperia* 25: 167–210.

———. 1961. "Five New Fragments of the Attic Stelai." *Hesperia* 30: 23–29.

Proietti, G. 1987. *Xenophon's Sparta: An Introduction*. Leiden: E. J. Brill.

Rasponi, S., and C. Tanzi. 1987. *The Arcimboldo Effect*. Milan: Electa Editrice.

Rau, P. 1967. *Paratragodia: Untersuchung einer komischen Form des Aristophanes*. Zetemata 45. Munich: Beck.

Raubitschek, A. E. 1948. "The Case against Alcibiades (Andocides IV)." *Transactions of the American Philological Association* 79: 191–210.

Rawlings, H. R. 1981. *The Structure of Thucydides' History*. Princeton, N.J.: Princeton University Press.

Redfern, W. 1984. *Puns*. Oxford: Blackwell.

Rhodes, P. J. 1972. *The Athenian Boule.* Oxford: Clarendon.

———. 1981. *A Commentary on the Aristotelian Athenaion Politeia.* Oxford: Clarendon.

Richardson, N. J. 1974. *The Homeric Hymn to Demeter.* Oxford: Clarendon.

Richler, M. 1990. *Solomon Gursky Was Here.* New York: Knopf.

Richter, G. M. A. 1965. *The Portraits of the Greeks.* London: Phaidon.

Robert, L. 1938. "Inscriptions du dème d'Acharnai." *Études épigraphiques et philologiques* (Bibliothèque de l'École des Hautes Études 272): 293–316.

Robinson, C. E. 1916. *The Days of Alkibiades.* New York: E. Arnold.

Rodnan, G. P. 1961. "A Gallery of Gout: Being a Miscellany of Prints and Caricatures from the Sixteenth Century to the Present Day." *Arthritis and Rheumatism* 4: 27–46.

Rogers, B. B. 1902. *The Frogs of Aristophanes.* London: George Bell.

———. 1906. *The Birds of Aristophanes.* London: George Bell.

———. 1910a. *The Acharnians of Aristophanes.* London: George Bell.

———. 1910b. *The Knights of Aristophanes.* London: George Bell.

———. 1916. *The Clouds of Aristophanes.* London: George Bell.

de Romilly, J. 1963. *Thucydides and Athenian Imperialism.* Oxford: Blackwell.

Rose, H. J. 1959. *A Handbook of Greek Mythology.* New York: E. P. Dutton.

Rosen, R. M. 1984. "The Ionian at Aristophanes *Peace* 46." *Greek, Roman and Byzantine Studies* 25: 389–396.

———. 1988a. "Hipponax, Boupalos, and the Conventions of the *Psogos*." *Transactions of the American Philological Association* 118: 29–41.

———. 1988b. *Old Comedy and the Iambographic Tradition.* Atlanta: Scholars Press.

Rosen, R. M., and J. Farrell, eds. 1993. *Nomodeiktes: Greek Studies in Honor of Martin Ostwald.* Ann Arbor, Mich.: University of Michigan Press.

Rotroff, S. I., and J. H. Oakley. 1992. *Debris from a Public Dining Place in the Athenian Agora. Hesperia,* suppl. 25.

Rötscher, H. T. 1827. *Aristophanes und sein Zeitalter.* Berlin: Voss.

Rova, E. 1987. "Usi del cristallo di rocca in area anatolica (fine III–inizi II mill. a.C." *Oriens antiquus* 26: 109–143.

Ruck, C. A. P. 1975. "Euripides' Mother: Vegetables and the Phallus in Aristophanes." *Arion,* n.s. 2: 13–57.

———. 1986. "Mushrooms and Philosophers." In Wasson, Kramisch, Ott, and Ruck 1986: 151–178.

Ruijgh, C. J. H. 1960. "Aristophane, Oiseaux 1372 sqq., Grenouilles 1316 sqq., et le sens de *póda kullón.*" *Mnemosyne* 13: 318–322.

Russell, D. A. 1966. "Plutarch, 'Alcibiades' 1–16." *Proceedings of the Cambridge Philological Society* 12: 37–47.

———. 1972. *Plutarch.* London: Duckworth.

Russo, C. F. 1962. *Aristofane, autore di Teatro.* Florence: Sansoni.

de Ste. Croix, G. M. A. 1972. *The Origins of the Peloponnesian War.* London: Duckworth.

von Saldern, A. 1966. "Glass." In *Nimrud and Its Remains,* by M. Mallowan, 623–634. London: Collins.

———. 1991. "Roman Glass with Decoration Cut in High Relief." In *Roman Glass: Two Centuries of Art and Invention,* edited by M. Newby and K. S. Painter, 111–121. Society of Antiquaries, Occasional Papers 13. London: Society of Antiquaries.

Sallares, R. 1991. *The Ecology of the Ancient Greek World.* Ithaca, N.Y.: Cornell University Press.

Sartori, F. 1957. *Le eterie nella vita politica ateniese del VI e V secolo a.C.* Rome: "L'Erma" di Bretschneider.

Sayle, M. 1988. "My Friend Kim." *Spectator* (21 May): 9–12.

Schachermeyr, F. 1965. "Stesimbrotos und seine Schrift über die Staatsmänner." *Sitzungsbericht der Akademie der Wissenschaften in Wien, Philosophisch-historische Klasse* 247/5.

———. 1969. *Perikles.* Stuttgart: Kohlhammer.

Schaeffer, A. 1949–1950. "Alkibiades und Lysander in Ionien." *Würzburger Jahrbücher für die Altertumswissenschaft* 4: 287–308.

Scheid, J., and J. Svenbro. 1994. *Le Métier de Zeus: Mythe du tissage et du tissu dans le monde gréco-romain.* Paris: Éditions la découverte.

Schlaifer, R. 1960. "Greek Theories of Slavery from Homer to Aristotle." In *Slavery in Classical Antiquity: Views and Controversies,* edited by M. Finley, 93–132. Cambridge: Cambridge University Press.

Schlegel, A. W. von. 1809. *Vorlesungen über dramatische Kunst und Literatur.* Vol. 1. Heidelberg.

Schmid, W., and O. Stählin. 1929–1948. *Geschichte der griechischen Literatur.* 5 vols. Munich: C. H. Beck.

Schmidt, E. 1957. *Persepolis 2: Contents of the Treasury and Other Discoveries.* Chicago: Oriental Institute.

Schmidt, M. 1860. *Hesychii Alexandrini Lexicon.* 2d ed. Jena: Hermann Dufft.

Schmitt, R. 1984. "Perser und Persisches in der alten attischen Komödie." In *Orientalia J. Duchesne-Guillemin emerito oblata,* Acta Iranica 23: 459–472.

Schouler, A. 1984. *La Tradition hellénique de Libanius.* Lille/Paris: Atelier national reproduction des thèses: Université de Lille III/Belles Lettres.

Schreiner, J. H. 1968. *Aristotle and Perikles: A Study in Historiography. Symbolae Osloenses,* suppl. 21. Oslo: Universitetsforlaget.

Schroff, A. 1901. "Zur Echtheitsfrage d. vierten Rede des Andokides." Diss., Erlangen.

Schwarze, J. 1971. *Die Beurteilung des Perikles durch die attische Komödie und ihre historische und historiographische Bedeutung. Zetemata* 51. Munich: C. H. Beck.

Seager, R. 1967. "Alcibiades and the Charge of Aiming at Tyranny." *Historia* 16: 6–18.

Sealey, R. 1956. "The Entry of Pericles into History." *Hermes* 84: 234–247.

Selig, K.-L., and E. Sears, eds. 1990. *The Verbal and the Visual: Essays in Honor of William Sebastian Heckscher.* New York: Italica.

Sharpley, H. 1905. *The Peace of Aristophanes.* Edinburgh: W. Blackwood and Sons.

Shear, T. L., Jr. 1993. "The Persian Destruction of Athens: Evidence from Agora Deposits." *Hesperia* 62: 383–482.

Shimron, B. 1989. *Politics and Belief in Herodotus. Historia* Einzelschrift 58. Stuttgart: Steiner.

Smith, R. R. R. 1990. "Late Roman Philosopher Portraits from Aphrodisias." *Journal of Roman Studies* 80: 127–155.

———. 1991. "Late Roman Philosophers." In *Aphrodisias.* Vol. 2: *The Theatre, a Sculptor's Workshop, Philosophers, and Coin Types,* ed. R. R. R. Smith and K. Erim, 144–158. *Journal of Roman Archaeology* supplementary series 2. Ann Arbor, Mich.

Smith, S. 1886. *The Wit and Wisdom of the Rev. Sidney Smith.* New ed. London: Longmans, Green and Co.

Solomos, A. 1974. *The Living Aristophanes.* Ann Arbor, Mich.: University of Michigan Press.

Sommerstein, A. H. 1980. *The Comedies of Aristophanes.* Vol. 1, *Acharnians.* Warminster: Aris and Phillips.

———. 1981. *The Comedies of Aristophanes.* Vol. 2, *Knights.* Warminster: Aris and Phillips.

———. 1982. *The Comedies of Aristophanes.* Vol. 3, *Clouds.* Warminster: Aris and Phillips.

———. 1983. *The Comedies of Aristophanes.* Vol. 4, *Wasps.* Warminster: Aris and Phillips.

———. 1985. *The Comedies of Aristophanes.* Vol. 5, *Peace.* Warminster: Aris and Phillips.

———. 1986. "The Decree of Syrakosios." *Classical Quarterly* 36: 101–108.

———. 1987. *The Comedies of Aristophanes.* Vol. 6, *Birds.* Warminster: Aris and Phillips.

Sourvinou-Inwood, C. 1995. *"Reading" Death to the End of the Classical Period.* Oxford: Clarendon.

Spacks, P. M. 1985. *Gossip.* Chicago: University of Chicago Press.

Spence, I. G. 1993. *The Cavalry of Classical Greece: A Social and Military History with Particular Reference to Athens.* Oxford: Clarendon.

Stadter, P. A. 1989. *A Commentary on Plutarch's Pericles.* Chapel Hill and London: University of North Carolina Press.

Stahl, H.-P. 1966. *Thukydides: Die Stellung des Menschen im Geschichtlichen Prozess. Zetemata* 40. Munich: Beck.

Stallbaum, G. 1861. *Platonis Opera Omnia 2/1: Gorgias.* Göttingen: Hennings.

Stanford, W. B. 1939. *Ambiguity in Greek Literature.* Oxford: Blackwell.

———. 1967. *The Sound of Greek: Studies in the Greek Theory and Practice of Euphony.* Berkeley and Los Angeles: University of California Press.

Starkie, W. J. M. 1897. *The Wasps of Aristophanes.* London: Macmillan.

———. 1909. *The Acharnians of Aristophanes.* London: Macmillan.

———. 1911. *The Clouds of Aristophanes.* London: Macmillan.

Steffig, J. R., and L. Casson, eds. 1991. *The Athlit Ram.* College Station, Tex.: Texas A&M University Press.

Stevens, F. G., and M. D. George. 1870–1954. *Catalogue of Political and Personal Satires . . . in the British Museum to 1832.* 12 vols. London: British Museum.

Stone, L. M. 1984. *Costume in Aristophanic Comedy.* Salem, N.H.: Ayer Co.

Storey, I. C. 1985. "The Symposium at *Wasps* 1299ff." *Phoenix* 39: 317–333.

———. 1989. "The 'Blameless Shield' of Kleonymus." *Rheinisches Museum für Philologie* 132: 247–261.

———. 1990. "Dating and Redating Eupolis." *Phoenix* 44: 1–30.

———. 1993. "The Dates of Aristophanes' *Clouds* II and Eupolis' *Baptae:* A Reply to E. C. Kopff." *American Journal of Philology* 114: 71–84.

Strasburger, H. 1958. "Thukydides und die politische Selbstdarstellung der Athener." *Hermes* 86: 17–40.

Strauss, B. S. 1986. *Athens after the Peloponnesian War: Class, Faction and Policy, 403–386 B.C.* London: Croom Helm.

———. 1989. Review of Garnsey 1988. *Food and Foodways* 3: 283–297.

———. 1990. "*Oikos/Polis:* Towards a Theory of Athenian Paternal Ideology, 450–399 B.C." *Classica et mediaevalia* 40: 101–127.

———. 1993. *Fathers and Sons in Athens: Ideology and Society in the Era of the Peloponnesian War.* Princeton, N.J.: Princeton University Press.

Stroud, R. 1994. "The Aiakeion and Tholos of Athens in P.Oxy 2087." *Zeitschrift für Papyrologie und Epigraphik* 103: 1–9.

Strycker, E. de. 1942. "Platonica I: L'Authenticité du *Premier Alcibiade.*" Études classiques 11: 135–151.

Süss, W. 1911. *Aristophanes und die Nachwelt.* Leipzig: Dieterich.

———. 1954. "Scheinbare und wirkliche Inkongruenzen in den Dramen des Aristophanes." *Rheinisches Museum für Philologie,* n.s. 97: 115–159; 229–316.

Sutton, D. F. 1988. "Dicaeopolis as Aristophanes, Aristophanes as Dicaeopolis." *Liverpool Classical Monthly* 13: 105–108.

Süvern, J. W. 1826. *Über Aristophanes Wolken.* Berlin: Ferdinand Dümmler.

———. 1827. *Über Aristophanes Vögel.* Berlin: Ferdinand Dümmler.

———. 1835. *Essay on "The Birds" of Aristophanes.* Translated by W. R. Hamilton. London: J. Murray.

———. 1836. *Two Essays on "The Clouds" and on the "Geras" of Aristophanes.* Translated by W. R. Hamilton. London: J. Murray.

Taillardat, J. 1965. *Les Images d'Aristophane.* Paris: Les Belles Lettres.

Taplin, O. 1978. *The Stagecraft of Aeschylus.* Oxford: Clarendon.

———. 1986. "Fifth-Century Tragedy and Comedy: A *Synkrisis.*" *Journal of Hellenic Studies* 106: 163–174.

Tate, J. 1927. "The Beginnings of Greek Allegory." *Classical Review* 41: 214–215.

Taylor, A. E. 1926. *Plato, the Man and His Work.* London: Methuen.

Taylor, C. C. W. 1976. *Plato Protagoras.* Oxford: Clarendon.

Thalheim, T. 1901. *Lysias.* Leipzig: Teubner.

Thiercy, P. 1986. *Aristophane: Fiction et dramaturgie.* Paris: Les Belles Lettres.

Thirlwall, C. 1845–1852. *The History of Greece.* 8 vols. London: Longmans.

Thompson, D. B. 1960. "The House of Simon the Shoemaker." *Archaeology* 13: 235–240.

Thompson, H. A. 1982. "The Pnyx in Models." In *Studies in Attic Epigraphy, History and Topography Presented to Eugene Vanderpool. Hesperia,* suppl. 19: 136–137.

———. 1988. "Building for a More Democratic Society: The Athenian Agora after Ephialtes." *Praktika tou XII diethnous sunedriou klasikes archaiologias Athena, 1983* 4: 198–204, pls. 70–72.

Thompson, H. A., and R. E. Wycherley. 1972. *The Agora of Athens. The Athenian Agora* 14. Princeton, N.J.: Princeton University Press.

Thompson, W. E. 1970. "The Kinship of Perikles and Alkibiades." *Greek, Roman and Byzantine Studies* 11: 27–33.

Thuasne, L. 1923. *François Villon: Oeuvres.* Paris: A. Picard.

Toepffer, J. 1894. "Alkibiades (2)." *RE* 1, no. 2: 1516–1532.

Tomin, J. 1987. "Socratic Gymnasium in the Clouds." *Symbolae Osloenses* 62: 25–32.

Tompkins, D. P. 1972. "Stylistic Characterization in Thucydides: Nicias and Alcibiades." *Yale Classical Studies* 22: 181–214.

———. 1993. "Archidamus and the Question of Characterization in Thucydides." In Rosen and Farrell 1993: 99–111.

Travlos, J. 1972. *Pictorial Dictionary of Athens.* London: Thames and Hudson.

Treheux, J. 1991. "Bulletin épigraphique: Attique." *Revue des études grecques* 104: 467–475.

Turato, F. 1972. *Il problema storico delle Nuvole di Aristofane.* Padua: Antenore.

Usener, H. 1905. "Keraunos." *Rheinisches Museum für Philologie* 60: 9–12.

Ussher, R. G. 1979. *Aristophanes. Greece and Rome* New Surveys in the Classics, no. 44. Oxford: Clarendon.

Vendryes, J. 1921. *Le Langage: Introduction linguistique à l'histoire.* Paris: Renaissance du Livre.

Vickers, M. 1978. *Greek Vases.* Oxford: Ashmolean Museum.

———. 1984. "The Influence of Exotic Materials on Attic White-Ground Pottery." In *Ancient Greek and Related Pottery,* edited by H. A. Brijder, 88–97. Allard Pierson series 5. Amsterdam: Allard Pierson Museum.

———. 1985. "Artful Crafts: The Influence of Metalwork on Athenian Painted Pottery." *Journal of Hellenic Studies* 105: 108–128, pls. 4–6.

———. 1987a. "Alcibiades on Stage: *Philoctetes* and *Cyclops.*" *Historia* 36: 171–197.

———. 1987b. "Lambdacism at Aristophanes *Clouds* 1381–2." *Liverpool Classical Monthly* 12: 143.

———. 1987c. "Value and Simplicity: Eighteenth-Century Taste and the Study of Greek Vases." *Past and Present* 116: 98–137.

———. 1989a. "Alcibiades on Stage: *Thesmophoriazusae* and *Helen*." *Historia* 38: 41–65.

———. 1989b. "Alcibiades on Stage: Aristophanes' *Birds*." *Historia* 38: 267–299.

———. 1990a. "Wandering Stones: Venice, Constantinople and Athens." In Selig and Sears 1990: 225–242.

———. 1990b. "Golden Greece: Relative Values, Minae and Temple Inventories." *American Journal of Archaeology* 94: 613–624.

———. 1990c. "The Impoverishment of the Past: The Case of Classical Greece." *Antiquity* 64: 455–463.

———. 1991. "A Contemporary Account of the Athenian Plague? (Aristophanes *Clouds* 694–734)." *Liverpool Classical Monthly* 16: 64.

———. 1993. "Alcibiades in Cloudedoverland." In Rosen and Farrell 1993: 603–618.

———. 1994. "Alcibiades and Critias in the *Gorgias*: Plato's 'Fine Satire'." *Dialogues d'histoire ancienne* 20, no. 2: 85–112.

———. 1995a. "Thucydides 6.53.3–59: Not a 'Digression'." *Dialogues d'histoire ancienne* 21, no. 1: 193–200.

———. 1995b. "Alcibiades at Sparta: Aristophanes *Birds*." *Classical Quarterly* 45: 339–354.

———. 1995c. "Heracles Lacedaemonius: The Political Dimensions of Sophocles *Trachiniae* and Euripides *Heracles*." *Dialogues d'histoire ancienne* 21, no. 2.

———. 1996. "Fifth-Century Chronology and the Coinage Decree." *Journal of Hellenic Studies* 116.

———. Forthcoming. *Images on Textiles: The Weave of Fifth-Century Athenian Art and Society. Xenia: Konstanzer Althistorische Vorträge und Forschungen.* Konstanz.

Vickers, M., and D. W. J. Gill. 1994. *Artful Crafts: Ancient Greek Silverware and Pottery*. Oxford: Clarendon.

Vidal-Naquet, P. 1983. *Le Chasseur noir: Formes de pensée et formes de societé dans le monde grec*. 2d ed. Paris: La Découverte/Maspero.

Vischer, W. [1843] 1877–1879. "Alkibiades und Lysandros." In *Kleine Schriften*, vol. 1, edited by H. Gelzer and A. Burckhardt. Leipzig: S. Hirzel.

Vocotopoulou, J. 1980. "Pilos Lakōnikos." *Stēlē, Tomos eis mnēmēn Nikoláou Kontoléontos* (Athens): 236–241, pls. 70–72.

Vogt, J. 1960. "Das Bild des Perikles bei Thukydides." In *Orbis: Ausgewählte Schriften zur Geschichte des Altertums*, 47–63. Freiburg: Herder.

Wade-Gery, H. T. 1932–1933. "Studies in Attic Inscriptions of the Fifth Century." *Annual of the British School at Athens* 33: 101–136.

———. 1957. *Essays in Greek History*. Oxford: Blackwell.

Walbank, M. 1978. *Athenian Proxenies of the Fifth Century B.C.* Toronto and Sarasota: S. Stevens.

Wallace, R. W. 1991. "Damone da Oa ed i suoi successori: Un analisi delle fonti." In *Harmonia Mundi: Music and Philosophy in the Ancient World*, edited by R. W. Wallace and B. MacLachlan, 30–53. *Quaderni urbinati di cultura classica*, suppl. 5.

———. 1993. "Private Lives and Public Enemies: Freedom of Thought in Classical Athens." In *Athenian Identity and Civic Ideology*, edited by A. Scafuro and A. Boegehold, 127–155. Baltimore, Md.: The Johns Hopkins University Press.

Wasson, R. G., S. Kramisch, J. Ott, and C. A. P. Ruck. 1986. *Persephone's Quest: Entheogens and the Origins of Religion*. New Haven, Conn.: Yale University Press.

West, A. B. 1924. "Pericles' Political Heirs." *Classical Philology* 19: 201–228.

West, M. L. 1968. "Two Passages of Aristophanes." *Classical Review* 82: 5–7.

———. 1972. *Iambi et elegi graeci*. Vol. 2. Oxford: Clarendon.

———. 1974. *Studies in Greek Elegy and Iambus*. Untersuchungen zur antiken Literatur und Geschichte, 14. Berlin: de Gruyter.

Westlake, H. D. 1938. "Alcibiades, Agis, and Spartan Policy." *Journal of Hellenic Studies* 58: 31–40.

———. 1960. "Athenian Aims in Sicily." *Historia* 9: 385–402.

———. 1968. *Individuals in Thucydides*. Cambridge: Cambridge University Press.

———. 1980. "The *Lysistrata* and the War." *Phoenix* 34: 38–54.

———. 1989. *Studies in Thucydides and Greek History*. Bristol: Bristol Classical Press.

White, J. W., and E. Cary. 1918. "Collations of the Manuscripts of Aristophanes' *Aves*." *Harvard Studies in Classical Philology* 29: 77–131.

Whitman, C. H. 1964. *Aristophanes and the Comic Hero*. Cambridge, Mass.: Harvard University Press.

Wide, S. 1893. *Lakonische Kulte*. Leipzig: Teubner.

von Wilamowitz-Moellendorff, U. 1924. "Lesefrüchte." *Hermes* 59: 248–273.

———. 1982. *History of Classical Scholarship*. Edited by H. Lloyd-Jones. London: Duckworth.

Williams, G. W. 1952. "The Curse of the Alkmaionidai — iii: Themistokles, Perikles and Alkibiades." *Hermathena* 80: 58–71.

Wind, E. 1966. *Pagan Mysteries in the Renaissance*. 2d ed. New York: Barnes and Noble.

Winkler, M. M. 1991. "Satire and the Grotesque in Juvenal, Arcimboldo, and Goya." *Antike und Abendland* 37: 22–42.

Wolf, P. 1954. "Libanios' Kampf um die hellenische Bildung." *Museum Helveticum* II: 231–242.

Woodhead, A. G. 1960. "Thucydides' Portrait of Cleon." *Mnemosyne* 13: 289–317.

Woodruff, P. 1982. *Plato, Hippias Major*. Oxford: Blackwell.

Wright, W. C. 1922. *Philostratus and Eunapius: The Lives of the Sophists*. London: Heinemann.

Wycherley, R. E. 1978. *The Stones of Athens*. Princeton, N.J.: Princeton University Press.

of, 10, 40; tribe, Leontis, 178, 183; tribute assessor, 20, 24, 32, 99, 103, 108, 176n; tyrannical disposition, *xxviii, xxxiii*, 2, 8, 31, 46, 57, 137, 144, 163, 169, 171, 179, 185; violence, propensity to, *xvii*, 47, 53, 54, 123, 129, 131, 137, 141, 147, 148, 153, 161, 164, 183, 191; wife's virtue tested, 47, 94; win, strong desire to, 47, 110; woman, characterised as a, 20; women, liaisons with, *xix*, 19, 46, 55, 94, 100, 112, 125, 158, 160, 167, 168, 171, 172, 174–177, 190; youth, relative, 43, 99n, 104, 111, 118, 141, 179; Zeus, descent from, 170

Alcibiades Jr., 44, 106, 126n; imitation of his father, *xvii, xxix;* speech impediment, *xvii*

Alcmaeon, Olympic victory, 33

Alcmaeonids: descent from Nestor, 33; family curse, 21, 69, 73, 78, 96, 105–106, 144

Allegory: "impersonated abstractions," *xxii;* political, *xvi–xxxiii*, 1–6, 16, 59, 140, 143, 154, 171, 188

Allókoton, Cleonian resonance, 126

Ambiguity, *xxii–xxiv, xxxiii*, 4–5

Amphipolis, 63, 67n, 180, 181

Amphitheus, in *Acharnians,* 108

Amynias, in *Clouds,* 54

Anaea, 194n

Anaxagoras (philosopher), 29, 30, 34, 37, 80, 89, 90, 116, 118, 127, 130–131, 150, 173, 174, 178, 184

Ancien régime, xxi, xxiii

Andocides (orator), 14

Anecdotal tradition, 6, 13, 15, 100, 132, 134, 137, 175

Anér, 104

Antiochus (friend of Alcibiades), 147n

Antiphon (orator), 14

Antisthenes (philosopher), 14, 175

Anytus (tanner), 114

Apatouria, 68

Aphrodite, 142

Apollo, 142, 186, 188

Apragmosúnē, 17, 137

Archestratus (male prostitute), 52n

Archidamus (Spartan king), 69, 164

Arcimboldo, Giuseppe, 31–32

Ares, 80n, 149, 179

Argos, *xxx,* 148n, 149, 153

Argument, Stronger, in *Clouds,* 16, 43, 44, 46–51, 121, 123, 146

Argument, Weaker, in *Clouds,* 16, 43, 44, 46–48, 51, 53, 121, 123

Aristodemus (Dorian hero), 166

Aristophanes: *Acharnians, xxx,* 7, 12, 13, 19, 59–96, 97, 100, 106, 108, 115, 119, 120, 123, 133, 134, 146, 151, 152, 165, 175, 179, 183, 190; audience, sophistication of, *xxiv; Babylonians, xv,* 95, 123n; *Banqueters,* 106, 118, 123, 131–132; *Birds, xviii, xix–xx, xxvi, xxx, xxxiii,* 1, 8, 154–189, 190, 191; *Clouds, xvii,* 1, 2, 7, 8, 11, 13, 16, 21, 22–58, 59, 61, 71, 96, 105, 115, 121–123, 125, 130, 136, 138, 143, 144, 146, 151, 155, 161, 165, 175, 183, 190, 191, 196, 197; composition of plays, 6; *Frogs,* 9, 12, 52, 191; *Knights, xviii,* 7, 8, 12, 14, 63, 97–120, 122, 126, 128, 136, 151, 163, 190, 194; *Lysistrata,* 94n, 168n, 186, 186n; obscenity, 16, 17; *Peace, xvi,* 8, 13, 138, 139–153, 175, 190, 197; plays found in Plato's deathbed, 192; plots, unity of, *xxvii,* 16, 44, 122, 138; political views, 12; puns, sophistication of, 26, 182; satire, effects of, 13; *Thesmophoriazusae,* 115; Thucydides, use by, 15, 39, 73, 96, 138, 145; *Wasps,* 7, 8, 11, 42, 110, 121–138, 146, 151, 190; Xenophon, use by, 15

Aristotle, speech impediment, *xvii*

Artabas (Bactrian), 65

Artemon, in *Acharnians,* 86

Aspasia, 180n, 182n, 183n, 189; Alcibiades, relations with, 174–178; fisticuffs, propensity to, 56; Helen of Troy, comparison with, 75; Hera, comparison with, 152n; and Lysicles, 73, 115, 125, 152, 193, 194; and Miletus, 71n, 152; and Pericles, 7–9, 32, 56, 90, 131, 134; Pericles' teacher in rhetoric, 183; philosophical interests, 31, 56, 90n; procuress, 72, 78, 115, 135; wordplay on name, 56n, 182n

Aspasius (son of Aeschines), 177

Athena Areia, 80n

Athena Hygieia, 116

Athena Parthenos, 89, 150, 173, 176

Athenaeus, *Deipnosophistae,* 26

Athens, 148n; Acropolis, 60, 179; cavalry, 108; fleet, 68; grain supply, 95; Odeum, 36, 39, 49, 65, 131, 182; Pelasgian precinct, 145; Pnyx, 61, 70n, 101, 114, 116, 125; Propylaea,

117; "School of Hellas," 50; Theatre of
Dionysus, 131, 182; walls, 64. *See also*
Agora of Athens
Athmonia, 140, 148
Aulós, 84, 187; accompaniment to marching
armies, 84; rejected by Alcibiades, 105
Axiochus (father of Aspasia), 177
Axiochus (uncle of Alcibiades), 177–178

Bacchylides, *xxiii,* 4, 162
Bathing, 24, 41, 45, 51, 116, 127
Bdelycleon, in *Wasps,* 11, 121–138, 190
Beak, metal (on ship), 64
Bentley, Richard, *xxi*
Blindness motif, 11, 48, 87, 91, 96, 115
Boeotia, 88, 159
Boulé, 150; extraordinary meeting, 65, 88
Boy, in *Wasps,* 122, 131, 132
Brasidas (Spartan ephor), 180–181
Bridesmaid, in *Acharnians,* 93, 94
Brumoy, Pierre, *xxvi,* 156–159, 163, 167

Callias (brother-in-law of Alcibiades), 31n,
32, 43, 112, 140, 161
Callicles, 44, 47, 109, 125, 156
Candaules, 169
Caria, 102, 194
Carthage, 102, 103
Catana, 162
Caunus, revolt of, 66, 179
Cecropis (Athenian tribe), 183
Cecrops, 183
Cephalus of Syracuse, 78n
Chaerephon, 25, 34
Chalcidice, 67, 180
Chalybes, 108
Charon, 183n
Chios, Chians, 112n, 153, 161, 162
Cholargus (deme), 87
Chorus: in *Acharnians,* 69, 70, 76, 82, 86,
90, 92, 95, 96; in *Birds,* 158, 160, 168–170,
177, 185–187; in *Clouds,* 28, 36, 55;
in Cratinus' *Dionysalexandros,* 194; in
Knights, 98n, 108, 110–111, 117, 122; in
Peace, 149–151, 185; in *Wasps,* 122, 130, 131
Chorus-leader: in *Birds,* 178; in *Wasps,* 122,
131, 132
Chronology, epigraphical, 83
Chrysilla of Corinth, 135
Chrysostom, Saint John, 18

Cimon, *xxiii,* 11, 55, 78, 135, 150
Cinesias (in *Birds*), 181–183; in *Lysistrata,*
182n
Cinesias (son of Meletus), 182–184
Classical scholarship, *xxi–xxii,* 2, 192
Cleinias (father of Alcibiades), 8, 27, 121n, 178
Cleon, *xv, xvi, xxxiii*n, *xxxiv,* 7, 9, 14, 20,
21, 83, 86n, 95, 97, 98, 105–110, 114, 115,
117–119, 121, 125, 126, 128, 132, 138, 143,
150, 190
Cleonymus, 86, 124
Cloudcuckooland, 157, 165, 167, 171, 178–179
Cock-fighting, 179
Coesyra, 23
Colone, brothel at, 163
Comedy: function of, 12; lampooning
by name, *xviii–xix,* 80, 86, 171, 183;
masks, *xvi,* 107, 122; usual targets of,
xv, xviii–xix, xxiv, xxx, 12, 18, 21, 188
Coronea, 27
Cotytto (Thracian deity), 188
Cowardice motif, 36, 60, 81, 86, 95, 105, 115,
124, 184
Crates (Cynic philosopher), 175
Cratinus, 7, 30, 86, 176; *Dionysalexandros,*
xv, 3, 9, 60, 152, 176, 193–195
Creditor, in *Clouds,* 32n, 52–54
Critias, 31n
Croton, 33n
Ctesias, in *Acharnians,* 86
Cyclades, 102
Cyclops, 130
Cynna (prostitute), 115
Cynosarges, Temple of Heracles, 112n
Cyzicus, Cyzicenes, 112n, 153

Damon (philosopher), 29, 30, 37, 53, 86, 90
Darius the Great, 65–66
Dead, laws against lampooning, 7
Death motif, 27, 46, 61, 74, 76, 81, 88, 95,
113, 172–173, 180
Decelea, fortification of, 154, 156–157, 159,
168, 171, 179
Deinomache (mother of Alcibiades), 8, 23,
175
Dékhas (prison at Sparta), 164
Delium, 20, 24, 94n, 106
Delos, 102
Delphi, *xxx,* 159, 163, 186, 188; bad portents,
xxx; Lesche of the Cnidians, *xxiv*

Demaratus (Spartan king), 75

Democrates (lover of Alcibiades), 100, 113

Dêmos, Athenian, forbidden to lampoon or defame, 156, 185

Demosthenes (general), 97, 107

Demosthenes (orator), 15, 45, 100, 101, 106; speech impediment, *xvii*

Demosthenes (slave), in *Knights,* 97–98, 100–107

Demus, in *Knights,* 97–120, 190

Demus (son of Pyrilampes), 114, 125, 127

Dercetes, in *Acharnians,* 87, 90–92, 108, 133

Dialects, 21; Ionian, 152; Laconian, 142, 147, 164n, 186; laconism, 166, 167; repetition in Laconian, 142, 186

Diallagē, 90

Dicaeopolis, 4, 19, 59, 108, 114, 124, 138, 146, 150, 151, 190

Diminutive nouns, 115, 145, 146, 152, 176, 184

Diogenes of Apollonia, 35

Dion of Syracuse, 7

Dionysius I or II (tyrant of Syracuse), 1, 57, 192

Dionysius of Halicarnassus, 5

Dionysus, 52, 71, 191

Diopeithes (accuser of Anaxagoras), 116

Dracontides, 130, 181

Dramatic festivals: civic aspect of, 12; Dionysia, 12, 22, 139; Lenaea, 9, 59, 97, 121, 132

Dramatists, restraints on freedom, 75

Duris of Samos, 9n, 14, 168

Earthquakes, 78, 194n

Eels, 87, 88

Eleusinian Mysteries, 84; initiation, 35, 174; profanation, *xviii,* 46, 174, 183

Elis, 148n, 158

Elpinice, 11, 55, 135

Emblem books, *xxi*

Emphasis, *xv, xxiii, xxiv, xxxiii, xxxiv,* 4, 10, 26, 40, 82, 86, 119, 122, 129, 132, 172, 176, 181

Enyalius, 149

Epicharmus, 146

Epidaurus, 39

Epískopos, in *Birds,* 161, 181

Epops, in *Birds,* 155–189, 190

Eros, 45, 169, 170

Etna. *See* Aetna

Euathlus (prosecutor of Thucydides, son of Milesias), 82

Euboea, 34

Eucrates (general), 98

Euelpides, 166, 176–178, 186

Eupolis, *xvii, xxv,* 7, 9, 55, 59n, 73, 99, 147, 183; *Baptae, xviii,* 188; *Demi,* 7, 9; *Kolakes,* 140

Euripides, 9, 55, 75, 76, 150, 179; epinician ode, 45, 161–162; *Telephus,* 65, 74, 75

Eurotas, 186

Euryptolemus, 135

Eutéleia, 86, 94

Euthymenes (archon), 63

Fabius Maximus, Q., 11n, 36n

Father-beating motif, 18, 54–56, 123, 129, 132, 137, 161, 181, 183

Figs, 129, 132

Fire hazards, 88

Flamingoes, 186

Forgetfulness motif, 11, 28, 81, 89, 93, 96, 114, 116, 118

Frontinus, 13, 37, 185

Funeral pyres, 93, 128, 129

Funerary wreath, 113

Generation gap, 8, 42, 44, 48, 136, 138, 178, 181

Genital loss motif, 11, 39, 71, 72, 84, 85, 87–89, 96, 124, 151, 172, 175

Geometría, 165

Glanis, 116

Glass. *See* Rock crystal

Gorgias, 155–156

Gossip, *xxiv–xxv, xxxiii,* 13, 15, 55, 62, 112, 154, 168, 174, 176

Graces, 142, 164n

Greek studies, *xx*

Gylippus, 157

Gymnopaidíai, 169

Hagnon, 63, 67n, 181

Half-allegory mode, 77

Halisarna, 75

Harmodius (sister of), 72n

Hegemon of Thasos, *xvii*

Helen of Troy, 75

Heliaea, 126, 173–174

Hera, 152n

Richler, Mordecai, *Solomon Gursky Was Here,* 17
Riddles, *xxi*
Rock crystal, confused with glass, 66n
Role transformation, 52, 122, 136, 137

Sabazius, 124
Sadocus (Thracian prince), 67, 68, 194
Salabaccho (prostitute), 115
Salaminia (Athenian state trireme), 155, 158, 161, 162
Samos, 11, 28, 37, 56, 59, 75, 85, 126, 129, 131–132, 146, 181, 184, 185
Satyrus, 14
Sausage-seller, 20, 21, 97–120, 122, 161, 190
Scambonidae (deme), 177, 178
Schinocephaly motif, 50, 65, 71, 73–76, 86, 96, 137, 173, 176, 184. *See also* Pericles, Schinocephaly
Segesta, Athenian treaty with, 82n
Servant: in *Birds,* 165, 166; in *Peace,* 151, 190
Sheep imagery, 73, 152–153, 194
Shoe motif, *xxvii, xxxi,* 25, 26, 30, 39, 43, 53–55, 127
Sicily, 102, 103, 157; Athenian designs on, 148; Athenian expedition, *xix–xxxiii,* 162–163, 172, 179–181
Siege-engines, 37, 85n, 129
Simaetha (prostitute), 99n
Simon (cobbler), 30
Simon (hipparch), 107
Simonides, 55, 161, 162
Sitalces (king of Odrysians), *xxix*n, 67, 68
Slave names, 122–123, 128
Smith, Rev. Sydney, *xxi–xxii*
Socrates, 7, 13, 19, 21–23, 25–26, 30–31, 34, 42–43, 54–58, 99, 104, 114, 123, 175, 191, 194
Solon, 7, 129n
Soothsayer, in *Birds,* 161, 162
Sophocles, and pederasty, 49, 114, 118, 136
Sosias (slave), in *Wasps,* 122–125, 128
Sparta, 35, 45, 48–50, 142–143, 154–192; aged, respect for, 50; *agōgē,* 49, 187; Agora, Skias (Tholos), 184; barley diet, 49, 142; *bibasis,* 168; boys silent, 49; boys' single garment, 49; camps circular, 181n; communal dining halls, 187; constitution, 188; corporal punishment, 49; deceit encouraged, 50, 187; *diakonía,* 166, 180;

dirty, 41, 51n, 142; doors at, 166; eirens, 186; ephors, 166, 168, 172, 180, 185, 187; exercise at, 51; expulsion of foreigners, 165; homosexual chastity, 50; hospitality, 169, 172; Hyacinthia, 187, 188; invasions of Attica, 9, 60, 133, 190, 194; iron currency, 163; *Krupteía,* 180; laws and customs immutable, 50, 187n; modesty encouraged, 50–51; musical conservatism, 49; oaths, monthly, 187n; pederasty, laws against, 49; Phobos, temple of, 187; Plataea, destruction of, 73, 96; religious conservatism, 188; at the run, orders carried out, 148n, 166, 172, 181; servitude at, 148, 164, 166, 180; shooting stars, 165, 186; shouting, at doors, 165; shouting, voting by, 49, 166n; soup, consumption of, 166; strangling, execution by, *xxix,* 164; swampy nature, *xxx,* 168n, 186n; *xénoi tróphimoi,* 187n
Speech disorders, *xvii, xxvii;* and behavioral problems, 46n. *See also* Alcibiades, speech impediment; Lambdacism
Sphacteria, 97, 99, 111, 126, 141
Spitting Image, 2
Statute-seller, in *Birds,* 161
Stesimbrotus of Thasos, 9n, 11, 72, 91
Strepsiades, in *Clouds,* 11, 13, 16, 22–58, 59, 114, 121, 122, 124, 130, 136, 138, 145, 146, 174, 190, 196, 197
Süvern, J. W., *xx, xxvi,* 23, 154–159, 173n
Swallows, *xxviii, xxxii,* 163
Sycophant: in *Acharnians,* 85, 88, 89, 108, 146; in *Birds,* 181
Sycophants, 81n, 129
Symbolic satire, *xix*
Syracosius, decree of, *xviii,* 171, 188

Taenarus, *xxix,* 78
Tarentum, 11n
Taureas (choregus), 183
Teleas of Corinth, 135
Telecleides (comic poet), 7
Telephus myth, 48, 75–76, 79
Teuthrania, 75n
Thales of Miletus, 127
Theban, in *Acharnians,* 87–89
Themistocles (general), 132
Theophrastus, 45, 87, 111
Theoria, 150, 152

INDEX LOCORUM

551	112	920–924	88
555	127n	936–939	89
556	79	960–962	89
566–575	80		90
580	81	963	196
	196	965	89
581–582	81		130
584–589	81	971	90
585	73	977–999	90
598	81	1003–1007	90
	179n	1017	93
607	81	1018–1036	87
620–627	81		91
680ff.	102	1037–1039	92
703–719	82	1041	196
716	64	1044–1046	92
	82	1047	72n
	100		93
	112	1048–1068	13
723	83		19
729–835	83		93
732	196		106
740–749	146n	1052–1055	94
751–764	84	1060	94
801–802	84		112n
	196	1061–1062	19
806	146n	1069–1142	94
808	84	1085–1142	xxx
	146n	1128	xxx
809–810	85	1198–1202	95
812	146n	1224–1234	95
818–828	88	1385	196
819	146n	Babylonians	123n
830	146n	Banqueters	106
832	85		118
833	73		123
	86		131–132
834	85n	Birds	
	146n	16	166
836–859	86–87	43	124n
844	86	55–59	172–173
	124n	60	165
850	196	70–74	166
881–882	87	75	172
881–894	196	77–80	166
888	87		182
889–890	151		186n
893	88		187
901–902	88	82	172
910ff.	88	82–84	180n